Susan Mortimer's

CREATE-A-NOTEBOOK BIBLE AND HISTORY SERIES:
BOOK 2

Remembering God's Chosen Children

TEACHER'S MANUAL

Written and Illustrated
by
Susan Mortimer

Intended for individual teacher use only.

Acknowledgements

Working on this book has been so much fun. To study the Bible every day as your job-what more could a person ask for?!

There are so many people whom I want to thank:

Esther Nordman, who has been great to work with. She has jumped in and willingly done whatever was needed to finish the book, and always did it with a joyful spirit.

Cammie Van Rooy who did artwork for me. She defeated cancer as a toddler only to have it come back as a young adult. However, her trust in God never wavers, and the beauty of the Lord radiates from her face.

Margaret Beasley, also fighting cancer, who proofread much of the text; and though she was often weak, she did it promptly and returned it with notes of encouragement.

Betty Smith, my sister, who came and helped with the last push to get the book fininished. She is a remarkable woman and a dear friend. And also her family for promoting the books at bookfairs across the country.

Adam Smith, my nephew, who makes my book covers come together on his computer.

My brother, Tom, and my father Dick, who keep my computers up and running and are willing to drop whatever they are doing to help.

Greg, my best friend and husband of 25 years, who built me an office where I can spread out my hundreds of books.

My daughter Wendy, and son Chris, who help with meals and cleaning up.

With each book I have written there has always been a baby born in the extended family! And with this book, my daughter Sheri and her husband Phillip, supplied the new baby–Taylor. Too wonderful for words!

Tammy Scholz, my dear friend, who worked with me and makes me take 'sanity' breaks. (That is what we call going out together and enjoying life.)

Thank you all so much, and may all your work go towards glorifying the Lord and touching the hearts of those who use this book.

TABLE OF CONTENTS

Open Letter to Students and Teacher

(Please read aloud together before beginning the course.)

Welcome to the beginning of a new course. We will be going over what you will be studying in the coming months.

Remembering God's Chosen Children is different from tradition textbooks that deal with only one subject. It is primarily Bible and history. However, it also includes creative writing assignments, teaches calligraphy and introduces beginning Hebrew. You will need to use a New International Version Bible for this course.

The point of each element is to give you a better understanding of the Bible. You will not be doing each subject every day, but you will be studying issues, playing with concepts, and mastering skills through all of the lessons.

Your student notebook is not an ordinary workbook. It is a creative effort to be shared with others. Therefore, corrections need to be done discretely. Writing assignments should be fully corrected before transcribing them into your notebook.

In Remembering God's Chosen Children, you will follow the Israelites as they leave slavery in Egypt and suffer with them during their forty years in the desert. You will march along as they conquer the Promised Land and watch the rise and fall of the judges and the kings of the United Kingdom. You will also interact with the laws and principles that unified them as a nation, from their beginnings to modern times.

The calligraphy lessons will prepare you to make an art of writing verses from God's Word, much like the ancient scribes. You will also learn to write Hebrew in calligraphy.

In the introduction to beginning Hebrew, you will learn to recognize the Hebrew letters with creative cartoons. Then, starting with some things you already know—Biblical names—you will quickly built your Hebrew vocabulary. For example, from 'Samuel' comes the Hebrew words that mean 'heard' and 'God;' from Bethlehem, we get the Hebrew words that mean 'house' and 'bread.' Soon you will have a good number of Hebrew words you can recognize.

Keep in mind that the end result should not be just the rote memorization of facts, but to gain wisdom, understanding, and a deeper love for God.

As always, the purpose of this book is to encourage you to delve into these subjects in greater depth. We've just touched the surface here and there is so much more to discover!

Sincerely,

Susan Mortimer

Introduction

BIBLE

Bible Reading: 2 Timothy 3:16-17

Notebook Page iv: Books of the Bible

Points to Bring Out: Make sure you know all the books of the Bible and their divisions. Color in the books as you study them.

Note to Teacher: Forms are in the back of this teacher's manual for the Books of the Bible without their names. These may be used to test the student.

BIBLE

Bible Reading: Review Exodus 1-3

Notebook Pages 1-4: Old Testament Timeline1 & 2, Interacting with the Timeline

Points to Bring Out: Have you ever tried to read through the Bible and gotten bogged down about Leviticus? Then this will be a refreshing and encouraging experience for you. As you begin the study of Remembering God's Chosen Children, you will see not only how God led His people from Egypt as an unorganized group of slaves but how he turned them into a formidable nation. You will learn many lessons from the accounts of the Israelite people—how they accepted a sacred covenant with God and broke it; how they were blessed by God and grumbled; and how God gave specific instructions and then they tried to do things their own way. The Bible is not only our most accurate source for ancient history, it is also our best handbook for daily living. We will begin by going over the history of the Bible beginning with Creation through the Old Testament in order for you to get an over-view. Put these pages together and go over them aloud as a group. When you are done, work out the Interacting with the Timeline page.

Note to Teacher: It is very important for your student to have a good understanding of these pages because this will provide a framework for studying the rest of the Old Testament.

CALLIGRAPHY

Notebook Pages 5-6: How to do Calligraphy, Calligraphy Strokes

Points to Bring Out: You will be learning to do calligraphy, an art form of handwriting, so that you can make beautiful copies of verses. Pages are included for practice.

Note to Teacher: Each student will need to have the supplies listed on the page. There are reproducible forms in the back of this manual for extra practice. In addition, the calligraphy (and Hebrew) lessons are to be done in conjunction with a Bible or History lesson, not by itself.

HISTORY

Bible Reading: Review Ex 4-6

Notebook Page 7: Timeline Crossword 1

Points to Bring Out: Use the information on the Old Testament Timeline to fill in the crossword puzzles. Then write ten questions about it.

Note to Teacher: Choose the best ones to use as a test for the timeline.

Moses—Exiting Egypt

HISTORY

Notebook Page 8: The Legend of Sargon

Points to Bring Out: The legend of Sargon and the story of Moses have many similarities. See what a lawyer could do with their stories.

HISTORY

Bible Reading: Review Ex 7-9

Notebook Page 9: Timeline Crossword 2

Points to Bring Out: Use the information on the Old Testament Timeline to fill in the crossword puzzles. Then write ten questions about it. Then divide into two teams and have each team ask the other questions about the information on the Timeline. Keep score!

Note to Teacher: Choose the best questions to use as a test for the timeline.

CALLIGRAPHY

Notebook Page 10: Calligraphy Strokes

Points to Bring Out: Practice doing your calligraphy.

HISTORY

Bible Reading: Review Ex 10-12

Notebook Pages 11, 13-18: Passover 1-4

Points to Bring Out: Passover has been celebrated continually for over three thousand years. We know now that much of what was being done in that celebration pointed to Jesus Christ the Messiah. You will cut out and glue these pages to make a Passover Seder plate. Go over each element on the page and read the booklets for each one.

Note to Teacher: If the students have never participated in a Passover celebration, try to have one this year.

BIBLE

Bible Reading: Ex 13

Notebook Page 12: Passover Crossword

Points to Bring Out: This crossword puzzle is to help the students become better acquainted with the Passover terms and to see how they all presented a picture of what Jesus would fulfill.

CALLIGRAPHY

Notebook Page 19: Calligraphy Strokes

Points to Bring Out: Practice doing your calligraphy.

BIBLE

Bible Reading: Ex 12:37-15:27

Notebook Page 20: Exiting Egypt 1

Points to Bring Out: You may do this over several days. Exodus is the story of 'exiting' Egypt. Under each picture write briefly about each location the Israelites moved to. This exercise will help you get a more complete view of their travels. Write enough to understand what happened at each point.

Note to Teacher: You may want to have your students work on several pages at once. As they read a chapter in Exodus, go ahead and have them fill in what they can on pages 20, 21 and 22.

CALLIGRAPHY

Notebook Page 21: English Calligraphy

Points to Bring Out: Practice doing your calligraphy.

BIBLE

Bible Reading: Ex 14-17 (may use several days to do this)

Notebook Page 22: Grumbling 1

Points to Bring Out: The Israelites saw all the miracles God performed to get them out of Egypt and out of slavery. However, the Israelites had been mistreated as slaves and even though they were free now, they still had a slave's mentality and believed they were still being mistreated. They looked at their circumstances as being unbearable. Instead of turning to God and asking for help and waiting with anticipation to see how He would answer, they grumbled and complained.

You will be following the Israelites' grumblings all through their time in the desert. The Israelites were never thankful, did not remember what God had done for them before, had a victim's spirit, and didn't trust that God would care for them.

Post-Discussion: Explore the idea that a person often becomes rebellious when he or she does not believe that those who provide protection and care have his or her best interest in mind.

CALLIGRAPHY

Notebook Page 23: English Calligraphy

Points to Bring Out: Practice doing your calligraphy.

BIBLE

Bible Reading: Ex 16:1-36 and John 6:26-69

Notebook Page 24: Bread from Heaven

Points to Bring Out: Manna means 'why', 'what', 'when', or 'how.' It also implies a hesitation or reluctance. This study will show you how Jesus is the Bread of Life or Manna from Heaven.

Post-Discussion: Compare your answers about the two types of bread from heaven.

BIBLE

Bible Reading: Ex 18

Notebook Page 25: Jethro's Counsel

Points to Bring Out: Meet Jethro and find out what he suggested to Moses.

Post-Discussion: Were Jethro's suggestions of how to govern the vast numbers of Israelites a good plan?

The Law and Covenant

BIBLE

Bible Reading: Selected verses from Ex 19, 20, 24, 31-34

Notebook Page 26: The Ups and Downs of Mt Sinai

Points to Bring Out: Moses did not make just one trip up and down Mt. Sinai to get the Ten Commandments, but seven trips. And he received many more than ten commands. He was the intermediary between God and the people of Israel.

CALLIGRAPHY

Notebook Page 27: Calligraphy Capital Letters

Points to Bring Out: Practice doing your calligraphy.

BIBLE

Bible Reading: Selected verses in Ex 19-40

Notebook Page 28: God's Covenant with Israel 1

Points to Bring Out: This page gives an overview of the roles of God, Moses, and the Israelites in the making of a covenant, much like the Jewish wedding.

Post-Discussion: Compare the following with what happened at Mt. Sinai between God and Israel.

JEWISH WEDDING

1. The marriage is arranged by a matchmaker
2. The bride may veto or agree to the marriage.
3. The bride has a cleansing bath.
4. The marriage contract is read aloud and agreed on before the wedding day.
5. The bride prepares herself for the wedding.
6. The bride and groom have a short, face-to-face talk before the wedding.
7. The wedding takes place under a hoopah (a canopy).
8. A house is built for the couple.
9. A husband cannot go to battle for a full year.

BIBLE

Bible Reading: Jeremiah 31:31-33

Notebook Page 29: God's Covenant with Israel 2

Points to Bring Out: God's Covenant with Israel was like a marriage contract. God proposes, and the people accept, but it doesn't take long for the Israelites to break the sacred covenant. God reestablishes the covenant and lives with them.

God often refers to the Israelites as His bride or wife. The story of God making a covenant with Israel follows many of the steps in a Jewish wedding.

BIBLE

Bible Reading: Review Ex 32:1-33:6

Notebook Page 30: The People Break the Covenant

Points to Bring Out: Once Moses went up Mt. Sinai, the Israelites began to lose sight of the promises that had been made between God and themselves. They questioned what had happened to Moses and demanded that a god be made that they could see. With the wild celebration that followed, the Israelites would probably have broken all the Ten Commandments at this time. Since they unfaithful to God, He wanted to destroy them, but Moses intervened on their behalf.

Post-Discussion: Discuss the character of each of the players in the story: Moses, Aaron, the people, the Levites, and the Lord.

BIBLE

Bible Reading: Ex 19, 20, 32

Notebook Page 31: The Voice of God

Points to Bring Out: This is a review of God speaking to Moses and the Israelites.

CALLIGRAPHY

Notebook Page: Calligraphy Capital Letters

Points to Bring Out: Practice doing your calligraphy. In a few lessons, you will be using scripture verses from your daily reading assignments for your calligraphy. As you read, select some verses that are special to you and make a note of them for the future.

BIBLE

Bible Reading: Ex 33:7-34:3

Notebook Page 32: Moses and the Lord

Points to Bring Out: Moses had already seen the power of the Lord in the plagues on Egypt and the miracles in the desert. He had seen the clouds, smoke, fire, and lightning on the mountain. He had heard the thunder, trumpets, and the voice of God. He had felt the mountain quake. He spoke with God face to face and God had granted many of his requests. Why did he ask, "Show me Your glory"? What did he want? MORE!!

Post-Discussion: Though Moses had a close relationship with the Lord, it was the desire of his heart to have an even closer relationship. He could not get enough! Think about your own relationship with God. Are you satisfied or do you, like Moses, want MORE?

HISTORY

Notebook Pages 33-34: History of Hebrew, Hebrew History Crossword

Points to Bring Out: Hebrew has the amazing distinction of being both one of the oldest and one of the youngest languages of the world today. How can that be? Write about it and then do the crossword puzzle on it.

HISTORY

Notebook Page 35: The Holocaust

Points to Bring Out: One of the terrible things that happened was the killing of over 6 million Jews during the Holocaust. But the amazing thing was that it led to the rebirth of Israel as country almost two thousand years after Israel as an entity had ceased to exist.

BIBLE

Bible Reading: Ex 34:6-7 and other selections.

Notebook Page 36: God's Self-Portrait

Points to Bring Out: Under each line of the verse on this page is another verse that elaborates on it. Discuss how each verse corresponds to the line above it. How does this description of God build your faith and trust in Him?

Post-Discussion: One of the hard things in the Bible is at the end of Ex 34:7, which state that God punishes children for the sins of their fathers. At first glance this seems to say that God punishes children for sins they did not commit. This does not agree with the rest of Scripture. Discuss these two views.

1. One likely meaning is that God will continue to punish people as long as they continue in the sinful footsteps of their parents; He will not become tolerant of sin over time. Think of some examples of this.

2. Another way children suffer for the sins of their fathers can be easily seen in that when a father abandons or abuses a child, the child grows up lacking the nurturing and the love he should have. It is hard for such a child to know how to be a good and faithful parent. Think of some examples of how a parent has harmed their children and the consequences continue in their lives as adults.

God can and does bring healing in one's life. With that healing, the punishment to future generations ends. (Read 2 Chr 7:14)

HISTORY

Notebook Page 37: The Need for Vowels

Points to Bring Out: Imagine what it would be like to try to read something if there were no vowels. Try this out on your page today.

BIBLE

Bible Reading: Ex 20:1-12 and selected verses from the Gospels.

Notebook Page 38: The Ten Commandments in the Words of Jesus 1

Points to Bring Out: Memorize Ex. 20:1-12. The next two pages will show that Jesus had something to say about each one of the Ten Commandments.

Post-Discussion: The Jews, the Catholics/Lutherans and Protestants divide the Commandments differently. Copy the following table on the blackboard. Discuss possible reasons for the differences.

Jewish	Catholic/ Lutheran	Protestants
1. I am the Lord 2. No other gods/ No graven images. 3. Lord's name 4. Sabbath 5. Honor parents 6. Not kill 7. No adultery 8. Not steal 9. No false witness 10. Not covet	1. No other gods/ No graven images 2. Lord's name 3. Sabbath 4. Honor parents 5. Not kill 6. No adultery 7. Not steal 8. No false witness 9. Not covet house 10. Not covet wife	1. No other gods 2. No graven images 3. Lord's name 4. Sabbath 5. Honor parents 6. Not kill 7. No adultery 8. Not steal 9. No false witness 10. Not covet

BIBLE

Bible Reading: Ex 20:13-17 and selected verses from the Gospels

Notebook Page 39: The Ten Commandments in the Words of Jesus 2

Points to Bring Out: The demands that Jesus makes on fulfilling the Ten Commandments are impossible. In fact, if you don't understand that, He then tells us to "be perfect, therefore, as your Heavenly Father is perfect." (Mt 5:48)

Post-Discussion: There are people, including some who claim Christianity, who believe they do obey all of the Ten Commandments and therefore are good enough to go to heaven. Discuss different religions that are based on having your good works outweigh your bad deeds. (For example, Islam, Hinduism, Mormonism, and so forth.) Not only is God's standard to be perfect, but the motivation for all our actions is to be love. What hope is there for any of us to fulfill this? (None, except through the blood of Jesus Christ.)

BIBLE

Bible Reading: Ex 20:3-17, and selected verses from the New Testament

Notebook Page 40: The Ten Commandments and Our Hearts

Points to Bring Out: See how well you can put the Ten Commandments together with what Jesus says.

Post-Discussion: Discuss and compare each others' summaries for each commandment.

Note to Teacher: At this point, a message of salvation by grace should be given. Here is one way you could explain. Go over each of these verses together and pray about how to apply them in your lives.

Rom. 3:23—All have sinned
Rom. 6:23—The wages of sin is death
Rom. 10:9-10—Confess Jesus
Rom. 5:1—We are justified by faith
Rom. 12:1-2—Our response to God's goodness

HEBREW

Notebook Pages 41-48: Hebrew Letter Cartoons 1-2, English Words with Hebrew Letters 1, Hebrew Bookmarks (Needed: 2 envelopes)

Points to Bring Out: You will be using the Hebrew Letter Cartoons flash cards to help you learn Hebrew letters. Review the cards you have studied daily until you know them well, and don't forget to use both sides of the card. Store the cards in an envelope.

For English Words with Hebrew Letters 1, get the cards shown at the top of the page. Then make the outline letters into cartoons. For your first lesson in Hebrew, you will be working with English word. However, they will be spelled with Hebrew letters.

Note to Teacher: The Hebrew (and calligraphy) lessons are to be done in conjunction with a Bible or History lesson, not by themselves. Have your student cut out the Hebrew Letter Cartoons 1-2 and store these cartoon flash cards in two envelopes—one containing the letters he haven't studied yet, and one with the letters he has learned. You will need these to teach several lessons. Cut out the bookmarks and use these to help learn Hebrew as well.

HEBREW

Notebook Page 38: Hebrew Letter Cartoons 3

Points to Bring Out: Draw in the cartoons for the letters you have studied. You will be filling the rest of the letters as you learn them. Remember to fill in this page with each future lesson.

BIBLE

Bible Reading: Ex 20:8-11, Isaiah 56:1-7, 58:13-14

Notebook Page 49: The Sabbath 1

Points to Bring Out: The Sabbath was instituted by God at creation—on the seventh day, He rested from all He had done. Read the page on the Sabbath and prepare to discuss it.

Post-Discussion: How would it change your week to have every day centered around either remembering and reflecting on the past Sabbath or preparing and anticipating the coming Sabbath? Think of ways to plan a Sabbath. Make the day fun, relaxing, and mindful of God. See if you can invite family friends for a meal and activities.

CALLIGRAPHY

Notebook Page 50: Calligraphy Capital Letters

Points to Bring Out: Practice doing your calligraphy.

BIBLE

Bible Reading: Ex 20:8-11, Psalms. 92

Notebook Page 51: The Sabbath 2

Points to Bring Out: God gave some specific instructions to His people about activities that should not be done on the Sabbath. Through the ages, people have not only applied these to their lives but have made new lists of regulations as well.

Post-Discussion: What are your thoughts about the Sabbath? What are some things that you can do to celebrate a day as to the Lord?

HEBREW

Notebook Page 52: Hebrew Vowel Boy

Points to Bring Out: Review your vowels with this page. It will help you remember the placement and sound of each one.

HEBREW

Notebook Page 53: English Words with Hebrew Letters 2

Points to Bring Out: Get the Hebrew Letters Cartoon cards shown at the top of the page. Then make the outline letters into cartoons. For your next lesson in Hebrew, you will be working with English words. However, they will be spelled with Hebrew letters. Remember to go back to the Hebrew Letter Cartoons and fill in the new letters.

CALLIGRAPHY

Notebook Page 54: Calligraphy Practice

Points to Bring Out: Practice doing your calligraphy.

BIBLE

Bible Reading: Lev 18:1-4, Psalms 19:7-14, Ps 119, Pr 3:5, Heb 5:14

Notebook Page 55: Reasons for the Law 1

Points to Bring Out: The law has been the molding tool of the Jewish people. It created their culture, kept them healthy, gave ways to settle disputes and much more.

Post-Discussion: How has Biblical law affected the whole world in legal and medical fields?

BIBLE

Bible Reading: Various references in Leviticus

Notebook Page 56: Reasons for the Law 2

Points to Bring Out: In our culture, we have separated what is contained in the law into many disciplines, such as lawyers, doctors, pastors and so forth. Yet God gave one law that contained it all. The priests were responsible for implementing it.

HEBREW

Notebook Page 57: English Words with Hebrew Letters 3

Points to Bring Out: Get the Hebrew Letters Cartoon cards shown at the top of the page. Then make the outline letters into cartoons. For your next lesson in Hebrew, you will be working with English words. However, they will be spelled with Hebrew letters. Remember to go back to the Hebrew Letter Cartoons and fill in the new letters.

BIBLE

Bible Reading: Read after doing the top of the notebook page; Ex 20:22-22:15

Notebook Page 58: Test on the Legal Code 1

Points to Bring Out: How well would you do as a lawyer in Israel – before reading the Biblical passage, go through and circle your guesses for each one with a blue pen. This is for fun; it does not matter if you get them right. Next read the passages and rework the page with a red pen. See how well you guessed.

BIBLE

Bible Reading: Read after doing the top of the notebook page; Ex 22:16-23:13

Notebook Page 59: Test on the Legal Code 2

Points to Bring Out: How well would you do as a lawyer in Israel – before reading the Biblical passage, go through and circle your guesses for each one with a blue pen. This is for fun; it does not matter if you get them right. Next read the passages and rework the page with a red pen. See how well you guessed.

Post-Discussion: Share the ideas you have written for the bottom section of the page. (Under the heading: My Anger Will be Aroused)

CALLIGRAPHY

Notebook Page 60: Calligraphy Practice

Points to Bring Out: Practice doing your calligraphy.

WRITING

Bible Reading: Psalms 119:9-16

Notebook Page 61 Law Summary

Points to Bring Out: Use what you've learned about the law in this writing exercise.

Post-Discussion: Read your summaries aloud to each other.

HEBREW

Notebook Page 62: English Words with Hebrew Letters 4

Points to Bring Out: Get the Hebrew Letters Cartoon cards shown at the top of the page. Then make the outline letters into cartoons. For your next lesson in Hebrew, you will be working with English words. However, they will be spelled with Hebrew letters. Remember to go back to the Hebrew Letter Cartoons and fill in the new letters.

CALLIGRAPHY

Notebook Page 63: Calligraphy Verses

Points to Bring Out: Pick a verse from your recent scripture readings and use your calligraphy skills on this page. Review page 5 in your notebook.

Note to Teacher: There are verses included in the teacher's manual for ideas for students who haven't chosen one on their own.

HISTORY

Bible Reading: Numbers 15:37-41

Notebook Pages 64-65: Tying the Tzitzit, Tzitzit to Remember Commands

Points to Bring Out: The tzitzit was commanded by God and is a distinguishing mark of the Israelites clothing. Jesus wore tzitzit on each corner of His garment. Try making one of your own.

Post-Discussion: Discuss how the Jews use the tzitzit as a mnemonic devise to help them remember the commandments.

HEBREW

Notebook Page 66: English Words with Hebrew Letters 5

Points to Bring Out: Get the Hebrew Letters Cartoon cards shown at the top of the page. Then make the outline letters into cartoons. For your next lesson in Hebrew, you will be working with English words. However, they will be spelled with Hebrew letters. Remember to go back to the Hebrew Letter Cartoons and fill in the new letters.

The Tabernacle, Priests & Offerings

BIBLE

Bible Reading: Ex 25-27

Notebook Pages 67, 69-70: The Tabernacle in the Wilderness 1 & 2

Points to Bring Out: The Tabernacle had to be built to exact specifications and God gave very specific instructions for each aspect of it. It was a symbol of God dwelling with the Israelites and being among them. All Israel was eager to contribute for the building of the Tabernacle. The Tabernacle also depicted Heave and was another "shadow of things to come."

BIBLE

Bible Reading: Heb 7-10

Notebook Pages 68, 71-73: A Shadow of Things to Come 1-4 (Do over several days)

Points to Bring Out: The Tabernacle was given as a picture of Jesus Christ. These pages show how He fulfilled each aspect that God had designed.

Post-Discussion: Talk through each page as it is completed.

HEBREW

Notebook Page 74: English Words with Hebrew Letters 6

Points to Bring Out: Get the Hebrew Letters Cartoon cards shown at the top of the page. Then make the outline letters into cartoons. For your next lesson in Hebrew, you will be working with English words. However, they will be spelled with Hebrew letters. Remember to go back to the Hebrew Letter Cartoons and fill in the new letters.

BIBLE

Bible Reading: Selected verses

Notebook Page 75: A Shadow of Things to Come 5

Points to Bring Out: The arrangement of the items in the court and Tabernacle form the shape of a cross. Each item covers some aspect of Jesus Christ.

HEBREW

Notebook Page 76: English Words with Hebrew Letters 7

Points to Bring Out: From your envelope, pull out the cards shown at the top of the page. Then make the outline letters into cartoons. For your next lesson in Hebrew, you will be working with English word. However, they will be spelled with Hebrew letters. Remember to go back to the Hebrew Letter Cartoons 3 and fill in the letters.

WRITING

Bible Reading: Ps 100

Notebook Page 77: Tabernacle Summary

Points to Bring Out: Use what you've learned about the Tabernacle in this writing exercise.

Post-Discussion: Read your summaries aloud to each other.

CALLIGRAPHY

Notebook Page 78: Calligraphy Verses

Points to Bring Out: Pick a verse from your recent scripture readings and try your calligraphy skills on this page.

Note to Teacher: There are verses included in the teacher's manual for ideas for students who haven't chosen one on their own. Also, continue to assign verses to be done in calligraphy every couple of weeks. This will keep up your students' skills as well has help them to learn and appreciate verses.

BIBLE

Bible Reading: Review Ex 16-39

Notebook Page 79: Exiting Egypt 2

Points to Bring Out: Review how God provided food, water, protection and direction for the Israelites.

HEBREW

Notebook Page 80: English Words with Hebrew Letters 8

Points to Bring Out: Get the Hebrew Letters Cartoon cards shown at the top of the page. Then make the outline letters into cartoons. For your next lesson in Hebrew, you will be working with English words. However, they will be spelled with Hebrew letters. Remember to go back to the Hebrew Letter Cartoons and fill in the new letters.

BIBLE

Bible Reading: Leviticus 1-7 and selected New Testament verses

Notebook Pages 81, 83-84: Offerings to God 1 & 2 (Do over several days.)

Points to Bring Out: There were specific rules and procedures for every kind of sacrifice and offering to be given. The Israelites didn't know why they were doing them this way, but God was giving them a picture of what Jesus Christ would do for us.

Post-Discussion: Talk about each of the types of offerings on the page.

Note to Teacher: Under the heading of "Duties", students are to only mark the duties to be done for the specific verses in that section.

HEBREW

Notebook Page 82: English Words with Hebrew Letters 9

Points to Bring Out: Get the Hebrew Letters Cartoon cards shown at the top of the page. Then make the outline letters into cartoons. For your next lesson in Hebrew, you will be working with English words. However, they will be spelled with Hebrew letters. Remember to go back to the Hebrew Letter Cartoons and fill in the new letters.

WRITING

Bible Reading: Psalms 40

Notebook Page 85: Offerings Summary

Points to Bring Out: Use what you've learned about the offerings in this writing exercise.

Post-Discussion: Read your summaries aloud to each other.

HEBREW

Notebook Page 86: English Words with Hebrew Letters 10

Points to Bring Out: Get the Hebrew Letters Cartoon cards shown at the top of the page. Then make the outline letters into cartoons. For your next lesson in Hebrew, you will be working with English words. However, they will be spelled with Hebrew letters. Remember to go back to the Hebrew Letter Cartoons and fill in the new letters.

CALLIGRAPHY

Notebook Page 87: Calligraphy Verses

Points to Bring Out: Pick a verse from your recent scripture readings and try your calligraphy skills on this page.

BIBLE

Bible Reading: Ex 28, Hebrews 4:14-16

Notebook Page 88: Priestly Garments

Points to Bring Out: The directions for the garments of the priest were very detailed and specific. Again God was giving His people a picture of the Messiah to come. As we saw when we did the Tabernacle pages, Jesus is our High Priest.

BIBLE

Bible Reading: Lev 8

Notebook Pages 89, 91-92: Ordination of Aaron and Sons 1 & 2

Points to Bring Out: Aaron and his sons were set apart with a special ceremony for their responsibilities as priests.

HEBREW

Notebook Page 90: Holocaust

Points to Bring Out: The word study today is on the word that means 'to go up'. The priests offered sacrifices that go up to heaven. How does this relate to the Holocaust?

HEBREW

Notebook Page 93: English Words with Hebrew Letters 11

Points to Bring Out: Get the <u>Hebrew Letters Cartoon</u> cards shown at the top of the page. Then make the outline letters into cartoons. For your next lesson in Hebrew, you will be working with English words. However, they will be spelled with Hebrew letters. Remember to go back to the <u>Hebrew Letter Cartoons</u> and fill in the new letters.

CALLIGRAPHY

Notebook Page 94: Hebrew Calligraphy Strokes

Points to Bring Out: Pick a verse from your recent scripture readings and try your calligraphy skills on this page.

BIBLE

Bible Reading: Lev 9 & 10

Notebook Page 95: Reverence of God

Points to Bring Out: There were very real consequences that happened to the people who violated God's specific instructions. This shows us that when God gives us directions to follow, we can't just do things any old way.

BIBLE

Bible Reading: Lev 11, 26-28, Deuteromony 14

Notebook Pages 96-97: Food for Thought 1 -2

Points to Bring Out: God gave specific descriptions of what living things His people were allowed to eat.

HEBREW

Notebook Page 98: Too Close for Comfort

Points to Bring Out: Many of the Hebrew letters look or sound alike. So be very careful in reading them.

HISTORY

Bible Reading: Romans 14:12-23

Notebook Page 99: Our Thoughts on Food

Points to Bring Out: Look closely at the list of animals. Most of these animals are eaten in various countries around the world.

Post-Discussion: How many of them do you eat? Would you be willing to eat them if they were offered to you by someone who considers them a delicacy? In cases like this, would the law of love override the dietary laws or personal preferences?

HEBREW

Notebook Page 100: Animals

Points to Bring Out: Figure out what these animals are with your knowledge of Hebrew letters.

WRITING

Bible Reading: Matthew 15:1-20

Notebook Page 101: Food Law Summary

Points to Bring Out: Use what you've learned about the food laws in this writing exercise.

Post-Discussion: Read your summaries aloud to each other.

HISTORY

Bible Reading: Lev 17:12, Ex. 23:19

Notebook Pages 102-104: Walls Around Walls 1 & 2

Points to Bring Out: The issue of cooking milk with meat would not have been a big problem to the early Israelites. Meat was a rare treat. In time, the Jews became very wary of disobeying the Law of God, and so they built "walls around walls" to keep themselves very far from any transgression.

Post-Discussion: Do you think that the walls that were built around these verses were a good idea? Also, discuss your answers to the question at the bottom of the page.

HISTORY

Bible Reading: Matt. 5:18

Notebook Page 105: The Scribe

Points to Bring Out: The same characteristics that built the "walls" and added more regulations to the original laws, were critical in passing the written law on to future generations. The scribes were perfectionists in copying the scriptures.

Post-Discussion: Discuss the page together and answer the questions.

HISTORY

Bible Reading: Dt 23:12-13, Lev 11:7-19

Notebook Page 106: Before its Time

Points to Bring Out: God gave dietary laws that prevented the spread of diseases even before people knew the cause of the diseases. Modern science has shown us that there are many good health reasons that are related to these dietary and cleanliness laws.

HEBREW

Notebook Page 107: Hebrew Alphabet Chart

Points to Bring Out: In the first column, under Hebrew Letters, write the letters of the Hebrew alphabet in order. The names of each letter are in the third column, under Name. (Hint: The first letter of each name is that letter.) Under the pronunciation, write out how you would pronounce the name of the letter. The rest of the chart will be filled out in later lessons.

HISTORY

Bible Reading: Lev 13

Notebook Page 108: Doctor! Doctor!

Points to Bring Out: The priests also played an important role in their communities as the medical authorities. They were expected to be able to diagnose and treat many diseases. With large groups of people, it was important to isolate and quarantine contagious diseases. God gave these instructions in His law and it prevented the spread of plagues and other disease.

Post-Discussion: Research and discuss the history of sterilization of medical equipment over the years.

HISTORY

Bible Reading: Luke 17:11-17

Notebook Page 109: Leprosy

Points to Bring Out: Leprosy in the Bible referred to many types of skin diseases and not just to what we call leprosy today. There are many spiritual applications to these diseases, and there are nine stories in the Bible about leprosy.

Post-Discussion: Talk about the information on this page and how it relates to you today.

HEBREW

Notebook Pages 110-111: The Source of Hebrew and Latin Letters 1 & 2

Points to Bring Out: Follow the instructions to match the Latin and Hebrew letters to their source—900 B.C. Hebrew. Then use that information to fill in the Hebrew Alphabet Chart. Note that the name 'alphabet' came from the first two letters of the Hebrew 'alef-beth.'

BIBLE

Bible Reading: Lev 18

Notebook Page 112: Scintillating Talk-Shows

Points to Bring Out: People have had a heart for evil since the beginning of time. The issues that are discussed, to their shame, on today's talk-shows are nothing new.

Discuss: Discuss how God feels about these relationships.

CALLIGRAPHY

Notebook Page 113: Hebrew Calligraphy Strokes

Points to Bring Out: Practice the strokes necessary to write Hebrew letters.

HISTORY

Bible Reading: Lev 19

Notebook Pages 114-115: Egyptian Code, I Am the Lord God

Points to Bring Out: Many people discredit the law God gave to Moses by saying that there were already many laws and codes in existence, such as the Egyptian Code, prior to Moses. However, there are only a few similarities and these could be attributed to the fact that any society needs similar types of governing laws to survive.

Seasons and Feasts

BIBLE

Bible Reading: Lev 23

Notebook Pages 116-118: The Lord's Appointed Feasts 1 & 2, Crossword for Feasts

Points to Bring Out: These pages give an overview of the biblical feasts and show how they represent God's plan of salvation through the centuries.

HEBREW

Notebook Page 119: Hebrew Alphabet & Modern Words

Points to Bring Out: The word 'alphabet' has no meaning to us other than that it represents our letters. In Hebrew, their word for 'alphabet' is 'alef-beth' and means, "ox-house." Many of the letters, with a few vowel changes, still have meaning today. You will need to memorize these names. (Try singing them to a familiar tune to help you remember them.) Not only do they have literal meanings, they represent numbers. The Hebrew letters also have spiritual meanings, which you may want to research on your own.

Note to Teacher: Give the following explanation of how to fill in the Hebrew numbers. Fill in the Hebrew

Alphabet Chart under Number, with the first ten numbers being 1-10. The next nine numbers go by ten's to 100 (20-100), and the last three go by hundred's to 400 (200, 300, and 400.)

HISTORY

Bible Reading: Lev 23

Notebook Pages 120-124: Seasons and Feasts 1-3, Schedule of Jewish Holidays

Points to Bring Out: The feasts are closely tied to the cycle of seasons. The celebration was related to farming activities. The Jewish calendar is different from the secular Western calendar. This causes the festivals to fall on different dates every year as seen on the Schedule of Jewish Holidays. If you choose to celebrate the biblical festivals, this chart will help you determine the dates.

HEBREW

Bible Reading: Various verses

Notebook Page 125: Atonement

Points to Bring Out: This is a word study of the word that is often translated "atone." The idea of "covering" is also included.

Post-Discussion: Discuss the page and how we have atonement through Jesus.

WRITING

Bible Reading: Zec 14

Notebook Page 126: The Feasts Summary

Points to Bring Out: Use what you've learned about the feasts in this writing exercise.

Post-Discussion: Read your summaries aloud to each other.

HEBREW

Notebook Page 127: Name Elements

Points to Bring Out: Soon you will be reading Hebrew names and seeing the elements that make them up.

HEBREW

Notebook Pages 128-130: Blessings for Passover & Sabbath 1-3 (Do over several days)

Points to Bring Out: Fill in these Hebrew blessings that are used for Sabbath and Passover services. Then choose one to practice your Hebrew Calligraphy.

Note to Teacher: There are verses included in the teacher's manual for ideas for students who haven't chosen one on their own. Also, continue to assign verses in Hebrew or English every couple of weeks to keep up your student's skills.

HEBREW

Notebook Page 131: Hebrew Calligraphy

Points to Bring Out: Practice your strokes for learning Hebrew letters.

HEBREW

Notebook Pages 132-133: Hebrew Names 1 & 2

Points to Bring Out: See how many of these names you know. Read the names written in Hebrew out loud together. The way these names are pronounced in Hebrew is not the way we say them when they are translated into English. Use the Hebrew Names 1 chart to help you fill in the Hebrew Names 2 page.

BIBLE

Bible Reading: Various verses

Notebook Page 134: Brought to You by the Number Seven

Points to Bring Out: The number seven is used symbolically in the Bible for the idea of completion and perfection.

BIBLE

Bible Reading: Numbers 2-3

Notebook Page 135: Organization of the Camp

Points to Bring Out: It is very helpful to visualize the number and placement of each tribe and its relationship to the Tabernacle.

CALLIGRAPHY

Notebook Page 136: Hebrew Calligraphy

Points to Bring Out: Practice the strokes necessary to write Hebrew letters.

HEBREW

Notebook Page 137: Hebrew Names 3

Points to Bring Out: See how many of these names you know. Read the names written in Hebrew out loud together. The way these names are pronounced in Hebrew is not the way we say them when they are translated into English. Also, note that Hebrew does not have a 'j' but uses a 'y' instead. That letter has been translated into English as a 'j'. For example, 'Jesus' is pronounced 'Yeshua' in Hebrew and literally means 'salvation.'

Forty Years in the Wilderness

BIBLE

Bible Reading: Nu 11-14,

Notebook Page 138: Grumbling 2 (Do over a couple of days)

Points to Bring Out: The children of Israel continue to complain about hardships, no good food, no water, and that Canaan is too dangerous.

WRITING

Bible Reading: Ps 136

Notebook Page 139: A Thankful Heart

Points to Bring Out: Thank God for the food that you have available to you. Think about how having the same food day after day would make you feel.

Post-Discussion: Read your prayers aloud to each other.

CALLIGRAPHY

Notebook Page 140: Grid for Hebrew Calligraphy

Points to Bring Out: Practice the strokes necessary for writing Hebrew letters.

BIBLE

Bible Reading: Nu 16, 20:1-13, 21:4-9

Notebook Page 141: Grumbling 3 (Do over a couple of days)

Points to Bring Out: The children of Israel continue to complain. Does this sound familiar?

Post-Discussion: What were some of the results of their grumbling?

HEBREW

Notebook Page 142: Hebrew Names 4

Points to Bring Out: See how many of these names you know. Read the names written in Hebrew out loud together. The way these names are pronounced in Hebrew is not the way we say them when they are translated into English. You will be using the Hebrew Names 1 chart to help you.

BIBLE

Bible Reading: Nu 11, 13, 16, 20

Notebook Page 143: Exiting Egypt 3 (Do over a couple of days)

Points to Bring Out: Write in enough information to tell the story of the wanderings of the Israelites.

HEBREW

Notebook Page 144: Hebrew Names 5

Points to Bring Out: See how many of these names you know. Read the names written in Hebrew out loud together. The way these names are pronounced in Hebrew is not the way we say them when they are translated into English. You will be using the Hebrew Names 1 chart to help you.

BIBLE

Bible Reading: Nu 21-25, 31:1-7

Notebook Page 145: Exiting Egypt 4 (Do over a couple of days)

Points to Bring Out: Write in enough information to tell the story of the wanderings of the Israelites.

HEBREW

Notebook Page 146: Hebrew Names 6

Points to Bring Out: See how many of these names you know. Read the names written in Hebrew out loud together. The way these names are pronounced in Hebrew is not the way we say them when they are translated into English. You will be using the Hebrew Names 1 chart to help you.

HISTORY

Bible Reading: Ps 106

Notebook Page 147: Exiting Egypt 5

Points to Bring Out: This map is a review of the journey of the children of Israel after they left Egypt.

WRITING

Bible Reading: Various verses

Notebook Pages 148-152: We Could be Back in Egypt Eating Onions 1-4 (Do over several days)

Points to Bring Out: You will be writing a play to act out about the Israelites and their grumbling. Make comments on what they should have done instead of grumbling.

Post-Discussion: When we have needs, how does God want us to approach Him for them?

HEBREW

Notebook Page 153: Hebrew Names 7

Points to Bring Out: See how many of these names you know. Read the names written in Hebrew out loud together. The way these names are pronounced in Hebrew is not the way we say them when they are translated into English. You will be using the Hebrew Names 1 chart to help you.

The Law Revisited

BIBLE

Bible Reading: Deuteronomy 1-8

Notebook Page 154: God's Care of His Chosen Children

Points to Bring Out: The beginning of Deuteronomy is addressed to the younger generation of the Israelites. Moses wanted to instruct and encourage them as they entered the Promised Land.

HEBREW

Notebook Page 155: Hebrew Names 8

Points to Bring Out: See how many of these names you know. Read the names written in Hebrew out loud together. The way these names are pronounced in Hebrew is not the way we say them when they are translated into English. You will be using the Hebrew Names 1 chart to help you.

BIBLE

Bible Reading: Dt 4-6, 9-10

Notebook Pages 156-157: Deuteronomy and the Ten Commandments 1 & 2 (Do over a couple of days)

Points to Bring Out: The Ten Commandments are repeated here and yet there is additional information included.

Post-Discussion: Why do you think scripture records the same events differently in other places?

HISTORY

Bible Reading: Various verses

Notebook Pages 158-159, 161-162: "Bayit" Box, A Sign on Your Hand and Forehead 1-2

Points to Bring Out: Instructions about the "Bayit" box are in scripture and have been done in this way by Jews for thousands of years.

Post-Discussion: Think of things that people wear as reminders of relationships in their lives. (wedding rings, crosses, ID's, WWJD bracelets)

HEBREW

Notebook Page 160, 163-166: Biblical Women's Names, Hebrew Word Cards 1 & 2 (You will need an envelope)

Points to Bring Out: See how many of these names you know. Read the names written in Hebrew out loud together. Then cut out and use the flash cards on Hebrew Word Cards 1 & 2 to help you learn more words.

BIBLE

Bible Reading: Dt 11

Notebook Page 167: Loving the Lord

Post-Discussion: How do we demonstrate our love for the Lord?

BIBLE

Bible Reading: Dt 15-19

Notebook Pages 168-169: The Law of Justice and Mercy 1 & 2 (Do over a couple of days)

Points to Bring Out: Micah 6:8 contains a summary of our relationship with God and man. Most laws are built on the elements in this verse: Justice, mercy, and your relationship with God.

Post-Discussion: What have you discovered in these laws about God's mercy?

HISTORY

Notebook Page 170: Hammurabi's Code

Points to Bring Out: There were other laws written down before Moses' time. Of the law codes found, Hammurabi's Law is the most famous.

Post-Discussion: Compare and contrast the law of Hammurabi with the Law of Moses.

HISTORY

Notebook Pages 171, 173-174: History of Names 1- 2

Points to Bring Out: Laws have governed the names that Jewish parents could name their children in several countries. Look at one list of acceptable names and see what you think about them. Then do the History of Names 2 and glue it on.

Post-Discussion: What was Hitler trying to accomplish by forcing Jews to have only certain names?

BIBLE

Bible Reading: Dt 24-27

Notebook Pages 172, 175: The Law of Justice and Mercy 3 & 4 (Do over a couple of days)

Points to Bring Out: Micah 6:8 contains a summary of our relationship with God and man. Most laws are built on the elements in this verse: Justice, mercy, and your relationship with God.

HISTORY

Bible Reading: Various verses

Notebook Page 176: Brought to You by the Number Forty

Points to Bring Out: The number forty shows up many times in the Bible. Check out the connections with forty in each situation on this page.

BIBLE

Bible Reading: Dt 31-34

Notebook Page 177: Moses' Last Days

Points to Bring Out: The number '40' was very significant in Moses' life. He lived as an Egyptian prince for 40 years. He herded sheep as a nobody for 40 years. He was on the mountain of God for 40 days. Then he led the people of Israel through the wilderness as a servant of God for 40 years. Moses at 120 years of age was still strong and a contributing leader of the Israelites. He was honored and respected, and his words were held in high esteem.

WRITING

Bible Reading: Ps 90 (written by Moses)

Notebook Page 178: Moses' Life

Points to Bring Out: Think of words that begin with each letter of the alphabet to tell something about Moses' life. Then write a sentence using that word to further explain the event or item.

Post-Discussion: Read your summaries aloud to each other.

BIBLE

Bible Reading: Ge 48:15-49:28

Notebook Page 179: Blessings of Jacob and Moses

Points to Bring Out: Compare the blessings Jacob gave his sons with the blessings Moses gave their descendents.

CALLIGRAPHY

Notebook Page 180: Hebrew Letter Embroidery (See supply list on page.)

Points to Bring Out: First select a Hebrew verse (if you have a Hebrew Bible), blessing, or the alef-beth, and plot it on the graph paper. If time or circumstances permit, embroider it on counted cross-stitch material.

BIBLE

Bible Reading: Ge 46:8-23, Nu 1:17-47, 26:1-51, 62, Ex 30:11-16

Notebook Page 181: Numbers-Tally it Up

Points to Bring Out: When the children of Israel went to Egypt, they were a small family group. When they left Egypt, they were a nation of over 600,000 men. When they entered the Promised Land, some tribes had increased in number and some had decreased, but God had sustained them as a nation through the desert.

BIBLE

Notebook Page 182: It Would Have Been

Points to Bring Out: The Jewish people sing a song called "Dayenu", which means, "It would have been enough." In contrast to the complaints and grumblings that the Israelites did, this song reminds them that at any point along the way, God's provision would have been enough. This grateful attitude should be evident in our walk as Christians, as in the words for "It would have been more than we deserved."

Joshua Conquers the Promised Land

BIBLE

Bible Reading: Various verses

Notebook Page 183: From Joshua Through Solomon

Points to Bring Out: This page will give you an overview of what you will be studying over the next few weeks.

HEBREW

Notebook Pages 184-185: Hebrew Vocabulary, Simple Hebrew Sentences 1

Points to Bring Out: The Hebrew Vocabulary will be used today as well as for future lessons. The words come from the names and the alef-beth that you have studied so far. As you look over it, you will see the connections.

Now you're ready to put Hebrew words together into sentences.

BIBLE

Bible Reading: Various verses

Notebook Page 186: Joshua's Heart

Points to Bring Out: This is an overview of Joshua's character and heart towards God.

HISTORY

Bible Reading: Lev 18:21, 20:1-5, Jer 32:30-35

Notebook Page 187: Commanded to Kill?!

Points to Bring Out: To some it seems harsh that God required the Israelites to kill their enemies. After you study this page, think about what would you say to someone who believes that God was cruel.

Post-Discussion: What would you say to someone who told you that the God of the Old Testament was harsh and cruel.

BIBLE

Bible Reading: Eph 6:10-18

Notebook Pages 188-189: The Armor of God 1 & 2 (Do over a couple of days)

Points to Bring Out: The Israelites are learning to be warriors so they can go in and conquer the land. Christians are also in a battle, but we have the resources for spiritual battle through Jesus.

Post-Discussion: Share your answers for how the armor of God protects.

HEBREW

Notebook Page 190: Hebrew Vocabulary, Adding 'The' in Hebrew 1

Points to Bring Out: Today you will see how 'the' is used with Hebrew words. Use the Hebrew Vocabulary if you need help.

HISTORY

Notebook Pages 191, 193-194: The Tale Told by a Tell 1 & 2

Points to Bring Out: Archeologists can learn many things about the past through their investigations of tells.

Post-Discussion: How is a tell formed? What sequence of events that can be learned from it?

BIBLE

Bible Reading: Various verses

Notebook Page 192: Practice for Joshua's Conquest Page

Points to Bring Out: This page is to help you understand and practice what you will be doing for the next couple of pages. You will be filling in the events and plotting the progress of Joshua and the Israelites in the conquest.

HISTORY

Bible Reading: Joshua 1-11

Notebook Pages 195, 197-198: Joshua's Conquests 1 & 2 (Do over several days)

Points to Bring Out: Read two or three chapters a day. You will be filling in the events and plotting the progress of Joshua and the Israelites in the conquest. You will be doing other pages as well that cover some of these chapters. As you read, fill in any information you find for this chart.

HISTORY

Bible Reading: Jos 6:26, 1 Kng 16:34

Notebook Page 196: The City of Jericho

Points to Bring Out: The first city that was conquered was the oldest, or longest inhabited, city in the world. They had the most time of any city to decide whether to sin or turn to God. They chose to sin and reaped the consequences.

BIBLE

Bible Reading: Jos 2-7

Notebook Page 199: He Said, She Said

Points to Bring Out: Figure out who each of these characters are by what they said.

BIBLE

Bible Reading: Jos 7-8

Notebook Page 200: Respecting God's Commands

Points to Bring Out: God has His reasons for the directions He gives His people. When they choose to disobey, there are serious consequences, not only for them, but for all Israel.

HISTORY

Bible Reading: Ex 20:24-36, Jos 8:30-35

Notebook Page 201: Joshua's Altar or is It?

Points to Bring Out: As you study archeological discoveries that relate to the Bible, you will find many contradictory conclusions. This page will give you an example of such a Post-Discussion.

Post-Discussion: What difference does the worldview of the archeologist make in regard to his conclusions about his discoveries?

HEBREW

Notebook Page 201: Adding 'The' in Hebrew 2

Points to Bring Out: Today you will see how 'the' is used with Hebrew words. Use the Hebrew Vocabulary if you need help.

BIBLE

Bible Reading: Jos 9-10

Notebook Page 203: Keeping Promises

Points to Bring Out: Joshua is tricked into a treaty and there are interesting consequences.

Post-Discussion: How did God feel about the validity of the treaty?

HEBREW

Notebook Page 204: Male and Female Words in Hebrew

Points to Bring Out: The Hebrew Vocabulary will be used today as well as for future lessons. Letters are added to Hebrew nouns and verbs to designate gender.

WRITING

Bible Reading: Jos 1:1-5

Notebook Page 205: Joshua's Life

Points to Bring Out: Use what you've learned about Joshua in this writing exercise.

Post-Discussion: Read your summaries aloud to each other.

HEBREW

Notebook Page 206: Hebrew Vocabulary, Simple Hebrew Sentences 2

Points to Bring Out: You'll be using the new things you've studied to make sentences today. Use the information on pages 201 and 204 if you need help.

BIBLE

Bible Reading: Ge 49:1-27

Notebook Page 207: Emblems of the Tribes of Israel

Points to Bring Out: Variations of these emblems have been used for the tribes ever since Jacob (Israel) blessed his children.

Post-Discussion: What kind of an emblem would you use to represent your family? (Make a banner with that emblem.)

BIBLE

Bible Reading: Jos 13-22

Notebook Page 208: Division of the Promised Land (Do this over several days-younger students will need help.)

Points to Bring Out: The Promised Land was divided between the tribes before they even conquered it. All the tribes were committed to help each other take control of their territory.

Post-Discussion: What happened to the tribes Simeon and Levi?

HEBREW

Notebook Pages 209-210: More Hebrew, Simple Hebrew Sentences 3

Points to Bring Out: Today you will see more elements that go into Hebrew sentences. Refer to past Hebrew lesson pages if you need help.

Overview of Jewish History

HISTORY

Bible Reading: Jos 23-24

Notebook Pages 211-221: Overview of Jewish History, Persecution 1-3, Interacting With Persecution (Do over several days)

Points to Bring Out: God promised the Israelites that He would bless them if they followed His commandments, but if they didn't they would suffer. The Jews sing the song, "Khad Gadyah", an allegory, to remember the persecution they have suffered at the hands of many nations for their continual disobedience.

HISTORY

Notebook Pages 222-223: Persecution of the Jews in Europe, Persecution Crossword

Points to Bring Out: Jews suffered terribly throughout the centuries of their life in Europe. Consequently, Europe is depicted as the 'Angel of Death' in their song, "Khad Gadyah."

Post-Discussion: Where do Jews still suffer persecution today? What are some reasons why it is difficult for a Jew to accept Jesus as Messiah?

Judges

HISTORY

Bible Reading: Various verses

Notebook Page 224: Family Trouble for the Israelites

Points to Bring Out: The Bible is a history book. It tells the stories of the people who made history. As we study the Israelites and the people they encounter, we need to know where they came from. Many of the enemies the Israelites faced were descendants of Abraham or his father, Terah. After working the Family Trouble for the Israelites, you can use it as a reference to refer to as you read your Bible.

BIBLE

Bible Reading: Judges 1-21

Notebook Pages 225, 227-230: Israel's Judges 1-3 (Do over several days; you will be doing other pages at the same time.)

Points to Bring Out: You will be filling out charts about the book of Judges over the next few days. You will also be working on other pages at the same time. As you find the answers to the charts, fill them in.

Post-Discussion: What pattern is repeated over and over again in the lives of the Israelites?

BIBLE

Bible Reading: Jdg 4-9

Notebook Page 226: Deborah, Gideon, & Abimelech

Points to Bring Out: Figure out who said what and write in the correct name below each statement.

BIBLE

Bible Reading: Jdg 13-17

Notebook Page 231: Samson's Heart

Points to Bring Out: This page will show you the contrast between the choices that Samson could have made and the choices he did make.

BIBLE

Bible Reading: Jdg 17-18

Notebook Page 232: Priest for Hire

Points to Bring Out: Even the priests do not have a good understanding of the scriptures and their lives reflect the downhill spiral of the nation.

BIBLE

Bible Reading: Jdg 19-21

Notebook Page 233: Horror in the Night

Points to Bring Out: Anarchy leads to chaos and catastrophe as each person does what is right in his own sight.

Post-Discussion: Why does God allow evil to happen? And why does God want it to be recorded in scripture?

BIBLE

Bible Reading: Various verses

Notebook Page 234: Location of Israel's Judges

Points to Bring Out: Unlike a royal dynasty that comes from one family, God chose judges from almost every tribe. His method of leadership did not put one group above another.

BIBLE

Bible Reading: Various verses

Notebook Page 235: Adding Up the Years

Points to Bring Out: Review the years of rest and the years of oppression in this 420 year time period.

BIBLE

Bible Reading: Various verses

Notebook Page 236: Name That Judge

Points to Bring Out: Remember the most important judges as you fill in this crossword puzzle.

WRITING

Bible Reading: Heb 11:29-40, 12:1-3

Notebook Page 237: Judges Summary

Points to Bring Out: Use what you've learned about the judges in this writing exercise.

Post-Discussion: Read your summaries aloud to each other.

Ruth

BIBLE

Bible Reading: Ruth 1-4

Notebook Page 238: Overview of Ruth

Points to Bring Out: Ruth is a good book to use to learn one way to do a book study on your own. Begin by reading the whole book to get an overview of the events. Then go back and read each chapter, asking questions. Put yourself into the place of the characters and try to understand what they were thinking and feeling.

BIBLE

Bible Reading: Ru 1-4

Notebook Pages 239-243: Gleanings From Ruth 1-4, Ruth (Do over several days)

Points to Bring Out: You will be gathering information from Ruth over the next few days as well as deciphering Hebrew words that are related to her name.

BIBLE

Bible Reading: Various verses

Notebook Page 244: Redeeming Ruth

Points to Bring Out: This page compares Jesus to Boaz as our redeemer.

BIBLE

Bible Reading: Ruth

Notebook Page 245: Ruth Scroll

Points to Bring Out: This is another way to outline and can be done with any book.

Samuel, King Saul and David

BIBLE

Bible Reading: 1 Samuel 1-3

Notebook Page 246: Birth of Samuel

Points to Bring Out: Fill out the crossword puzzle to learn about the amazing events that lead to the birth of one of Israel's greatest prophets.

BIBLE

Bible Reading: 1 Sa 4-7

Notebook Page 247: Rats! Foiled Again!

Points to Bring Out: Follow the events that lead to the capture and loss of the Ark of God.

BIBLE

Bible Reading: 1 Sa 8

Notebook Page 248: The Hearts of Fathers and Sons

Points to Bring Out: Just because the father is godly does not mean that his children will follow in his footsteps.

Post-Discussion: What does the saying, 'God has no grandchildren' mean? (Our parents can't give us their salvation. We must individually be born again and become His child.)

BIBLE

Bible Reading: 1 Sa 8-10

Notebook Page 249: Crowning a King

Points to Bring Out: Samuel warns the people of all the hardships they will experience if they have a king. They still want one, so he reluctantly gives them Saul as their king.

BIBLE

Bible Reading: 1 Sa 15

Notebook Pages 251-252: Saul's Family Tree, Saul's Family Tree Crossword

Points to Bring Out: This is a review of Saul's family and the relationships and conflicts between them.

BIBLE

Bible Reading: 1 Sa 11, 13, 14, 31

Notebook Page 252: First King of Israel

Points to Bring Out: Here is an overview of Saul's life as king, including the battles and conflicts he had. Notice that he began his reign as king differently than he ended it.

Post-Discussion: If you are seeking to follow God in your life now, will you automatically be righteous the rest of your life? What do we need to do to stay close to God, day by day?

BIBLE

Bible Reading: 1 Sa 15

Notebook Page 253: Saul's Heart

Points to Bring Out: Again, look at what Saul could have done and what he did do, thus revealing his heart.

Post-Discussion: What does what you DON'T do reveal about your character?

WRITING

Bible Reading: Psalms 78

Notebook Page 254: A Rebellious Heart

Points to Bring Out: Write a play with a main character who feels he is above any authority. Use at least five of the arguments that Saul used for why he didn't have to completely obey.

BIBLE

Bible Reading: 1 Sa 16-17

Notebook Page 255: Qualifications 1

Points to Bring Out: David had developed personal integrity, skills as a musician, a relationship with God, and had learned to be a good protector of his flocks. He used his time wisely during the lonely hours of watching the sheep to compose music. He had many skills which he shared with others. When Saul needed someone, David was ready.

Post-Discussion: Are you using your time to develop your relationship with God and your personal skills so that you will be ready to be used when an opportunity arises?

WRITING

Bible Reading: Ps 1 & 23

Notebook Page 256: The Poetry of the Psalms

Points to Bring Out: This is a short assignment to learn how Hebrew poetry works.

BIBLE

Bible Reading: Various verses

Notebook Page 257: The Good Shepherd

Points to Bring Out: David was a good shepherd and God and Jesus are often depicted as good shepherds.

WRITING

Bible Reading: Ps 23

Notebook Page 258: The Lord is my Shepherd

Points to Bring Out: Take each line from Psalm 23 and figure out what it means.

WRITING

Bible Reading: Matt. 6:5-14, 25-34

Notebook Page 259: God is my Heavenly Father

Points to Bring Out: Not all fathers are good to their children. But our Heavenly Father is better to His children than the best earthly father ever could be.

BIBLE

Bible Reading: 1 Sa 17

Notebook Page 260: Qualifications 2

Points to Bring Out: Man's qualifications and God's qualifications are very different.

Post-Discussion: Have you even been in a situation that seemed to be impossible from a human perspective but that God worked out in a miraculous way?

WRITING

Bible Reading: Ps 19, 100, 103

Notebook Pages 261-263: Types of Psalms, Psalm of Praise, My Own Psalm of Praise

Points to Bring Out: There are many different ways of looking at the psalms. The <u>Types of Psalms</u> is a reference page that we will be using to study the Psalms. The first type that you will study is a psalm of praise. Then you will write your own psalm of praise to God.

Post-Discussion: Read your psalms aloud to each other.

BIBLE

Bible Reading: 1 Sa 18, 19

Notebook Page 264: Saul's Jealousy 1

Points to Bring Out: Jealousy is a heart issue as you will find in this study about Saul.

Post-Discussion: Share your examples of ways that seem right to men but lead to death.

BIBLE

Bible Reading: 1 Sa 16—2 Sa 5

Notebook Pages 265, 267-268: David on the Run 1 & 2 (Do over several days while you work on other pages)

Points to Bring Out: You will be plotting and filling in the events of David's life over several days while you work on other pages.

WRITING

Bible Reading: 1 Sa 21:1-22:1; Ps 15, 32, 24

Notebook Pages 266, 269: Psalm to Teach Wisdom 1, My Own Psalm to Teach Wisdom

Points to Bring Out: Today you will study a psalm to teach wisdom. Then you will write your own psalm to teach wisdom.

Post-Discussion: Read your psalms aloud to each other.

BIBLE

Bible Reading: 1 Sa 22, Ps 37, 52

Notebook Page 270: Psalm to Teach Wisdom 2

Points to Bring Out: David was inspired to write many Psalms about difficult circumstances and events. What event happened prior to the writing of Psalm 52?

BIBLE

Bible Reading: 1 Sa 14-23

Notebook Page 271: Jonathan's Heart

Points to Bring Out: David and Jonathan had a special friendship that withstood many tests. Find out what characteristics of Jonathan contributed to his loyalty to David.

WRITING

Bible Reading: 1 Sa 24; Ps 18

Notebook Pages 272-273: Psalm of Thanksgiving, My Own Psalm of Thanksgiving

Points to Bring Out: Psalms of thanksgiving flowed from a heart rejoicing in God's goodness and deliverance. Write one to thank God for helping you in a difficult experience.

Post-Discussion: Read your psalms aloud to each other.

HEBREW

Bible: Mt 21:42, Eph 2:19-22, 1 Pe 2:4-8a

Notebook Page 274: Ahead of the Game

Points to Bring Out: In Hebrew, the word for 'head' is used to create many other words. As in English, the word has the connotation of 'first', 'chief', or 'excellent.' The 'cornerstone' had the significance of being the first stone that was laid for a building and by which all other stones were aligned to. When Jesus is described as the chief cornerstone in the scriptures above, it is an illustration of Him being the foundation of our faith and a word picture of how we, as believers in Him, are being built together into a holy temple in the Lord.

BIBLE & WRITING

Bible Reading: 1 Sa 19-31

Notebook Page 275: Saul's Jealousy 2

Points to Bring Out: Jealousy often blinds our intellect and keeps us from making wise decisions. See how it affects Saul and all of his relationships.

Post-Discussion: What could you do if you were feeling jealous of someone? What if they were jealous of you?

HEBREW

Bible Reading: Selected verses

Notebook Page 276: Hear and Obey 1

Points to Bring Out: In Hebrew, the word for 'hear' means much more than just to hear with our ears. It includes 'paying attention', 'listening', 'granting requests' and 'obeying.' See how this word relates to many aspects of Samuel's life.

Post-Discussion: Talk about a time that you asked someone to do something but they didn't do it. How did you respond?

WRITING

Bible Reading: Review1 Sa 1-28

Notebook Page 277: Hear and Obey 2

Points to Bring Out: Rewrite the story of Samuel using as many of the synonyms for the Hebrew word for 'hear' as possible.

Post-Discussion: Read your stories aloud to each other.

HISTORY

Bible Reading: Various verses

Notebook Pages 278-279: Family Tree of David, David's Family Tree Crossword

Points to Bring Out: By working with David's family tree, you will be able to better understand who the characters are and why they do what they do.

Post-Discussion: How were some of David's problems related to relatives?

King David

BIBLE

Bible Reading: 2 Samuel 1-5

Notebook Pages 280-281: God Gives David the Kingdom 1 & 2 (Do over a couple of days)

Points to Bring Out: The position of King did not come to David without a price. He lost his best friend, the Israelites were divided in their acceptance of him, and his relatives plotted against him. Yet David put his trust in God and God was faithful to help him.

WRITING

Bible Reading: Ps 119

Notebook Pages 282-283: Psalm 119 – An Acrostic, My Acrostic Psalm

Points to Bring Out: Acrostics are usually poems where the first letter of each line spells a word or writes out the alphabet. Psalm 119 is written as an acrostic psalm, with each section beginning with a letter of the Hebrew alphabet in order. It was written in this way in order to make it easier to memorize. Write your own acrostic psalm.

Post-Discussion: Read your psalms aloud to each other.

BIBLE

Bible Reading: 2 Sa 6, 1 Chronicles 13, 15, 16

Notebook Page 284: David Gets the Ark

Points to Bring Out: Bringing the Ark back to the City of David was not accomplished without danger. Yet, to have a symbol of God's presence in their midst was worth it. They learned that God had no tolerance for those who did not follow His commands exactly.

BIBLE

Bible Reading: 2 Sa 7

Notebook Page 285: God Builds David's House

Points to Bring Out: David wants to do something special to show his gratitude to God. But instead God blesses him even more.

HEBREW

Bible Reading: Various NT verses

Notebook Page 286: House of David

Points to Bring Out: God's promises to David were fulfilled in many loving ways. You will be learning about some of these and the Hebrew meaning of his name today.

BIBLE

Bible Reading: 2 Sa 8:15-18, 1 Chr 18:14-17

Notebook Page 287: God's Kindness

Points to Bring Out: David reflected God's kindness in dealing with Saul's grandson. He demonstrates the kindness that God shows us as well.

BIBLE

Bible Reading: 2 Sa 11

Notebook Page 288: David's Downfall

Points to Bring Out: David didn't set out to betray God, his family, or his country. But his actions led him quickly into serious sin. What could he have done differently to escape from sinning?

Post-Discussion: What are some things that you can do to keep from getting into a compromising situation?

WRITING

Bible Reading: 1 Cor. 10:13

Notebook Page 289: Road to Downfall

Points to Bring Out: Write a story about the downfall of an individual. Then counter each step of his wrong actions with a creative way of escape.

Post-Discussion: Share your stories and ideas.

HEALTH

Bible Reading: Prov. 20:1, 23: 20-21, 29-35, 31:4-7

Notebook Pages 290-291: Reasons for Using Drugs or Alcohol, The Low Down on Getting High,

Points to Bring Out: Over the next few lessons, we will be discussing mind-altering agents and addictions. Alcohol was the earliest recorded drug to be used. There were warnings against its abuse even then.

Post-Discussion: Discuss why people use drugs in the first place. Then, talk about some of the 'price tags' that make drugs and alcohol too expensive for you.

Note to Teacher: For the next four lessons, there are pages in the back of the teacher's manual to help you lead the discussions about these important issues.

HEALTH

Bible Reading: Rom 6:15-23

Notebook Pages 292-295: Drugs and the Body 1 & 2, Everything Has Gone up in Smoke, Wicked Game

Points to Bring Out: One of the ways we can avoid the temptation to use drugs is to decide before the situation arises what choices we will make. By looking at the effects of each of these agents on our body and mind, as well as the hidden high costs, we will be better prepared to stand up for righteousness.

Post-Discussion: Talk about some of the physical costs that make drugs and smoking too expensive for you and discuss the poem, "Wicked Game."

HEALTH

Bible Reading: Rom 7:14-8:39

Notebook Pages 296-297: Drugs and the Body 3 & 4

Points to Bring Out: Christians are free from the power of sin and death. Now we are slaves to God and whatever we do should be pleasing to Him.

Post-Discussion: Prepare a good response to give for someone who wants you to try drugs.

HEALTH

Bible Reading: Rom 12:1-2, I Cor 3:16-17

Notebook Pages 298-299: Drugs and the Body 5 & 6

Points to Bring Out: Our bodies are the temple of the Holy Spirit. As such, we must take care not to defile or abuse our temple.

Post-Discussion: Prepare a good argument to encourage someone not to try drugs.

WRITING

Bible Reading: 1 Sa 12; Ps 51

Notebook Page 300: Vocabulary of Psalm 51

Points to Bring Out: Although David sinned, he repented of his sin. By acknowledging to God and others that he had sinned and was sorry, his relationship to God was restored.

Post-Discussion: How did David's response differ from Saul's response after each sinned?

WRITING

Bible Reading: 2 Sa 14-18, Ps 51

Notebook Pages 301-302: Psalm of Petition, My Own Psalm of Petition

Points to Bring Out: As our Heavenly Father, God wants us to come to Him with our problems and needs. The psalms of petition do just this. Write your own psalm of petition for a need in your life.

Note to Teacher: If the student has written of a private matter, he may not want to share his psalm with others. Be sensitive to this.

BIBLE

Bible Reading: 2 Sa 12:26-31; 13

Notebook Page 303: Trouble in David's Family 1

Points to Bring Out: Figure out the name of each of the speakers and write it in.

HEALTH

Bible Reading: 1 Cor. 6:13-20

Notebook Pages 304-305: Reasons for Sex Outside of Marriage, The High Price of Free Love

Points to Bring Out: We are bombarded by appeals to our sexual appetites in advertisements, movies, magazines and so forth. They are not telling you all of the heartache that goes along with sex outside of marriage.

Post-Discussion: Talk about why people have sex outside of marriage. Then discuss some of the 'price tags' that make sex outside of marriage too expensive for you.

BIBLE

Bible Reading: 2 Sa 15-17

Notebook Page 306: Trouble in David's Family 2

Points to Bring Out: Trouble continues to plague David in his own family.

WRITING

Bible Reading: Ps 3, 40, 2 Sa 14-18

Notebook Pages 307-308: Psalm of Petition 2, My Own Psalm of Petition 2

Points to Bring Out: Psalm 3 was composed as David fled from Absolam. Write another psalm of petition of your own.

BIBLE

Bible Reading: 2 Sa 18-20

Notebook Page 309: The Conspiracy Fails

Points to Bring Out: Look over the Family Tree of David to help you understand some of the background for this attempted coup.

WRITING

Bible Reading: Selected Psalms

Notebook Page 310: The Psalms 1 (May do over several days)

Points to Bring Out: You have covered the various kinds of psalms. Now take a psalm and summarize it, find the author, identify the type of psalm, and figure out if it was written for an individual or a group.

BIBLE

Bible Reading: 2 Sa 7, 1 Kings 1 and 1 Chr17

Notebook Page 311: Nathan

Points to Bring Out: When a leader sins, it is difficult for the people under him to confront him. Nathan, God's prophet, courageously brought a message to David from God. Yet God revealed to him how to make a proper appeal to the King's conscience.

Post-Discussion: What advise does the Bible have to offer about confronting sin in other's lives? Is there a special caution about doing this?

BIBLE

Bible Reading: 1 Chr 18-28, and selected verses

Notebook Page 312: David's Part in Building the Temple

Points to Bring Out: Although David made mistakes in his life that even caused the death of some of his people, he wanted to honor God by building a temple for Him. But God said, "No." Instead David did what he could to get everything ready to build the Temple.

WRITING

Bible Reading: Selected Psalms

Notebook Page 313: The Psalms 2 (May do over several days)

Points to Bring Out: You have covered the various kinds of psalms. Now take a psalm and summarize it, find the author, identify the type of psalm, and figure out if it was written for an individual or a group.

Note to Teacher: You may make copies of this page from the teacher's manual if you wish your students to cover more (or all) of the psalms. You may also assign particular ones or let your students choose their own.
Here is a list of psalms to analyze:

Petition: 3, 12, 13, 17, 22, 42, 44, 69, 71, 74, 79, 80, 88, 102
Thanksgiving: 30, 34, 41, 66, 67, 75, 92, 107, 116, 118, 124, 129, 136, 138
Praise: 65, 68, 93, 100, 117, 134, 146, 150
Wisdom: 13, 14, 19, 37, 49, 78, 92, 112, 119, 127, 128, 133

BIBLE

Bible Reading: 2 Sa 9b-12

Notebook Page 314: Sword Will Never Depart

Points to Bring Out: Our sin may be forgiven when we repent, but we still have to reap the consequences of our actions. See what happened to David and his family as a result of his sins.

WRITING

Bible Reading: Various verses

Notebook Page 315: Consequences of Sin

Points to Bring Out: Sin is never private. Think about why God takes it so seriously and who sin affects.

BIBLE

Bible Reading: Various verses

Notebook Page 316: Crossword for David

Points to Bring Out: This crossword puzzle will review the life of David. He was the ancestor of the Messiah, Jesus Christ.

BIBLE

Bible Reading: Various verses

Notebook Page 317: Memorable Songs

Points to Bring Out: As David's life came to an end, he was able to say that in spite of all the problems, his house was right with God. Write your own song of victory.

Post-Discussion: Read your song of victory aloud.

HISTORY

Bible Reading: Various verses

Notebook Page 318: Lists and Notes

Points to Bring Out: Keeping records are an important aspect of history. They document that real people lived and did noteworthy deeds. Today you will be working on some of those records.

King Solomon

BIBLE

Bible Reading: 2 Chr 1

Notebook Page 319: God Speaks to Solomon 1

Points to Bring Out: Solomon was not David's oldest son and yet he was chosen by God to succeed David. When God made an offer to him, he made the right choice and was blessed even more.

Post-Discussion: What might your choice be if God offered you whatever you wanted?

WRITING

Bible Reading: Verses from Pr 1-3

Notebook Page 320: The Beginning of Wisdom

Points to Bring Out: Proverbs is a collection of observations on life. The short, clever statements teach wisdom and give advise on how to deal with life.

Post-Discussion: Have your ever worked really hard for something you wanted? Tell about what it was and how you got it.

ART

Bible Reading: Various Proverbs

Notebook Page 321: Picturesque Proverbs 1

Points to Bring Out: Proverbs is full of interesting word pictures that help to convey the ideas. Draw illustrations of these Proverbs.

BIBLE

Bible Reading: Proverbs

Notebook Page 322: Honey for the Soul

Points to Bring Out: Hebrew children learned to associate scripture with honey. As they memorized it, their mothers would give them a taste of honey. Pr. 24 :13-14 says that honey is sweet to your taste and wisdom is sweet to your soul. Give your soul a treat.

BIBLE

Bible Reading: Psa. 31:18, Psa. 52, Prov. 6:16-19, 10:18, 12:19-22, Jer. 29:23

Notebook Pages 323-324: Reasons Why People Lie, A Little White Lie

Points to Bring Out: There are many reasons why people lie. However, no matter what the motivation, there are common consequences to this sin.

Post-Discussion: Define a lie. Is being deceitful always wrong? What if your motivation for being misleading is to save someone's life, as in Rahab protecting the spies?

WRITING

Bible Reading: Pr 10

Notebook Page 325: Written on the Tablets of the Heart

Points to Bring Out: The heart is used symbolically to represent the spiritual state of a person. Find the characteristics of a righteous heart and of an evil heart.

ART

Bible Reading: Various Proverbs

Notebook Page 326: Picturesque Proverbs 2

Points to Bring Out: Practice your drawing skills again today to illustrate these Proverbs.

WRITING

Bible Reading: Pr 31:10-31

Notebook Page 327: A Virtuous Woman

Points to Bring Out: Far from being repressive to women, the Israelites honored women, protected them and extolled their achievements at home and in the marketplace.

Post-Discussion: What is the position of women in countries that do not accept the Word of God?

WRITING

Bible Reading: Pr 5, 6, 9

Notebook Page 328: An Immoral Woman

Points to Bring Out: The descriptions of an immoral woman in Proverbs can be an invaluable help in discerning the character of people you meet.

BIBLE

Bible Reading: 2 Chr 3-4

Notebook Page 329: Solomon's Temple

Points to Bring Out: David's son, Solomon, was given the privilege of building the temple. Though very different from the Tabernacle, God was pleased with this offering to Him.

BIBLE

Bible Reading: 2 Chr 5, 6

Notebook Page 330: Solomon Dedicates the Temple

Points to Bring Out: The Temple was dedicated with a great celebration and a prayer by Solomon.

BIBLE

Bible Reading: 2 Chr 7

Notebook Page 331: God Speaks to Solomon 2

Points to Bring Out: Solomon began his reign pleasing God. But in spite of all that God did for him, he fell away from God in his old age. See why this happened as you work through your lesson.

BIBLE

Bible Reading: SS 1:1-2:16

Notebook Page 332: Song of Songs 1

Points to Bring Out: The Song of Solomon presents many unanswered questions. Some of these are mentioned in the outline of this book. But no matter which view you choose to take, you will find the book to present a beautiful love story.

WRITING

Bible Reading: SS 3:1-7

Notebook Pages 333-334: Song of Songs 2, Your Eyes Are Doves

Points to Bring Out: The lover in the song uses many similes and metaphors to describe his beloved. Find out what they are and then try writing some yourself.

BIBLE

Bible Reading: SS 6:4-8:14

Notebook Page 335: Song of Songs 3

Points to Bring Out: The conclusion of the song includes a well-known declaration of love.

HISTORY

Bible Reading: Various verses

Notebook Page 336: Solomon's Check List

Points to Bring Out: Solomon broke many of the laws God had ordained for kings. He became rich at the expense of his people and replaced his love for God with lust for wives.

HISTORY

Bible Reading: Various verses

Notebook Page 337: Double Trouble

Points to Bring Out: There are many examples of polygamy in the Bible. As you work through this page, see what some of the complications can be.

Post-Discussion: Some ethnic groups still practice polygamy today. From a biblical perspective, what would be your advice to a new Christian about what to do with his 'extra' wives?

BIBLE

Bible Reading: Ecc 1-3

Notebook Pages 338-339: Under the Sun 1, A Time for Everything

Points to Bring Out: Ecclesiastes is attributed by most people to Solomon. It is the account of a man's search for meaning in life and presents the extremes of meaninglessness 'under the sun' to extolling God's goodness. Notice the symbols for these as you work through the next few pages.

BIBLE

Bible Reading: Ecc 4-5

Notebook Page 340: Under the Sun 2

Points to Bring Out: The 'preacher' observed oppression, loneliness and the meaninglessness of riches.

BIBLE

Bible Reading: Ecc 6-8

Notebook Page 341: Under the Sun 3

Points to Bring Out: The debate goes on. Is life going to be worth living?

BIBLE

Bible Reading: Ecc 9-10

Notebook Page 342: Under the Sun 4

Points to Bring Out: We all have a common destiny—death. And life is not fair.

BIBLE

Bible Reading: Ecc 11-12

Notebook Page 343: Under the Sun 5

Points to Bring Out: Here are the surprising conclusions of a disillusioned man who has tried it all.

WRITING

Bible Reading: Review Ecclesiastes

Notebook Page 344: Fear God

Points to Bring Out: Present your own points for debate on the issues of life.

REMEMBERING GOD'S CHOSEN CHILDREN

EXTRA PAGES TO EXPAND LESSONS

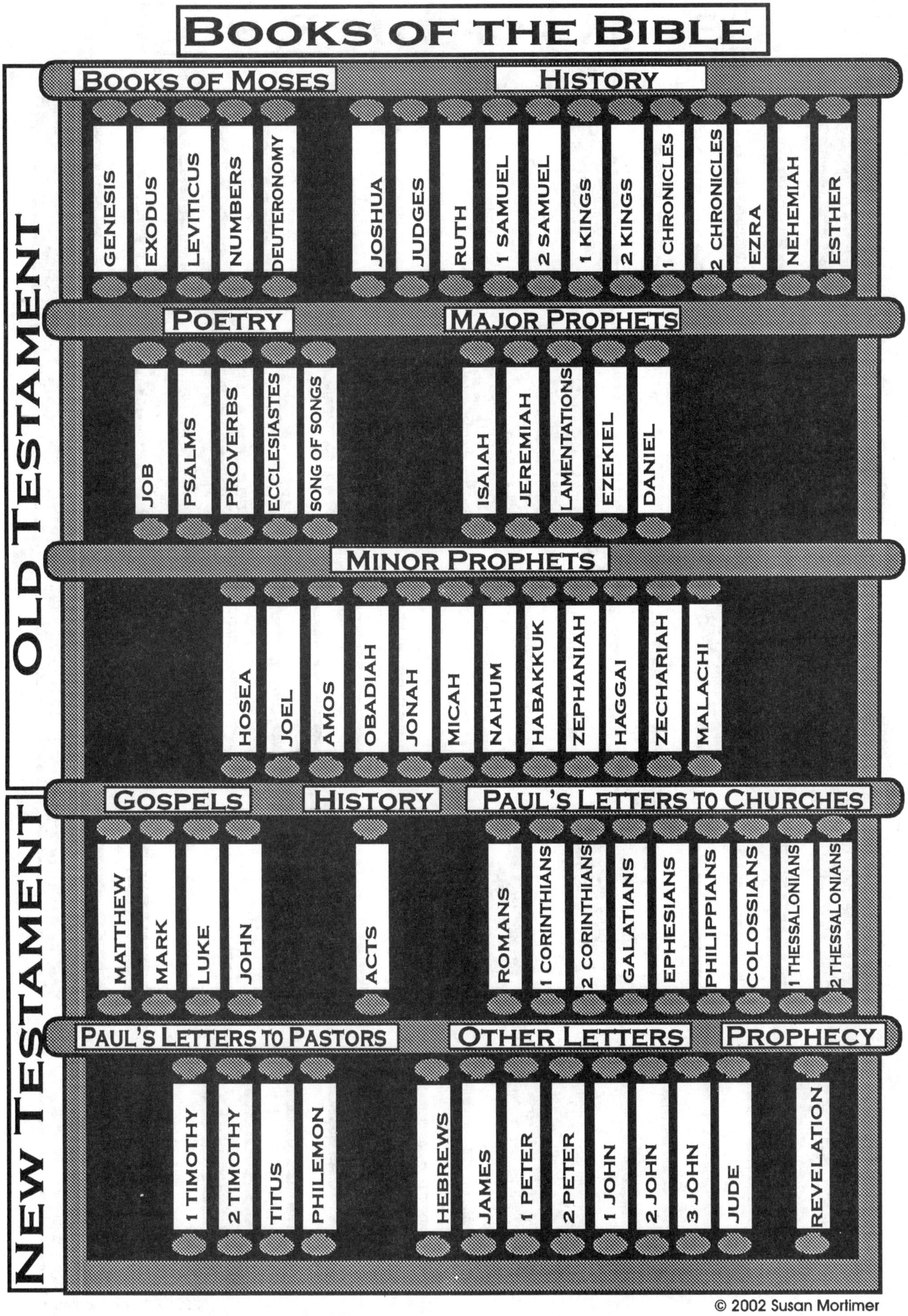

Books of the Bible

Old Testament

Books of Moses
Genesis, Exodus, Leviticus, Numbers, Deuteronomy

History
Joshua, Judges, Ruth, 1 Samuel, 2 Samuel, 1 Kings, 2 Kings, 1 Chronicles, 2 Chronicles, Ezra, Nehemiah, Esther

Poetry
Job, Psalms, Proverbs, Ecclesiastes, Song of Songs

Major Prophets
Isaiah, Jeremiah, Lamentations, Ezekiel, Daniel

Minor Prophets
Hosea, Joel, Amos, Obadiah, Jonah, Micah, Nahum, Habakkuk, Zephaniah, Haggai, Zechariah, Malachi

New Testament

Gospels
Matthew, Mark, Luke, John

History
Acts

Paul's Letters to Churches
Romans, 1 Corinthians, 2 Corinthians, Galatians, Ephesians, Philippians, Colossians, 1 Thessalonians, 2 Thessalonians

Paul's Letters to Pastors
1 Timothy, 2 Timothy, Titus, Philemon

Other Letters
Hebrews, James, 1 Peter, 2 Peter, 1 John, 2 John, 3 John, Jude

Prophecy
Revelation

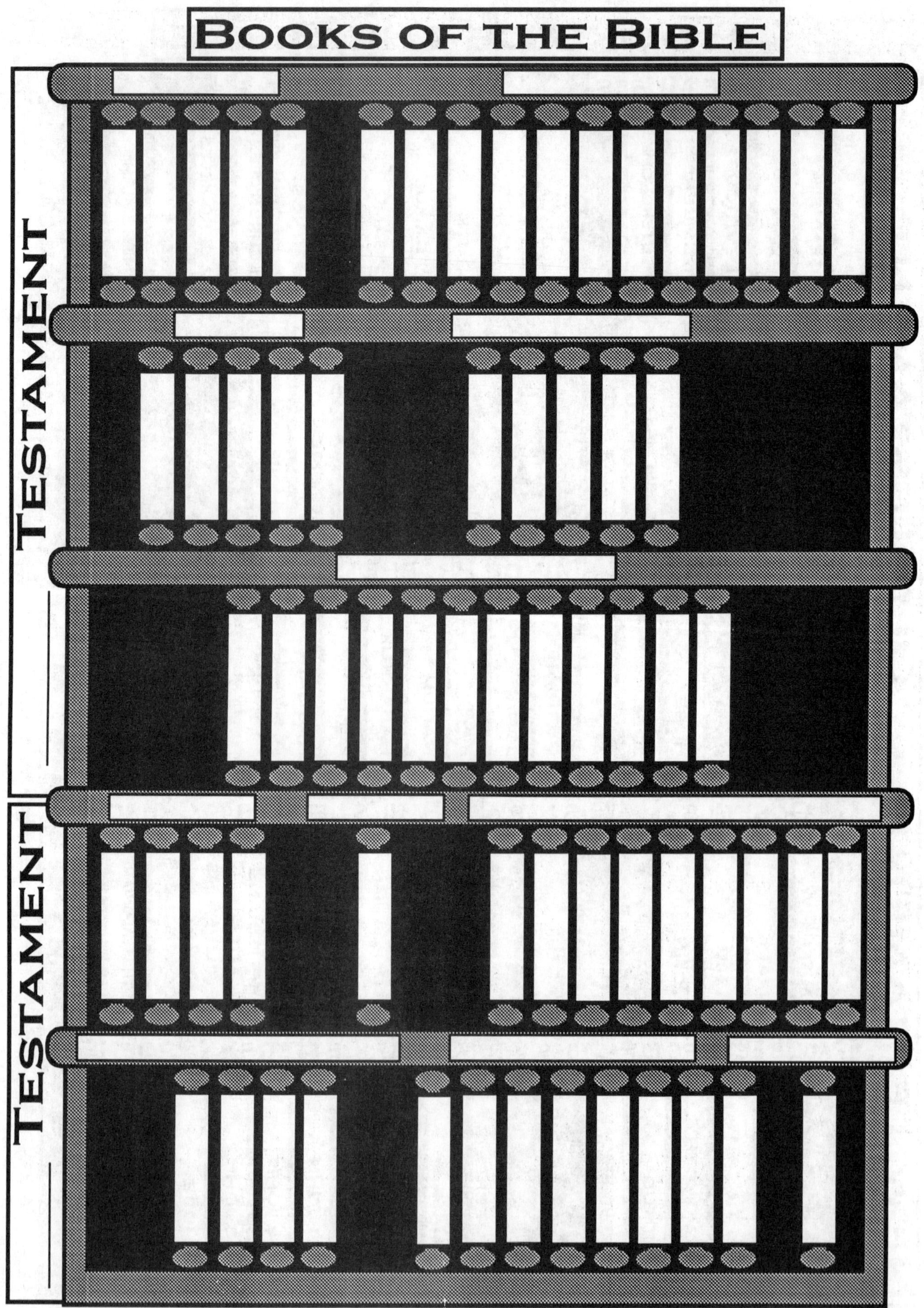
Books of the Bible
Testament
Testament

Hebrew Letter Bookmarks can be photocopied, cut apart and laminated. Use as bookmarks and for quick reference during Hebrew activities.

Hebrew Letter Bookmark

Letter	Sound	Value
א	ʻ (No sound)	1
בּ ב	b (bird) v	2
גּ	g (goat)	3
דּ ד	d (drill)	4
ה	h (horse)	5
ו	v (violin) w	6
ז	z (zoo)	7
ח	kh (Bach)	8
ט	t (tail)	9
י	y (yam)	10
כּ כ ך	k (kitten) kh	20
ל	l (lion)	30
מ ם	m (mouse)	40
נ ן	n (nail)	50
ס	s (sun)	60
ע	ʻ (silent)	70
פּ פ ף	p (penguin) f	80
צ ץ	ts (ants)	90
ק	k (kite)	100
ר	r (rabbit's ear)	200
שׂ שׁ	s (sea) sh	300
תּ ת	t (turban) th	400

Vowel Markings

ַ =å (scar) ָ =ŏ (sob) ֶ =ĕ (freckle)

ִ =ĭ (itch) ֻ = ŭ (buttons) ִי =ē (tweet)

ֵ =ā (ate) or וֹ =ō (over) ֻ or וּ =ü (flute)

Hebrew Letter Bookmark

Letter	Sound	Value
א	ʻ (No sound)	1
בּ ב	b (bird) v	2
גּ	g (goat)	3
דּ ד	d (drill)	4
ה	h (horse)	5
ו	v (violin) w	6
ז	z (zoo)	7
ח	kh (Bach)	8
ט	t (tail)	9
י	y (yam)	10
כּ כ ך	k (kitten) kh	20
ל	l (lion)	30
מ ם	m (mouse)	40
נ ן	n (nail)	50
ס	s (sun)	60
ע	ʻ (silent)	70
פּ פ ף	p (penguin) f	80
צ ץ	ts (ants)	90
ק	k (kite)	100
ר	r (rabbit's ear)	200
שׂ שׁ	s (sea) sh	300
תּ ת	t (turban) th	400

Vowel Markings

ַ =å (scar) ָ =ŏ (sob) ֶ =ĕ (freckle)

ִ =ĭ (itch) ֻ = ŭ (buttons) ִי =ē (tweet)

ֵ =ā (ate) or וֹ =ō (over) ֻ or וּ =ü (flute)

© 2002 Susan Mortimer

Hebrew Letter Bookmark

Letter	Sound	Value
א	ʻ (No sound)	1
בּ ב	b (bird) v	2
גּ	g (goat)	3
דּ ד	d (drill)	4
ה	h (horse)	5
ו	v (violin) w	6
ז	z (zoo)	7
ח	kh (Bach)	8
ט	t (tail)	9
י	y (yam)	10
כּ כ ך	k (kitten) kh	20
ל	l (lion)	30
מ ם	m (mouse)	40
נ ן	n (nail)	50
ס	s (sun)	60
ע	ʻ (silent)	70
פּ פ ף	p (penguin) f	80
צ ץ	ts (ants)	90
ק	k (kite)	100
ר	r (rabbit's ear)	200
שׂ שׁ	s (sea) sh	300
תּ ת	t (turban) th	400

Vowel Markings

ַ =å (scar) ָ =ŏ (sob) ֶ =ĕ (freckle)

ִ =ĭ (itch) ֻ = ŭ (buttons) ִי =ē (tweet)

ֵ =ā (ate) or וֹ =ō (over) ֻ or וּ =ü (flute)

© 2002 Susan Mortimer

CALLIGRAPHY STROKES

Practice the following strokes. Fill in each row. Use a calligraphy pen with a 3.5 nib or tip.

ENGLISH CALLIGRAPHY

Write your name in calligraphy on the top line. Trace over each line and then write it again on the lines directly below it. This sentence uses every letter in the alphabet. Use a calligraphy pen with a 3.5 nib or tip.

NAME:

In excitement, his

In excitement, his

followers gazed up

fo

as Jesus quickly rose

as

above the clouds.

ab

CALLIGRAPHY CAPITAL LETTERS

Trace over each line and then write it again on the lines directly below it. This sentence uses every letter in the alphabet. Use a calligraphy pen with a 3.5 nib or tip.

IN EXCITEMENT,

HIS FOLLOWERS

GAZED UP AS JESUS

QUICKLY ROSE ABOVE

THE CLOUDS. CLOUDS

CALLIGRAPHY PRACTICE

This sentence uses every letter in the alphabet. Trace over the letters in the darkened sentence. Then write it on the line directly below it. Use a calligraphy pen with a 2.00 mm nib or tip.

In excitement, his followers

In excitement, his followers

gazed up as Jesus quickly

ga

rose above the clouds.

ro

In excitement, his followers

gazed up as Jesus quickly

rose above the clouds.

In

ga

ro

CALLIGRAPHY VERSES

Write verse lightly in pencil. Center on the midline. Then write over with calligraphy pen.

HEBREW CALLIGRAPHY STROKES

Practice your Hebrew calligraphy. Go over every stroke. Start at the left and go to the right.

Use the following lines to practice the stokes that are giving you trouble.

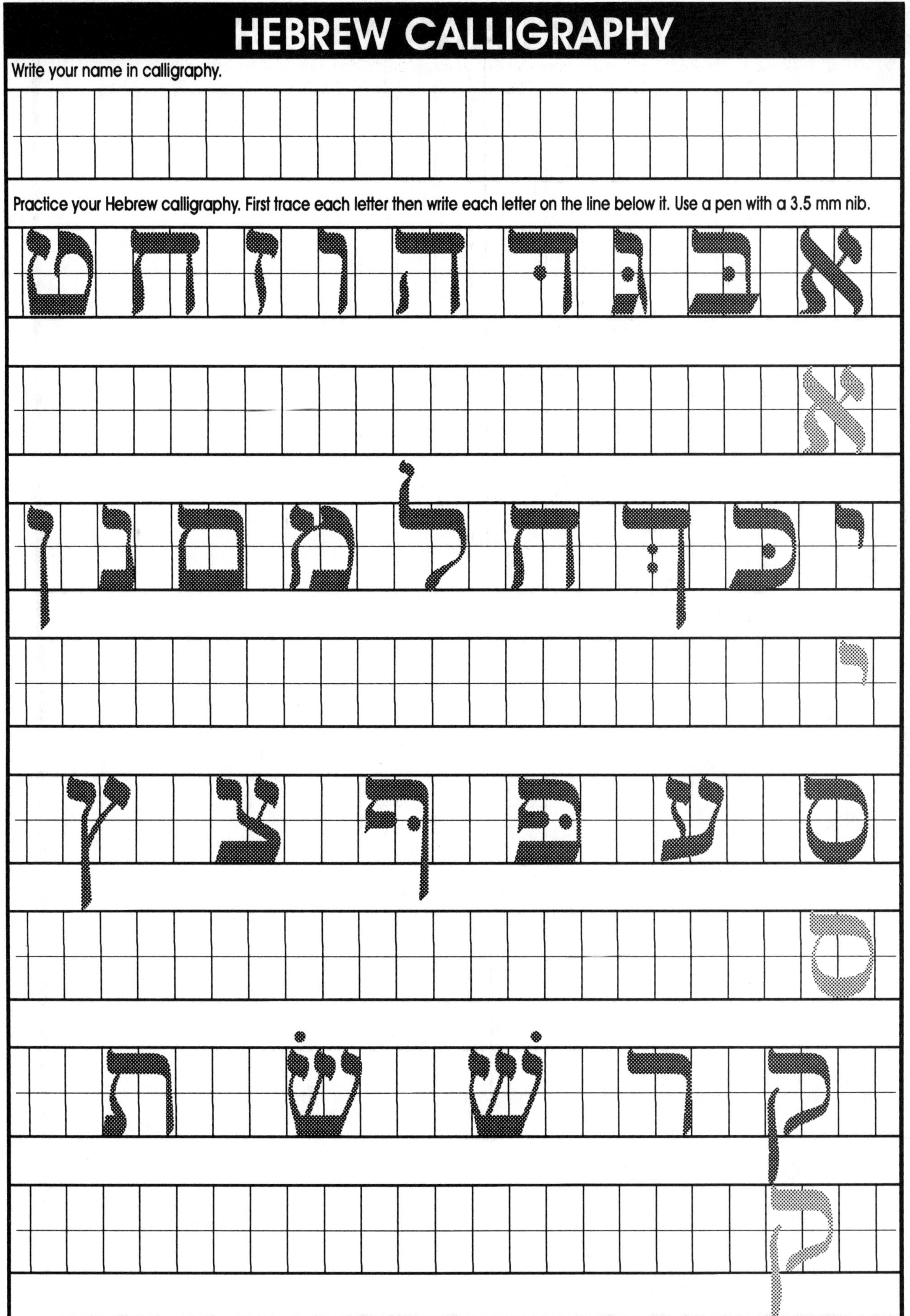
HEBREW CALLIGRAPHY
Write your name in calligraphy.
Practice your Hebrew calligraphy. First trace each letter then write each letter on the line below it. Use a pen with a 3.5 mm nib.

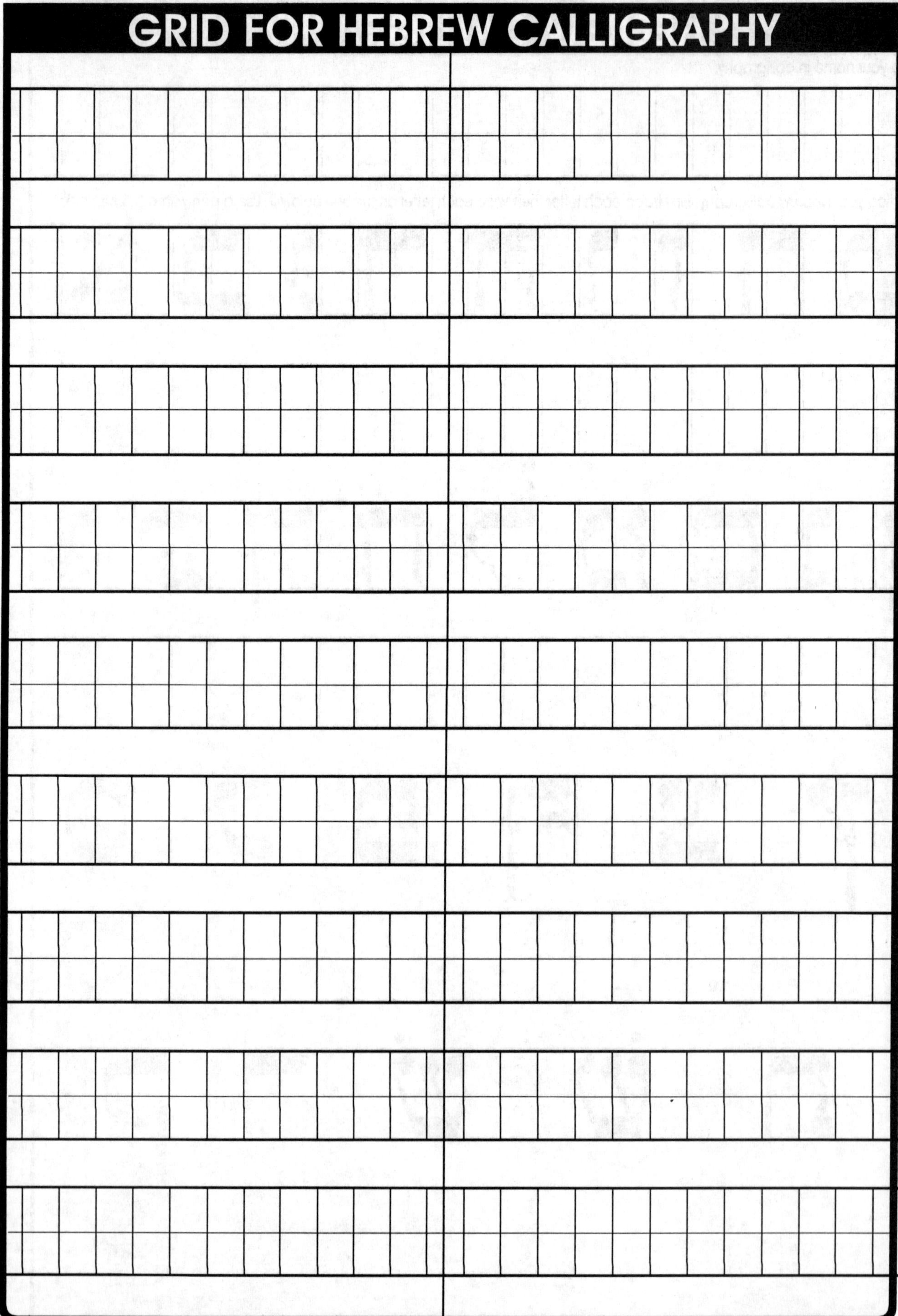
GRID FOR HEBREW CALLIGRAPHY

HEBREW ALPHABET CHART

Hebrew letters	English sounds	Name	Pronunciation	Meaning	Number	Proto-Canaanite	900 B.C. Hebrew	Latin Letters
א	ʻ VOWEL HELPER (No sound)	אָלֶף	*ʻŏlĕf*	ox	1			A
בּ	b (bird)	בֵּית	*bāyth*	house	2			B
גּ	g (goat)	גִּמֶל	*gēmĕl*	camel	3			C
דּ ד	d (drill)	דָּלֶת	*dŏlĕth*	door	4			D
ה	h (horse)	הֵא	*hāʼ*	lattice	5			E
ו	VOWEL HELPER v (violin) w	וָו	*vŏv*	hook	6			F
ז	z (zoo)	זַיִן	*zåyĭn*	weapon	7			Z
ח	kh (Bach)	חֵית	*khāyth*	fence	8			H
ט	t (tall) =תּ	טֵית	*tāyth*	serpent	9			———
י	y VOWEL HELPER (yam)	יוֹד	*yōd*	hand	10			I
כּ ךְ	k (kitten)=ק	כַּף	*kåf*	palm of hand	20			K
ל	l (lion)	לָמֶד	*lŏmĕd*	ox-goad	30			L
מ ם	m (mouse)	מֵם	*mām*	water	40			M
נ ן	n (nail)	נוּן	*nün*	fish	50			N
ס	s (sun)=שׂ	סָמֶךְ	*sŏmĕk*	support	60	———		X
ע	ʻ VOWEL HELPER (Silent as a giraffe)	עַיִן	*ʻåyĭn*	eye	70			O
פּ ף	p (penguin)	פֵּה	*pāh*	mouth	80			P
צ ץ	ts (ants)	צָדֵי	*tsŏdāy*	fish hook	90	———		———
ק	k (kite) =כּ	קוֹף	*kōf*	back of head	100			Q
ר	r (rabbit's ear)	רֵישׁ	*rāysh*	head	200			R
שׂ	s (sea) =ס	שִׂין	*sēn*	tooth	300			S
תּ	t (turban) = ט	תָּו	*tŏv*	———	400			T

ב=v (vine) כ=kh (Bach) פ=f (ph)(pharmacy) (farm) שׁ=sh (ship) ת=th (throne)

ַ =å (scar) ָ =ŏ (sob) ֶ =ĕ (freckle) ִ =ĭ (itch) ֻ =ŭ (buttons) ִי =ē (tweet) ֵ =ā (ate) ֹ or וֹ =ō (over) ֻ or וּ =ü (flute)

Overview Scroll 3

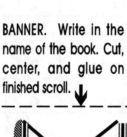

BANNER. Write in the name of the book. Cut, center, and glue on finished scroll.

SCROLL HANDLE. Add to end of scroll outline.

Cut on dotted line

To make an Overview Scroll for a Bible book follow these steps:

1. Cut and glue the scroll together.
2. Write an outline of the book on lines that say 'outline'. Use short phrases. Intersperse illustrations.
3. Figure out the chapter numbers, focus, topics, and divisions of the book. Write them on the lines above the outline. Overview Scroll 2 tells where everything goes.
4. Find verses that are good to memorize and write them in the box below the scroll. Draw arrows to the location of the verses in the outline.
5. Copy and add more pages of Overview Scroll 2 if you need more lines.
6. When you are finished with your outline cut out the scroll handle on the dotted line. Glue it onto the scroll just past the last used line. Trim off any extra.
7. Write the name of the book in the banner. Cut and glue it above the scroll. Try to center it.

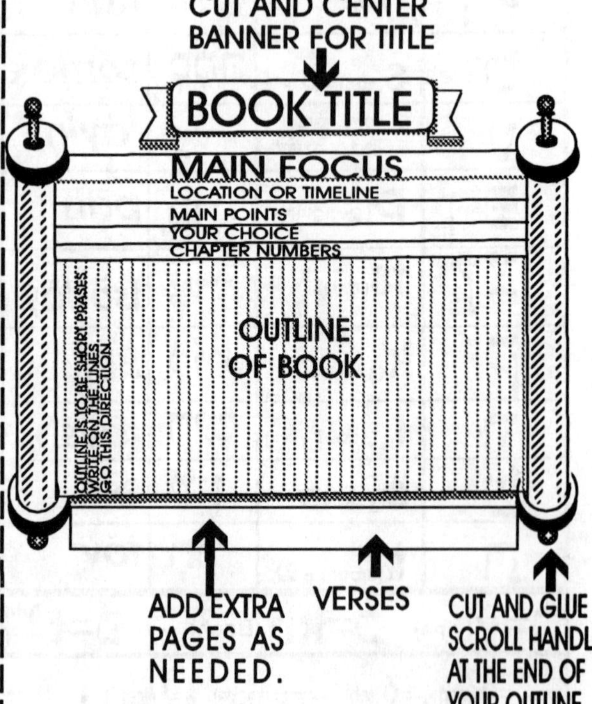

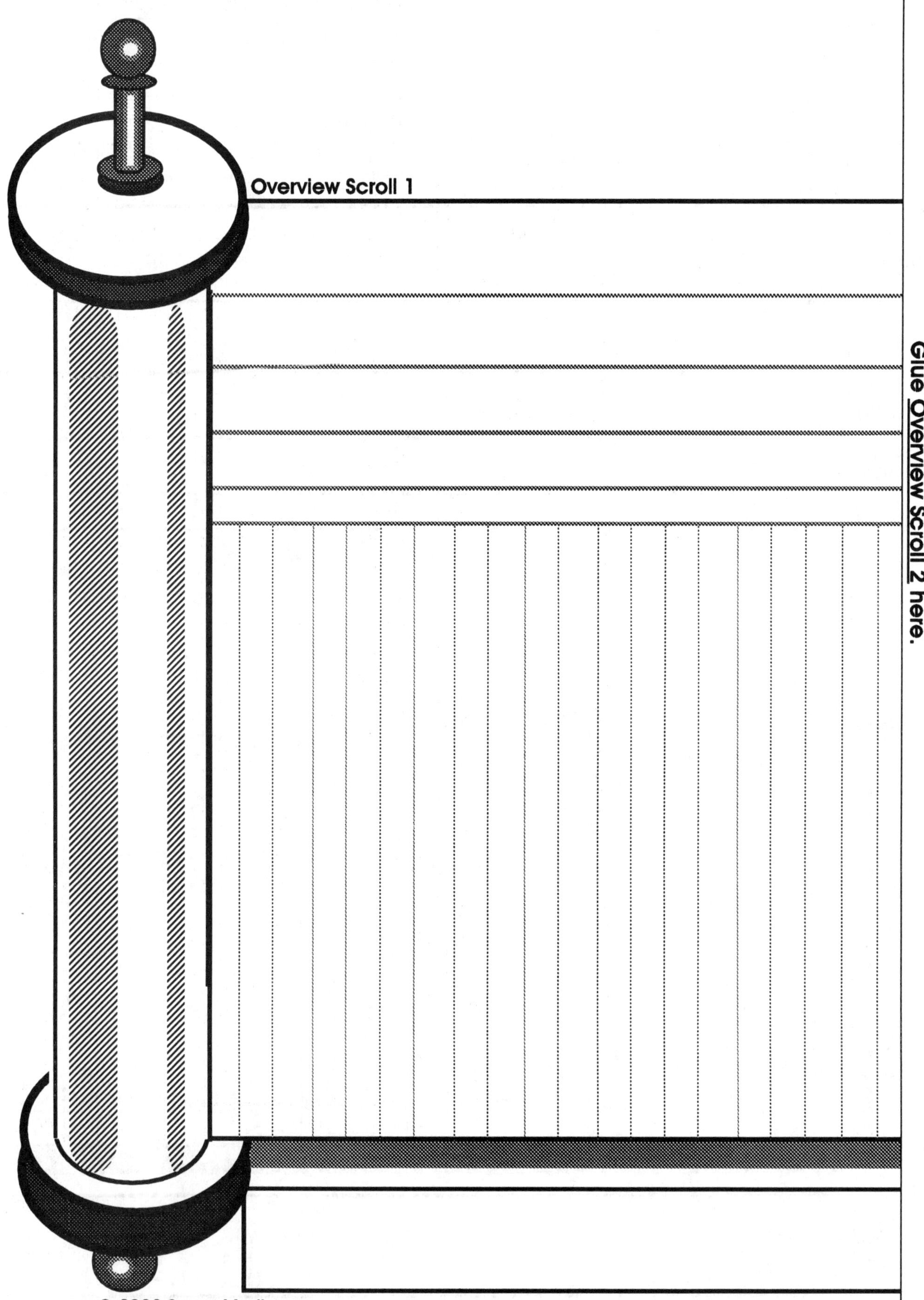
Overview Scroll 1
Glue Overview Scroll 2 here.

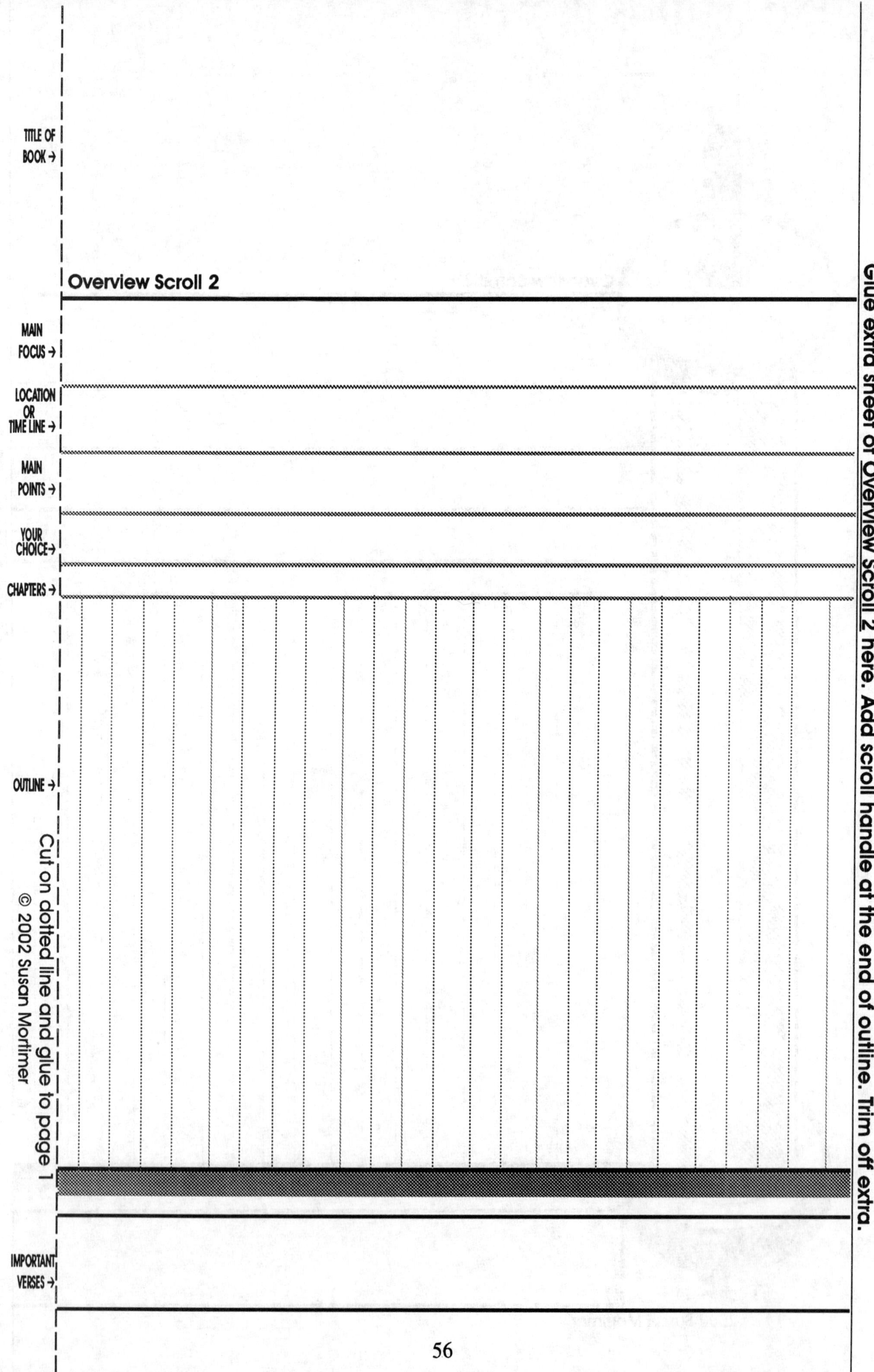
TITLE OF BOOK →
Overview Scroll 2
MAIN FOCUS →
LOCATION OR TIME LINE →
MAIN POINTS →
YOUR CHOICE →
CHAPTERS →
OUTLINE →
IMPORTANT VERSES →
Glue extra sheet of Overview Scroll 2 here. Add scroll handle at the end of outline. Trim off extra.
Cut on dotted line and glue to page 1
© 2002 Susan Mortimer

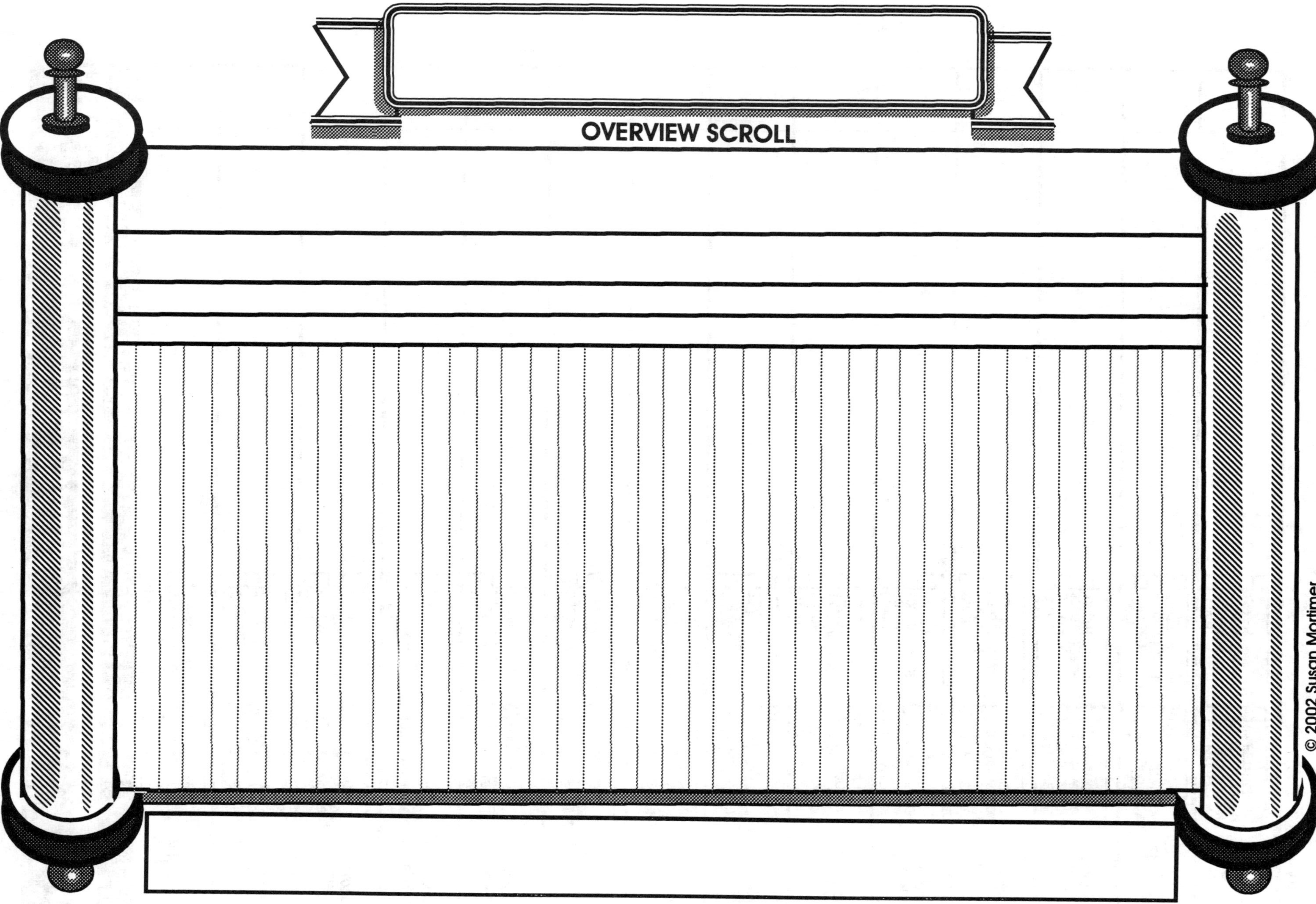
OVERVIEW SCROLL

THE PSALMS

Fill in the information for each Psalm.

NUMBER	WHAT THE PSALM IS ABOUT	AUTHOR	TYPE OF PSALM	WRITTEN FOR
		☐ DAVID ☐ SOLOMON ☐ SONS OF KORAH ☐ ASAPH ☐ ______	☐ OF PRAISE ☐ OF THANKSGIVING ☐ TO TEACH WISDOM ☐ OF PETITION ☐ ______	☐ INDIVIDUAL ☐ GROUP
		☐ DAVID ☐ SOLOMON ☐ SONS OF KORAH ☐ ASAPH ☐ ______	☐ OF PRAISE ☐ OF THANKSGIVING ☐ TO TEACH WISDOM ☐ OF PETITION ☐ ______	☐ INDIVIDUAL ☐ GROUP
		☐ DAVID ☐ SOLOMON ☐ SONS OF KORAH ☐ ASAPH ☐ ______	☐ OF PRAISE ☐ OF THANKSGIVING ☐ TO TEACH WISDOM ☐ OF PETITION ☐ ______	☐ INDIVIDUAL ☐ GROUP
		☐ DAVID ☐ SOLOMON ☐ SONS OF KORAH ☐ ASAPH ☐ ______	☐ OF PRAISE ☐ OF THANKSGIVING ☐ TO TEACH WISDOM ☐ OF PETITION ☐ ______	☐ INDIVIDUAL ☐ GROUP
		☐ DAVID ☐ SOLOMON ☐ SONS OF KORAH ☐ ASAPH ☐ ______	☐ OF PRAISE ☐ OF THANKSGIVING ☐ TO TEACH WISDOM ☐ OF PETITION ☐ ______	☐ INDIVIDUAL ☐ GROUP
		☐ DAVID ☐ SOLOMON ☐ SONS OF KORAH ☐ ASAPH ☐ ______	☐ OF PRAISE ☐ OF THANKSGIVING ☐ TO TEACH WISDOM ☐ OF PETITION ☐ ______	☐ INDIVIDUAL ☐ GROUP
		☐ DAVID ☐ SOLOMON ☐ SONS OF KORAH ☐ ASAPH ☐ ______	☐ OF PRAISE ☐ OF THANKSGIVING ☐ TO TEACH WISDOM ☐ OF PETITION ☐ ______	☐ INDIVIDUAL ☐ GROUP
		☐ DAVID ☐ SOLOMON ☐ SONS OF KORAH ☐ ASAPH ☐ ______	☐ OF PRAISE ☐ OF THANKSGIVING ☐ TO TEACH WISDOM ☐ OF PETITION ☐ ______	☐ INDIVIDUAL ☐ GROUP
		☐ DAVID ☐ SOLOMON ☐ SONS OF KORAH ☐ ASAPH ☐ ______	☐ OF PRAISE ☐ OF THANKSGIVING ☐ TO TEACH WISDOM ☐ OF PETITION ☐ ______	☐ INDIVIDUAL ☐ GROUP
		☐ DAVID ☐ SOLOMON ☐ SONS OF KORAH ☐ ASAPH ☐ ______	☐ OF PRAISE ☐ OF THANKSGIVING ☐ TO TEACH WISDOM ☐ OF PETITION ☐ ______	☐ INDIVIDUAL ☐ GROUP
		☐ DAVID ☐ SOLOMON ☐ SONS OF KORAH ☐ ASAPH ☐ ______	☐ OF PRAISE ☐ OF THANKSGIVING ☐ TO TEACH WISDOM ☐ OF PETITION ☐ ______	☐ INDIVIDUAL ☐ GROUP
		☐ DAVID ☐ SOLOMON ☐ SONS OF KORAH ☐ ASAPH ☐ ______	☐ OF PRAISE ☐ OF THANKSGIVING ☐ TO TEACH WISDOM ☐ OF PETITION ☐ ______	☐ INDIVIDUAL ☐ GROUP
		☐ DAVID ☐ SOLOMON ☐ SONS OF KORAH ☐ ASAPH ☐ ______	☐ OF PRAISE ☐ OF THANKSGIVING ☐ TO TEACH WISDOM ☐ OF PETITION ☐ ______	☐ INDIVIDUAL ☐ GROUP
		☐ DAVID ☐ SOLOMON ☐ SONS OF KORAH ☐ ASAPH ☐ ______	☐ OF PRAISE ☐ OF THANKSGIVING ☐ TO TEACH WISDOM ☐ OF PETITION ☐ ______	☐ INDIVIDUAL ☐ GROUP

REMEMBERING GOD'S CHOSEN CHILDREN

VERSES FOR CALLIGRAPHY

Verses for Calligraphy

Students may look over these verses to find something they would like to use for their calligraphy assignments. Use verses from the chapters you have studied or verses that relate to those chapters. In parentheses are notes and summaries for your information, not for copying. All verses are from the NIV.

Exodus 15:21
Sing to the Lord, for He is highly exalted.
The horse and its rider He has hurled into the sea.

Exodus 15:26
If you listen carefully to the voice of the Lord your God
and do what is right in His eyes,
if you pay attention to His commands
and keep all His decrees,
I will not bring on you any of the diseases
I brought on the Egyptians,
for I am the Lord Who heals you.

Exodus 18:16
Whenever they have a dispute, it is brought to me,
and I decide between the parties
and inform them of God's decrees and laws.

Exodus 19:4-6
You yourselves have seen what I did to Egypt,
and how I carried you on eagles' wings
and brought you to Myself.
Now if you obey Me fully and keep My covenant,
then out of all nations you will be My treasured possession.
Although the whole earth is Mine,
you will be for Me a kingdom of priests and a holy nation.

Exodus 22:28
Do not blaspheme God
or curse the ruler of your people.

Exodus 23:9
Do not oppress an alien;
you yourselves know how it feels to be aliens,
because you were aliens in Egypt.

Exodus 24:8
Moses then took the blood,
sprinkled it on the people and said,
"This is the blood of the covenant
that the Lord has made with you
in accordance with all these words."

Matthew 26:28
Jesus said, "This is my blood of the covenant,
which is poured out for many
for the forgiveness of sins."

Exodus 24:22
There, above the cover between the two cherubim
that are over the ark of the Testimony,
I will meet with you
and give you all My commands for the Israelites.

Exodus 28:29
Whenever Aaron enters the Holy Place,
he will bear the names of the sons of Israel
over his heart on the breastpiece of decision
as a continuing memorial before the Lord.

Exodus 29:42-43
For the generations to come
this burnt offering is to be made regularly
at the entrance to the Tent of Meeting
before the Lord.
There I will meet you and speak to you;
there also I will meet with the Israelites
and the place will be consecrated by My glory.

Romans 1:22, 23
Although they claimed to be wise,
they became fools
and exchanged the glory of the immortal God
for images made to look like mortal man
and birds and animals and reptiles.

Exodus 29:45-46
Then I will dwell among the Israelites
and be their God.
They will know that I am the Lord their God,
Who brought them out of Egypt
so that I might dwell among them.
I am the Lord their God.

Exodus 30:2-6
See, I have chosen Bezalel...
and I have filled him with the Spirit of God,
with skill, ability and knowledge
in all kinds of crafts...
Also, I have given skill to all the craftsmen
to make everything I have commanded you...

Exodus 34:6b-7
The Lord, the compassionate and gracious God,
slow to anger,
abounding in love and faithfulness,...
maintaining love to thousands,
and forgiving wickedness, rebellion, and sin.
Yet He does not leave the guilty unpunished..."

Exodus 40:34
Then the cloud covered the Tent of Meeting,
and the glory of the Lord filled the tabernacle.

Leviticus 18:30
Keep my requirements
and do not follow any of the detestable customs
that were practiced before you came
and do not defile yourselves with them.
I am the Lord your God.

Leviticus 19:34
The alien living with you must
be treated as one of your native-born.
Love him as yourself,
for you were aliens in Egypt.
I am the Lord.

Verses for Calligraphy

Numbers 6:24-26
The Lord bless you and keep you;
the Lord make his face shine upon you
and be gracious to you;
the Lord turn his face toward you
and give you peace.

Numbers 27:15-17
Moses said to the Lord,
"May the Lord,
the God of the spirits of all mankind,
appoint a man over this community
to go out and come in before them,
one who will lead them out and bring them in,
so the Lord's people will not be like
sheep without a shepherd."

Deuteronomy 6:4-5
Hear, O Israel:
The Lord our God,
the Lord is one.
Love the Lord your God
with all your heart
and with all your soul
and with all your strength.

Deuteronomy 6:6
These commandments that I give you today
are to be upon your hearts.

Deuteronomy 8: 2
Remember how the Lord your God led you
all the way in the desert these forty years,
to humble you and to test you
in order to know what was in your heart,
whether or not you would keep his commands.

Deuteronomy 8:3
He humbled you, causing you to hunger
and then feeding you with manna,
which neither you nor your fathers had known,
to teach you that man does not live on bread alone
but on every word that comes from the mouth of the Lord.

Deuteronomy 8:18a
But remember the LORD your God,
for it is He Who gives you the ability to produce wealth...

Deuteronomy 10:12-13
And now, O Israel,
what does the Lord your God ask of you
but to fear the Lord your God,
to walk in all His ways,
to love Him,
to serve the Lord your God
with all your heart and with all your soul,
and to observe the Lord's commands and decrees
that I am giving you today for your own good?

Deuteronomy 11:11-12
But the land you are crossing the Jordan
to take possession of
is a land of mountains and valleys
that drinks rain from heaven.
It is a land the Lord your God cares for;
the eyes of the Lord your God are continually on it
from the beginning of the year to the end.

Deuteronomy 18:10
Let no one be found among you
who sacrifices his son or daughter in the fire,
who practices divination or sorcery,
interprets omens, engages in witchcraft, or casts spells,
or who is a medium or spiritist
or who consults the dead.

Deuteronomy 29:29
The secret things belong to the Lord our God,
but the things revealed belong to us
and to our children forever,
that we may follow all the words of this law.

Joshua 1:8-9
Do not let this Book of the Law depart from your mouth;
meditate on it day and night,
so that you may be careful to do everything written in it.
Then you will be prosperous and successful.
Have I not commanded you?
Be strong and courageous. Do not be terrified.
Do not be discouraged,
for the Lord your God will be with you wherever you go.

Joshua 24:15
...choose for yourselves this day whom you will serve...
But as for me and my household,
we will serve the Lord.

Joshua 24:31
Israel served the Lord throughout the lifetime of Joshua
and of the elders who outlived him
and who had experienced everything
the Lord had done for Israel.

Judges 2:10-11
After that whole generation had been gathered to their fathers,
another generation grew up,
who knew neither the Lord nor what He had done for Israel.
The Israelites did evil in the eyes of the Lord
and served the Baals.

Judges 6:31
...Are you going to plead Baal's cause?
Are you trying to save him?...
If Baal really is a god,
he can defend himself when someone breaks down his altar.

Judges 21:25
In those days Israel had no king; everyone did as he saw fit.

Verses for Calligraphy

Ruth 1:16
...Don't urge me to leave you
or to turn back from you.
Where you go I will go,
and where you stay I will stay.
Your people will be my people
and your God my God.

Ruth 2:12
May the Lord repay you for what you have done.
May you be richly rewarded by the Lord,
the God of Israel, under whose wings
you have come to take refuge.

Ruth 4:14-15
Praise be to the Lord,
who this day has not left you without a kinsman-redeemer.
May he become famous throughout Israel!
He will renew your life
and sustain you in your old age...

1 Samuel 2:26
And the boy Samuel continued to grow in stature
and in favor with the LORD and with men.

1 Samuel 3:10b
Speak, for your servant is listening.

1 Samuel 15:22a, 23a
Does the LORD delight in burnt offerings and sacrifices
as much as in obeying the voice of the LORD?
For rebellion is like the sin of divination,
and arrogance like the evil of idolatry.

1 Samuel 16:7
...The Lord does not look at the things man looks at.
Man looks at the outward appearance,
but the Lord looks at the heart.

1 Samuel 18:7
Saul has slain his thousands,
and David his tens of thousands.

1 Samuel 23:16
And Saul's son Jonathan went to David at Horesh
and helped him find strength in God.

1 Samuel 24:12
May the Lord judge between you and me.
And may the Lord avenge the wrongs you have done to me,
but my hand will not touch you.
and the old saying goes,
'From evildoers come evil deeds,'
so my hand will not touch you.

2 Samuel 1:26-27
I grieve for you, Jonathan my brother;
you were very dear to me.
Your love for me was wonderful,
more wonderful than that of women.
How the mighty have fallen!
The weapons of war have perished!

2 Samuel 6:14
David, wearing a linen ephod,
danced before the Lord with all his might,
while he and the entire house of Israel brought up
the ark of the Lord
with shouts and the sound of trumpets.

2 Samuel 6:21-22
...I will celebrate before the Lord.
I will become even more undignified than this...

2 Samuel 15:21
As surely as the Lord lives,
and as my lord the king lives,
wherever my lord the king may be,
whether it means life or death,
there will your servant be.

2 Samuel 23:3-4
When one rules over men in righteousness,
when he rules in the fear of God,
he is like the light of morning at sunrise
on a cloudless morning,
like the brightness after rain
that brings the grass from the earth.

2 Samuel 11:4
As Solomon grew old,
his wives turned his heart after other gods,
and his heart was not fully devoted
to the Lord his God,
as the heart of David his father had been.

Verses for Calligraphy

Psalm 1
(Delighting in God's law.)

Psalm 4:1
Answer me when I call to You,
O my righteous God.
Give me relief from my distress;
be merciful to me and hear my prayer.

Psalm 4:8
I will lie down and sleep in peace,
for You alone, O Lord,
make me dwell in safety.

Psalm 5:7-8
But I, by Your great mercy,
will come into Your house;
in reverence will I bow down
toward Your holy temple.
Lead me, O Lord, in Your righteousness
because of my enemies--
make straight Your way before me.

Psalm 6 or 13
(Sorrow, a cry for mercy.)

Psalm 8
(What is man that You care for him?)

Psalm 10:17-18
You hear, O Lord, the desire of the afflicted;
You encourage them, and You listen to their cry,
defending the fatherless and the oppressed,
in order that man, who is of the earth,
may terrify no more.

Psalm 15
(Who may dwell in Your sanctuary?)

Psalm 16
(Praise for many blessings.)

Psalm 19
(Praising God's work and law.
Forgive my hidden faults.

Psalm 23
(The Good Shepherd.)

Psalm 25:4-10
(Teach me Your ways.
Remember Your mercy and love.)

Psalm 27:7-11
(Seeking His face.
Though father & mother forsake...)

Psalm 28:9
Save Your people and bless Your inheritance;
be their shepherd and carry them forever.

Psalm 29:11
The Lord gives strength to His people;
the Lord blesses His people with peace.

Psalm 30: 4-5
Sing to the Lord, you saints of His;
praise His holy name.
For His anger lasts only a moment,
but His favor lasts a lifetime;
weeping may remain for a night,
but rejoicing comes in the morning.

Psalm 30:6-7
When I felt secure, I said,
"I will never be shaken."
O Lord, when You favored me,
You made my mountain stand firm;
but when You hid Your face,
I was dismayed.

Psalm 31:7
I will be glad and rejoice in Your love,
for You saw my affliction
and knew the anguish of my soul.

Psalm 31:22
In my alarm I said,
"I am cut off from Your sight!"
Yet You heard my cry for mercy
when I called to You for help.

Psalm 32:1-5
(Acknowledging sin)

Psalm 32:8-9
I will instruct you and teach you in the way you should go;
I will counsel you and watch over you.
Do not be like the horse or the mule,
which have no understanding
but must be controlled by bit and bridle
or they will not come to you.

Psalm 33:1-5
(Making music to a God Who is faithful,
righteous, just, loving.)

Psalm 33:16-22
(Depending on God and not on military strength.)

Psalm 34
(Taste and see that the Lord is good.)

Psalm 36
(Sinfulness of the wicked vs.
the love, faithfulness, righteousness and justice of God.)

Psalm 37
(Do not fret because of evil men.)

Psalm 38
(I am troubled by my sin, pain, sickness, guilt.)

Verses for Calligraphy

Psalm 39:4-6
Show me, O Lord, my life's end
and the number of my days;
let me know how fleeting is my life.
You have made my days a mere handbreadth;
the span of my years is as nothing before You.
Each man's life is but a breath.
Man is a mere phantom as he goes to and fro:
He bustles about, but only in vain;
he heaps up wealth, not knowing who will get it.

Psalm 40:5
Many, O Lord my God,
are the wonders You have done.
The things You planned for us
no one can recount to You;
were I to speak and tell of them,
they would be too many to declare.

Psalm 42
(Why are you downcast, O my soul?)

Psalm 46
(Be still and know that I am God.
I will be exalted among the nations.)

Psalm 47
(God is King of all the earth)

Psalm 49:7-9
No man can redeem the life of another
or give to God a ransom for him--
the ransom for a life is costly,
no payment is ever enough--
that he should live on forever
and not see decay.

Psalm 49:14-15
Like sheep they are destined for the grave,
and death will feed on them.
The upright will rule over them in the morning;
the their forms will decay in the grave,
far from their princely mansions.
But God will redeem my life from the grave;
He will surely take me to Himself.

Psalm 51:12-13
Restore to me the joy of Your salvation
and grant me a willing spirit, to sustain me.
Then I will teach transgressors your ways,
and sinners will turn back to you.

Psalm 56:3-4
When I am afraid,
I will trust in You.
In God, Whose word I praise,
in God I trust; I will not be afraid.
What can mortal man do to me?

Psalm 57:9-11
I will praise You, O Lord, among the nations;
I will sing of You among the peoples.
For great is Your love, reaching to the heavens;
Your faithfulness reaches to the skies.
Be exalted, O God, above the heavens;
let Your glory be over all the earth.

Psalm 62
(My soul finds rest in God alone.
He is strong and loving.)

Psalm 63
(Seeking God.
I have seen You in the sanctuary.
Your power and glory.)

Psalm 65:9-13
(God cares for the land)

Psalm 66:18
If I had cherished sin in my heart,
the Lord would not have listened.

Psalm 67
(May God bless our nation.
May the nations praise Him.)

Psalm 68:5, 6
A father to the fatherless, a defender of widows,
is God in His holy dwelling.
God sets the lonely in families,
He leads forth the prisoners with singing;
but the rebellious live in a sun-scorched land.

Psalm 68:24-27
(A procession praising God)

Psalm 71:20-21
Though You have made me see troubles,
many and bitter,
You will restore my life again;
from the depths of the earth
You will again bring me up.
You will increase my honor
and comfort me once again.

Psalm 73:1-3, 16-17
(Envy of the arrogant)

Psalm 73:21-26
(God's presence in grief and bitterness)

Psalm 74:9, 22
We are given no miraculous signs;
no prophets are left,
and none of us knows how long this will be.
Rise up, O God, and defend Your cause;
remember how fools mock You all day long.

Verses for Calligraphy

Psalm 75:6-7
No one from the east of the west
or from the desert can exalt a man.
But it is God who judges:
He brings one down; He exalts another.

Psalm 84:10
Better is one day in Your courts
than a thousand elsewhere;
I would rather be a doorkeeper
in the house of my God
than dwell in the tents of the wicked.

Psalm 85:8-9
I will listen to what God the Lord will say;
He promises peace to His people, His saints--
but let them not return to folly.
Surely His salvation is near those who fear Him,
that His glory may dwell in our land.

Psalm 86
(A cry for mercy)

Psalm 90
(A prayer of Moses)

Psalm 91:14-16
"Because he love Me," says the Lord, "I will rescue him;
I will protect him, for he acknowledges My name.
He will call upon Me, and I will answer him;
I will be with him in trouble,
I will deliver him and honor him.
With long life will I satisfy him
and show him My salvation."

Psalm 97:6
The heavens proclaim His righteousness,
and all the peoples see His glory.

Psalm 93:5
Your statues stand firm;
holiness adorns your house for endless days, O Lord.

Psalm 94:1-15
(Judgment on the wicked
and discipline of individuals and nations for blessing.)

Psalm 95:1-3
Come, let us sing for joy to the Lord;
let us shout aloud to the Rock of our salvation.
Let us come before Him with thanksgiving
and extol Him with music and song.
For the Lord is the great God,
the great King above all gods.

Psalm 98
(God's salvation, righteousness, love, faithfulness to
Israel.
Rejoice, all nations and all nature.)

Psalm 99
(The Lord reigns. Moses, Aaron, Samuel, pillar of cloud.
Forgiving though You punished.)

Psalm 100
(Praise. We are His sheep.)

Psalm 101
(Dedication to living a blameless life
because of God's love and justice.)

Psalm 103
(Compare with Ex 34:6-7)

Psalm 105
(God keeps His promise.)

Psalm 106
(Israel's rebelliousness)

Psalm 109:21-22
But You, O Sovereign Lord,
deal well with me for Your name's sake;
out of the goodness of Your love, deliver me.
For I am poor and needy,
and my heart is wounded within me.

Psalm 111
(Remember the faithfulness of God)

Psalm 113:5-6
Who is like the Lord our God,
the One Who sits enthroned on high,
Who stoops down to look
on the heavens and the earth?

Psalm 115:1-8
(God vs gods.)

Psalm 116:12
How can I repay the Lord
for all His goodness to me?

Psalm 116:15
Precious in the sight of the Lord
is the death of His saints.

Psalm 118:8-9
It is better to take refuge in the Lord
than to trust in man.
It is better to take refuge in the Lord
than to trust in princes.

Psalm 119:1-8
(Blessed are those who seek God.)

Psalm 119:67-68
Before I was afflicted I went astray,
but now I obey Your word.
You are good, and what You do is good;
teach me Your decrees.

Verses for Calligraphy

Psalm 119:73
Your hands made me and formed me;
give me understanding to learn Your commands.

Psalm 119:97, 99
Oh, how I love Your law!
I meditate on it all day long.
I have more insight than all my teachers,
for I meditate on Your statutes.

Psalm 119:126
It is time for You to act, O Lord:
Your law is being broken.

Psalm 119:136
Streams of tears flow from my eyes,
for Your law is not obeyed.

Psalm 119:150-151
Those who devise wicked schemes are near,
but they are far from your law.
Yet You are near, O Lord,
and all Your commands are true.

Psalm 119:173
May Your hand be ready to help me,
for I have chosen Your precepts.
for I have not forgotten Your commandments.

Psalm 121
(The blessings of God's personal care.)

Psalm 122
(A prayer for the peace of Jerusalem)

Psalm 127:1
Unless the Lord builds the house,
its builders labor in vain.

Psalm 127:2
In vain you rise early and stay up late,
toiling or food to eat--
for He grants sleep to those He loves.

Psalm 127:3
Sons are a heritage from the Lord,
children a reward from Him.

Psalm 128
(Blessings of the Lord on the family.)

Psalm 130:3, 4
If You, O Lord, kept a record of sins,
O Lord, who could stand?
But with You there is forgiveness;
therefore You are feared.

Psalm 131
(I have stilled and quieted my soul.)

Psalm 132
(About bringing the ark to Jerusalem.)

Psalm 133
(The blessing of unity among brothers.)

Psalm 134
(Encouragement for ministers.)

Psalm 135
(Idols of silver and gold.)

Psalm 136
(God's care for creation and for Israel.)

Psalm 139
(God's intimate knowledge of
and care for the individual.)

Psalm 141:1-2
(Worship at the temple is pattern for personal worship.)

Psalm 141:3-4
(Lead us not into temptation.)

Psalm 141:5
Let a righteous man strike me--it is a kindness;
let him rebuke me--it is oil on my head.
My head will not refuse it.

Psalm 142
(A cry for help when no one cares.)

Psalm 143
(David cries for help)

Psalm 145:3-7
(Remembering God's awesome acts.)

Psalm 145:8-9
The Lord is gracious and compassionate,
slow to anger and rich in love.
The Lord is good to all;
He has compassion on all He has made.

Psalm 146:5-9
(God helps those in trouble--
the oppressed, hungry, prisoners, blind,
bowed down, alien, fatherless, widow--
and loves the righteous.)

Psalm 147:22
The Lord delights in those who fear Him,
who put their hope in His unfailing love.

Psalm 148
(Let every thing praise the Lord.)

Psalm 150
(Praise God for His greatness.
Praise Him with music and dancing.)

VERSES FOR CALLIGRAPHY

Proverbs 1:7
The fear of the LORD is the beginning of knowledge,
but fools despise wisdom and discipline.

Proverbs 3:11-12
My son, do not despise the LORD's discipline,
and do not resent His rebuke,
because the LORD disciplines those He loves,
as a father the son he delights in.

Ecclesiastes 3:11
He has made everything beautiful in its time.
He has also set eternity in the hearts of men;
yet they cannot fathom what God has
done from beginning to end.

Ecclesiastes 3:12-13
I know that there is nothing better
for men than to be happy
and do good while they live.
That everyone may eat and drink,
and find satisfaction in all his toil - this is the gift of God.

Ecclesiastes 5:10
Whoever loves money never has money enough;
whoever loves wealth is never satisfied with his income.
This too is meaningless.

1 Timothy 6:9-10
People who want to get rich
fall into temptation and a trap
and into many foolish and harmful desires
that plunge men into ruin and destruction.
For the love of money is a root of all kinds of evil.
Some people, eager for money,
have wandered from the faith
and peirced themselves with many griefs.

Ecclesiastes 10:17
The quiet words of the wise are more to be heeded
than the shouts of a ruler of fools.

Ecclesiastes 12:13-14
Now all has been heard;
here is the conclusion of the matter:
Fear God and keep His commandments,
for this is the whole duty of man.
For God will bring every deed into judgment,
including every hidden thing,
whether it is good or evil.

All verses are from the NIV.

Remembering God's Chosen Children

Answer Pages

INTERACTING WITH THE TIMELINE

1 *Before Abraham*	7 THE CYCLES OF THE JUDGES
2 THE PATRIARCHS	8 UNITED KINGDOM
3 THE YEARS IN EGYPT	9 THE DIVIDED KINGDOM OF ISRAEL
4 EXITING EGYPT	10 THE DISPERSION
5 THE WANDERING	11 THE DIVIDED KINGDOM OF JUDAH
6 CONQUEST OF CANAAN	12 70 YEARS OF CAPTIVITY

13 THE RETURN

Show which era each of the following events belongs to by writing the era's number (from your work above) by each event. The first one is done as an example.

1 God created Adam and Eve. They brought sin into the world.
2 Jacob with Rachel and Leah had 12 sons. Jacob's name became Israel.
7 Ruth came to Israel with Naomi & became the grandmother of King David.
8 Samuel was a priest and prophet who ruled Israel justly.
1 Job, a godly man, suffers greatly as Satan tries to turn him from God.
4 God gave the Ten Commandments and made a covenant with Israel.
9 The first king, Jeroboam, led the Israelites to worship two calf-idols.
8 David, a shepherd, killed Goliath and ruled as king for 40 years.
9 Elijah challenged 400 priests of Baal. The Lord responded. Baal did not.
13 Esther used her position as queen of Persia to save the Jews.
8 Solomon was a wise king, built the Temple, but turned from God.
12 Daniel served kings but never compromised even when thrown to lions.
7 The Israelites would repeatedly rebel, be oppressed, repent, and be redemed.
8 Jonathan, Saul's son but David's best friend, died in battle.
9 King Ahab and evil wife Jezebel tried to kill the prophet Elijah.
11 King Josiah turned to the Lord like no other king before or after him.
6 Joshua lead Israel to conquer the Promised Land of Canaan.
13 The last writing prophet before the birth of Jesus was Malachi.
2 God called Abraham out of Ur to Canaan. He took Lot and Sarah.
2 Isaac, the promised son, married Rebekah. They had twins Jacob & Esau.
4 God had them build a Tabernacle and lived among them.
8 When the people asked for a king, God gave them Saul.
11 King Manasseh, the most evil, sacrificed his son in the fire.
12 Ezekiel taught the exiles that God is sovereign everywhere.
10 Assyria conquered and scattered Israel. They are not heard of again.
5 The Israelites rejected God and wandered the wilderness for 40 years.

TIMELINE CROSSWORD 1

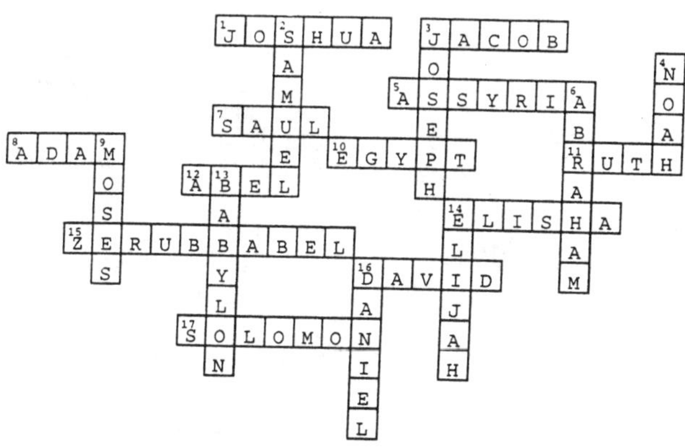

THE LEGEND OF SARGON

This is the story of Sargon an ancient king of Akkad in what is now Iraq. He was the first to rule a great empire in history.

"My father knew not of me. My mother conceived me and bore me in secret. She set me in a basket of rushes and sealed the lid with tar. Then she cast me into the river that carried me down to Akki.

"There a gardener drew me out of the water and raised me as his son. I became a gardener and Ishtar granted me her love and I became a king and ruled the black-haired people."

SOME HIGHLY EDUCATED INDIVIDUALS TEACH THAT MOSES DID NOT EXIST.
Their reasoning is as follows:

1. Sargon was put in a basket of rushes and put in a river.
   Moses was put in a basket of rushes and put in a river.
2. Sargon was taken out of the river and became a leader of many people.
   Moses was taken out of the river and became a leader of many people.
3. Sargon comes before Moses' time.
4. These similarities are too close to be two different stories.
5. Therefore Moses is not a real person but is only story based on the legend of Sargon.

BUT THIS LOGIC IS FAULTY.

See how a lawyer could use this kind of logic (that things only happen once) to prove a young lady did not abandon her baby at the laundry mat in a plastic basket.

"The young lady did not abandon her baby at the laundry mat in a plastic basket - it is but a story based on a young lady in 1950 who abandon her baby in a stroller in a park. And she is but a story based on a young lady from 1802 who abandoned baby in a basket on the church steps. And she, in turn, is but a story based on Sargon who was abandoned by his mother in a basket in the river. Therefore; the young girl is innocent of all charges."

What they are saying is that events only happen once. Think of something that has happened, and with their logic, prove it did not happen.

ANSWERS MAY VARY

TIMELINE CROSSWORD 2

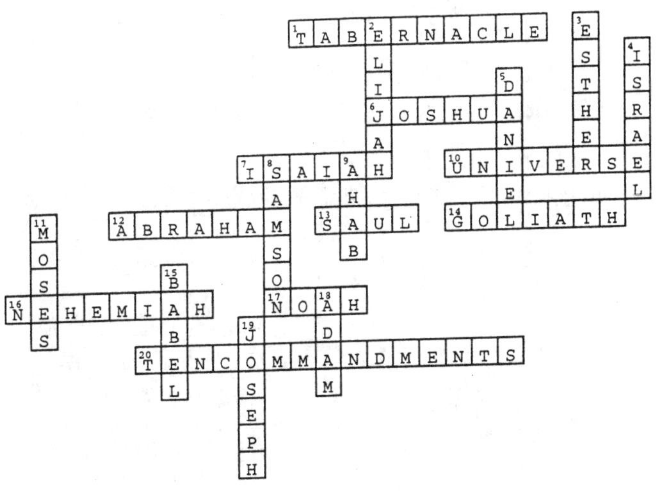

PASSOVER CROSSWORD

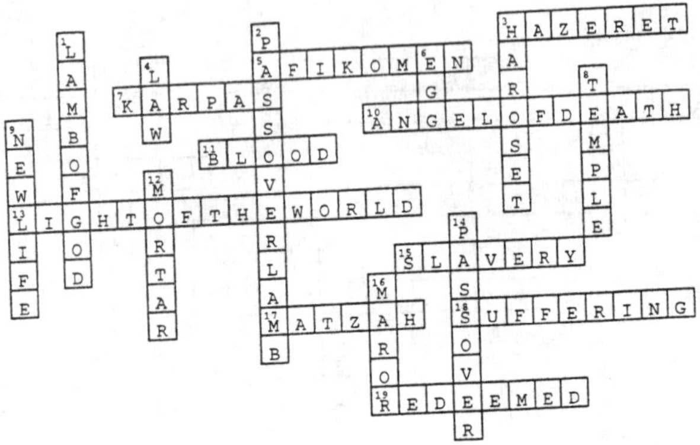

12

EXITING EGYPT 1

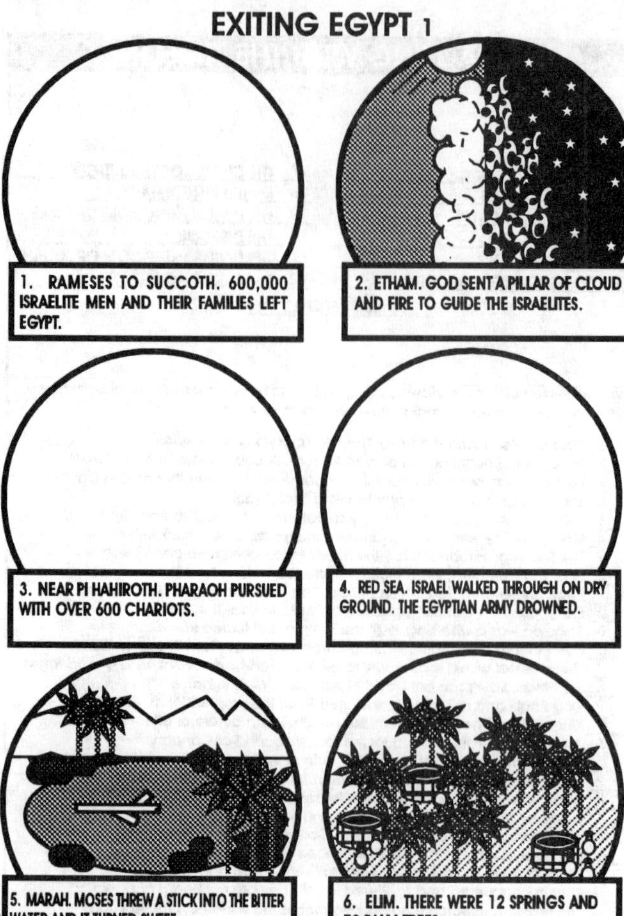

1. RAMESES TO SUCCOTH. 600,000 ISRAELITE MEN AND THEIR FAMILIES LEFT EGYPT.
2. ETHAM. GOD SENT A PILLAR OF CLOUD AND FIRE TO GUIDE THE ISRAELITES.
3. NEAR PI HAHIROTH. PHARAOH PURSUED WITH OVER 600 CHARIOTS.
4. RED SEA. ISRAEL WALKED THROUGH ON DRY GROUND. THE EGYPTIAN ARMY DROWNED.
5. MARAH. MOSES THREW A STICK INTO THE BITTER WATER AND IT TURNED SWEET.
6. ELIM. THERE WERE 12 SPRINGS AND 70 PALM TREES.

20

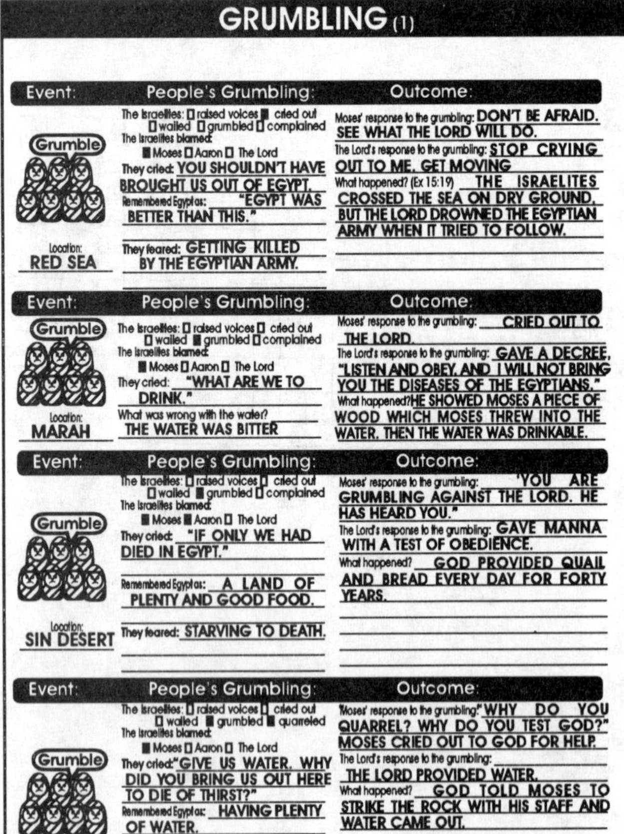

GRUMBLING (1)

Event: | People's Grumbling: | Outcome:

Location: RED SEA

The Israelites: ☐ raised voices ■ cried out ☐ wailed ☐ grumbled ☐ complained
The Israelites blamed: ■ Moses ☐ Aaron ☐ The Lord
They cried: YOU SHOULDN'T HAVE BROUGHT US OUT OF EGYPT.
Remembered Egypt as: "EGYPT WAS BETTER THAN THIS."
They feared: GETTING KILLED BY THE EGYPTIAN ARMY.

Moses' response to the grumbling: DON'T BE AFRAID. SEE WHAT THE LORD WILL DO.
The Lord's response to the grumbling: STOP CRYING OUT TO ME. GET MOVING
What happened? (Ex 15:19) THE ISRAELITES CROSSED THE SEA ON DRY GROUND, BUT THE LORD DROWNED THE EGYPTIAN ARMY WHEN IT TRIED TO FOLLOW.

Event: | People's Grumbling: | Outcome:

Location: MARAH

The Israelites: ☐ raised voices ☐ cried out ☐ wailed ■ grumbled ☐ complained
The Israelites blamed: ■ Moses ☐ Aaron ☐ The Lord
They cried: "WHAT ARE WE TO DRINK."
What was wrong with the water? THE WATER WAS BITTER

Moses' response to the grumbling: CRIED OUT TO THE LORD.
The Lord's response to the grumbling: GAVE A DECREE, "LISTEN AND OBEY, AND I WILL NOT BRING YOU THE DISEASES OF THE EGYPTIANS."
What happened? HE SHOWED MOSES A PIECE OF WOOD WHICH MOSES THREW INTO THE WATER. THEN THE WATER WAS DRINKABLE.

Event: | People's Grumbling: | Outcome:

Location: SIN DESERT

The Israelites: ☐ raised voices ☐ cried out ☐ wailed ■ grumbled ☐ complained
The Israelites blamed: ■ Moses ■ Aaron ☐ The Lord
They cried: "IF ONLY WE HAD DIED IN EGYPT."
Remembered Egypt as: A LAND OF PLENTY AND GOOD FOOD.
They feared: STARVING TO DEATH.

Moses' response to the grumbling: "YOU ARE GRUMBLING AGAINST THE LORD. HE HAS HEARD YOU."
The Lord's response to the grumbling: GAVE MANNA WITH A TEST OF OBEDIENCE.
What happened? GOD PROVIDED QUAIL AND BREAD EVERY DAY FOR FORTY YEARS.

Event: | People's Grumbling: | Outcome:

Location: REPHIDIM MASSAH & MERIBAH

The Israelites: ☐ raised voices ☐ cried out ☐ wailed ■ grumbled ■ quarreled
The Israelites blamed: ■ Moses ☐ Aaron ☐ The Lord
They cried: "GIVE US WATER. WHY DID YOU BRING US OUT HERE TO DIE OF THIRST?"
Remembered Egypt as: HAVING PLENTY OF WATER.
They feared: DYING OF THIRST.

Moses' response to the grumbling: "WHY DO YOU QUARREL? WHY DO YOU TEST GOD?" MOSES CRIED OUT TO GOD FOR HELP.
The Lord's response to the grumbling: THE LORD PROVIDED WATER.
What happened? GOD TOLD MOSES TO STRIKE THE ROCK WITH HIS STAFF AND WATER CAME OUT.

22

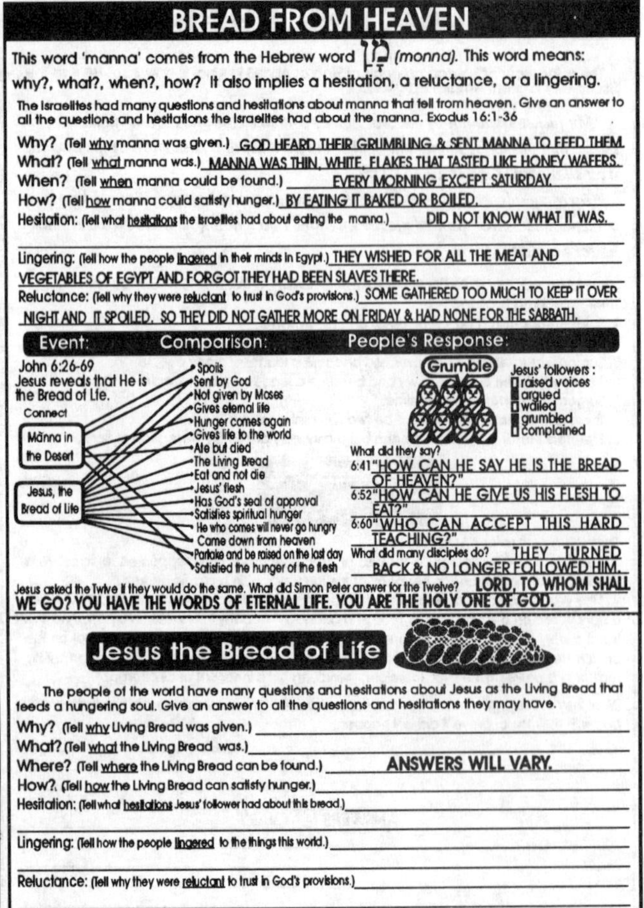

BREAD FROM HEAVEN

This word 'manna' comes from the Hebrew word מָן *(monna)*. This word means: why?, what?, when?, how? It also implies a hesitation, a reluctance, or a lingering.

The Israelites had many questions and hesitations about manna that fell from heaven. Give an answer to all the questions and hesitations the Israelites had about the manna. Exodus 16:1-36

Why? (Tell why manna was given.) GOD HEARD THEIR GRUMBLING & SENT MANNA TO FEED THEM.
What? (Tell what manna was.) MANNA WAS THIN, WHITE, FLAKES THAT TASTED LIKE HONEY WAFERS.
When? (Tell when manna could be found.) EVERY MORNING EXCEPT SATURDAY.
How? (Tell how manna could satisfy hunger.) BY EATING IT BAKED OR BOILED.
Hesitation: (Tell what hesitations the Israelites had about eating the manna.) DID NOT KNOW WHAT IT WAS.
Lingering: (Tell how the people lingered in their minds in Egypt.) THEY WISHED FOR ALL THE MEAT AND VEGETABLES OF EGYPT AND FORGOT THEY HAD BEEN SLAVES THERE.
Reluctance: (Tell why they were reluctant to trust in God's provisions.) SOME GATHERED TOO MUCH TO KEEP IT OVER NIGHT AND IT SPOILED. SO THEY DID NOT GATHER MORE ON FRIDAY & HAD NONE FOR THE SABBATH.

Event: | Comparison: | People's Response:

John 6:26-69
Jesus reveals that He is the Bread of Life.
Connect
Mãnna in the Desert
Jesus, the Bread of Life

- Spoils
- Sent by God
- Not given by Moses
- Gives eternal life
- Hunger comes again
- Gives life to the world
- Ate but died
- The Living Bread
- Eat and not die
- Jesus' flesh
- Has God's seal of approval
- Satisfies spiritual hunger
- He who comes will never go hungry
- Came down from heaven
- Partake and be raised on the last day
- Satisfied the hunger of the flesh

Jesus' followers: ☐ raised voices ■ argued ☐ wailed ■ grumbled ☐ complained

What did they say?
6:41 "HOW CAN HE SAY HE IS THE BREAD OF HEAVEN?"
6:52 "HOW CAN HE GIVE US HIS FLESH TO EAT?"
6:60 "WHO CAN ACCEPT THIS HARD TEACHING?"
What did many disciples do? THEY TURNED BACK & NO LONGER FOLLOWED HIM.

Jesus asked the Twlve if they would do the same. What did Simon Peter answer for the Twelve? LORD, TO WHOM SHALL WE GO? YOU HAVE THE WORDS OF ETERNAL LIFE. YOU ARE THE HOLY ONE OF GOD.

Jesus the Bread of Life

The people of the world have many questions and hesitations about Jesus as the Living Bread that feeds a hungering soul. Give an answer to all the questions and hesitations they may have.

Why? (Tell why Living Bread was given.)
What? (Tell what the Living Bread was.)
Where? (Tell where the Living Bread can be found.) ANSWERS WILL VARY.
How?. (Tell how the Living Bread can satisfy hunger.)
Hesitation: (Tell what hesitations Jesus' follower had about this bread.)
Lingering: (Tell how the people lingered to the things this world.)
Reluctance: (Tell why they were reluctant to trust in God's provisions.)

24

JETHRO'S COUNSEL

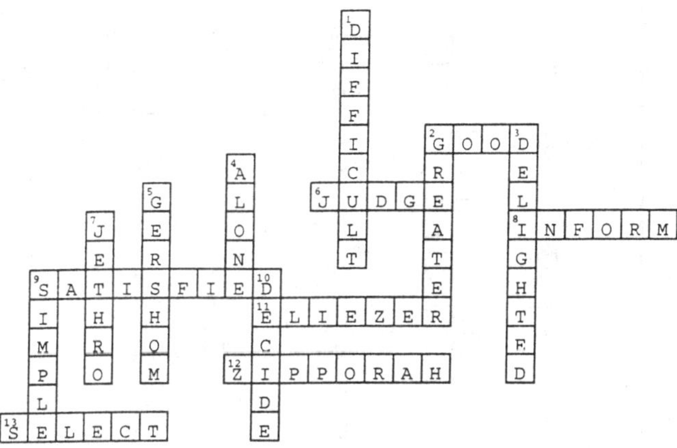

THE UPS AND DOWNS OF MT SINAI

5 Moses, AARON, Nadab, Abihu and the 70 elders see God. They ATE & drink in His presence. Moses and JOSHUA go up further. For 6 days the GLORY of the Lord settles on Mt Sinai. Moses stays 40 days. God gives him the two tablets of the TESTIMONY made of STONE and written by the FINGER of God.

4 God explains more laws and instruction. God tells Moses, 'Go get Aaron, his sons, and the 70 elders of Israel.'

2 God says, 'I will SPEAK aloud. Let the people get consecrated and ready.'

7 Moses arrives with two stone tablets. God PASSES in front of Moses. He restates His covenant and tells Moses to write it all down. Moses stays 40 days and returns with the 10 Commandments on stone tablets.

3 God says, 'Go down and WARN the people to stay back." Moses says, 'You have warned them." God says, 'Go down and bring AARON up -- warn the people not to FORCE their way through."

6 Moses pleads for the lives of the nation. God says, 'I will NOT go with you stiff-necked people to the land I promised because I might DESTROY you. Take off your ORNAMENTS. I will soon decide what to do with you.'

1 God says, 'Tell the Israelites that that if they will keep My covenant, they will be My treasured POSSESSION

REFERENCES FOR WHEN MOSES WENT UP OR DOWN THE MOUNTAIN:

TRIP 1: UP EX 19:3, DOWN EX 19:7
TRIP 2: UP EX 19:8, DOWN EX 19:14
TRIP 3: UP EX 19:20, DOWN EX 19:25
TRIP 4: UP EX 20:21, DOWN EX 24:3
TRIP 5: UP (LARGE GROUP) EX 24:9, (MOSES & JOSHUA) 24:13, (MOSES) 24:18, DOWN EX 32:15
TRIP 6: UP EX 32:31 DOWN IS SUPPLIED
TRIP 7: UP EX 34:4, DOWN EX 34:29

5 Moses finds the Israelites worshiping a CALF of gold. Moses throws down the TABLETS. He grinds the calf into POWDER and makes the people DRINK it. About 3,000 were killed for sinning.

2 The people get ready and assemble near the mountain. Fire and SMOKE billow up. Mt Sinai trembles VIOLENTLY. The TRUMPET sounds grow loud. Moses speaks & God ANSWERS.

4 Moses writes God's words. The next day he reads the Book of the TESTIMONY to the people. They say, "We will do EVERYTHING the Lord has said." Moses sprinkles the blood of the covenant on them.

1 The people CAMP in front of Mt. Sinai. When Moses tells them what God said, they say, "We will do EVERYTHING the Lord has said."

7 God tells Moses to bring two stone TABLETS. When Moses returns with them to camp, his face is RADIANT from speaking with the Lord.

6 The PEOPLE mourn when they hear this.

3 God speaks the 10 Commandments. The people tremble with FEAR and beg Moses, "SPEAK to us yourself and we will LISTEN. But do not have God SPEAK to us or we will DIE."

GOD'S COVENANT WITH ISRAEL 1

GOD	MOSES	ISRAELITES
		THEY ACCEPT Ex 19:8 We will do everything the Lord has said.
		THEY GET READY Ex 19:14 Moses CONSECRATES them, and they wash their CLOTHES.
		THEY ACCEPT Ex 20:19a SPEAK TO US YOURSELF AND WE WILL LISTEN
		THEY CONFIRM COVENANT Exodus 24:7 WE WILL DO EVERYTHING THE LORD HAS SAID; WE WILL OBEY.
		THEY BREAK THE COVENANT ☆ Covered in "The People Break the Covenant." Exodus 32:1a COME, MAKE US GODS WHO WILL GO BEFORE US.
		THEY ARE PUNISHED & REPENT 3,000 people are killed, and God sends a plague. Ex 33:4 The people MOURN and no one puts on any ORNAMENTS.
		THEY PREPARE FOR GOD'S ARRIVAL Ex 35:21 And EVERYONE whose HEART moved him brought an OFFERING to the Lord for the Tent of MEETING.
		THEY LIVE IN GOD'S PRESENCE Ex 40:38 The cloud was over the TABERNACLE in the SIGHT of all Israel during all their TRAVELS.

GOD'S COVENANT WITH ISRAEL 2

A Jewish Wedding	*God's Covenant With Israel*
1. The marriage is often arranged by a 'matchmaker.'	[5] Israel was told to prepare by washing their clothes and getting ready.
2. The bride has a right to veto the marriage.	[2] Israel agrees to the Covenant.
3. The bride is to have a *mikveh*, a ritual bath in a body of water, like a lake, or river.	[3] Israel passed through the Red Sea (Reed Sea).
4. There is a marriage contract (ketubah) that is much like a prenuptial agreement. It is a legal document negotiated long before the wedding. It states what each party is to do. It is read aloud and agreed upon.	[1] Moses is the go-between for Israel and God.
5. The bride is to prepare herself for the wedding.	[7] The Covenant took place under the shadow of Mt Sinai and the Cloud of God's glory.
6. Before the wedding, the bride and groom have a short face-to-face meeting to affirm their intentions.	[9] The Israelites stayed at the foot of Mt Sinai and fought no battles for a year.
7. The wedding takes place under a canopy (or *chuppah*).	[6] God meets Israel and speaks to them; they are afraid, but they say they will listen and do their part of the contract.
8. The couple is now to live together. A house must be built.	[4] God had Moses write out the Covenant and read it aloud to the Israelites. They repeatedly stated their agreement to the terms.
9. According to Old Testament law, a husband cannot go to battle for a full year after the wedding.	[8] Israel builds the Tabernacle for the Lord, and He comes down to live among the people.

"The time is coming," declares the Lord, "When I will make a NEW *covenant with the house of Israel and with the house of Judah. It will not be like the* COVENANT *I made with their* FOREFATHERS *when I took them by the* HAND *to lead them out of Egypt, because they* BROKE *my* COVENANT *though I was a* HUSBAND *to them," declares the Lord.*

"This is the COVENANT *I will make with the house of Israel after that time," declares the Lord. "I will put my* LAW *in their* MINDS *and write it on their* (heart) *. I will be their* GOD*, and they will be My* PEOPLE*."*

Jeremiah 31:31-33 NIV

THE PEOPLE BREAK THE COVENANT

OUTLINE

1. THE ISRAELITES' PROBLEM
2. THE PEOPLE'S DEMAND
3. AARON'S SOLUTION
4. ISRAEL'S DECLARATION ABOUT CALF
5. AARON'S FESTIVAL
6. GOD'S ANGER
7. GOD'S NEW PLAN FOR MOSES
8. MOSES' PERSUASIVE SPEECH
9. GOD'S RESPONSE TO MOSES' SPEECH
10. MOSES' RESPONSE TO THE IDOLATRY
11. THE LEVITES' LOYALTY TO THE LORD
12. MOSES' RESPONSE TO THE LEVITES
13. MOSES' PLEA TO GOD
14 GOD'S ANSWER TO MOSES' PLEA
15. THE PEOPLE'S HUMILITY

2	"Make us gods to lead us."
1	Moses is long in coming down from the mountain. "Moses brought us up out of Egypt, but we don't know what happened to him."
5	Builds an altar in front of the golden calf and announces a festival to "the Lord." The next day the people sacrifice offerings, eat, drink, & indulge in revelry.
10	He becomes very angry, breaks the tablets. He burns and grinds the calf to powder then makes the people drink it. He confronts Aaron. He calls for those who are for the Lord, orders them to start killing people.
7	"I'll make of you a great nation."
4	"These are your gods, who brought you out of Egypt."
13	"Please forgive this horrible sin. If not, then blot me out of the book You have written."
3	"Give me your gold earrings." Makes a cast idol and fashions it with tools.
8	"Why should Your anger burn against Your people whom You brought out of Egypt? The Egyptians will say that You brought them out here to destroy them? Remember your promise to Abraham, Isaac & Israel."
6	"Your people you brought out of Egypt are corrupt, quick to turn away from what I commanded. They have made and worshiped an idol. They are stiff-necked. Let me destroy them."
9	He relents.
15	They remove their ornaments and mourn while they wait for the Lord to decide what to do with them.
12	He blesses them for siding with God to the point of killing their own relatives.
14	"Whoever sins against Me I will blot out of My book. Lead the people to the promised land. I'll send an angel before you, but I will punish whenever it is time to punish." He sent a plague as punishment for idolatry.
11	They obey Moses and kill about 3,000 revelers.

ANSWERS MAY VARY

5, 8	Moses	1. Forgetful of God's awesome acts	5. Remembered God's promise
1, 2, 3, 4	Aaron	2. Unable to wait patiently	6. Able to wait patiently
1, 2, 3	The people	3. Unfaithful to promises	7. Faithful to promises
8	The Levites	4. Quick to side with the people	8. Quick to side with the Lord
5, 7	The Lord		

VOICE OF GOD

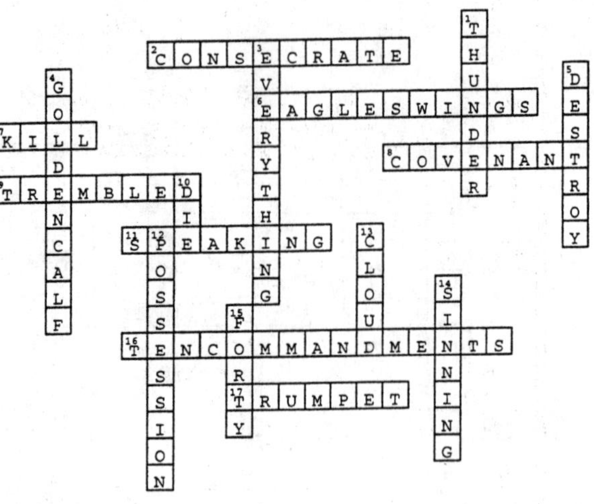

MOSES AND THE LORD

Moses used to meet with God in a TENT outside the camp. The CLOUD of God came and stayed at the ENTRANCE. God spoke with Moses FACE to FACE as a man speaks with his FRIEND. Here are some of their talks in the Tent of Meetings.

Moses said,

You keep telling me, 'LEAD these people.' But whom will You SEND with me? You've said,' I KNOW you by NAME and you have found FAVOR with me.' Then TEACH me Your WAYS so that I may KNOW You and continue to find FAVOR with you. Remember that this nation is YOUR people.

The Lord said, My PRESENCE will go with you, and I will GIVE you REST.

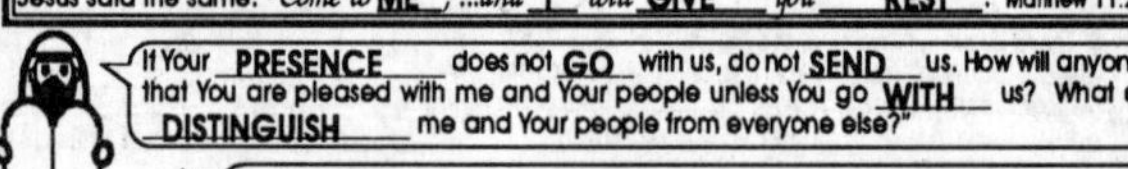

Jesus said the same. *"Come to* ME *, ...and* I *will* GIVE *you* REST *."* Matthew 11:28-30

If Your PRESENCE does not GO with us, do not SEND us. How will anyone know that You are pleased with me and Your people unless You go WITH us? What else will DISTINGUISH me and Your people from everyone else?

I will go with you, because I am PLEASED with you and I KNOW you by name.

"The prayer of a RIGHTEOUS *man is powerful and* EFFECTIVE *."* James 5:16b

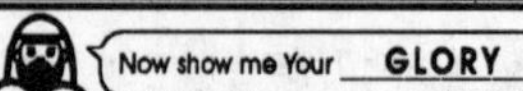

Now show me Your GLORY.

What had Moses already seen? MIRACLES, FIRE, SMOKE, DARK CLOUDS, LIGHTNING
What had he heard? THE VOICE OF GOD, THUNDER, TRUMPETS
He had spoken with God and God had ANSWERED AND GRANTED MERCY
Put yourself in Gods' place. Was Moses asking for too much? ANSWERS WILL VARY

Stand near Me on a rock. When My GLORY passes by, I'll put you in a CLEFT of the rock and COVER you with My hand. When I have gone by, I'll remove My hand so that you may see My BACK. My FACE must not be seen. The Lord came down in a cloud and STOOD there with him and proclaimed His NAME.

"The Lord, the Lord the COMPASSIONATE *and* GRACIOUS *God, slow to* ANGER*, abounding in* LOVE *and* FAITHFULNESS*, maintaining* LOVE *to thousands, and forgiving* WICKEDNESS*,* REBELLION *and* SIN*. Yet He does not leave the* GUILTY *unpunished; He punishes the children & their children for the* SINS *of the fathers to the 3rd and 4th generation."* Ex 34:6,7 NIV

If I have found favor in Your eyes, please GO with us. Even though these people are STIFF-NECKED, forgive our SINS and take us as Your INHERITANCE.

The Lord agreed to continue the covenant, even though the people had broken it. Moses took God's answer to the people, but they were afraid of him--Moses' face was RADIANT from speaking with the Lord. He explained all the Lord's words and then covered his face with a VEIL. Whenever he entered the tent, he took the VEIL off to speak with the Lord.

"And we who with UNVEILED *faces all* REFLECT *the Lord's* GLORY*, are being transformed into His* LIKENESS *with ever-increasing* GLORY*, which comes from the* LORD*, Who is the* SPIRIT*.* 2 Corinthians 3:18 NIV

HEBREW HISTORY CROSSWORD

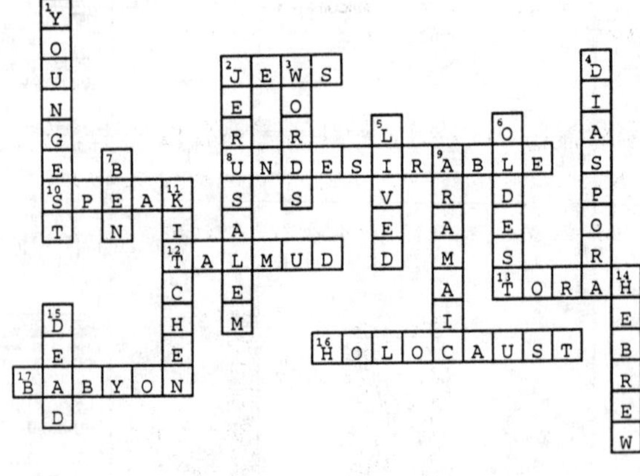

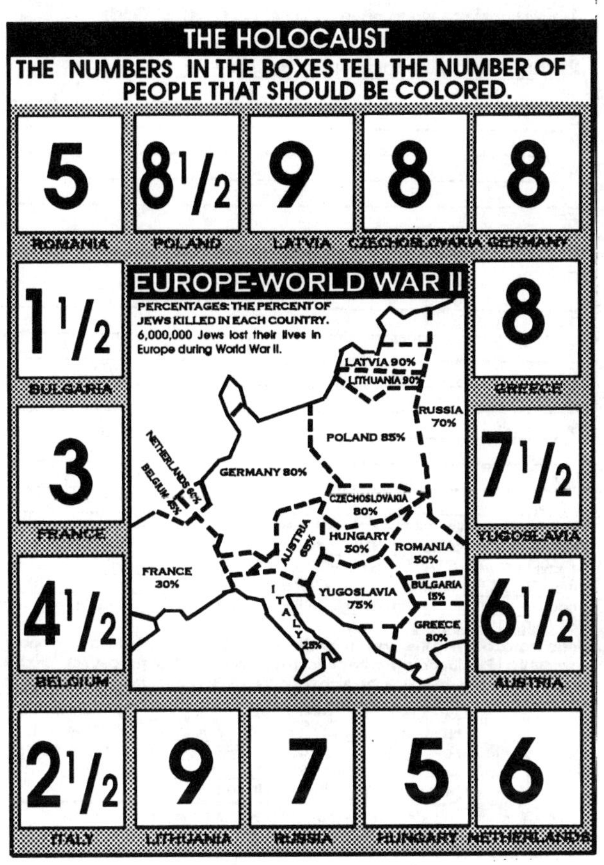

35

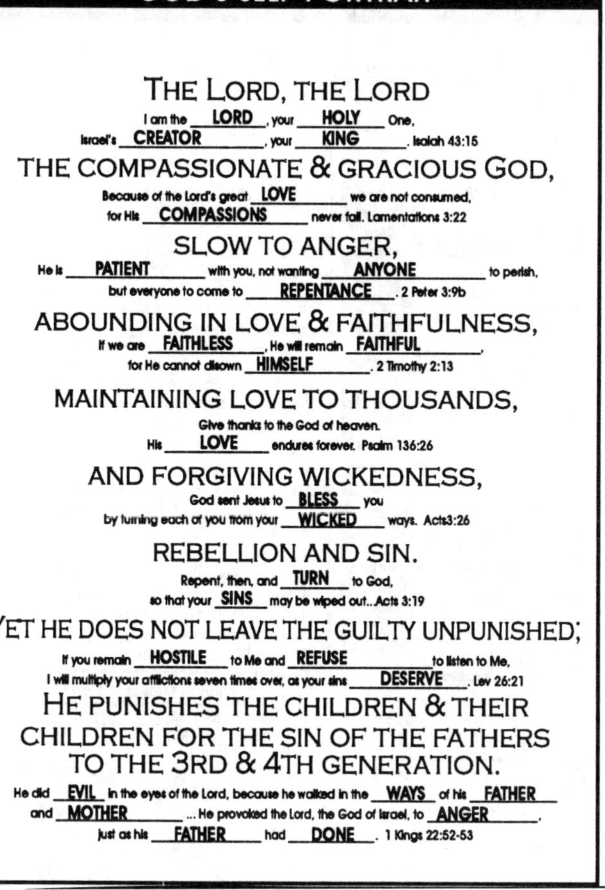

GOD'S SELF-PORTRAIT

THE LORD, THE LORD

I am the __LORD__, your __HOLY__ One,
Israel's __CREATOR__, your __KING__. Isaiah 43:15

THE COMPASSIONATE & GRACIOUS GOD,

Because of the Lord's great __LOVE__ we are not consumed,
for His __COMPASSIONS__ never fail. Lamentations 3:22

SLOW TO ANGER,

He is __PATIENT__ with you, not wanting __ANYONE__ to perish,
but everyone to come to __REPENTANCE__. 2 Peter 3:9b

ABOUNDING IN LOVE & FAITHFULNESS,

If we are __FAITHLESS__, He will remain __FAITHFUL__,
for He cannot disown __HIMSELF__. 2 Timothy 2:13

MAINTAINING LOVE TO THOUSANDS,

Give thanks to the God of heaven.
His __LOVE__ endures forever. Psalm 136:26

AND FORGIVING WICKEDNESS,

God sent Jesus to __BLESS__ you
by turning each of you from your __WICKED__ ways. Acts3:26

REBELLION AND SIN.

Repent, then, and __TURN__ to God,
so that your __SINS__ may be wiped out... Acts 3:19

YET HE DOES NOT LEAVE THE GUILTY UNPUNISHED;

If you remain __HOSTILE__ to Me and __REFUSE__ to listen to Me,
I will multiply your afflictions seven times over, as your sins __DESERVE__. Lev 26:21

HE PUNISHES THE CHILDREN & THEIR CHILDREN FOR THE SIN OF THE FATHERS TO THE 3RD & 4TH GENERATION.

He did __EVIL__ in the eyes of the Lord, because he walked in the __WAYS__ of his __FATHER__
and __MOTHER__ ... He provoked the Lord, the God of Israel, to __ANGER__,
just as his __FATHER__ had __DONE__. 1 Kings 22:52-53

36

THE NEED FOR VOWELS

Many ancient writing systems, like the one for Hebrew, did not use vowels. The use of writing spread from Canaan to the Greeks and the rest of Europe by sea trade. There were problems, since these languages depended greatly on the vowels as well as consonants to distinguish similar words from each other. For example, different vowels used with the same consonants create different words with totally different meanings. In order to deal with this confusion, the Greeks decided to make vowels from some of the Hebrew consonants they did not need for Greek words.

In order for you to see how difficult it would be not to have vowels, try to read the following sentence. On the line below write the words with vowels.

RDNGWLDBVRYHRDFTHRWRNVWLS

READING WOULD BE VERY HARD IF THERE WERE NO VOWELS.

OR AS A JOKE IT COULD BE:
"RIDING WILD BEAVER, YOU HEAR DEAF THROW RAY ON VIEWLESS."

R D

RADIO	RID	RIDE	READ
READY	ROAD	RAID	ROD
RODE	ROWDY	RODEO	RUDE
REED	RED	ARID	REEDY
ERRED	AIRED	ROWED	REDO

STUDENTS WILL NOT GET ALL OF THESE.

37

THE TEN COMMANDMENTS IN THE WORDS OF JESUS (1)

JESUS STATES THE TWO MOST IMPORTANT COMMANDS.

Matthew 22:36-40
Jesus replied: "'__LOVE__ the __LORD__ your __GOD__.' This is the __FIRST__ and __GREATEST__ commandment. And the second is like it: '__LOVE__ your __NEIGHBOR__ as __YOURSELF__.' All the __LAW__ and the __PROPHETS__ hang on these __TWO__ commandments."

JESUS EXPANDS THE MEANING OF LOVE.

Matthew 5:43 You have heard ...'Love your __NEIGHBOR__ and hate your __ENEMY__.' But I tell you: __LOVE__ your __ENEMY__ and pray for those who __PERSECUTE__ you.

IN THE WORDS OF JESUS

Read the references and complete each commandment. You may need to shorten some.

Jesus said all laws hang on loving God or loving your neighbor. COLOR THE ONE THAT APPLIES.

WRITE HOW JESUS EXPANDED THE TEN COMMANDMENTS.

EX 20:3 — 1. You shall have NO	OTHER GODS	GOD / NEIGHBOR	Mark 12:30 "Love the Lord your God with all your __HEART__ and with all your __SOUL__ and with all your __MIND__ and with all your __STRENGTH__."
EX 20:4 — 2. You shall NOT	MAKE IDOLS	GOD / NEIGHBOR	Matthew 6:24 "No one can serve __TWO__ masters. ... He will hate the one and __LOVE__ the other... You can not serve both __GOD__ and __MONEY__."
EX 20:7 — 3. You shall NOT	MISUSE THE NAME OF THE LORD	GOD / NEIGHBOR	Matthew 5:34-37 "... I tell you, Do not __SWEAR__ at __ALL__: either by heaven for it is __GOD'S THRONE__; or by earth, for it is his __FOOTSTOOL__ ... Simply let your __YES__ be __YES__ and your __NO__ __NO__."
EX 20:8 — 4. REMEMBER	THE SABBATH TO KEEP IT HOLY	GOD / NEIGHBOR	Matthew 12:12 "It is __LAWFUL__ to do __GOOD__ on the Sabbath." Mark 2:27 ..."The __SABBATH__ was made for __MAN__, not __MAN__ for the __SABBATH__."
EX 20:12 — 5. HONOR	YOUR FATHER AND MOTHER	GOD / NEIGHBOR	Matthew 15:4-6 God said, 'Honor your __FATHER__ and __MOTHER__.' But you say ...If a man says to his father or mother, 'Whatever help you might have __RECEIVED__ from me is a __GIFT__ devoted to __GOD__,'...Thus you have __NULLIFIED__ the word of God for the sake of your __TRADITION__.

38

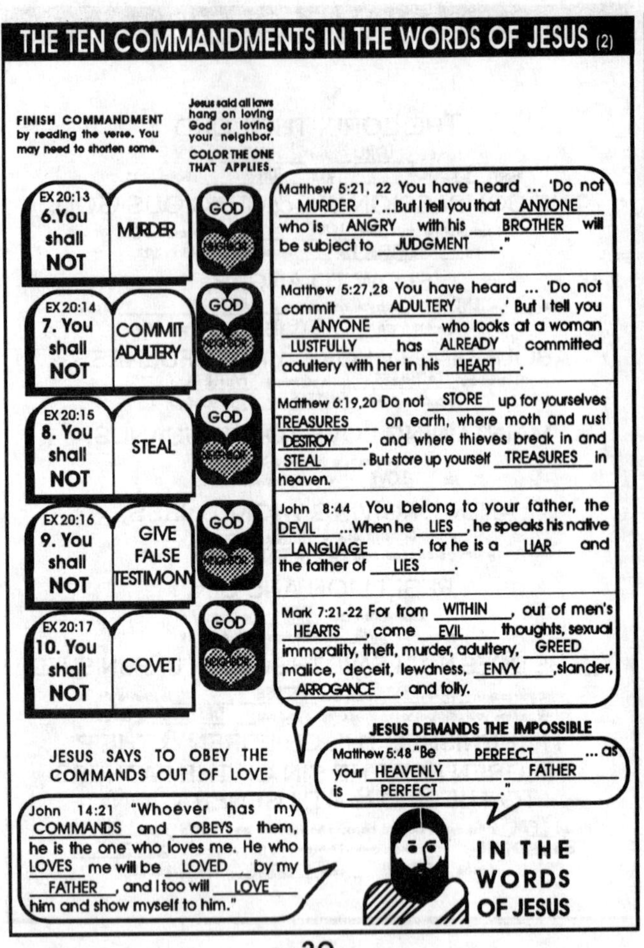

THE TEN COMMANDMENTS IN THE WORDS OF JESUS (2)
FINISH COMMANDMENT by reading the verse. You may need to shorten some.
Jesus said all laws hang on loving God or loving your neighbor.
COLOR THE ONE THAT APPLIES.
EX 20:13 6. You shall NOT MURDER
GOD
Matthew 5:21, 22 You have heard ... 'Do not MURDER.' ...But I tell you that ANYONE who is ANGRY with his BROTHER will be subject to JUDGMENT."
EX 20:14 7. You shall NOT COMMIT ADULTERY
Matthew 5:27,28 You have heard ... 'Do not commit ADULTERY.' But I tell you ANYONE who looks at a woman LUSTFULLY has ALREADY committed adultery with her in his HEART.
EX 20:15 8. You shall NOT STEAL
Matthew 6:19,20 Do not STORE up for yourselves TREASURES on earth, where moth and rust DESTROY, and where thieves break in and STEAL. But store up yourself TREASURES in heaven.
EX 20:16 9. You shall NOT GIVE FALSE TESTIMONY
John 8:44 You belong to your father, the DEVIL ...When he LIES, he speaks his native LANGUAGE, for he is a LIAR and the father of LIES.
EX 20:17 10. You shall NOT COVET
Mark 7:21-22 For from WITHIN, out of men's HEARTS, come EVIL thoughts, sexual immorality, theft, murder, adultery, GREED, malice, deceit, lewdness, ENVY, slander, ARROGANCE, and folly.
JESUS DEMANDS THE IMPOSSIBLE
Matthew 5:48 "Be PERFECT ... as your HEAVENLY FATHER is PERFECT."
JESUS SAYS TO OBEY THE COMMANDS OUT OF LOVE
John 14:21 "Whoever has my COMMANDS and OBEYS them, he is the one who loves me. He who LOVES me will be LOVED by my FATHER, and I too will LOVE him and show myself to him."
IN THE WORDS OF JESUS
39

THE TEN COMMANDMENTS AND OUR HEARTS

In your own words write the Ten Commandments adding Jesus' statements. Follow the format shown below.

1. Not only are we to have no other gods before God, but we are to love Him with everything we have and are.
2. Not only are we not to make idols, but
3.
4.
5.
6. ANSWERS WILL VARY
7.
8.
9.
10.

Fill in the verses below, and discuss what you learn.

Romans 3:23 For all have SINNED and fall short of the GLORY of God.

1 John 1:8 If we CLAIM to be without SIN, we DECEIVE ourselves and the TRUTH is not in us. If we CONFESS our SINS, he is FAITHFUL and JUST and will FORGIVE us our SINS and PURIFY us from all UNRIGHTEOUSNESS.

Jesus makes obeying the Law impossible by including our heart attitude. No one is able to meet this high standard and be perfect as our heavenly Father is perfect. The dilemma then is: What can we do? Is there no hope for us? Fill in what Jesus says about that.

John 3:16, 17 "For GOD so LOVED the world that he gave his ONE and ONLY Son, that WHOEVER believes in him shall not PERISH but have ETERNAL life. For God did NOT send his Son into the WORLD to CONDEMN the world, but to SAVE the world through him."

Have you accepted Jesus into your life to purify you from sin and give you eternal life?

ENGLISH WORDS WITH HEBREW LETTERS (1)

ב=b ט=t ד=d מ=m פ=p ל=L

פט 5 pŏt — t=טט=t 2 tŏt — b=מב=m 7 mŏb

(The line with a tear drop under a consonant is short o.) =ŏ (sŏb)

START HERE

לט lŏt — בלב 4 blŏb — פלט plŏt — פלד 1 plŏd

בט 6 bŏt — דט 3 dŏt — בב bŏb — פד pŏd

THE SABBATH 1

In English, the days of the week are named after different Roman and Norse gods and/or their planets. The Jewish names are based on their relation to the Sabbath. Sunday is called 'the first day from Sabbath,' Monday 'the second day from Sabbath,' and so on.

Genesis 2:3 says, *"God BLESSED the SEVENTH day and made it HOLY, because on it He RESTED from all the WORK of CREATING that He had done."* In Exodus 20:8 God says, *"REMEMBER the SABBATH day by keeping it HOLY."*

The Jews honor the Sabbath is a weekly 'holy day,' the most sacred of all the Lord's festivals. For them, the week revolves around the Sabbath with Wednesday through Friday to prepare for and anticipate the coming Sabbath, and Sunday through Tuesday to remember and reflect on the past Sabbath.

Observe *Deuteronomy 5:12* — PREPARE FOR AND ANTICIPATE THE COMING SABBATH

Sabbath: 6. Friday, 1. Sunday, 5. Thursday, 2. Monday, 4. Wednesday, 3. Tuesday

Remember *Exodus 20:8* — REMEMBER AND REFLECT ON THE PAST SABBATH

To the Jews the Sabbath is like one's wedding day--a time to put aside everyday work. It is a day of rest, have wonderful food, and dedication to God--a weekly taste of heaven. In addition, those who believe in Jesus can anticipate the day when He returns for His bride, the Church (Mt 25).

For a Jewish family preparation for the coming Sabbath starts on Wednesday. Daily scripture readings and prayers guide one's thoughts. Special food is set aside so even the poor can feast like royalty. New clothes are often saved to be worn for the first time on that day. On Friday, final preparations keep everyone busy.

- ☐ 1. The house is cleaned.
- ☐ 2. The Hallah bread is baked.
- ☐ 3. The Sabbath food is cooked.
- ☐ 4. The table is set.
- ☐ 5. The candle sticks are polished and set up.
- ☐ 6. Just before sunset, fresh clean clothes are put on.

When Sabbath begins at sunset, all the work is finished, and the whole family is together. All the worries and cares of the week are put aside so everyone can rest, relax, and worship God together. The following rich feast of thoughts on the meaning of the Sabbath developed over the centuries.

- Remember the Sabbath - do no work. ~ *Honor the day God rested from His work.*
- Refresh body, soul, and mind. ~ *Just be human and enjoy God's love.*
- Rest from fighting to survive. ~ *Remember your dependence on God.*
- Rest from physical, creative acts. ~ *Honor God as the Creator of all.*
- Rest from controlling the world. ~ *Acknowledge God as Lord of the Universe.*

Exodus 20:8-11 states the Sabbath law from the Ten Commandments:

REMEMBER the Sabbath day by keeping it HOLY. SIX days you shall LABOR and do all your WORK, but the SEVENTH day is a Sabbath to the LORD your GOD. On it you shall not do any WORK, neither YOU, nor your SON or DAUGHTER, nor your MANSERVANT or MAIDSERVANT, nor your ANIMALS, nor the ALIEN within your gates. For in SIX days the Lord made the HEAVENS and the EARTH, the SEA, and all that is in them, but He RESTED on the SEVENTH day. Therefore the Lord BLESSED the Sabbath day and made it HOLY.

In this law, God shows His great mercy and protection. He shows His mercy on slaves and wives, who in other cultures had to continue working while only the men or the wealthy relaxed. He even gave animals a day off. He made sure they did not suffer even though their owners rested. Since the day begins and ends at sunset, their owners could feed and water them Friday just before sunset and again Saturday just after sunset. The idea of taking a day off from the daily struggles of life was God's idea.

THE SABBATH 2

In the following list, check the acts that you would not classify as work. (You will be instructed on how to use the lines later.)

- ☐ Making cookies ____ 5
- ☐ Painting a watercolor 8
- ☐ Writing a letter____ 7
- ☐ Tying shoelaces____ 2
- ☐ Using a coffee grinder ____ 1
- ☐ Picking flowers ____ 3
- ☐ Going for a drive ____ 4
- ☐ Ordering food at a restaurant 6

Now let's find out what those who practice the Jewish faith think of them, and why.

WE NEED A DAY OF REST!

Thousands of years ago, thirty-nine acts were forbidden on the Sabbath by the rabbis. As times changed and new situations arose, the forbidden acts were expanded. For example, in early days, farming was the common way of life. Reaping was work and was forbidden on the Sabbath. As people moved away from farming to other forms of livelihood, 'reaping' came to mean cutting any plant from its place of growth. This meant that picking flowers, breaking tree branches, or plucking blades of grass was work and must not be done on the Sabbath. It may be surprising to find out that all the activities listed at the top of the page are considered work. See if you can figure out why:

In the list below are a few of the original 39 acts forbidden on the Sabbath. Chose one for each of the activities listed at the top of the page. Write its number after the related current-day activity. Use each number only once.

1. Grinding 2. Tying a knot 3. Reaping 4. Lighting a fire (turning on an engine or electricity)
5. Baking 6. Selecting 7. Writing 8. Dyeing

The purpose of all the restrictions on the Sabbath is not to make it boring. The day is set aside for physical and spiritual refreshment, of enjoying your relationship with God, family, and friends. Sleep in. Slow your life down. Take long walks. Reconnect with family and friends. Sing. Dance. Feast. Pray. Meditate. Study. Talk. Smile. Laugh. Read a book. Play board games. Engage in community activities such as singing groups, religious folk dances, discussion groups, refreshments, and socializing.

Those who observe the Sabbath would say it is the only one of the Ten Commandments most Christians do not observe. Are they legalistic or right? Should Christians celebrate the Sabbath or dismiss it as something that is no longer important? Some Christians worship God on Saturday (the Sabbath) while other Christians worship God on Sunday. Each can give reasons for what they do. Paul wrote to people who had similar questions way back in the first century. See what he had to say.

Read Romans 14:5-13 and fill in the blanks:

One man considers one DAY *more* SACRED *than another; another man considers* EVERY *day* ALIKE. *Each one should be fully* CONVINCED *in his own* MIND. *He who regards* ONE *day as* SPECIAL *does so to the* LORD *...So then, each of* US *will give an* ACCOUNT *of himself to* GOD. *Therefore let* US *stop passing* JUDGMENT *on one* ANOTHER.

Read Colossians 2:16-17 and fill in the blanks:

Therefore do not let anyone JUDGE *you by what you* EAT *or* DRINK, *or with regard to a* RELIGIOUS FESTIVAL, *a New Moon* CELEBRATION, *or a* SABBATH DAY. *These are* SHADOW *of things that were to* COME; *the* REALITY, *however, is found in* CHRIST.

What are your thoughts on the Sabbath? ANSWERS WILL VARY

The Scripture says that what anyone does, he 'does so to the Lord.' Rethink your week including the day you worship God. Are you doing it as to the Lord? Write some ideas on how to get back to celebrating a day as to the Lord.

ANSWERS WILL VARY

51

HEBREW VOWEL BOY

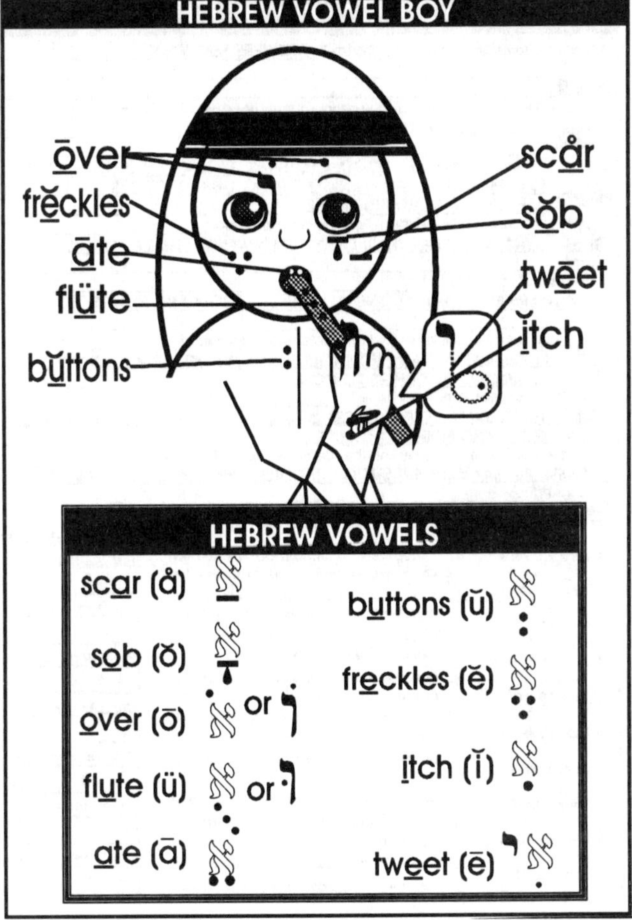

52

ENGLISH WORDS WITH HEBREW LETTERS (2)

53

REASONS FOR THE LAW 1

1. One reason for the Law was to provide a **MEDICAL MANUAL**. There were laws about cleanliness, disposing of waste, and the washing or getting rid of contaminated items. Diseases and other conditions were subject to quarantine, repeated washing, waiting and rechecking. This kept down the spread of disease and contributed to better health.

2. Another reason for the Law was to create a new and distinct **CULTURE**. The family of Jacob with its 70 members had grown to around 2 million by the time they left Egypt over 400 years later. They came out of Egypt as a broken, victimized people. To become God's chosen children, a new and distinct people, they had to have a separate culture. Culture involves all aspects of a community's life, and the laws had to cover it all. The laws told the Israelites what food, clothing, farming methods, family life, marriage, government, and religious practices to have in order to form their unique culture. God repeatedly warned them against becoming like the other peoples.

Lev 18:1-4. *"You must not do as they do in* EGYPT *where you used to* LIVE, *and you must not do as they do in the land of* CANAAN, *where I am bringing you. Do not follow their* PRACTICES. *You must obey my* LAWS *and be careful to follow my* DECREES. *I am the* LORD *your* GOD."

3. A third reason for the Law was to give the Israelites a clearly defined and unpolluted way of **WORSHIP**. Many of the Israelites had adopted the religions of Egypt and other peoples. All these religions featured gods who were immoral, cruel, and fickle. And those who worshipped these gods did immoral and cruel things such as sacrificing their own children and they visiting temple prostitutes; and they constantly tried to please fickle gods. The religion God gave the Israelites sharply contrasted with the common ways. It was a holy and righteous way to worship, a way that was in line with His character.

4. God's Law taught **DISCERNMENT**. It gave clear instructions on how to distinguish the acceptable from the unacceptable. A recurring command is: "Do not make yourselves unclean by these things...You must distinguish between the unclean and the clean." Lev 10:10-11, 11:44-47, 15:31, 18:1-5, 18:29-19:2, 20:25-26. Believers need to practice discernment, to learn what pleases God.

Heb 5:14. *"But solid food is for the* MATURE, *who by* CONSTANT USE *have trained themselves to* DISTINGUISH *good from evil."*

5. Other reason for the Law was to **MIRROR SPIRITUAL TRUTHS**. A husband's relationship with his wife was to be a picture of God's relationship with His people. A father's treatment of his children was to reflect God as our Heavenly Father. The laws on relationships were to prevent abuse that would mar the picture of a holy and loving God. God gave laws about animal sacrifices for sin to show the seriousness of sin and to explain the way to approach God. These sacrifices pointed to Jesus Christ who became our sin sacrifice. The Tabernacle and festivals were laid out in great detail as a 'shadow' of things to come thousands of years later, revealing God's full plan for salvation.

6. God's Law included a **LEGAL CODE**. This taught how people should treat each other, and guided judges in court when individuals could not work out their differences. Some people view these laws as harsh; in reality they limited the punishment that the powerful might inflict on the ordinary person.

7. Much of the law was **HOW TO TREAT OTHERS**. The law tells how to give a helping hand to the poor, the weak, the orphan, the widow, the slave and the foreigner. It is done with dignity and respect.

GOD SAID

The Israelites realized that the **REASON** for the Law did not matter; it was enough that God said it. They could see the purpose for some laws, but not for others. They did not know about germs, nor did they know that many of the things they did were a 'shadow' of what was to come. Look up Proverbs 3:5. How can you bring yourself to obey the Lord if you do not understand why He gives a certain command?

ANSWERS WILL VARY

55

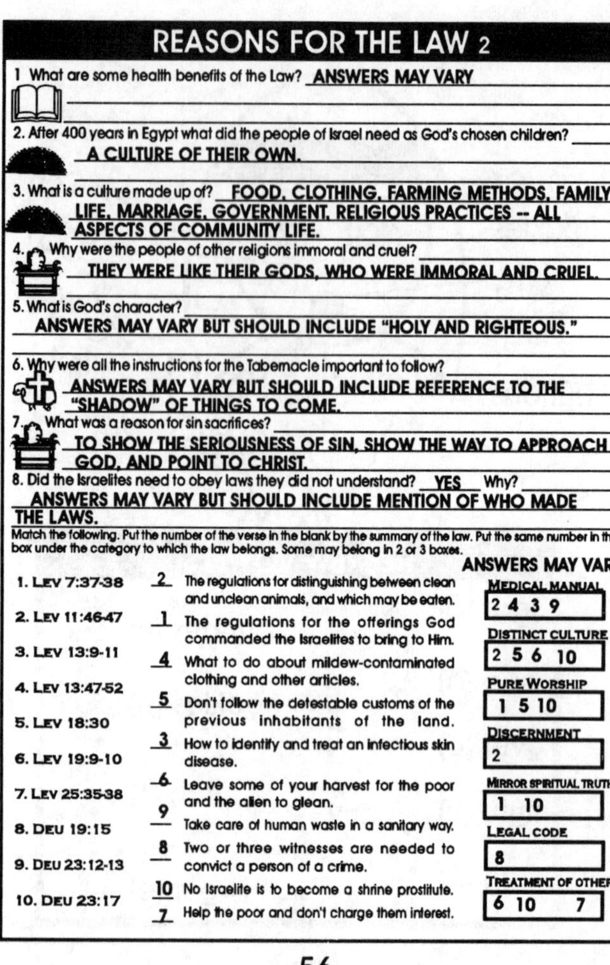

REASONS FOR THE LAW 2

1 What are some health benefits of the Law? ANSWERS MAY VARY

2. After 400 years in Egypt what did the people of Israel need as God's chosen children? A CULTURE OF THEIR OWN.

3. What is a culture made up of? FOOD, CLOTHING, FARMING METHODS, FAMILY LIFE, MARRIAGE, GOVERNMENT, RELIGIOUS PRACTICES -- ALL ASPECTS OF COMMUNITY LIFE.

4. Why were the people of other religions immoral and cruel? THEY WERE LIKE THEIR GODS, WHO WERE IMMORAL AND CRUEL.

5. What is God's character? ANSWERS MAY VARY BUT SHOULD INCLUDE "HOLY AND RIGHTEOUS."

6. Why were all the instructions for the Tabernacle important to follow? ANSWERS MAY VARY BUT SHOULD INCLUDE REFERENCE TO THE "SHADOW" OF THINGS TO COME.

7. What was a reason for sin sacrifices? TO SHOW THE SERIOUSNESS OF SIN, SHOW THE WAY TO APPROACH GOD, AND POINT TO CHRIST.

8. Did the Israelites need to obey laws they did not understand? YES Why? ANSWERS MAY VARY BUT SHOULD INCLUDE MENTION OF WHO MADE THE LAWS.

Match the following. Put the number of the verse in the blank by the summary of the law. Put the same number in the box under the category to which the law belongs. Some may belong in 2 or 3 boxes.

ANSWERS MAY VARY

Reference	Answer	Summary
1. Lev 7:37-38	2	The regulations for distinguishing between clean and unclean animals, and which may be eaten.
2. Lev 11:46-47	1	The regulations for the offerings God commanded the Israelites to bring to Him.
3. Lev 13:9-11	4	What to do about mildew-contaminated clothing and other articles.
4. Lev 13:47-52	5	Don't follow the detestable customs of the previous inhabitants of the land.
5. Lev 18:30	3	How to identify and treat an infectious skin disease.
6. Lev 19:9-10	6	Leave some of your harvest for the poor and the alien to glean.
7. Lev 25:35-38	9	Take care of human waste in a sanitary way.
8. Deu 19:15	8	Two or three witnesses are needed to convict a person of a crime.
9. Deu 23:12-13	10	No Israelite is to become a shrine prostitute.
10. Deu 23:17	7	Help the poor and don't charge them interest.

Medical Manual	2 4 3 9
Distinct Culture	2 5 6 10
Pure Worship	1 5 10
Discernment	2
Mirror Spiritual Truths	1 10
Legal Code	8
Treatment of Others	6 10 7

56

57

TEST ON THE LEGAL CODE 1

1. Altars are to be made of
   a. stones cut to fit together perfectly.
   b. earth with steps up the front.
   c. earth or naturally shaped stones.
2. A Hebrew servant
   a. is to be freed in the seventh year.
   b. is your property to sell to anyone.
   c. is not to marry until freed.
3. A servant will remain a servant for life if
   a. he is not a good worker.
   b. he wants to stay with his wife and master.
   c. if you gave him a wife.
4. If a female servant is not provided with food, clothing or martial rights, she is
   a. to be sold to foreigners.
   b. allowed to go free.
   c. to pay for her freedom.
5. The death penalty is for all of the following offences except
   a. one who attacks his father or mother.
   b. one who accidently kills a man and flees to a designated place.
   c. one who schemes and commits murder.
   d. a kidnapper.
   e. one who curses his parents.
6. If a person seriously injures another, which punishment is not listed? (Ex 20:23-25)
   a. life for a life — b. eye for an eye
   c. tooth for tooth — d. hand for a hand
   e. toe for toe — f. burn for a burn
   g. wound for wound — h. bruise for a bruise
7. A servant may not go free if the master
   a. destroys an eye.
   b. beats him with a rod.
   c. knocks a tooth out.
8. If a bull gores a person to death,
   a. it is stoned to death and eaten.
   b. the owner is held responsible.
   c. it is stoned and not eaten.
9. If a bull, known to gore, kills a free person
   a. the owner is put to death or may pay whatever amount is demanded.
   b. the owner is warned.
   c. the owner must pay 30 shekels.
10. If a man digs a pit and an animal falls in
    a. he gives the dead animal to its owner and pays for the loss.
    b. he keeps the dead animal but pays for the loss.
11. If a man's bull injures a bull of another
    a. they divide the money from the dead bull.
    b. if the animal is known to gore, he gives him a live bull and keeps the dead one.
12. If a man steals an animal
    a. his hand must be cut off.
    b. he must pay back five head of cattle for an ox or four sheep for a sheep.
    c. he is to be sold as a slave.
13. If a thief is killed while breaking in, the defender
    a. is always guilty of bloodshed.
    b. is never guilty of blood shed.
    c. is guilty if he kills the thief after the sunrise.
14. A thief must
    a. make restitution and be sold as a slave.
    b. be sold only if he can not make restitution.
    c. have his hand cut off
15. If a stolen animal is found alive with a thief
    a. he must pay back five fold.
    b. he must go to jail.
    c. he must have his hand cut off.
    d. he must pay back double.
16. If an animal grazes in another person's field or vineyard, his owner
    a. must give of his best fields or vineyards.
    b. must pay back five fold.
    c. must give him his animals.
17. If a fire is started and destroys property,
    a. the one who started it will be burnt to death.
    b. everyone will take care of his own property.
    c. the one who started it must make restitution.
18. If someone steals silver or goods that one is safekeeping for a neighbor
    a. if the thief is caught he must pay back both the owner and safekeeper.
    b. the safekeeper must go to court and prove he didn't steal it.
    c. the owner must accept the loss.
19. If a donkey, ox or sheep is in one's care and it comes to harm, which is not true?
    a. Restitution is always required.
    b. The safekeeper must take an oath saying he did not lay hands on it.
    c. Evidence must be shown if it was killed by other animal.
20. If an animal is hired and it dies,
    a. restitution must be made.
    b. the money paid for hire covers the loss.
    c. it must be paid for four times over.

58

TEST ON THE LEGAL CODE 2

1. If a man seduces and sleeps with a virgin
   a. he must pay the bride-price and she will be his wife.
   b. he must pay for damaging her reputation.
   c. he must marry her if she is pregnant.
2. If a man sleeps with a virgin, which is not true?
   a. Her father may refuse to give her to him.
   b. He has to pay bride-price
   c. He pays the bride-price and marries her.
   d. Her father must give his daughter to him.
3. True or False (write T or F)
   F Allow a sorceress to live.
   T Kill those who have sex with an animal.
   F Support those who sacrifice to other gods.
   F Give no aid to aliens.
4. If you take advantage of a widow or orphan,
   a. God will hear their cry and punish you.
   b. it doesn't matter; they are on their own.
   c. it is fine; they can't take you to court.
5. If you lend money to the needy
   a. charge a high interest rate.
   b. charge a low interest rate.
   c. charge no interest.
6. If a neighbor gives his coat as a pledge,
   a. keep it until he pays you back.
   b. return it to him by sunset.
   c. hope that the cold nights will make him pay you back quickly.
7. True or False (write T or F)
   T Do not blaspheme God.
   T Curse your evil rulers.
   F Keep back offerings if you need them.
   T Give your firstborn sheep and cattle.
   T Sacrifice your firstborn son.
   F Spread false reports.
   F Follow the crowd no matter what they are doing.
   T Help your enemy's ox or donkey.
   F Deny justice to the poor.
   T Do not accept bribes.
   F Oppress aliens; they should go home.
8. Sow your fields
   a. every year.
   b. for 6 years and let the land rest the 7th.
   c. but let no one get food from it in the 7th year.
9. On the seventh day
   a. work hard
   b. you may rest as your slave cooks.
   c. you, your animalsand slaves must not work.

MY ANGER WILL BE AROUSED

Read Exodus 22:22-27

In these verses God says that war comes because of wrongs against the poor and helpless. In the world today, what cries can you imagine coming to God from the following?

The poor:
The hungry: ANSWERS WILL VARY
The sexually abused:
The emotionally abused:
Widows:
Orphans:
Unborn babies:
Abandoned wives:
Children of divorce:
The elderly:
Families of drug users or alchoholics:

Who will hear their cry? GOD How will they be answered? GOD WILL KILL THE OPPRESSORS WITH THE SWORD. THEIR WIVES AND CHILDREN WILL BECOME WIDOWS AND ORPHANS.

If we want a country safe from terror, what must be done? ANSWERS MAY VARY: JUSTICE AND MERCY, COMPASSION ON THE ORPHANS, ETC. TREAT OTHERS AS YOU WISH TO BE TREATED, ETC.

59

ENGLISH WORDS WITH HEBREW LETTERS (4)

כּ=k  ו=v or w 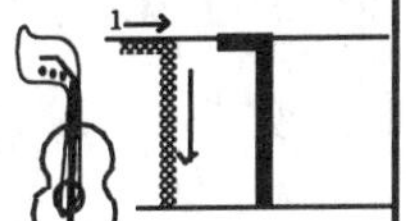

•= ĭ (itch) ⁘ = ĕ (freckle) ᵀ = ŏ (sob) ‾ = å (scar)

סְפֵּד sped	סוַמפּס 2 swåmps	t= כִּט =k =i kit START HERE	• = ĭ
כִּד kid	כִּס kis	וֶט (2 words) wĕt, vĕt	הִס his
סכָּלד skåld	סוֶל swĕl	סטִל 3 stil	בלֶס blĕs
בלִס blis	גלִב 4 glib	כלֹד 6 klŏd	כלֹג klŏg
טוִנכל 9 twinkl	לֹנגֶסט 8 lŏngĕst	סמָל smål	
ספלֶנדִד splĕndid	וִטנֶס witnĕs	ונָט 7 wånt	
סוֶפּט 1 swĕpt	וֶסט (2 words) west, vĕst	וֶנט (2 words) 5 wĕnt, vĕnt	וֶפּט wĕpt

62

TZITZIT TO REMEMBER COMMANDS

1. The two colors used in the tzitzit. BLUE and WHITE	1. The colors of the sky and clouds. BLUE and WHITE
2. Number of double knots. 5	5 (Ge, Ex, Lev, Nu, Dt = books of Moses =Torah) 2. How many books are in the Torah?
3. Number of sets of coils. 4	4 3. Number of letters in יהוה the Holy Name of God.
4. Number of coils in 1st set of coils. 7 Number of coils 2nd set of coils. 8 Number of coils in 3rd set of coils. 11 Total number of coils in 1st, 2nd & 3rd sets of coils. 26	Add up the number values for the letters in boxes 4 & 5. 4. יהוה the Holy Name of God. 26 =Total 5 = ה 6 = ו 5 = ה 10 = י
5. The numbers of coils in the 4th set of coils. 13 Add the number values for the letters in this word:	5. אֶחָד (ekhod) 'One.' 13 =Total 4 = ד 8 = ח 1 = א
6. ציצית (tzitzit) means tassel Total ת=400 י=10 צ=90 י= 10 צ= 90= 600 7. Add the total value of the Hebrew letters in 'tzitzit' and the number of coils in the last set of coils. 613	613 7. The number of laws in the books of Moses.

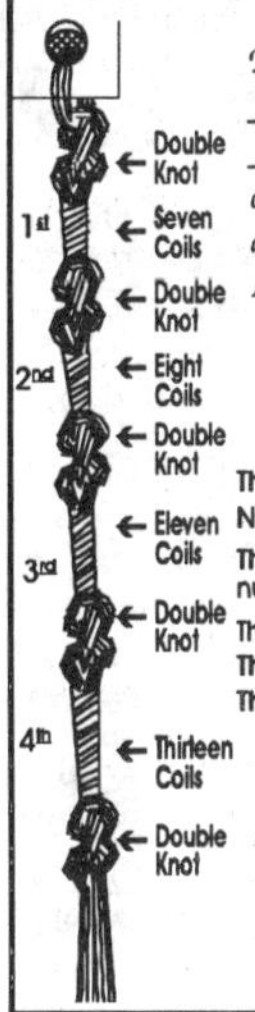

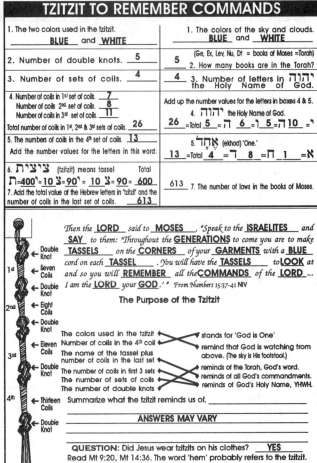

Then the LORD *said to* MOSES *, "Speak to the* ISRAELITES *and* SAY *to them: 'Throughout the* GENERATIONS *to come you are to make* TASSELS *on the* CORNERS *of your* GARMENTS *with a* BLUE *cord on each* TASSEL *. You will have the* TASSELS *to* LOOK *at and so you will* REMEMBER *all the* COMMANDS *of the* LORD *... I am the* LORD *your* GOD *.'"* From Numbers 15:37-41 NIV

The Purpose of the Tzitzit

The colors used in the tzitzit	stands for 'God is One'
Number of coils in the 4th coil	remind that God is watching from above. (The sky is His footstool.)
The name of the tassel plus number of coils in the last set	reminds of the Torah, God's word.
The number of coils in first 3 sets	reminds of all God's commandments.
The number of sets of coils	reminds of God's Holy Name, YHWH.
The number of double knots	

Summarize what the tzitzit reminds us of. ________________

ANSWERS MAY VARY

QUESTION: Did Jesus wear tzitzits on his clothes? YES
Read Mt 9:20, Mt 14:36. The word 'hem' probably refers to the tzitzit.

65

ENGLISH WORDS WITH HEBREW LETTERS (5)

ז=z 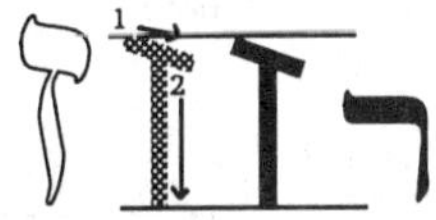 ר=r 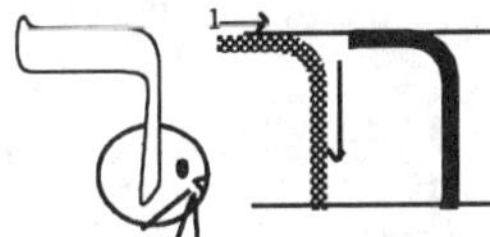

⁚ = ŭ (button) • = ĭ (itch) ⁘ = ĕ (freckle) ᵀ = ŏ (sob) ‾ =å (scar)

גרֻב grŭb	ספֹּטלֶס spŏtlĕs	t= רֻט =r =u rŭt START HERE	⁚ = ŭ
טרֻמפֶּט trŭmpĕt	טרִנכֶּט 4 trinkĕt	סוָנז 8 swånz	ספָּרכל 5 spårkl
הֻנדרֶד 6 hŭndrĕd	סֻנסֶט 3 sŭnsĕt	הִז 1 hiz	דרֻג drŭg
ברֻנט brŭnt	סטרֻנג strŭng	בֻּז bŭz	טרֹד trŏd
סלֻג 7 slŭg	סטרֻט strŭt	סטָרִנג støring	בלֻנט blŭnt
גרִל gril	פּרֹד prŏd	פּלֻג plŭg	דֻל dŭl
סנֻב snŭb	דֻז 2 dŭz	סמָרט smårt	כּרִב krib

66

The Tabernacle in the Wilderness 1

Pillar of Cloud & Fire
By day: ■ cloud ☐ fire
By night: ☐ cloud ■ fire
TO SHOW GOD'S PRESENCE & LEAD ISRAEL ON THEIR TRAVELS.

Ark of Testimony & Atonement Cover
M: ☐ bronze ■ wood ■ gold ☐ silver
L: 2 1/2 C W: 1 1/2 C H: 1 1/2 C

Golden Lampstand
M: ☐ bronze ☐ wood ■ gold ☐ silver
WEIGHT: 1 TALENT

Most Holy Place
Who: ☐ any priest
■ Aaron ☐ any Israelite
When?
☐ morning ☐ every Sabbath
☐ evening ■ once a year
TO MAKE ATONEMENT FOR ALL THE SINS OF ISRAEL.

Altar of Incense
M: ■ wood ■ gold ☐ silver
L: 1c W: 1c H: 2c
FOR THE BURNING OF INCENSE REGULARLY BEFORE THE LORD.

Inner Curtain
M: ■ linen
C: ■ blue ■ purple
■ white ☐ red ■ scarlet
■ cherubim ■ gold hooks
TO SEPARATE THE HOLY PLACE FROM THE MOST HOLY PLACE.

Table of the Bread of the Presence
M: ☐ bronze ■ gold ■ wood ☐ silver
L: 2c W: 1c H: 1 1/2c
TO HOLD THE BREAD OF THE PRESENCE.

Holy Place
Lamps — Table — Altar
• 12 loaves
• any time
• morning & twilight
• kept burning
• every Sabbath
• once a year
• burn incense

Entrance Curtain
M: ■ linen ☐ skins ☐ goat hair
C: ■ white ■ blue ■ purple
■ scarlet ☐ red ■ gold hooks

Altar of Sacrifices
M: ■ bronze ☐ gold
☐ silver ■ wood
L: 5c W: 5c H: 3c
TO BURN OFFERINGS TO THE LORD

Bronze Basin
M: ■ bronze ☐ gold ☐ silver
FOR THE PRIESTS TO WASH BEFORE APPROACHING THE ALTAR OR TABERNACLE

Curtains to Courtyard
M: ■ linen ☐ skins
☐ goat hair
C: ■ white ■ blue
■ purple ■ scarlet

The Courtyard
Curtains: ☐ skins ☐ goat hair ■ linen
Posts: ■ bronze ☐ gold ■ silver
L: 100c W: 50c H: 5c
FOR PEOPLE TO ENTER AND BRING THEIR OFFERINGS TO GOD.

Tabernacle in the Wilderness 2

First Cover
M: ■ linen ☐ ram skins ☐ goat hair ☐ sea cow hides
C: ■ blue ■ purple ■ scarlet ■ white ☐ red
☐ brown ■ with cherubim ■ gold clasps

Second Cover
M: ☐ linen ☐ ram skins ■ goat hair ☐ sea cow hides
C: ☐ blue ☐ purple ☐ scarlet ■ white ☐ red
☐ brown ☐ with cherubim ■ bronze clasps

Third Cover
M: ☐ linen ■ ram skins ☐ goat hair ☐ sea cow hides
C: ☐ blue ☐ purple ☐ scarlet ☐ white ■ red
☐ brown ☐ with cherubim ☐ gold clasps

Fourth Cover
M: ☐ linen ☐ ram skins ☐ goat hair ■ sea cow hides
C: ☐ blue ☐ purple ☐ scarlet ☐ white ☐ red
■ brown ☐ with cherubim ☐ gold clasps

KEY:
M: MADE OF:
C: COLOR:
C CUBITS
L: LENGTH
W: WIDTH:
H: HEIGHT

67

A Shadow of Things to Come 1

TABERNACLE:

A shadow of things to come: Heb. 8:5 *They serve at a* SANCTUARY *that is a* COPY *and* SHADOW *of what is in* HEAVEN. *This is why Moses was* WARNED *when he was about to* BUILD *the* TABERNACLE*: "See to it that you* MAKE *everything* ACCORDING *to the* PATTERN *shown you on the* MOUNTAIN*."*

Heb. 9:24 *For* CHRSIT *did not enter a* MAN - MADE *sanctuary that was* ONLY *a copy of the* TRUE *one; He* ENTERED HEAVEN *itself, now to* APPEAR *for us in God's* PRESENCE.

Explain how it was 'a shadow of things to come.' THE TABERNACLE WAS A COPY OF HEAVEN AND BEING IN GOD'S PRESENCE.

THE COVERS OF THE TABERNACLE:

A. THE OUTER COVER OF HIDES:

A shadow of things to come: Is. 53:2b *He had no* BEAUTY *or* MAJESTY *to attract us to* HIM, NOTHING *in His* APPEARANCE *that we should* DESIRE *Him.*

John 1:14 *The* WORD *(Jesus) became* FLESH *and made his* DWELLING *among us.*

Explain how it was 'a shadow of things to come.' JESUS' 'TENT' WAS A HUMAN BODY. HE LOOKED THE SAME AS EVERYONE ELSE, YET WAS GOD IN HUMAN FORM.

B. THE RED RAM SKIN COVER:

A shadow of things to come: Eph. 1:7 *In Him (Jesus) we have* REDEMPTION *through His* BLOOD, *the* FORGIVENESS *of* SINS, *in accordance with the* RICHES *of God's* GRACE.

Explain how it was 'a shadow of things to come.' JESUS SHED HIS BLOOD FOR OUR GOOD.

C. THE WHITE GOAT HAIR COVER:

A shadow of things to come: Heb. 4:15b *We have* ONE *(Jesus) who has been* TEMPTED *in* EVERY *way, just as we* ARE *— yet was* WITHOUT SIN.

Is. 1:18 *Though your* SINS *are like* SCARLET, *they shall be as* WHITE *as* WOOL; *though they are* RED *as* CRIMSON, *they shall be like* WOOL.

Explain how it was 'a shadow of things to come.' JESUS WAS PURE AND THROUGH HIM WE ARE MADE PURE.

D. THE EMBROIDERED LINEN COVER:

A shadow of things to come:

1. WHITE LINEN shows GLORY Matt. 17:2 *There He (Jesus) was* TRANSFIGURED *before them. His face* SHONE *like the* SUN, *and his* CLOTHES *became as* WHITE *as the light.*
2. BLUE depicts HEAVEN. Ex. 24:10 *Moses and Aaron... saw the* GOD *of Israel. Under His* FEET *was something like a* PAVEMENT *made of* SAPPHIRE, *clear as the* SKY *itself.*
3. PURPLE AND SCARLET show wealth and ROYALTY. Mark 15:17 *They put a* PURPLE *robe on Him (Jesus), then twisted together a* CROWN *of thorns and* SET *it on Him.*

Explain how it was 'a shadow of things to come.' JESUS IS GLORIOUS, FROM HEAVEN, A WEALTHY KING.

68

A Shadow of Things to Come 2

ALTAR OF SACRIFICES

A shadow of things to come: Heb. 10:1 *The law is only a* SHADOW *of the* GOOD *things that are* COMING *— not the realities themselves. For this reason it can* NEVER, *by the same* SACRIFICES *repeated* ENDLESSLY *year after year, make* PERFECT *those who draw near to worship.*

Heb. 9:25, 28 *Nor did He (Jesus) enter* HEAVEN *to offer Himself* AGAIN *and* AGAIN, *the way the high priest enters the Most Holy Place every year with* BLOOD *that is not his* OWN. *...So Christ was* SACRIFICED *once to take away the* SINS *of* MANY *people; and he will* APPEAR *a second time,* NOT *to bear sin, but to bring* SALVATION *to those who are* WAITING *for him.*

Explain how it was 'a shadow of things to come.' THE SACRIFICES COULD NOT PERFECT THE WORSHIPPER, BUT JESUS WAS SACRIFICED ONCE TO REMOVE ALL OUR SINS.

BRONZE BASIN

A shadow of things to come: Heb. 10:21, 22 *Since we have a great* PRIEST *(Jesus) over the house of God, let us draw* NEAR *to God with a* SINCERE *heart in full* ASSURANCE *of faith, having our hearts sprinkled to* CLEANSE *us from a guilty* CONSCIENCE *and having our bodies* WASHED *with* PURE WATER.

Eph. 5:25-27 *...Christ* LOVED *the church and gave* HIMSELF *up for her to make her* HOLY, *cleansing her by the* WASHING *with water through the* WORD, *and to present her to Himself as a* RADIANT *church, without* STAIN *or wrinkle or any other* BLEMISH, *but holy and* BLAMELSS.

Explain how it was 'a shadow of things to come.' CHRIST LOVED THE CHURCH AND MADE HER HOLY BY WASHING WITH WATER THROUGH THE WORD TO PRESENT HER TO HIMSELF HOLY AND BLAMELESS

TABLE OF THE BREAD OF THE PRESENCE

A shadow of things to come: Acts 2:46 *Every day they* CONTINUED *to meet* TOGETHER *in the* TEMPLE *courts. They* BROKE BREAD *in their homes and ate* TOGETHER *with glad and* SINCERE *hearts.*

Rev. 3:20 *(Jesus said,) "Here I am! I* STAND *at the* DOOR *and knock. If anyone* HEARS *my voice and* OPENS *the door, I will* COME *in and* EAT *with him, and* HE *with* ME*."*

Explain how it was 'a shadow of things to come.' WE CAN HAVE FELLOWSHIP WITH EACH OTHER. JESUS WANTS TO COME INTO OUR HEARTS AND HAVE FELLOWSHIP WITH US.

GOLDEN LAMPSTAND

A shadow of things to come: John 8:12 *When Jesus* SPOKE *again to the people, he said, "I am the* LIGHT *of the* WORLD. *Whoever follows me will never* WALK *in* DARKNESS, *but will have the* LIGHT *of* LIFE*."*

Eph. 5:9 *(for the fruit of the* LIGHT *consists in all* GOODNESS, RIGHTEOUSNESS *and* TRUTH*)*

Matt. 5:16 *In the same way, let* YOUR *light* SHINE *before men, that they may see your* GOOD *deeds and* PRAISE *your* FATHER *in heaven.*

Explain how it was 'a shadow of things to come.' JESUS IS THE LIGHT OF THE WORLD. WHEN WE WALK IN HIS LIGHT OUR DEEDS BRING PRAISE TO HIM - WE REFLECT GOD'S GOODNESS. 'LIGHT' INCLUDES GOODNESS, RIGHTEOUSNESS, AND TRUTH.

71

A Shadow of Things to Come 3

ALTAR OF INCENSE:

Psa. 141:2 *May my* PRAYERS *be set before you like* INCENSE; *may the* LIFTING *up of my* HANDS *be like the evening* SACRIFICE.

A shadow of things to come: Heb. 7:24, 25 *Because Jesus lives* FOREVER, *He has a* PERMANENT *priesthood. Therefore he is* ABLE *to save* COMPLETE *those who* COME *to God through* HIM, *because He always* LIVES *to* INTERCEDE *for them.*

Explain how it was 'a shadow of things to come.' THE INCENSE WAS LIKE JESUS WHO IS ALWAYS INTERCEDING FOR US TO GOD, AND WE CAN PRAY TO HIM AT ALL TIMES.

INNER CURTAIN:

A shadow of things to come: Matt. 27:50-51 *And when Jesus had* CRIED *out again in a loud* VOICE, *He gave up His* SPIRIT. *At that moment the* CURTAIN *of the* TEMPLE *was* TORN *in two from* TOP *to bottom.*

Explain how it was 'a shadow of things to come.' THE BARRIER BETWEEN GOD AND MAN WAS TORN IN TWO WHEN JESUS DIED ON THE CROSS.

HOLY OF HOLIES:

Heb. 9:7 *But only the high priest* ENTERED *the inner room, and that only* ONCE *a year, and* NEVER *without* BLOOD, *which he offered for* HIMSELF *and for the* SINS *the people had committed in* IGNORANCE.

A shadow of things to come: Heb. 9:12 *He (Jesus) did not* ENTER *by means of the* BLOOD *of* GOATS *and* CALVES; *but He* ENTERED *the Most Holy* PLACE *once for* ALL *by His* OWN *blood, having obtained* ETERNAL REDEMPTION.

Heb. 10:19, 20 *Therefore,* BROTHER, *since we have* CONFIDENCE *to enter the Most* HOLY *Place by the* BLOOD *of Jesus, by a* NEW *and* LIVING *way opened for us* THROUGH *the* CURTAIN, *that is, His* BODY.

Explain how it was 'a shadow of things to come.' WE CAN GO RIGHT INTO THE MOST HOLY PLACE, GOD'S PRESENCE, BECAUSE JESUS OPENED THE CURTAIN, THAT IS HIS BODY.

PILLAR OF CLOUD AND FIRE

Ex. 40:35 *Moses could not* ENTER *the Tent of* MEETING *because the* CLOUD *had settled* UPON *it, and the* GLORY *of the* LORD FILLED *the tabernacle.*

A shadow of things to come: Ezek. 10:4 *Then the* GLORY *of the* LORD *rose from* ABOVE *the* CHERUBIM *and moved to the threshold of the* TEMPLE. *The* CLOUD *filled the temple, and the* COURT *was full of the* RADIANCE *of the* GLORY *of the* LORD.

Matt. 24:30 *"At that time the* SIGN *of the Son of Man (Jesus) will* APPEAR *in the* SKY, *and all the* NATIONS *of the earth will* MOURN. *They will see the Son of Man* COMING *on the* CLOUDS *of the sky, with* POWER *and great* GLORY.

Explain how it was 'a shadow of things to come.' THE PILLAR SHOWED GOD'S PRESENCE AND JESUS (GOD) WILL COME IN A CLOUD IN POWER AND GREAT GLORY.

72

A Shadow of Things to Come 4

ARK OF TESTIMONY AND ATONEMENT COVER:

A shadow of things to come: Hebrews 4:14, 16 *Therefore, since we have a great high* PRIEST *who has gone through the* HEAVENS, JESUS *the Son of God, let us hold firmly to the* FAITH *we profess. Let us then approach the* THRONE *of* GRACE *with* CONFIDENCE, *so that we may receive* MERCY *and find* GRACE *to help us in our time of* NEED.

Explain how it was 'a shadow of things to come.' THE PRIEST WENT ONCE A YEAR TO THE ARK TO RECEIVE MERCY. JESUS HAS GONE INTO HEAVEN, AND NOW WE CAN COME TO GOD FOR MERCY.

IN THE ARK WERE THREE ITEMS: Hebrews 9:4 THE JAR OF MANNA, AARON'S STAFF AND THE STONE TABLETS OF THE COVENANT.

STONE TABLETS WITH TEN COMMANDMENTS:

A shadow of things to come: Heb. 10:10, 16 *...We have been made* HOLY *through the* SACRIFICE *of the body of* JESUS *Christ once for all... "This is the* COVENANT *I will make with them after that time, says the Lord. I will put my* LAWS *in their* HEARTS, *and I will* WRITE *them on their* MINDS*."*

1. You shall have NO OTHER GODS	6. You shall NOT MURDER
2. You shall NOT MAKE IDOLS	7. You shall NOT COMMIT ADULTERY
3. You shall NOT MISUSE THE LORD'S NAME	8. You shall NOT STEAL
4. Remember THE SABBATH TO KEEP IT HOLY	9. You shall NOT GIVE FALSE TESTIMONY
5. Honor YOUR FATHER AND MOTHER	10. You shall NOT COVET

Explain how it was 'a shadow of things to come.' INSTEAD OF REPEATED SACRIFICES, WE HAVE ONE SACRIFICE, JESUS, WHO MAKES US HOLY. INSTEAD OF LAWS ON STONE, WE HAVE THE DESIRE IN OUR HEARTS TO LOVE AND OBEY THE LORD.

MANNA:

A shadow of things to come: John 6:49-51 *(Jesus said,) "Your forefathers ate the* MANNA *in the desert, yet they* DIED. *But here is the* BREAD *that comes down from heaven, which a* MAN *may eat and not* DIE. *I am the* LIVING *bread that comes down from* HEAVEN. *If a man eats of this bread, he will* LIVE FOREVER*."*

Explain how it was 'a shadow of things to come.' PHYSICAL MANNA SUSTAINED PHYSICAL LIFE TEMPORARILY. JESUS IS THE SPIRITUAL BREAD THAT FEEDS OUR SOULS AND GIVES US ETERNAL LIFE.

AARON'S ROD:

A shadow of things to come: John 2:11 *This, the first of his* MIRACULOUS *signs, Jesus performed ... He thus* REVEALED *His glory, and his* DISCIPLES *put their* FAITH *in him.*

Explain how it was 'a shadow of things to come.' JUST AS AARON'S ROD SHOWED GOD'S POWER BY DOING MIRACLES, SO JESUS DID MIRACLES AND SHOWED HE HAD THE POWER AND GLORY OF GOD.

73

ENGLISH WORDS WITH HEBREW LETTERS (6)
VOWEL HELPER
=' No sound
=ts
= ē (tweet) = ŭ (button) = ĭ (itch) = ĕ (freckle) = ŏ (sob) = å (scar)
=ē START HERE
'ĕnd
1 mēt
12 'årtsē
'ēt (eat)
'ŭpsĕt
'ēvĕnĭng
2 'ŭngŏdlē
5 'åtŭmz
'ŏd
twēt
11 grēd
4 ĭtse-bĭtsē
3 pētsŭ
9 krēpē
6 kŭrtsē
14 'ŭphĭl
13 'ŭndŭr
8 tsår
10 pårtē
7 krŏsbrēd

74

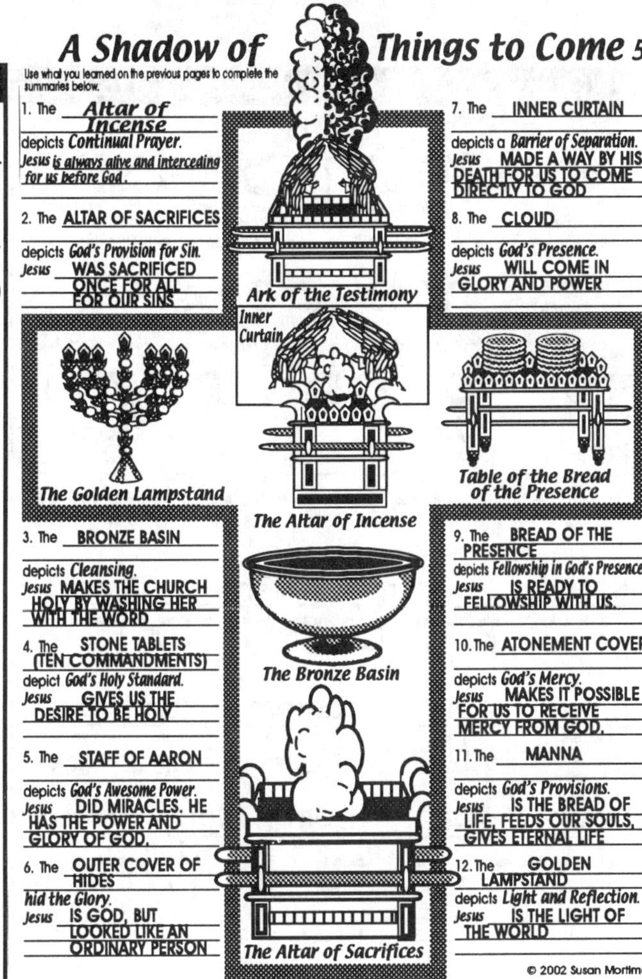

A Shadow of Things to Come 5
Use what you learned on the previous pages to complete the summaries below.
1. The Altar of Incense
depicts Continual Prayer.
Jesus is always alive and interceding for us before God.
2. The ALTAR OF SACRIFICES
depicts God's Provision for Sin.
Jesus WAS SACRIFICED ONCE FOR ALL FOR OUR SINS
3. The BRONZE BASIN
depicts Cleansing.
Jesus MAKES THE CHURCH HOLY BY WASHING HER WITH THE WORD
4. The STONE TABLETS (TEN COMMANDMENTS)
depict God's Holy Standard.
Jesus GIVES US THE DESIRE TO BE HOLY
5. The STAFF OF AARON
depicts God's Awesome Power.
Jesus DID MIRACLES. HE HAS THE POWER AND GLORY OF GOD.
6. The OUTER COVER OF HIDES
hid the Glory.
Jesus IS GOD, BUT LOOKED LIKE AN ORDINARY PERSON
7. The INNER CURTAIN
depicts a Barrier of Separation.
Jesus MADE A WAY BY HIS DEATH FOR US TO COME DIRECTLY TO GOD
8. The CLOUD
depicts God's Presence.
Jesus WILL COME IN GLORY AND POWER
9. The BREAD OF THE PRESENCE
depicts Fellowship in God's Presence.
Jesus IS READY TO FELLOWSHIP WITH US.
10. The ATONEMENT COVER
depicts God's Mercy.
Jesus MAKES IT POSSIBLE FOR US TO RECEIVE MERCY FROM GOD.
11. The MANNA
depicts God's Provisions.
Jesus IS THE BREAD OF LIFE, FEEDS OUR SOULS, GIVES ETERNAL LIFE
12. The GOLDEN LAMPSTAND
depicts Light and Reflection.
Jesus IS THE LIGHT OF THE WORLD
Ark of the Testimony
Inner Curtain
The Golden Lampstand
Table of the Bread of the Presence
The Altar of Incense
The Bronze Basin
The Altar of Sacrifices
© 2002 Susan Mortimer

75

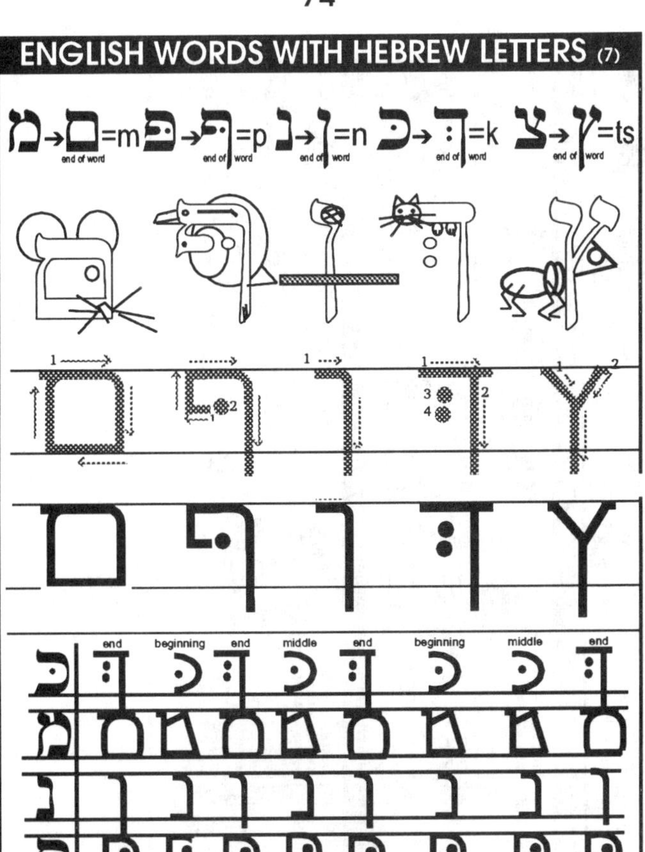

76

EXITING EGYPT 2

7. DESERT OF SIN. GOD SENT MANNA AND QUAIL FOR THE FIRST TIME.
8. REPHIDIM. GOD GAVE WATER OUT OF THE ROCK OF HOREB.
9. REPHIDIM. ISRAEL FOUGHT THE AMALEKITES. MOSES PRAYED WITH HIS HANDS HELD UP BY AARON & HUR.
TEN COMMANDMENTS
10. MOUNT SINAI. GOD GAVE THE LAW AND THE PEOPLE WORSHIPPED A GOLDEN CALF.
11. MT SINAI. THE ISRAELITES BUILT THE TABERNACLE AS GOD HAD INSTRUCTED.

79

80

82

OFFERINGS TO GOD 1

TYPE OF OFFERING	PURPOSE OF OFFERING	ANIMALS USED FOR OFFERING	DUTIES DONE BY	DUTIES	WHO RECEIVES PORTIONS OF OFFERING
LEVITICUS 1 ■ BURNT ☐ GRAIN ☐ FELLOWSHIP ☐ SIN ☐ GUILT	☐ THANKSGIVING ☐ COMPLETING A VOW ■ A PLEASING AROMA TO GOD ■ ATONEMENT FOR SIN ☐ FORGIVENESS OF SIN ☐ UNINTENTIONAL SIN ☐ KNOWING SIN ☐ VIOLATING THE LORD'S HOLY THINGS ☐ DOING WHAT IS FORBIDDEN ☐ DISHONEST GAIN	MALE • FEMALE • YOUNG • NO DEFECT HERD FLOCK ■ LAMB/SHEEP GOAT ■ DOVE PIGEON	INDIVIDUAL PRIEST	• ENTRANCE TO TENT OF MEETING • LAY HAND ON THE HEAD • SLAUGHTER • SPRINKLE BLOOD ON ALTAR • BURN FAT, KIDNEYS, COVERING OF LIVER • BURN MEAT ON ALTAR • GIVE SILVER AS RESTITUTION • ADD A FIFTH OF THE VALUE • SKIN & CUT INTO PIECES • BURN OUTSIDE OF CAMP	LEV 7:8 GOD (ON ALTAR): All that was burnt. PRIEST: HIDE INDIVIDUAL: none **PICTURE OF JESUS** EPHESIANS 5:2 JESUS GAVE HIMSELF AS A FRAGRANT OFFERING TO GOD
LEVITICUS 2 ☐ BURNT ■ GRAIN ☐ FELLOWSHIP ☐ SIN ☐ GUILT	■ THANKSGIVING ☐ COMPLETING A VOW ■ A PLEASING AROMA TO GOD ☐ ATONEMENT FOR SIN ☐ FORGIVENESS OF SIN ☐ UNINTENTIONAL SIN ☐ KNOWING SIN ☐ VIOLATING THE LORD'S HOLY THINGS ☐ DOING WHAT IS FORBIDDEN ☐ DISHONEST GAIN	ITEMS USED FOR OFFERING: FINE FLOUR FIRST FRUITS NEW GRAIN GRAIN FRUIT CAKES/WAFERS	INDIVIDUAL PRIEST	• ADD SALT • ADD OIL • ADD INCENSE • ADD NO YEAST • ADD NO HONEY • MAY COOK IN PAN • MAY BAKE IN OVEN • MAY COOK ON GRIDDLE • MAY ROAST • PRESENT TO PRIEST • BURN A MEMORIAL PORTION ON ALTAR	LEV 6:14-18, 7:9-10 GOD (ON ALTAR): A HANDFUL PRIEST: THE REST INDIVIDUAL: NONE **PICTURE OF JESUS** LUKE 22:14-19 JESUS GAVE HIS BODY FOR US, LIKE BREAD, GOOD, LIFE-GIVING, AND BROKEN.
LEVITICUS 3, 7:11-18 ☐ BURNT ☐ GRAIN ■ FELLOWSHIP ☐ SIN ☐ GUILT	■ THANKSGIVING ■ COMPLETING A VOW ■ A PLEASING AROMA TO GOD ☐ ATONEMENT FOR SIN ☐ FORGIVENESS OF SIN ☐ UNINTENTIONAL SIN ☐ KNOWING SIN ☐ VIOLATING THE LORD'S HOLY THINGS ☐ DOING WHAT IS FORBIDDEN ☐ DISHONEST GAIN	MALE • FEMALE • YOUNG • NO DEFECT HERD FLOCK ■ LAMB GOAT ☐ DOVE PIGEON	INDIVIDUAL PRIEST	• ENTRANCE TO TENT OF MEETING • LAY HAND ON THE HEAD • SLAUGHTER • SPRINKLE BLOOD ON ALTAR • BURN FAT, KIDNEYS, AND COVERING OF LIVER • THROW HANDFUL ON ALTAR • GIVE SILVER FOR RESTITUTION • ADD A FIFTH OF THE VALUE • SKIN & CUT INTO PIECES • BURN OUTSIDE OF CAMP	LEV 7:11-36 GOD (ON ALTAR): FAT, KIDNEYS, ETC PRIEST: BREAST, RIGHT THIGH INDIVIDUAL: THE REST **PICTURE OF JESUS** COLOSSIANS 3:17 WE SHOULD ALWAYS GIVE THANKS TO GOD THROUGH THE LORD JESUS.

81

TYPE OF OFFERING	PURPOSE OF OFFERING	ANIMALS USED FOR OFFERING	DUTIES DONE BY	DUTIES	WHO RECEIVES PORTIONS OF OFFERING
☐ BURNT ☐ GRAIN ☐ FELLOWSHIP ■ SIN ☐ GUILT	☐ THANKSGIVING ☐ COMPLETING A VOW ☐ A PLEASING AROMA TO GOD ■ ATONEMENT FOR SIN ☐ FORGIVENESS OF SIN ■ UNINTENTIONAL SIN ☐ KNOWING SIN ☐ VIOLATING THE LORD'S HOLY THINGS ■ DOING WHAT IS FORBIDDEN ☐ DISHONEST GAIN	PRIEST COMMUNITY LEADER MEMBER • Male • Young • No Defect • Female HERD FLOCK GOAT ■ LAMB	DUTIES OF PRIEST	■ ENTRANCE TO TENT OF MEETING ■ LAY HAND ON THE HEAD ■ SLAUGHTER ■ SPRINKLE BLOOD IN TENT ■ SOME BLOOD ON ALTAR ■ POUR BLOOD BY ALTAR ■ BURN FAT, KIDNEYS, COVERING OF LIVER ☐ THROW HANDFUL ON ALTAR ■ BURN THE HIDE, FLESH AND INNARDS OUTSIDE CAMP	GOD (ON ALTAR): ALL PRIEST: NONE INDIVIDUAL: NONE **PICTURE OF JESUS** 2 CORINTHIANS 5:21 JESUS WAS SINLESS. GOD MADE HIM TO BE SIN FOR US SO WE MAY BECOME RIGHTEOUS.
☐ BURNT ☐ GRAIN ☐ FELLOWSHIP ☐ SIN ■ GUILT	☐ THANKSGIVING ☐ COMPLETING A VOW ☐ A PLEASING AROMA TO GOD ■ ATONEMENT FOR SIN ■ FORGIVENESS OF SIN ■ UNINTENTIONAL SIN ■ KNOWING SIN ■ VIOLATING THE LORD'S HOLY THINGS ■ DOING WHAT IS FORBIDDEN ■ DISHONEST GAIN	MALE • FEMALE • YOUNG • NO DEFECT • PROPER VALUE HERD FLOCK ☐ LAMB GOAT ☐ DOVE PIGEON	INDIVIDUAL PRIEST	• ENTRANCE TO TENT OF MEETING • LAY HAND ON THE HEAD • SLAUGHTER • SOME BLOOD ON ALTAR • SPRINKLE BLOOD IN TENT • BURN FAT, KIDNEYS, COVERING OF LIVER • GIVE SILVER AS RESTITUTION • ADD A FIFTH OF THE VALUE • SKIN & CUT INTO PIECES • BURN OUTSIDE OF CAMP	GOD (ON ALTAR): FAT, KIDNEYS, ETC PRIEST: MEAT AND HIDE INDIVIDUAL: NONE **PICTURE OF JESUS** HEBREWS 10:19-22 THE BLOOD OF JESUS, SPRINKLED ON OUR HEARTS, CLEANSES US FROM A GUILTY CONSCIENCE

83

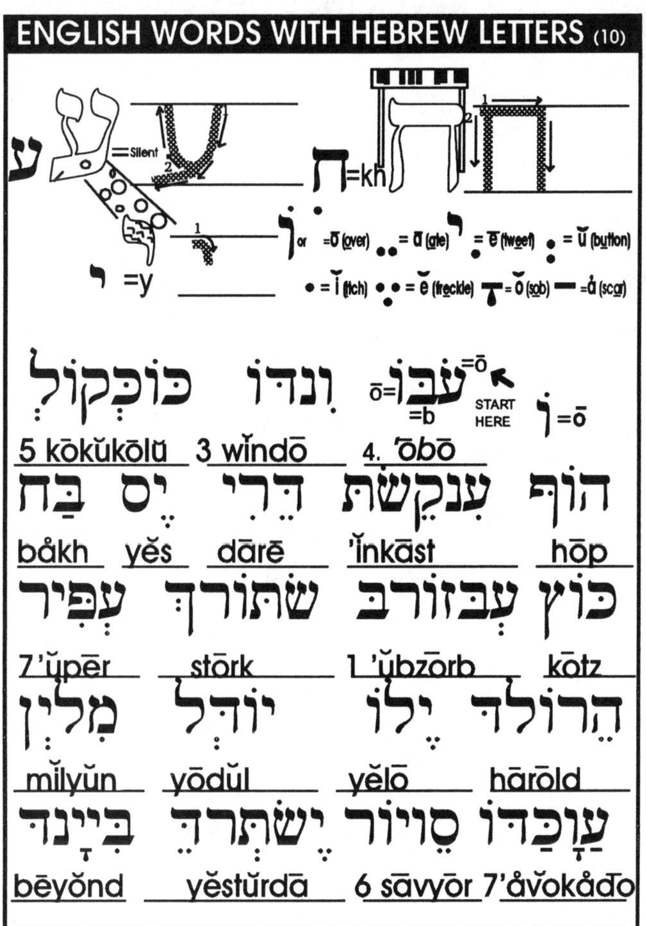

86

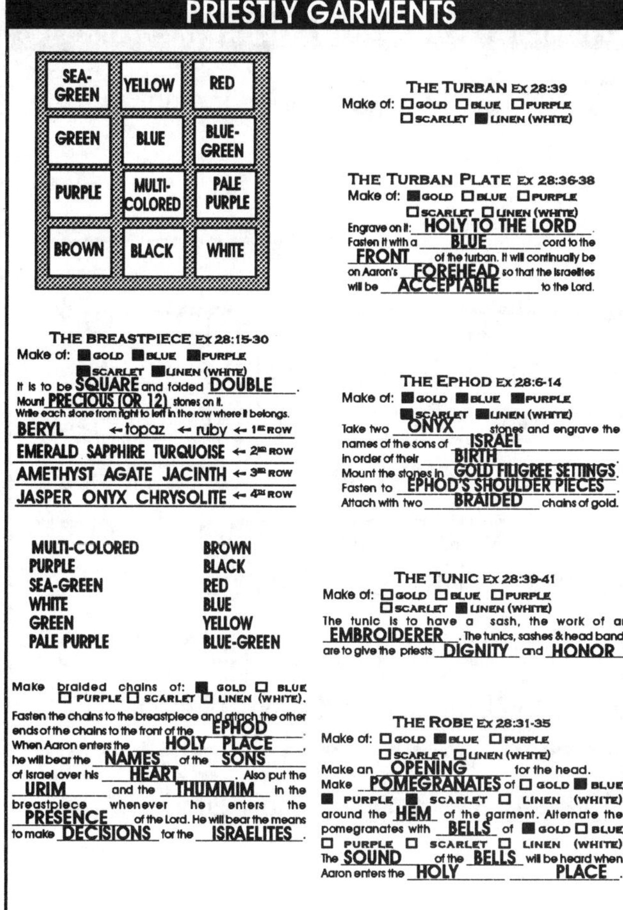

PRIESTLY GARMENTS
SEA-GREEN
YELLOW
RED
GREEN
BLUE
BLUE-GREEN
PURPLE
MULTI-COLORED
PALE PURPLE
BROWN
BLACK
WHITE
THE TURBAN Ex 28:39
Make of: GOLD BLUE PURPLE SCARLET LINEN (WHITE)
THE TURBAN PLATE Ex 28:36-38
Make of: GOLD BLUE PURPLE SCARLET LINEN (WHITE)
Engrave on it: HOLY TO THE LORD.
Fasten it with a BLUE cord to the FRONT of the turban. It will continually be on Aaron's FOREHEAD so that the Israelites will be ACCEPTABLE to the Lord.
THE BREASTPIECE Ex 28:15-30
Make of: GOLD BLUE PURPLE SCARLET LINEN (WHITE)
It is to be SQUARE and folded DOUBLE.
Mount PRECIOUS (OR 12) stones on it.
Write each stone from right to left in the row where it belongs.
BERYL ← topaz ← ruby ← 1ST ROW
EMERALD SAPPHIRE TURQUOISE ← 2ND ROW
AMETHYST AGATE JACINTH ← 3RD ROW
JASPER ONYX CHRYSOLITE ← 4TH ROW
THE EPHOD Ex 28:6-14
Make of: GOLD BLUE PURPLE SCARLET LINEN (WHITE)
Take two ONYX stones and engrave the names of the sons of ISRAEL in order of their BIRTH.
Mount the stones in GOLD FILIGREE SETTINGS.
Fasten to EPHOD'S SHOULDER PIECES.
Attach with two BRAIDED chains of gold.
MULTI-COLORED
PURPLE
SEA-GREEN
WHITE
GREEN
PALE PURPLE
BROWN
BLACK
RED
BLUE
YELLOW
BLUE-GREEN
THE TUNIC Ex 28:39-41
Make of: GOLD BLUE PURPLE SCARLET LINEN (WHITE)
The tunic is to have a sash, the work of an EMBROIDERER. The tunics, sashes & head bands are to give the priests DIGNITY and HONOR.
Make braided chains of: GOLD BLUE PURPLE SCARLET LINEN (WHITE).
Fasten the chains to the breastpiece and attach the other ends of the chains to the front of the EPHOD.
When Aaron enters the HOLY PLACE, he will bear the NAMES of the SONS of Israel over his HEART. Also put the URIM and the THUMMIM in the breastpiece whenever he enters the PRESENCE of the Lord. He will bear the means to make DECISIONS for the ISRAELITES.
THE ROBE Ex 28:31-35
Make of: GOLD BLUE PURPLE SCARLET LINEN (WHITE)
Make an OPENING for the head.
Make POMEGRANATES of GOLD BLUE PURPLE SCARLET LINEN (WHITE) around the HEM of the garment. Alternate the pomegranates with BELLS of GOLD BLUE PURPLE SCARLET LINEN (WHITE)
The SOUND of the BELLS will be heard when Aaron enters the HOLY PLACE.

88

ORDINATION OF AARON AND SONS 1

Read Leviticus 8. Fill in the blanks. In the space provided, glue the priest's garments from the Ordination...2 page.

1. **Assembly Gathers:** Moses summoned everyone to the entrance of the TENT of MEETING.
2. **Washed:** Moses brought Aaron and his sons forward and WASHED them with water.
3. **Dressed:** He put the TUNIC on Aaron, tied on the SASH, clothed him with the ROBE and put the EPHOD on him. He placed the BREASTPIECE on him and put the URIM and the THUMMIM in it. He then placed the TURBAN on Aaron's head and the GOLD plate on its front.
4. **Anointed:** Moses took the ANOINTING oil and anointed the TABERNACLE and everything in it, CONSECRATING them. He sprinkled oil on the altar SEVEN times. He anointed the ALTAR and all its UTENSILS and the BASIN with its STAND. Then he poured some ANOINTING oil on Aaron's HEAD to CONSECRATE him. Then Moses dressed Aaron's sons.
5. **Sin Offering:** Moses presented a BULL for the SIN offering. He SLAUGHTERED the bull, and with his FINGER put BLOOD on the horns of the altar. He poured the rest of the BLOOD at the base of the altar. He burnt the fat from the inner parts and kidneys on the ALTAR. The rest was burned OUTSIDE the camp.
6. **Burnt Offering:** Moses presented a RAM for the BURNT offering. Aaron and his sons laid their HANDS on its HEAD. Moses burnt the whole RAM as an offering made to the Lord by FIRE.
7. **Offering of Ordination:** Moses presented a RAM for the ordination. Aaron and his sons laid their HANDS on its HEAD. Moses slaughtered it and put some BLOOD on Aaron's right EAR, on the THUMB of his right HAND and on the big toe of his right FOOT. Moses did the same to Aaron's sons. He took the fat, kidneys and right THIGH. From the bread made without yeast, he took a cake of BREAD, and one with OIL and a wafer. Aaron and his sons WAVED them before the Lord. Then Moses burnt them on the altar.
8. **Consecration:** Moses used OIL and BLOOD to sprinkle Aaron, his sons and their GARMENTS
9. **Seven-Day Feast:** Moses told Aaron and his sons to cook the MEAT and eat it with the BREAD at the Tent's entrance. They were to burn up the rest and stay there SEVEN days.

Art work by Cammie Van Rooy.

89

HOLOCAUST

ע.ל.ה. 'to go up,' 'above,' 'high'

1. עָלָה	3 'ōlōh verb that means 'to go up'	1 comes up on a tree
2. עָלִי	1 'ōleh means 'leaf'	8 the Most High One
3. עָלָה	4 mă'ălōh means 'virtue'	5 space above the main floors
4. מַעֲלָה	5 'ăleyōh the honor reading the Torah	2 a child whose intellect is above others
5. עֲלִיָּה	9 'ōleh immigrant to Israel	9 ones who come to this land often go up to the high capital city
6. עוֹלָה	6 'ōlōh means 'burnt offering,' 'holocaust'	7 a moving platform that moves up and down
7. מַעֲלִית	8 'ĕlyōn means 'the Supreme' (God)	6 items go up in smoke
8. עֶלְיוֹן	4 mă'ălōh means 'stair'	4 a series of these leads up
9. עוֹלֶה	5 'ăleyōh means 'attic'	4 moral excellence, uprightness
10. עַל	2 'ĭlūy means 'young genius'	10 how far up something goes.
	10 'ōl means 'height'	3 verb that means ascend up, bring up, burn up, climb up, get up, lift oneself up, set up.
	7 mă'ălēth means 'elevator'	5 going up front to read the Torah

Holocaust is the word that is used for the 'burnt offering.' It is also the word used for what happened to the Jews under Hitler. Explain why you think they used this word.

They were killed and burned up in ovens or crematoriums.

90

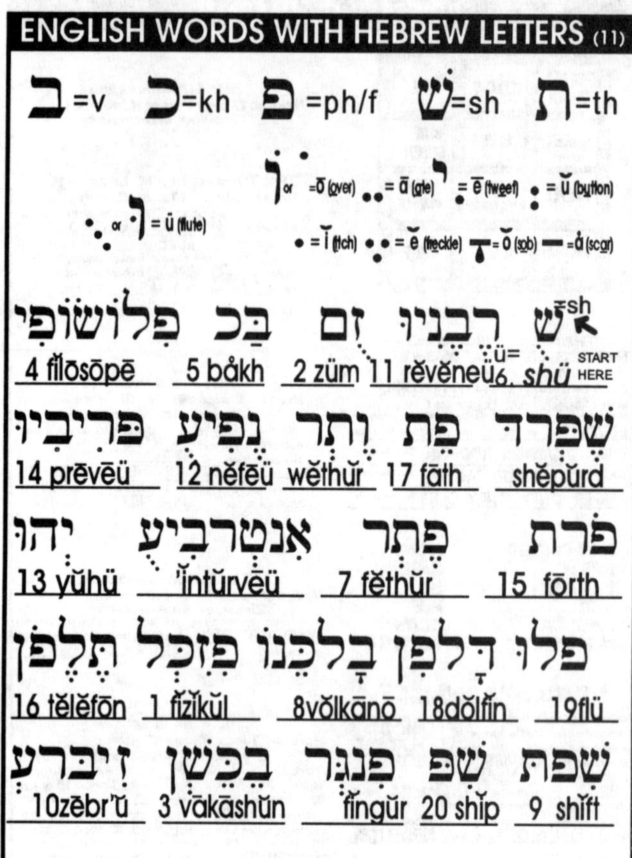

ENGLISH WORDS WITH HEBREW LETTERS (11)
=v =kh =ph/f =sh =th
START HERE
4 fĭlōsōpē 5 bǻkh 2 züm 11 rĕvĕnēü 6. shü
14 prēvēü 12 nĕfēü wĕthŭr 17 fāth shĕpŭrd
13 yŭhü ĭntŭrvēü 7 fĕthŭr 15 fōrth
16 tĕlĕfōn 1 fĭzĭkŭl 8vŏlkānō 18dŏlfĭn 19flü
10zēbr'ŭ 3 vākāshŭn fĭngŭr 20 shĭp 9 shĭft

REVERENCE OF GOD

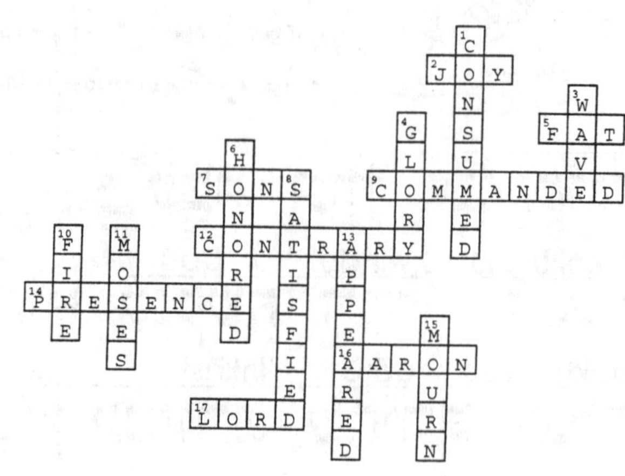

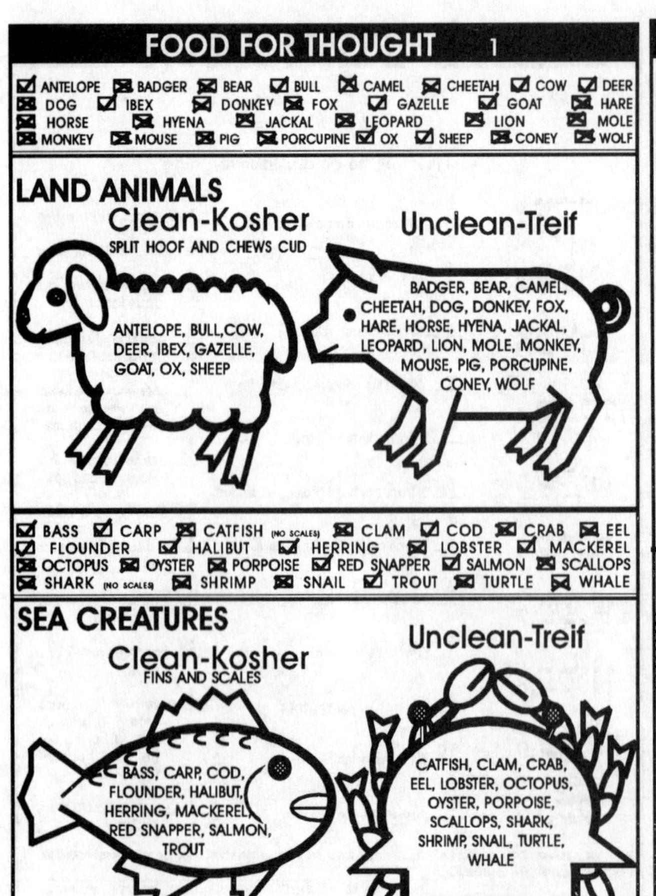

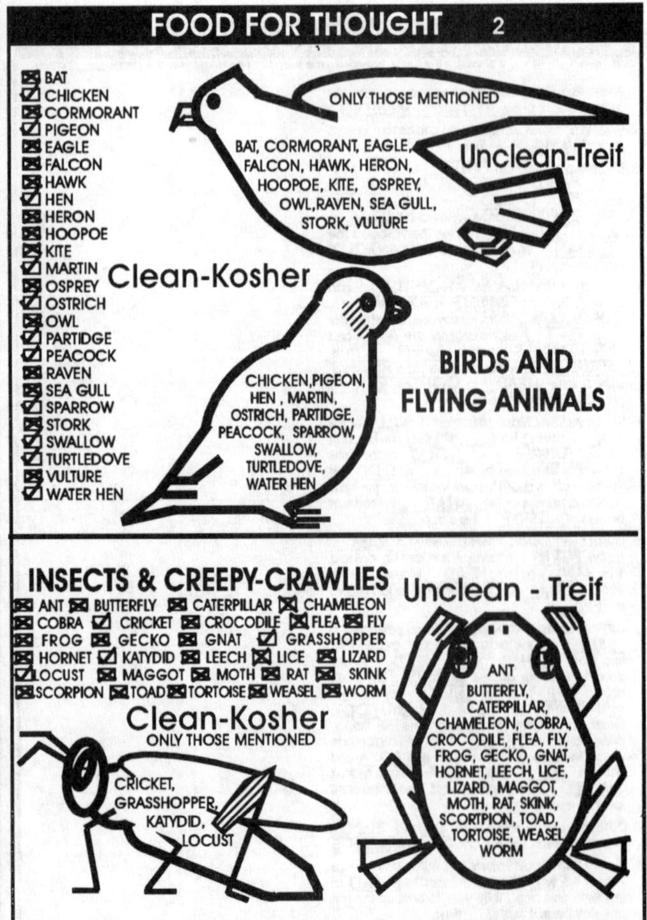

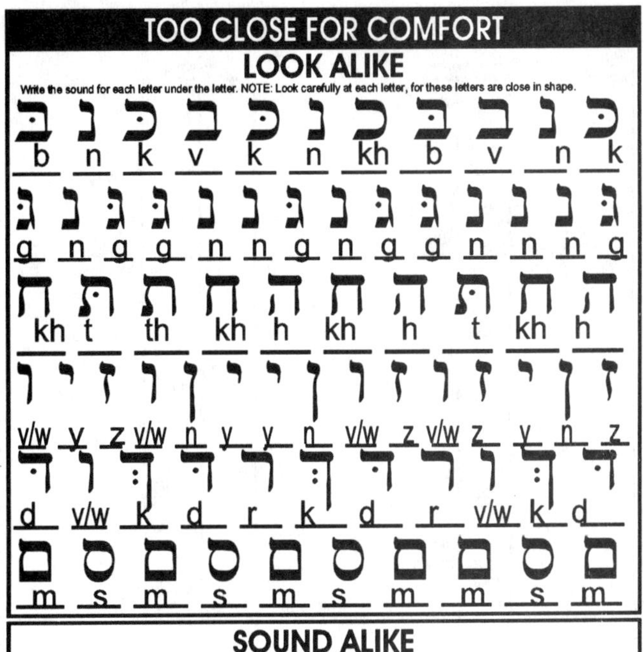

TOO CLOSE FOR COMFORT

LOOK ALIKE

Write the sound for each letter under the letter. NOTE: Look carefully at each letter, for these letters are close in shape.

בּ	נ	כּ	ב	כּ	נ	כ	בּ	ב	נ	כּ
b	n	k	v	k	n	kh	b	v	n	k

ג	נ	ג	ג	נ	נ	ג	נ	ג	ג	נ	נ	נ	ג
g	n	g	g	n	n	g	n	g	g	n	n	n	g

ח	תּ	ת	ח	ה	ח	ה	תּ	ח	ה
kh	t	th	kh	h	kh	h	t	kh	h

ו	י	ז	ו	ן	י	י	ן	ו	ז	ו	ז	י	ן	ז
v/w	y	z	v/w	n	y	y	n	v/w	z	v/w	z	y	n	z

ד	ו	ךְ	ד	ר	ךְ	ד	ר	ו	ךְ	ד
d	v/w	k	d	r	k	d	r	v/w	k	d

ם	ס	ם	ס	ם	ס	ם	ם	ס	ם
m	s	m	s	m	s	m	m	s	m

SOUND ALIKE

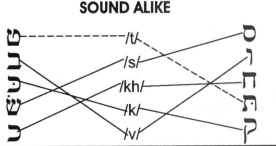

98

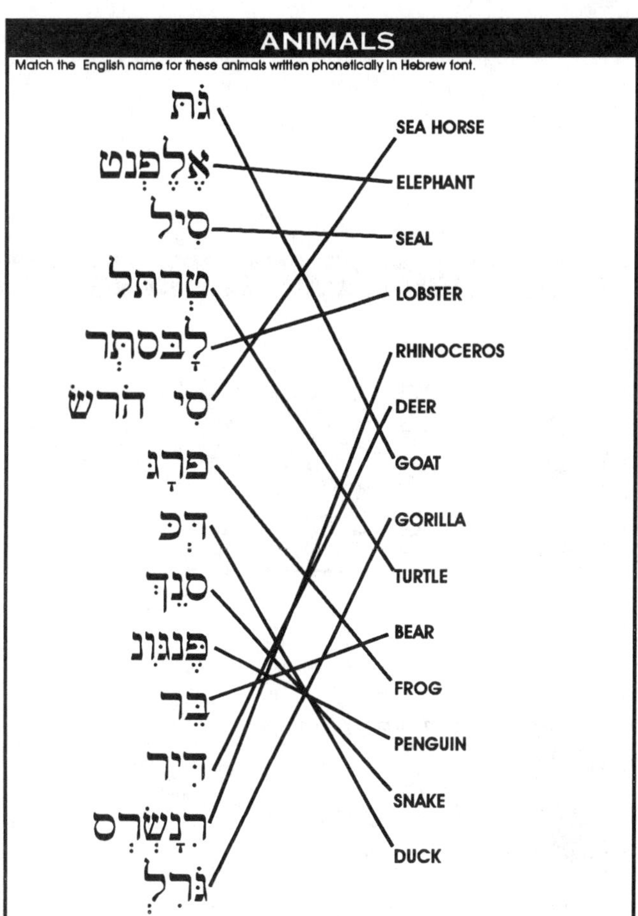

ANIMALS

Match the English name for these animals written phonetically in Hebrew font.

100

BEFORE ITS TIME

Deu. 23:12-13. Since the Israelites had no flush toilets, God told them to go to a place OUTSIDE the camp, DIG a hole, and when they were done, to COVER it up. Lev. 11:7-8, 13-19. God did not allow the Israelites to EAT or even touch the carcass of many creatures we classify as scavengers and carnivores. These animals tend to carry many more parasites and diseases than do herbivores. Read the paragraph about tapeworms at the bottom of the page and then fill in the blanks.

1. The head of the tapeworm is SMALL. It has HOOKS on its head to attach to the lining of the INTESTINE.
2. The tapeworm's largest sections are near the (head/end).
3. Tapeworms can grow 10 feet and live 20 years.
3. A mature section is full of EGGS. It BREAKS off and is expelled in the FECES. A tapeworm can produce 594 MILLION eggs in its life time.

TAPEWORM:

106

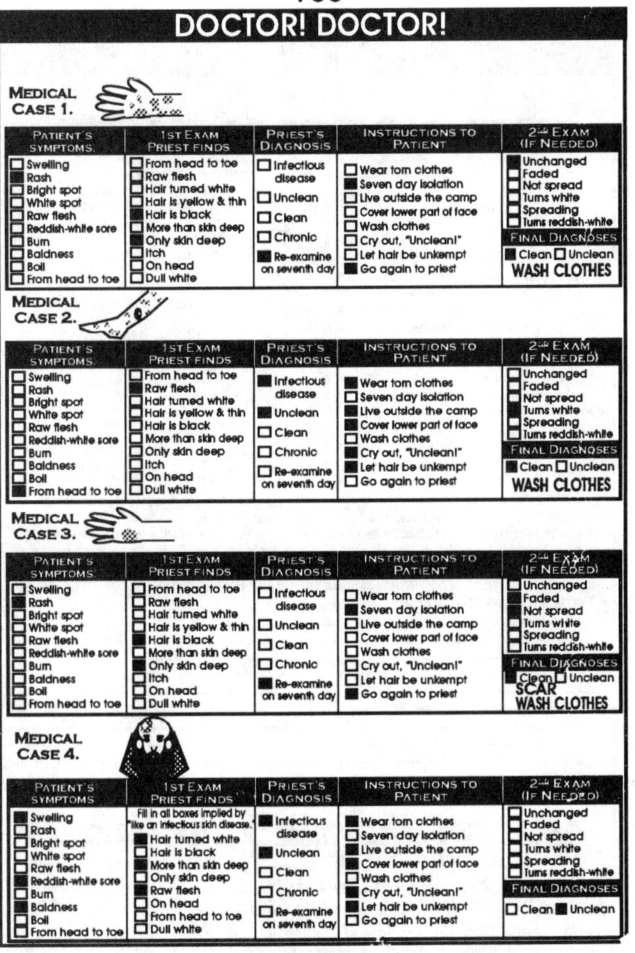

DOCTOR! DOCTOR!

MEDICAL CASE 1.

PATIENT'S SYMPTOMS	1ST EXAM PRIEST FINDS	PRIEST'S DIAGNOSIS	INSTRUCTIONS TO PATIENT	2ND EXAM (IF NEEDED)
☐ Swelling	☐ From head to toe	☐ Infectious disease	☐ Wear torn clothes	■ Unchanged
■ Rash	☐ Raw flesh	☐ Unclean	■ Seven day isolation	☐ Faded
☐ Bright spot	☐ Hair turned white	☐ Clean	☐ Live outside the camp	☐ Not spread
☐ White spot	☐ Hair is yellow & thin	☐ Chronic	☐ Cover lower part of face	☐ Turns white
☐ Raw flesh	■ Hair is black	■ Re-examine on seventh day	☐ Wash clothes	☐ Spreading
☐ Reddish-white sore	☐ More than skin deep		☐ Cry out, "Unclean!"	☐ Turns reddish-white
☐ Burn	■ Only skin deep		☐ Let hair be unkempt	FINAL DIAGNOSES
☐ Baldness	☐ Itch		■ Go again to priest	■ Clean ☐ Unclean
☐ Boil	☐ On head			WASH CLOTHES
☐ From head to toe	☐ Dull white			

MEDICAL CASE 2.

PATIENT'S SYMPTOMS	1ST EXAM PRIEST FINDS	PRIEST'S DIAGNOSIS	INSTRUCTIONS TO PATIENT	2ND EXAM (IF NEEDED)
☐ Swelling	☐ From head to toe	■ Infectious disease	■ Wear torn clothes	☐ Unchanged
☐ Rash	■ Raw flesh	■ Unclean	☐ Seven day isolation	☐ Faded
☐ Bright spot	☐ Hair turned white	☐ Clean	■ Live outside the camp	☐ Not spread
☐ White spot	☐ Hair is yellow & thin	☐ Chronic	■ Cover lower part of face	■ Turns white
☐ Raw flesh	☐ Hair is black	☐ Re-examine on seventh day	☐ Wash clothes	☐ Spreading
☐ Reddish-white sore	☐ More than skin deep		■ Cry out, "Unclean!"	☐ Turns reddish-white
☐ Burn	☐ Only skin deep		■ Let hair be unkempt	FINAL DIAGNOSES
☐ Baldness	☐ Itch		☐ Go again to priest	■ Clean ☐ Unclean
☐ Boil	☐ On head			WASH CLOTHES
■ From head to toe	☐ Dull white			

MEDICAL CASE 3.

PATIENT'S SYMPTOMS	1ST EXAM PRIEST FINDS	PRIEST'S DIAGNOSIS	INSTRUCTIONS TO PATIENT	2ND EXAM (IF NEEDED)
☐ Swelling	☐ From head to toe	☐ Infectious disease	☐ Wear torn clothes	☐ Unchanged
■ Rash	☐ Raw flesh	☐ Unclean	■ Seven day isolation	■ Faded
☐ Bright spot	☐ Hair turned white	☐ Clean	☐ Live outside the camp	■ Not spread
☐ White spot	☐ Hair is yellow & thin	☐ Chronic	☐ Cover lower part of face	☐ Turns white
☐ Raw flesh	■ Hair is black	■ Re-examine on seventh day	☐ Wash clothes	☐ Spreading
☐ Reddish-white sore	☐ More than skin deep		☐ Cry out, "Unclean!"	☐ Turns reddish-white
☐ Burn	■ Only skin deep		☐ Let hair be unkempt	FINAL DIAGNOSES
☐ Baldness	☐ Itch		■ Go again to priest	■ Clean ☐ Unclean
☐ Boil	☐ On head			SCAR
☐ From head to toe	☐ Dull white			WASH CLOTHES

MEDICAL CASE 4.

PATIENT'S SYMPTOMS	1ST EXAM PRIEST FINDS	PRIEST'S DIAGNOSIS	INSTRUCTIONS TO PATIENT	2ND EXAM (IF NEEDED)
■ Swelling	Fill in all boxes implied by "like an infectious skin disease."	■ Infectious disease	■ Wear torn clothes	☐ Unchanged
☐ Rash	■ Hair turned white	■ Unclean	☐ Seven day isolation	☐ Faded
☐ Bright spot	☐ Hair is black	☐ Clean	■ Live outside the camp	☐ Not spread
☐ White spot	■ More than skin deep	☐ Chronic	■ Cover lower part of face	☐ Turns white
☐ Raw flesh	☐ Only skin deep	☐ Re-examine on seventh day	☐ Wash clothes	☐ Spreading
■ Reddish-white sore	■ Raw flesh		■ Cry out, "Unclean!"	☐ Turns reddish-white
☐ Burn	☐ On head		■ Let hair be unkempt	FINAL DIAGNOSES
■ Baldness	☐ From head to toe		☐ Go again to priest	☐ Clean ■ Unclean
☐ Boil	☐ Dull white			
☐ From head to toe				

108

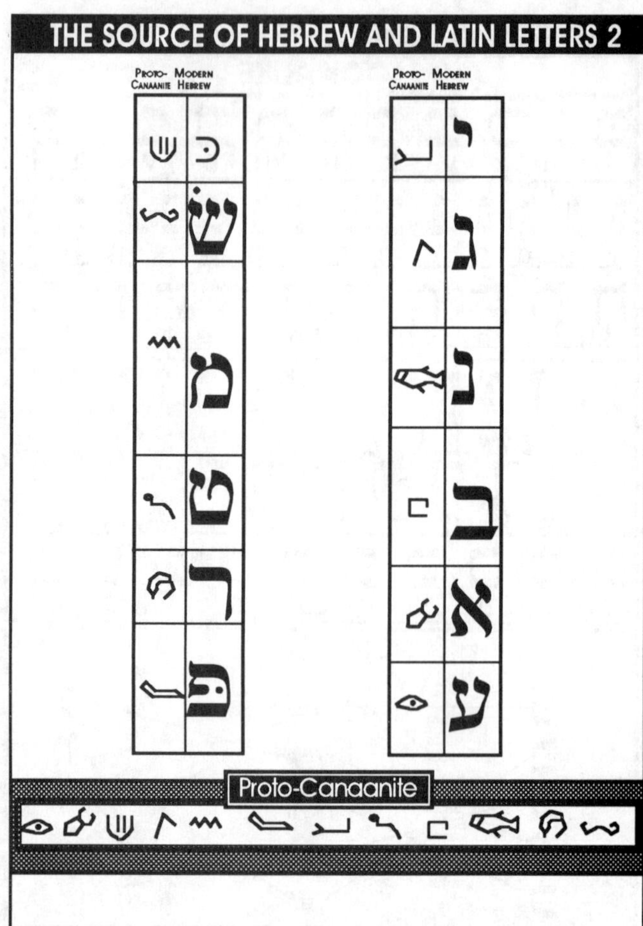

111

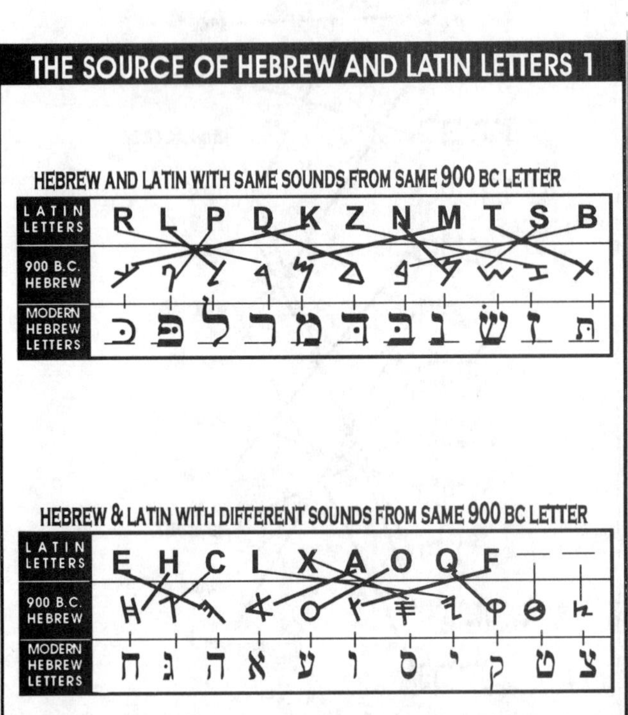

110

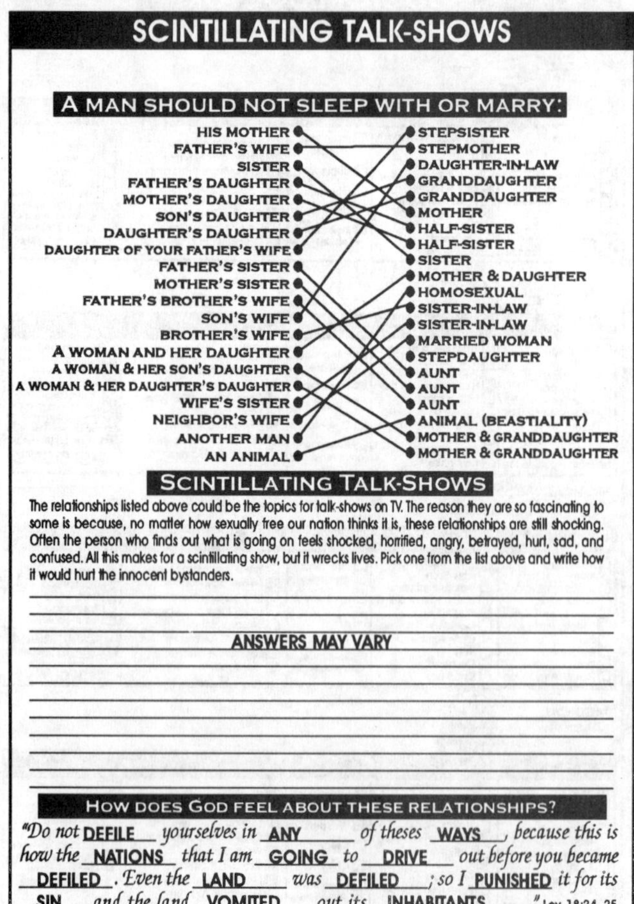

SCINTILLATING TALK-SHOWS
A MAN SHOULD NOT SLEEP WITH OR MARRY:
HIS MOTHER
FATHER'S WIFE
SISTER
FATHER'S DAUGHTER
MOTHER'S DAUGHTER
SON'S DAUGHTER
DAUGHTER'S DAUGHTER
DAUGHTER OF YOUR FATHER'S WIFE
FATHER'S SISTER
MOTHER'S SISTER
FATHER'S BROTHER'S WIFE
SON'S WIFE
BROTHER'S WIFE
A WOMAN AND HER DAUGHTER
A WOMAN & HER SON'S DAUGHTER
A WOMAN & HER DAUGHTER'S DAUGHTER
WIFE'S SISTER
NEIGHBOR'S WIFE
ANOTHER MAN
AN ANIMAL
STEPSISTER
STEPMOTHER
DAUGHTER-IN-LAW
GRANDDAUGHTER
GRANDDAUGHTER
MOTHER
HALF-SISTER
HALF-SISTER
SISTER
MOTHER & DAUGHTER
HOMOSEXUAL
SISTER-IN-LAW
SISTER-IN-LAW
MARRIED WOMAN
STEPDAUGHTER
AUNT
AUNT
AUNT
ANIMAL (BEASTIALITY)
MOTHER & GRANDDAUGHTER
MOTHER & GRANDDAUGHTER
SCINTILLATING TALK-SHOWS
The relationships listed above could be the topics for talk-shows on TV. The reason they are so fascinating to some is because, no matter how sexually free our nation thinks it is, these relationships are still shocking. Often the person who finds out what is going on feels shocked, horrified, angry, betrayed, hurt, sad, and confused. All this makes for a scintillating show, but it wrecks lives. Pick one from the list above and write how it would hurt the innocent bystanders.
ANSWERS MAY VARY
HOW DOES GOD FEEL ABOUT THESE RELATIONSHIPS?
"Do not DEFILE yourselves in ANY of theses WAYS, because this is how the NATIONS that I am GOING to DRIVE out before you became DEFILED. Even the LAND was DEFILED; so I PUNISHED it for its SIN, and the land VOMITED out its INHABITANTS." Lev 18:24, 25

112

EGYPTIAN CODE

	Respectful of gods	Respectful of man	Respectful of animals & plants	Vague or impossible	
1.	□	■	□	■	I have not done evil to mankind.
2.	□	■	□	■	I have not opposed family members.
3.	□	■	□	■	I have no knowledge of worthless men.
4.	□	■	□	□	I have sought no honors.
5.	■	□	□	□	I have not scorned the gods.
6.	□	■	□	□	I have not murdered.
7.	□	■	□	□	I have not ordered it done for me.
8.	■	□	□	□	I have not defrauded the temples.
9.	■	□	□	□	I have not stolen cakes from the gods.
10.	□	■	■	■	I have not caused pain.
11.	□	■	□	□	I have not committed fornication.
12.	□	■	□	□	I have not encroached on the fields of others.
13.	□	■	□	□	I have not oppressed the poor.
14.	□	■	□	□	I have not laid labor on any free man that he did not offer.
15.	□	■	□	□	I have not mistreated my servants.
16.	□	■	□	□	I have not starved any man.
17.	□	■	□	■	I have not made anyone weep.
18.	□	■	□	□	I have not added weights to the scales of balance.
19.	□	■	□	□	I have not taken milk from the mouths of children.
20.	□	□	■	□	I have not driven cattle from their pastures.
21.	■	□	■	□	I have not snared birds of the gods.
22.	□	□	■	□	I have not caught fish with bait made of the same kind of fish.
23.	□	■	■	□	I have not stopped the flow of water into canals.
24.	□	■	□	□	I have not extinguished a fire when it should burn.
25.	□	■	□	□	I have not lied or borne false witness.
26.	□	■	□	□	I have given bread to the hungry,
27.	□	■	□	□	I have given drink to the thirsty.
28.	□	■	□	□	I have clothed the naked with garments.
29.	□	■	□	□	I have not stolen, nor treated any man with treachery.
30.	□	■	□	□	I have not given false accusations (slandered).

114

I AM THE LORD GOD

18 = Z   25 = D   29 = F   30 = K

	Respectful of God	Respectful of man	Respectful of animals & plants	Vague or impractical	
A.	□	■	□	□	Respect mother and FATHER.
B.	■	□	□	□	Do not turn to IDOLS or make GODS of cast METAL.
C.	□	■	□	□	Do not REAP the very EDGES of your FIELD or go over your VINEYARD a 2nd time. Leave it for the POOR and alien.
D.	□	■	□	□	Do not LIE. Do not DECEIVE one another.
E.	■	□	□	□	Do not SWEAR falsely by My NAME.
F.	□	■	□	□	Do not DEFRAUD your neighbor or ROB him.
G.	□	■	□	□	Do not hold back the WAGES of a HIRED man overnight.
H.	□	■	□	□	Do not curse the DEAF or put a STUMBLING block in front of the BLIND.
I.	□	■	□	□	Do not PERVERT justice.
J.	□	■	□	□	Do not show partiality to the POOR or FAVORITISM to the rich.
K.	□	■	□	□	Do not spread SLANDER.
L.	□	■	□	□	Do not do anything to ENDANGER your neighbor's LIFE.
M.	□	■	□	□	Do not HATE your brother in your HEART.
N.	□	■	□	□	Do not seek REVENGE.
O.	□	□	■	□	Do not MATE DIFFERENT kinds of ANIMALS.
P.	□	□	■	□	Do not PLANT your fields with two kinds of SEED.
Q.	■	□	■	□	Do not eat any MEAT with the BLOOD still in it.
R.	■	□	□	□	Do not practice divination or SORCERY.
S.	?	□	□	□	Do not cut the HAIR at the sides of your HEAD.
T.	□	■	□	□	Do not CUT your BODIES for the dead or put TATOO marks on yourselves.
U.	□	■	□	□	Do not degrade your DAUGHTER by making her a PROSTITUTE.
V.	■	■	■	□	Observe the SABBATH.
W.	■	□	□	□	Do not turn to MEDIUMS or seek out SPIRITISTS.
X.	□	■	□	□	Rise in the presence of the AGED; show RESPECT for the ELDERLY.
Y.	□	■	□	□	As to the alien, do not MISTREAT him.
Z.	□	■	□	□	Do not use DISHONEST standards when measuring LENGTH, WEIGHT or QUALITY.

115

CROSSWORD FOR FEASTS

3 FIFTY
5 CAMPING
7 TRUMPETS
9 PASSOVER
11 RESURRECTED
14 HOMES
15 FALL
16 SABBATH
19 SEVEN

1 ATONEMENT
2 BURIED
4 YEAST
6 PURIM
8 SEASONS
10 CRUCIFIED
12 CIVIL
13 WHEAT
17 BARLEY
18 TEN

118

HEBREW ALPHABET & MODERN WORDS

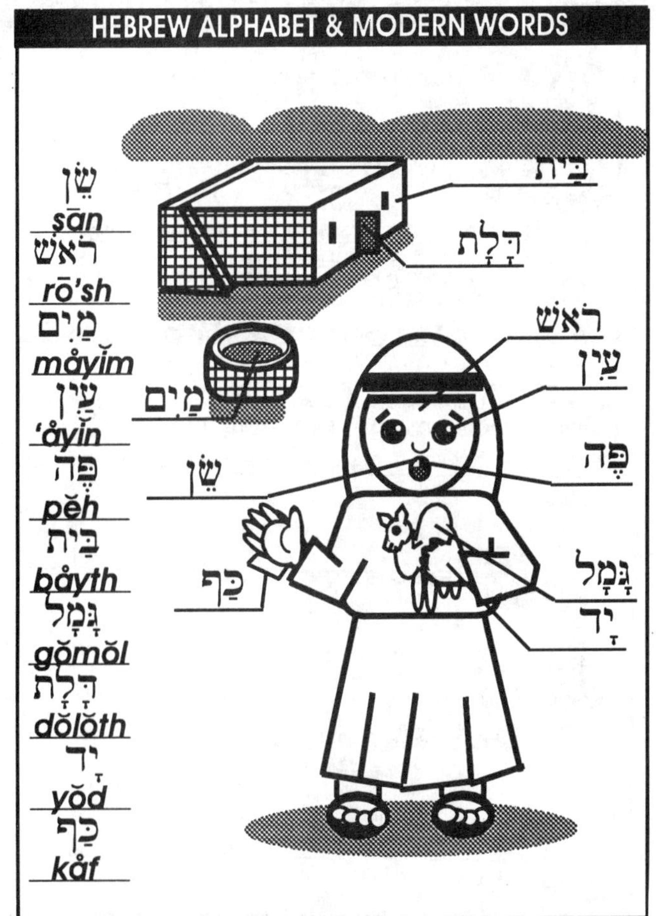

119

SEASONS AND FEASTS 1

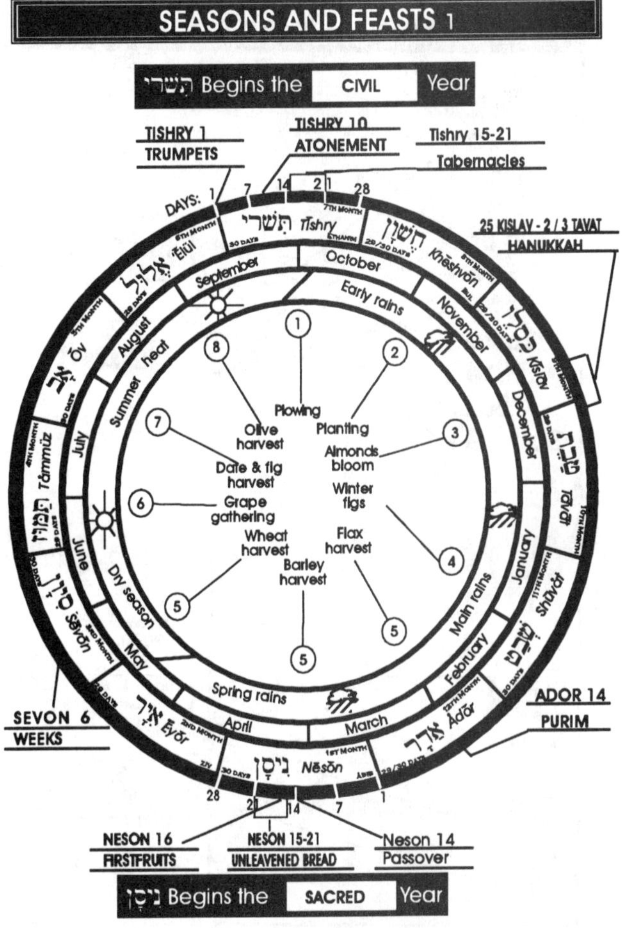

120

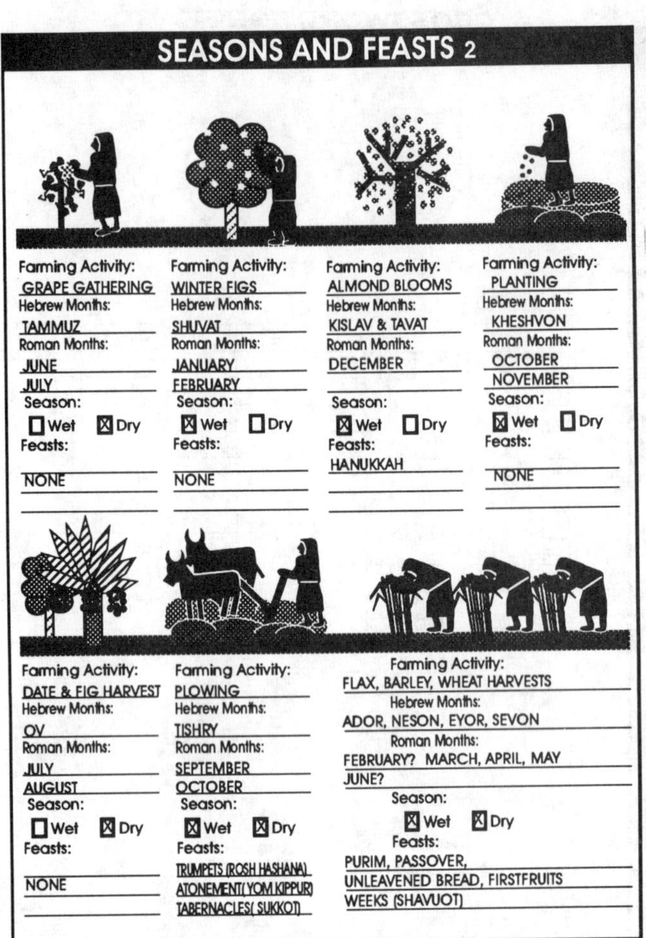

SEASONS AND FEASTS 2

Farming Activity:	Farming Activity:	Farming Activity:	Farming Activity:
GRAPE GATHERING	WINTER FIGS	ALMOND BLOOMS	PLANTING
Hebrew Months: TAMMUZ	Hebrew Months: SHUVAT	Hebrew Months: KISLAV & TAVAT	Hebrew Months: KHESHVON
Roman Months: JUNE, JULY	Roman Months: JANUARY, FEBRUARY	Roman Months: DECEMBER	Roman Months: OCTOBER, NOVEMBER
Season: ☐ Wet ☒ Dry	Season: ☒ Wet ☐ Dry	Season: ☒ Wet ☐ Dry	Season: ☒ Wet ☐ Dry
Feasts: NONE	Feasts: NONE	Feasts: HANUKKAH	Feasts: NONE

Farming Activity:	Farming Activity:	Farming Activity:
DATE & FIG HARVEST	PLOWING	FLAX, BARLEY, WHEAT HARVESTS
Hebrew Months: OV	Hebrew Months: TISHRY	Hebrew Months: ADOR, NESON, EYOR, SEVON
Roman Months: JULY, AUGUST	Roman Months: SEPTEMBER, OCTOBER	Roman Months: FEBRUARY? MARCH, APRIL, MAY, JUNE?
Season: ☐ Wet ☒ Dry	Season: ☒ Wet ☒ Dry	Season: ☒ Wet ☒ Dry
Feasts: NONE	Feasts: TRUMPETS (ROSH HASHANA), ATONEMENT (YOM KIPPUR), TABERNACLES (SUKKOT)	Feasts: PURIM, PASSOVER, UNLEAVENED BREAD, FIRSTFRUITS, WEEKS (SHAVUOT)

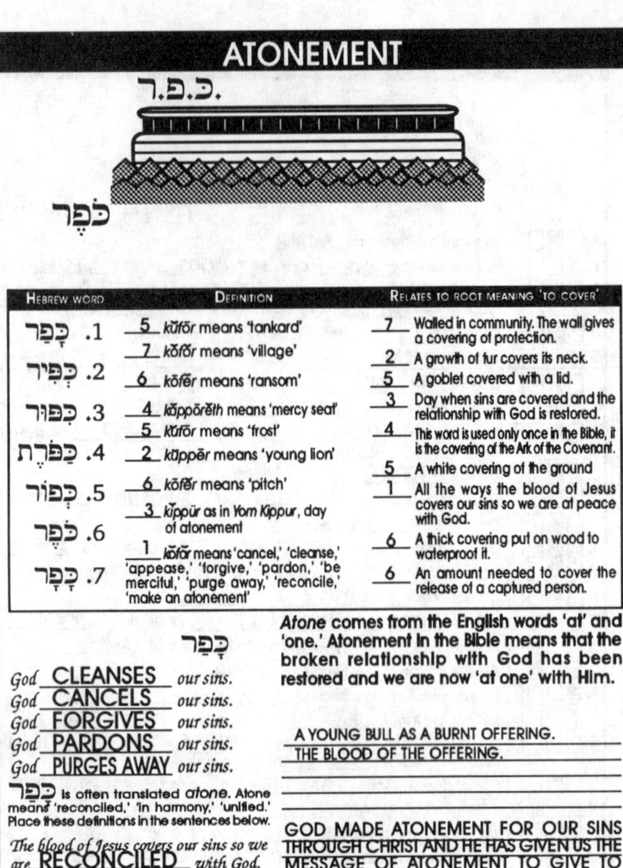

ATONEMENT

כ.פ.ר.

כִּפֵּר

Hebrew word	Definition	Relates to root meaning 'to cover'
1. כָּפַר	5 kŭfŏr means 'tankard'	7 Walled in community. The wall gives a covering of protection.
2. כְּפִיר	7 kŏfŏr means 'village'	2 A growth of fur covers its neck.
3. כִּפּוּר	6 kŏfĕr means 'ransom'	5 A goblet covered with a lid.
4. כַּפֹּרֶת	4 kăppōrĕth means 'mercy seat'	3 Day when sins are covered and the relationship with God is restored.
5. כְּפוֹר	5 kŭfŏr means 'frost'	4 This word is used only once in the Bible, it is the covering of the Ark of the Covenant.
6. כֹּפֶר	2 kŭppēr means 'young lion'	5 A white covering of the ground
7. כָּפָר	6 kŏfĕr means 'pitch'	1 All the ways the blood of Jesus covers our sins so we are at peace with God.
	3 Kĭppŭr as in Yom Kippur, day of atonement	6 A thick covering put on wood to waterproof it.
	1 kŏfŏr means 'cancel,' 'cleanse,' 'appease,' 'forgive,' 'pardon,' 'be merciful,' 'purge away,' 'reconcile,' 'make an atonement'	6 An amount needed to cover the release of a captured person.

כִּפֵּר

God CLEANSES our sins.
God CANCELS our sins.
God FORGIVES our sins.
God PARDONS our sins.
God PURGES AWAY our sins.

כִּפֵּר is often translated *atone*. Atone means 'reconciled,' 'in harmony,' 'unified.' Place these definitions in the sentences below.

The blood of Jesus covers our sins so we are RECONCILED *with God.*
The blood of Jesus covers our sins so we are IN HARMONY *with God.*
The blood of Jesus covers our sins so we are UNIFIED *with God.*

Atone **comes from the English words 'at' and 'one.' Atonement in the Bible means that the broken relationship with God has been restored and we are now 'at one' with Him.**

A YOUNG BULL AS A BURNT OFFERING.
THE BLOOD OF THE OFFERING.

GOD MADE ATONEMENT FOR OUR SINS THROUGH CHRIST AND HE HAS GIVEN US THE MESSAGE OF ATONEMENT TO GIVE TO EVERYONE. GOD MADE ATONEMENT WHILE WE WERE STILL SINNERS- BY THE DEATH OF HIS SON.

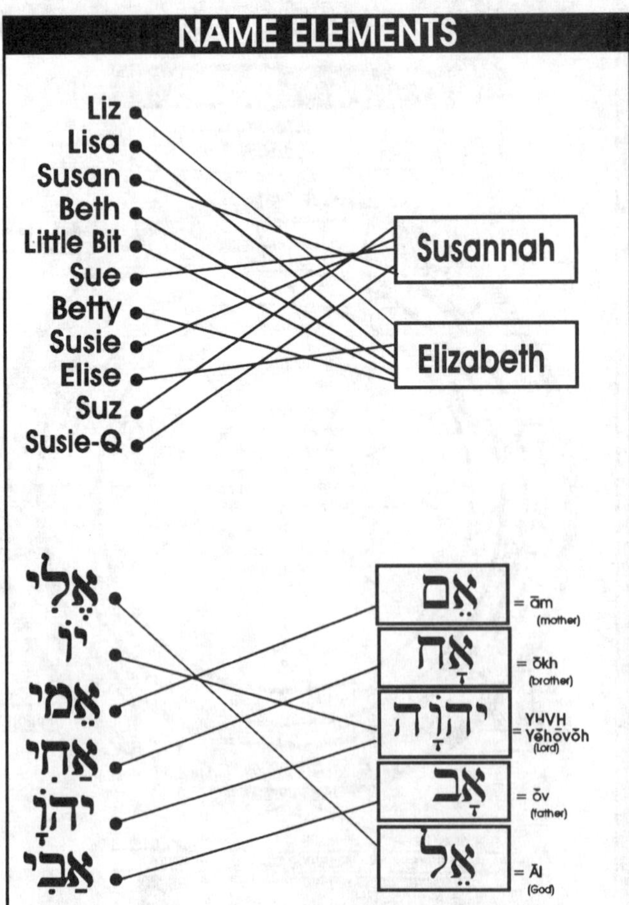

NAME ELEMENTS

Liz
Lisa
Susan
Beth
Little Bit
Sue
Betty
Susie
Elise
Suz
Susie-Q

Susannah
Elizabeth

אֱלִי
יוֹ
אִמִּי
אָחִי
יְהוֹ
אָבִי

אֵם = ām (mother)
אָח = ŏkh (brother)
יְהֹוָה = YHVH Yĕhōvŏh (Lord)
אָב = ŏv (father)
אֵל = Āl (God)

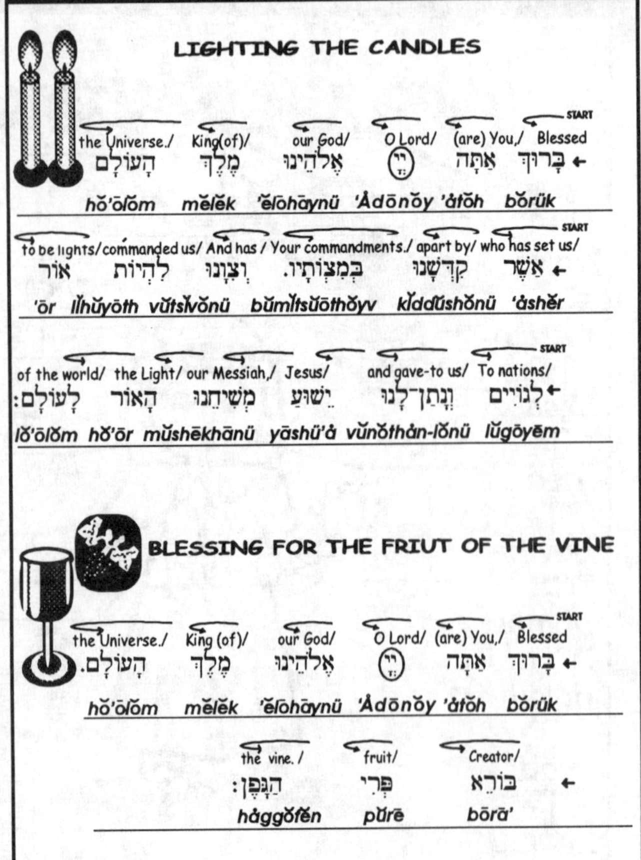

BLESSINGS FOR PASSOVER & SABBATH 1

LIGHTING THE CANDLES

START

Blessed/ (are) You,/ O Lord/ our God/ King(of)/ the Universe./
בָּרוּךְ אַתָּה יי אֱלֹהֵינוּ מֶלֶךְ הָעוֹלָם
bŏrŭk 'ătŏh 'Ădōnŏy 'ĕlōhāynū mĕlĕk hŏ'ōlŏm

who has set us/ apart by/ Your commandments./ And has / commanded us/ to be lights/
אֲשֶׁר קִדְּשָׁנוּ בְּמִצְוֹתָיו. וְצִוָּנוּ לִהְיוֹת אוֹר
'ăshĕr kĭddŭshŏnū bŭmĭtsŭōthŏyv vŭtsĭvŏnū lĭhŭyōth 'ōr

To nations/ and gave-to us/ Jesus/ our Messiah,/ the Light/ of the world/
לְגוֹיִים וְנָתַן־לָנוּ יֵשׁוּעַ מְשִׁיחֵנוּ הָאוֹר לְעוֹלָם:
lŭgōyēm vŭnŏthăn-lŏnū yāshŭ'ă mŭshēkhānū hŏ'ōr lŏ'ōlŏm

BLESSING FOR THE FRIUT OF THE VINE

START

Blessed/ (are) You,/ O Lord/ our God/ King (of)/ the Universe./
בָּרוּךְ אַתָּה יי אֱלֹהֵינוּ מֶלֶךְ הָעוֹלָם.
bŏrŭk 'ătŏh 'Ădōnŏy 'ĕlōhāynū mĕlĕk hŏ'ōlŏm

Creator/ fruit/ the vine./
בּוֹרֵא פְּרִי הַגָּפֶן:
bōrā' pŭrē hăggŏfĕn

BLESSINGS FOR PASSOVER & SABBATH 2

BLESSING THE SERVICE

the Universe,/	King (of)/	our God/	O Lord/	(are) You,/	Blessed (START)
הָעוֹלָם	מֶלֶךְ	אֱלֹהֵינוּ	יְיָ	אַתָּה	← בָּרוּךְ
hŏ'ōlŏm	mĕlĕk	'ĕlōhāynü	'Ådōnŏy	'åtŏh	bŏrük

this/	to season/	and brought us/	and established us,/	who has given us life,/ (START)
הַזֶּה:	לַזְּמַן	וְהִגִּיעָנוּ	וְקִיְּמָנוּ.	← שֶׁהֶחֱיָנוּ.
håzĕh	låzŭmån	vŭhĭggē'ŏnü	vŭkĭyymŏnü	shĕhĕkhĕyŏnü

BLESSING OF THE GREENS

the Universe,/	King (of)/	our God/	O Lord/	(are) You,/	Blessed (START)
הָעוֹלָם	מֶלֶךְ	אֱלֹהֵינוּ	יְיָ	אַתָּה	← בָּרוּךְ
hŏ'ōlŏm	mĕlĕk	'ĕlōhāynü	'Ådōnŏy	'åtŏh	bŏrük

(from) the ground./	fruit/	who created
הָאֲדָמָה:	פְּרִי	בּוֹרֵא
hŏ'ŭdŏmŏh	pŭrē	bōrā'

BLESSING FOR SEARCHING OUT LEAVEN

the Universe,/	King (of)/	our God/	O Lord/	(are) You,/	Blessed (START)
הָעוֹלָם	מֶלֶךְ	אֱלֹהֵינוּ	יְיָ	אַתָּה	← בָּרוּךְ
hŏ'ōlŏm	mĕlĕk	'ĕlōhāynü	'Ådōnŏy	'åtŏh	bŏrük

leaven./	to burn/	concerning/	and commanded us/	with His commands/	sanctified us/	who/
חָמֵץ:	בִּעוּר	עַל	וְצִוָּנוּ	בְּמִצְוֹתָיו	קִדְּשָׁנוּ	אֲשֶׁר
khŏmāts	bĭ'ür	'ål	vŭtsĭvŏnü	bŭmĭtsŭōthŏyv	kĭddŭshŏnü	'åshĕr

BLESSINGS FOR PASSOVER & SABBATH 3

BLESSING OF THE BITTER HERBS

the Universe./	King(of)/	our God/	O Lord/	(are) You,/	Blessed (START)
הָעוֹלָם	מֶלֶךְ	אֱלֹהֵינוּ	יְיָ	אַתָּה	← בָּרוּךְ
hŏ'ōlŏm	mĕlĕk	'ĕlōhāynü	'Ådōnŏy	'åtŏh	bŏrük

bitter (herbs)./	eating/	and commanded us concerning/	with His commandments./	made us Holy/	Who
מָרוֹר:	עַל־אֲכִילַת	וְצִוָּנוּ	בְּמִצְוֹתָיו	קִדְּשָׁנוּ	אֲשֶׁר
mŏrōr	'ål-'åkhēlü	vŭtsĭvŏnü	bŭmĭtsŭythŏyv	kĭddŭshŏnü	'åshĕr

WASHING OF HANDS

of the Universe./	King/	our God/	O Lord/	are You,/	Blessed
הָעוֹלָם	מֶלֶךְ	אֱלֹהֵינוּ	יְיָ	אַתָּה	← בָּרוּךְ
hŏ'ōlŏm	mĕlĕk	'ĕlōhāynü	'Ådōnŏy	'åtŏh	bŏrük

the hands./	us to wash/	and has commanded /	with his commandment/	has sanctified us/	who
יָדָיִם:	עַל־נְטִילַת	וְצִוָּנוּ	בְּמִצְוֹתָיו	קִדְּשָׁנוּ	אֲשֶׁר
yŏdŏyĭm	'ål-nŭtēlåth	vŭtsĭvŏnü	bŭmĭtsŭythŏyv	kĭddŭshŏnü	'åshĕr

BLESSING OF THE UNLEAVENED BREAD

of the Universe./	King/	our God/	O Lord/	are You,/	Blessed
הָעוֹלָם	מֶלֶךְ	אֱלֹהֵינוּ	יְיָ	אַתָּה	← בָּרוּךְ
hŏ'ōlŏm	mĕlĕk	'ĕlōhāynü	'Ådōnŏy	'åtŏh	bŏrük

from the earth./	bread/	The One brought forth
מִן־הָאָרֶץ	לֶחֶם	הַמּוֹצִיא
mĭn-hŏ'ŏrĕts	lĕkhĕm	håmmōtsē'

HEBREW NAMES 1

Use this page to figure out the meaning of the Hebrew names on the following pages.

יְהֹוָה	YHVH Yehōvŏh (eternal Lord)	אָב	'ŏv (father)	זָכַר	zŏkhår (remembered)
יָהּ	Yŏh (short for Jehovah)	אֵם	'ām (mother)	לֶחֶם	lĕkhĕm (bread, food)
אֵל	'Ēl (God)	בֵּן	bĕn (son)	שָׁמַע	shŏmå' (heard)
אֲדוֹנָי	'Ŏdōnŏy (Lord)	בַּת	båth (daughter)	רָאָה	rŏ'ŏh (saw)
מֶלֶךְ	mĕlĕk (king)	אָח	'ŏkh (brother)	יָסַף	yŏsåf (added)
שָׁפַט	shŏfåt (to judge)	עַם	'åm (people)	שָׁלוֹם	shŏlōm (peace)
דָּן	dŏn (judge)	בַּיִת	båyĭth (house)	עֵדֶן	'ēdĕn (pleasure)
דּוֹד	dōd (love)	בְּאֵר	bĭ'ēr (well)	עֲרָבָה	'ărŏvŏh (desert)
שֶׁבַע	shĕvå' (oath)	גִּיל	gēl (joy)	רוּם	rüm (high, exalted)
יָשַׁע	yŏshå' (saved)	נָתַן	nŏthån (gave)	לֹא	lō' (no, not)

HEBREW NAMES 2

Hebrew Name:	Hebrew Name in English:	Meaning of Name:
1. דָּנִאֵל	3 Elimelech 'ĕlēmĕlĕk	4 God is his father
2. אֶלְדָּד	2 Eldad 'ĕldŏd	5 God of his God
3. אֱלִימֶלֶךְ	5 Eliel 'ĕlē'ēl	3 My God is the king
4. אֱלִיאָב	7 Elnathan 'ĕlŭnŏthŏn	6 Heard of God
5. אֱלִיאֵל	1 Daniel dŏnĭ'āl	2 God has loved
6. שְׁמוּאֵל	8 Malechiel målŭky'āl	7 God is the giver
7. אֶלְנָתָן	6 Samuel shŭmü'āl	1 Judge from God
8. מַלְכִּיאֵל	4 Eliab 'ĕlĭ'ŏv	8 King of God

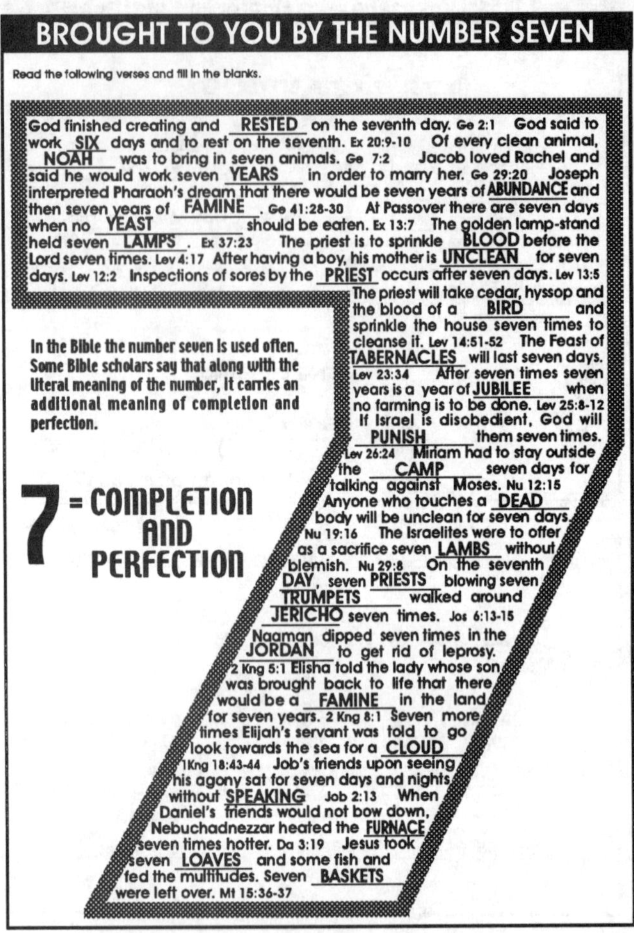

BROUGHT TO YOU BY THE NUMBER SEVEN

Read the following verses and fill in the blanks.

God finished creating and RESTED on the seventh day. Ge 2:1 God said to work SIX days and to rest on the seventh. Ex 20:9-10 Of every clean animal, NOAH was to bring in seven animals. Ge 7:2 Jacob loved Rachel and said he would work seven YEARS in order to marry her. Ge 29:20 Joseph interpreted Pharaoh's dream that there would be seven years of ABUNDANCE and then seven years of FAMINE. Ge 41:28-30 At Passover there are seven days when no YEAST should be eaten. Ex 13:7 The golden lamp-stand held seven LAMPS. Ex 37:23 The priest is to sprinkle BLOOD before the Lord seven times. Lev 4:17 After having a boy, his mother is UNCLEAN for seven days. Lev 12:2 Inspections of sores by the PRIEST occurs after seven days. Lev 13:5 The priest will take cedar, hyssop and the blood of a BIRD and sprinkle the house seven times to cleanse it. Lev 14:51-52 The Feast of TABERNACLES will last seven days. Lev 23:34 After seven times seven years is a year of JUBILEE when no farming is to be done. Lev 25:8-12 If Israel is disobedient, God will PUNISH them seven times. Lev 26:24 Miriam had to stay outside the CAMP seven days for talking against Moses. Nu 12:15 Anyone who touches a DEAD body will be unclean for seven days. Nu 19:16 The Israelites were to offer as a sacrifice seven LAMBS without blemish. Nu 29:8 On the seventh DAY, seven PRIESTS blowing seven TRUMPETS walked around JERICHO seven times. Jos 6:13-15 Naaman dipped seven times in the JORDAN to get rid of leprosy. 2 Kng 5:1 Elisha told the lady whose son was brought back to life that there would be a FAMINE in the land for seven years. 2 Kng 8:1 Seven more times Elijah's servant was told to go look towards the sea for a CLOUD. 1Kng 18:43-44 Job's friends upon seeing his agony sat for seven days and nights without SPEAKING. Job 2:13 When Daniel's friends would not bow down, Nebuchadnezzar heated the FURNACE seven times hotter. Da 3:19 Jesus took seven LOAVES and some fish and fed the multitudes. Seven BASKETS were left over. Mt 15:36-37

In the Bible the number seven is used often. Some Bible scholars say that along with the literal meaning of the number, it carries an additional meaning of completion and perfection.

7 = COMPLETION AND PERFECTION

134

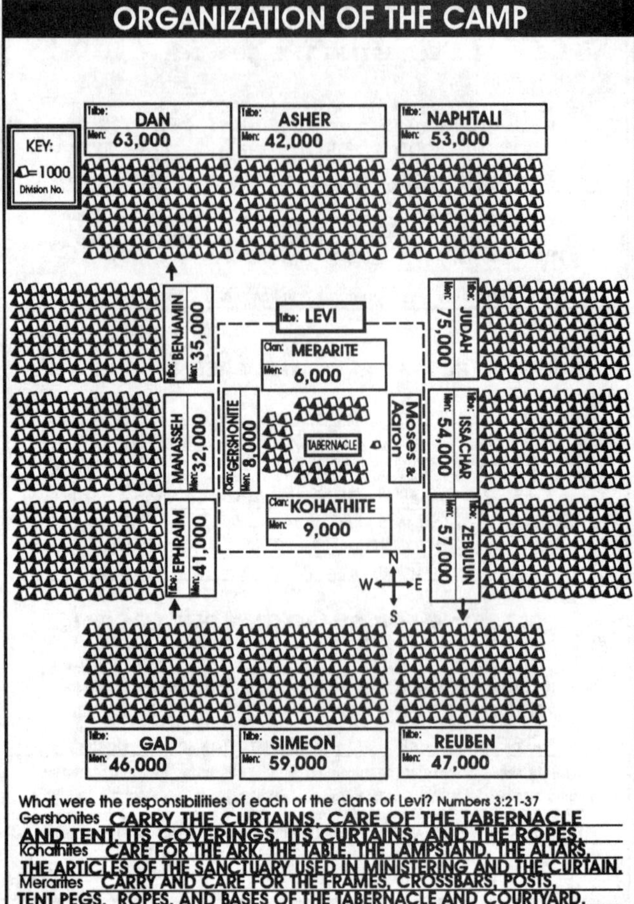

ORGANIZATION OF THE CAMP

What were the responsibilities of each of the clans of Levi? Numbers 3:21-37

Gershonites CARRY THE CURTAINS, CARE OF THE TABERNACLE AND TENT, ITS COVERINGS, ITS CURTAINS, AND THE ROPES.

Kohathites CARE FOR THE ARK, THE TABLE, THE LAMPSTAND, THE ALTARS, THE ARTICLES OF THE SANCTUARY USED IN MINISTERING AND THE CURTAIN.

Merarites CARRY AND CARE FOR THE FRAMES, CROSSBARS, POSTS, TENT PEGS, ROPES, AND BASES OF THE TABERNACLE AND COURTYARD.

135

HEBREW NAMES 3

Hebrew Name:	Hebrew Name in English:	Meaning of Name:
יוֹאָח 1.	6 Amaziah (strengthened) 'åmåtsŭyŏhŭ	2 Jehovah is God
יוֹאֵל 2.	4 Joseph yŏsāf	4 Let Jehovah add
זְכַרְיָהוּ 3.	3 Zachariah zŭkhårŭyŏhŭ	7 King of Jehovah
יוֹסֵף 4.	1 Joah yō'ŏkh	10 Jehovah saved
אֲדֹנִיָּהוּ 5.	8 Jehoshaphat yŭhōshŏfŏt	6 Strenghtened of Jehovah
אֲמַצְיָהוּ 6.	0 Joshua yŭhōshŭ'å	3 Remembered by Jehovah
מַלְכִּיָּהוּ 7.	9 Dodajah dōdyŏhŏŭå	5 Lord of Jehovah
יְהוֹשָׁפָט 8.	2 Joel yō'āl	9 Loved by Jehovah
דּוֹדָיָהוּ 9.	7 Malchijah målŭkkēŏhŭ	1 Jehovah brothered
יְהוֹשׁוּעַ 10.	5 Adonijah 'ådōnēåhŭ	8 Jehovah judges

137

GRUMBLING (2)

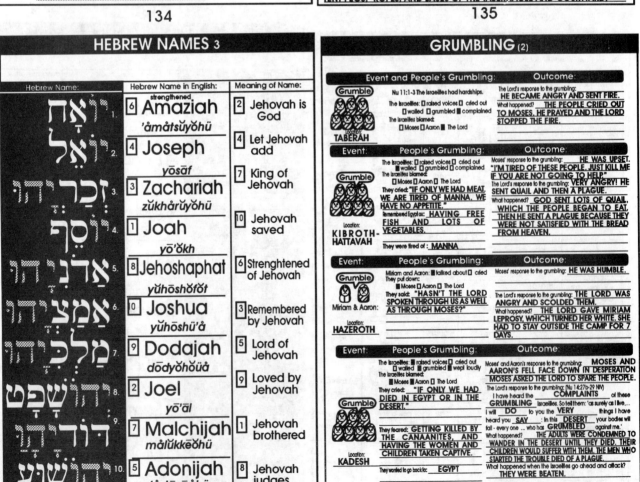

Event and People's Grumbling: / Outcome:

Location: TABERAH

Nu 11:1-3 The Israelites had hardships.
The Israelites: ☐ raised voices ☐ cried out ☐ wailed ☐ grumbled ■ complained
The Israelites blamed: ☐ Moses ☐ Aaron ■ The Lord

The Lord's response to the grumbling: HE BECAME ANGRY AND SENT FIRE.
What happened? THE PEOPLE CRIED OUT TO MOSES. HE PRAYED AND THE LORD STOPPED THE FIRE.

Event: / People's Grumbling: / Outcome:

Location: KIBROTH-HATTAVAH

The Israelites: ☐ raised voices ☐ cried out ■ wailed ☐ grumbled ☐ complained
The Israelites blamed: ☐ Moses ☐ Aaron ☐ The Lord
They cried: "IF ONLY WE HAD MEAT. WE ARE TIRED OF MANNA. WE HAVE NO APPETITE."
Remembered Egypt as: HAVING FREE FISH AND LOTS OF VEGETABLES.
They were tired of: MANNA

Moses' response to the grumbling: HE WAS UPSET. "I'M TIRED OF THESE PEOPLE. JUST KILL ME IF YOU ARE NOT GOING TO HELP."
The Lord's response to the grumbling: VERY ANGRY! HE SENT QUAIL AND THEN A PLAGUE.
What happened? GOD SENT LOTS OF QUAIL, WHICH THE PEOPLE BEGAN TO EAT. THEN HE SENT A PLAGUE BECAUSE THEY WERE NOT SATISFIED WITH THE BREAD FROM HEAVEN.

Event: / People's Grumbling: / Outcome:

Miriam & Aaron:
Location: HAZEROTH

Miriam and Aaron: ■ talked about ☐ cried
They put down: ■ Moses ☐ Aaron ☐ The Lord
They said: "HASN'T THE LORD SPOKEN THROUGH US AS WELL AS THROUGH MOSES?"

Moses' response to the grumbling: HE WAS HUMBLE.
The Lord's response to the grumbling: THE LORD WAS ANGRY AND SCOLDED THEM.
What happened? THE LORD GAVE MIRIAM LEPROSY, WHICH TURNED HER WHITE. SHE HAD TO STAY OUTSIDE THE CAMP FOR 7 DAYS.

Event: / People's Grumbling: / Outcome:

Location: KADESH

The Israelites: ■ raised voices ☐ cried out ☐ wailed ■ grumbled ■ wept loudly
The Israelites blamed: ■ Moses ■ Aaron ☐ The Lord
They cried: "IF ONLY WE HAD DIED IN EGYPT OR IN THE DESERT."
They feared: GETTING KILLED BY THE CANAANITES, AND HAVING THE WOMEN AND CHILDREN TAKEN CAPTIVE.
They wanted to go back to: EGYPT

Moses' and Aaron's response to the grumbling: MOSES AND AARON'S FELL FACE DOWN IN DESPERATION. MOSES ASKED THE LORD TO SPARE THE PEOPLE.
The Lord's response to the grumbling: (Nu 14:27b-29 NIV)
I have heard the COMPLAINTS of these GRUMBLING Israelites. So tell them: 'as surely as I live,... I will DO to you the VERY things I have heard you SAY: In this DESERT your bodies will fall - every one ... who has GRUMBLED against me.'
What happened? THE ADULTS WERE CONDEMNED TO WANDER IN THE DESERT UNTIL THEY DIED. THEIR CHILDREN WOULD SUFFER WITH THEM. THE MEN WHO STARTED THE TROUBLE DIED OF A PLAGUE.
What happened when the Israelites go ahead and attack? THEY WERE BEATEN.

138

GRUMBLING (3)

Event:	People's Grumbling:	Outcome:
Grumble	Korah and 250 Israelites: ■ rose up ☐ wailed ☐ grumbled ■ complained. The Israelites blamed: ■ Moses ■ Aaron ☐ The Lord. They cried: WHY DO YOU THINK YOU ARE BETTER THAN US?" Remembered Egypt as: AS A LAND FLOWING WITH MILK AND HONEY. They feared: DYING IN THE DESERT. DIDN'T WANT TO OBEY MOSES AND AARON.	Moses' response to the grumbling: HE WAS VERY ANGRY & FELL FACE DOWN. The Lord's response to the grumbling: THE LORD WANTED TO KILL THE WHOLE GROUP. What happened? GOD HAD THE EARTH OPEN UP AND SWALLOW THE REBELS AND THEIR FAMILIES. FIRE KILLED 250 FOLLOWERS.
Grumble	The Israelites: ☐ raised voices ☐ cried out ☐ wailed ■ grumbled ☐ complained. The Israelites blamed: ■ Moses ■ Aaron ☐ The Lord. They cried: "YOU KILLED THE LORD'S PEOPLE."	Moses' response to the grumbling: HE CHALLENGED THEM TO SEE WHO GOD HAD CHOSEN. The Lord's response to the grumbling: THE LORD WAS ANGRY, AND SENT A PLAGUE. What happened? THE PLAGUE KILLED 14,700. AARON RAN BETWEEN DEAD AND LIVING WITH INCENSE. THE PLAGUE STOPPED.
Grumble. Location: KADESH OR DESERT OF ZIN	The Israelites: ☐ raised voices ■ quarreled ☐ wailed ☐ grumbled ☐ complained. The Israelites blamed: ☐ Moses ■ Aaron ☐ The Lord. They cried: "IF ONLY WE HAD DIED WITH KORAH AND THE REST." Remembered Egypt as: FRUITFUL, WITH GOOD FOOD AND PLENTY TO DRINK. They feared: DYING OF THIRST ALONG WITH THEIR LIVESTOCK.	Moses' response to the grumbling: HE FELL ON HIS FACE BEFORE GOD. What did the Lord tell Moses to do? THE LORD TOLD MOSES TO SPEAK TO THE ROCK. What happened? MOSES ANGRILY SCOLDED THE ISRAELITES. HE THEN STRUCK THE ROCK. What was the Lord's response to Moses? "YOU WILL NOT ENTER CANAAN BECAUSE YOU DID NOT TRUST ME."
Grumble. Location: BETWEEN MT. HOR & THE RED SEA	The Israelites: ☐ raised voices ☐ cried out ☐ wailed ☐ grumbled ☐ complained. The Israelites blamed: ■ Moses ☐ Aaron ■ The Lord. They cried: "WHY HAVE YOU BROUGHT US HERE TO DIE? WE DETEST THIS MISERABLE FOOD." Remembered Egypt as: HAVING WATER AND FOOD. They feared: DYING OF THIRST.	Moses' response to the grumbling: The Lord's response to the grumbling: HE WAS ANGRY, AND SENT SNAKES TO KILL THEM. What happened? THEY ASKED MOSES TO PRAY FOR THEM. MOSES MADE A BRONZE SNAKE. ANYONE WHO LOOKED AT IT WOULD LIVE.

141

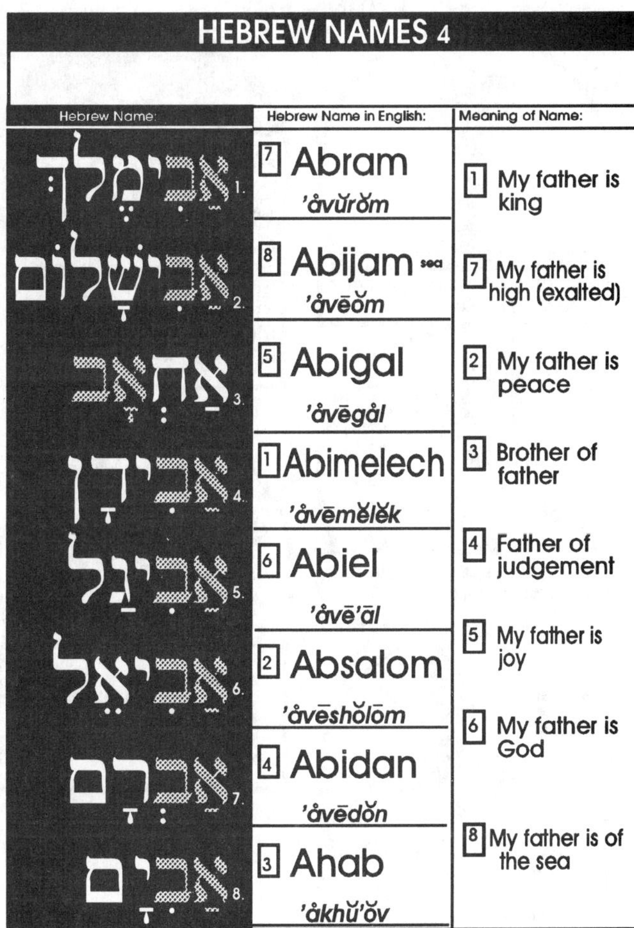

HEBREW NAMES 4

Hebrew Name:	Hebrew Name in English:	Meaning of Name:
אֲבִימֶלֶךְ 1.	7 Abram 'åvŭrŏm	1 My father is king
אֲבִישָׁלוֹם 2.	8 Abijam sea 'åvēŏm	7 My father is high (exalted)
אַחְאָב 3.	5 Abigal 'åvēgål	2 My father is peace
אֲבִידָן 4.	1 Abimelech 'åvēmĕlĕk	3 Brother of father
אֲבִיגַל 5.	6 Abiel 'åvē'ăl	4 Father of judgement
אֲבִיאֵל 6.	2 Absalom 'åvēshŏlŏm	5 My father is joy
אַבְרָם 7.	4 Abidan 'åvēdŏn	6 My father is God
אֲבִיָּם 8.	3 Ahab 'åkhŭ'ŏv	8 My father is of the sea

142

EXITING EGYPT 3

12. TABERAH. THE PEOPLE COMPLAINED AND GOD SENT A FIRE THROUGH THE CAMP.

13. KIBROTH HATTAAVAH. THE PEOPLE COMPLAINED ABOUT THE MANNA. GOD SENT QUAIL AND THEN A PLAGUE.

14. KADESH. MOSES SENT TWELVE SPIES TO EXPLORE CANAAN. ONLY TWO GAVE A GOOD REPORT.

15. KEDESH. REBELLION OF KORAH. THE EARTH OPENS UP AND SWALLOWS THEM.

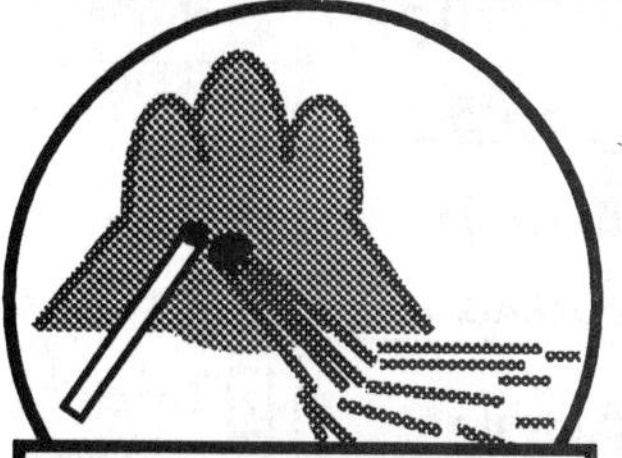

16. KADESH. MOSES DID NOT SPEAK TO THE ROCK, BUT STRUCK IT. GOD PROHIBITED MOSES FROM GOING INTO THE PROMISED LAND.

17. EDOM. EDOM WOULD NOT LET THE ISRAELITES PASS THROUGH.

143

HEBREW NAMES 5

Hebrew Name:	Hebrew Name in English:	Meaning of Name:
בַּת שֶׁבַע 1.	10 Benjamin right hand bånŭyŏmĕn	9 Mother
בַּת 2.	7 Achiam 'åkhē'ŏm	2 Daughter (Means apple of the eye.)
בֶּן עַמִּי 3.	3 Ben-Ammi bĕn 'åm(m)ē	8 Daughter Jehovah
רְאוּבֵן 4.	8 Bithiah bĭthyåh	10 Son of my right hand
בַּת שׁוּעַ 5.	6 Ben bān	3 Son of my people
בֵּן 6.	5 Bath Shua wealth båth shĕŭ'å	5 Daughter of wealth
אֲחִיאָם 7.	2 Bath båth	7 Brother of my mother
בִּתְיָה 8.	9 Ahiam 'ām	6 son (Means: builder of family name)
אֵם 9.	1 Bathsheba båth shĕvå'	1 Daughter of an oath
בִּנְיָמִין 10.	4 Reuben rŭ'ūbān	4 See a son

144

EXITING EGYPT 4

18. FROM MT. HOR TOWARDS THE RED SEA. GOD SENT SNAKES. THOSE WHO LOOKED AT THE BRONZE SNAKE LIVED.

19. ISRAEL CAMPED AT: (NU 21:10) OBOTH (21:11) IYE ABARIM (21:12) ZERED VALLEY (21:13) ARNON (21:16) BEER (21:18) MATTANAH (21:19) NAHALIEL (21:19) BAMOTH (21:20) VALLEY OF MOAB

20. MOAB BALAK TRIED TO CURSE ISRAEL BUT COULDN'T. HIS DONKEY SPOKE TO HIM.

22. ISRAEL FOUGHT:
CANAANITES FROM THE NEGEV
AMORITES (SIHON)
BASHAN (OG)
MIDIANITES

21. SHITTIM. GOD SENT A PLAGUE BECAUSE ISRAEL WORSHIPPED THE MOABITES' GODS.

145

HEBREW NAMES 6

Hebrew Name:	Hebrew Name in English:	Meaning of Name:
1. נְתַן מֶלֶךְ	5 Shemaiah *shŭmå'yŏh*	1 Given of the king
2. שִׁמְעוֹן	3 Jonathan *yŏnŏthŏn*	5 Heard by Jehovah
3. יוֹנָתָן	6 Nathan *nŏthŏn*	6 Given or gift
4. נְתַנְיָה	8 Samuel *shŭmå'āl*	8 Heard by God
5. שְׁמַעְיָה	7 Nathanel *nŭthånŭāl*	4 Given of Jehovah
6. נָתָן	2 Simeon *shŏmŏ'ōōn*	3 Jehovah-given
7. נְתַנְאֵל	4 Nethaniah *nŭthånŭyŏh*	7 Given of God
8. שְׁמוּאֵל	1 Nathan-melech *nŭthån mĕlĕk*	2 Hearing

146

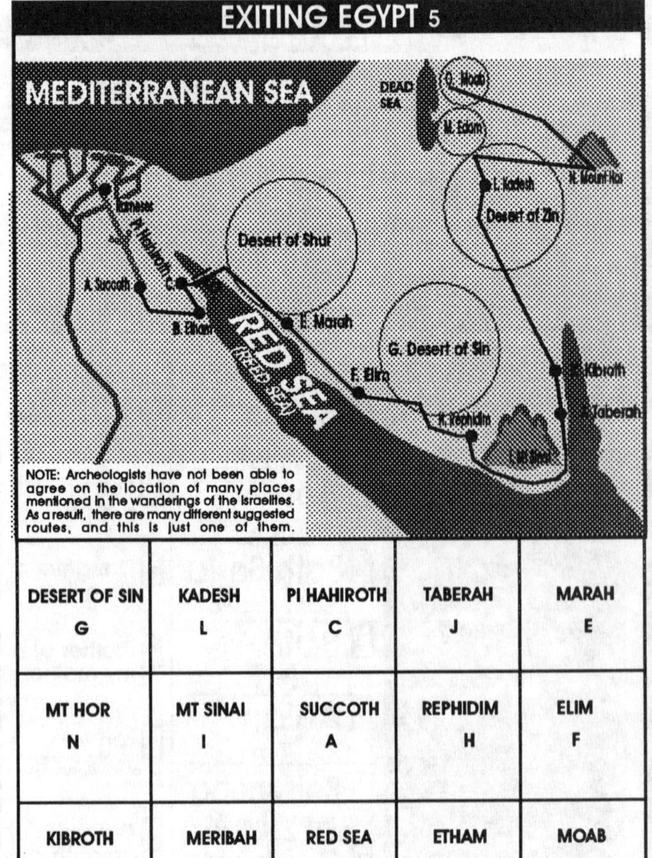

EXITING EGYPT 5

NOTE: Archeologists have not been able to agree on the location of many places mentioned in the wanderings of the Israelites. As a result, there are many different suggested routes, and this is just one of them.

DESERT OF SIN G	KADESH L	PI HAHIROTH C	TABERAH J	MARAH E
MT HOR N	MT SINAI I	SUCCOTH A	REPHIDIM H	ELIM F
KIBROTH K	MERIBAH M	RED SEA D	ETHAM B	MOAB O

147

HEBREW NAMES 7

Hebrew Name:	Hebrew Name in English:	Meaning of Name:
1. אֲחִירָם	5 Ahimelech *'åkhēmĕlĕkh*	3 People of God
2. עַמְרָם	1 Ahiram *'åkhērŏm*	1 My brother is high (exalted)
3. עַמִּיאֵל	8 Eliam *'ĕlē'ŏm*	6 Brother of Jehovah.
4. אַחְאָב	2 Amram *'åmŭrŏm*	8 God of my people
5. אֲחִימֶלֶךְ	7 Lo-ammi *lō' 'åmē*	4 Brother of father
6. אֲחִיָּהוּ	3 Ammiel *'åmĭ'āl*	5 Brother of king
7. לֹא עַמִּי	6 Ahjah *'åkhēŏhū*	7 Not my people
8. אֱלִיעָם	4 Ahab *'åkhŭ'ŏv*	2 People are high

153

GOD'S CARE OF HIS CHOSEN CHILDREN

Read Deuteronomy 1

1. The book of Deuteronomy states that Moses spoke these words to all of Israel in the fortieth year, on the first day of the eleventh month. What is the significance of this day? (Numbers 14:26-35.) GOD HAD SAID THEY WOULD WANDER 40 YEARS AND ALL THOSE OVER 20 WOULD DIE BEFORE THE REST WOULD BE ABLE TO ENTER CANAAN.

2. Which two men over 60 would be able to go into the promised land? Why? (Numbers 14:28-38) CALEB AND JOSHUA--BECAUSE THEY GAVE A GOOD REPORT.

Read Deuteronomy 2,3

3. How do we know that God cared for the other descendants of Abraham's family? (Look at *The Family Tree of Abraham*.) HE GAVE THEM THEIR OWN LANDS, AND ISRAEL WAS NOT TO TAKE THEM.

4. What command did Moses give when he gave land to the tribes of Reuben, Gad, and Manasseh? FIGHT ALONGSIDE ISRAEL UNTIL ALL HAD THEIR LAND.

5. When Moses prayed to be able to go into the promised land, what did Lord say? NO. STOP TALKING ABOUT IT. BUT I WILL LET YOU SEE THE LAND.

Read Deuteronomy 7,8

6. What did God tell the Israelites to do with the nations in the land they were to possess? DESTROY THEM TOTALLY WITH ALL THEIR ALTARS AND IDOLS.

7. What were the Israelites to remember when they felt the nations were too strong? REMEMBER WHAT GOD DID TO PHARAOH AND EGYPT.

8. There is much debate over the locations of the cities and landmarks on the route the Israelites took when they left Egypt. There are over six possible locations for Mount Sinai. Archeologists have found very little evidence of the Israelites' stay in the desert. What does Dt 8:4 have to do with it? THEY DID NOT LEAVE WORN OUT CLOTHES--THE CLOTHES DID NOT WEAR OUT.

9. When did Jesus quote Dt 8:3 b? See Matthew 4:1-11? WHEN SATAN TEMPTED JESUS TO TURN ROCKS INTO BREAD.

10. What were some of the reasons God's people forget Him in 'good times'? THEY MAY BECOME SATISFIED AND PROUD AND FEEL LIKE THEY BECAME RICH BY THEIR OWN STRENGTH.

HEBREW NAMES 8

Hebrew Name:	Hebrew Name in English:	Meaning of Name:
1. בית הערבה	5 Bethlehem *bāyth lĕkhĕm*	7 House of God
2. באר לחיראי	7 Bethel *bāyth 'āl*	1 House of the Desert
3. בית עדן	4 Beth Shalom *bāyth shŏlōm*	2 Well of the living One, my seer
4. בית שלום	2 Beer la Choy Roiy (living One) *bŭ'ār låkhåyr'ē*	3 House of pleasure
5. בית לחם	1 Beth Ha-Arabah (the) *bāyth hŏ'ārŏvŏh*	4 House of peace
6. בית הרם	8 Beer-shebah *bŭ'ār shĕvå'*	5 House of bread
7. בית אל	6 Betharam *bāyth hŏrŏm*	6 House is high
8. באר שבע	3 Beth Eden *bāyth 'ādĕn*	8 Well of oath

DEUTERONOMY AND THE TEN COMMANDMENTS 1

Read Deuteronomy 4,5,6

1. What did the Israelites see and hear when God gave the Ten Commandments? THEY SAW FIRE, BLACK CLOUDS AND DARKNESS. THEY HEARD GOD'S VOICE AND HIS WORDS.

2. What did they not see? THEY SAW NO FORM OF GOD.

3. Why is God above all other gods? (Dt 5:32-35) HE IS THE ONLY ONE WHO TOOK A NATION OUT OF ANOTHER NATION BY MIRACLES, WAR AND POWER.

NOTE: When the Bible goes over the same subject several times it means it is of great importance and you should take notice. Compare the Ten Commandments in Deuteronomy 5 with those in Exodus 20.

4. What is the reason stated in Exodus 20 for keeping the Sabbath? Ex 20:11 THE LORD RESTED ON THE SEVENTH DAY AFTER CREATING THE WORLD.

5. What is the reason stated in Deuteronomy 5 for keeping the Sabbath? Dt 5:15 GOD FREED THE ISRAELITES FROM SLAVERY IN EGYPT.

6. What additional promise does of Dt 5:16 have when compared with Ex 20:12? THAT IT MAY GO WELL WITH YOU.

7. How do the 'You shall not covet...' verses compare? EX. MENTIONED THE HOUSE FIRST, DT MENTIONED THE WIFE FIRST AND ALSO INCLUDED THE LAND.

8. Did the two tablets include all the laws or just the 10 Commandments? 10 COMMANDMENTS

9. This is the only time God spoke to a large group of people. Why? THE PEOPLE WERE AFRAID AND ASKED MOSES TO BE THE MEDIATOR.

10. How did God say He would communicate to them from now on? Dt 18:16-20 HE WOULD ONLY SPEAK TO THEM THROUGH PROPHETS.

11. What did God say He wanted from His people? Write out Dt 5:29. OH THAT THEIR HEARTS WOULD BE INCLINED TO FEAR ME AND KEEP ALL MY COMMANDMENTS ALWAYS, SO THAT IT MAY GO WELL WITH THEM AND THEIR CHILDREN.

12. Write out Dt 6:4-7. Underline the verse Jesus quoted as the most important commandment. Mark 12:29,30

HEAR O ISRAEL: THE LORD OUR GOD THE LORD IS ONE. LOVE THE LORD YOUR GOD WITH ALL YOUR HEART AND WITH ALL YOUR SOUL AND WITH ALL YOUR STRENGTH. THESE COMMANDMENTS THAT I GIVE YOU TODAY ARE TO BE UPON YOUR HEARTS. IMPRESS THEM ON YOUR CHILDREN. TALK ABOUT THEM WHEN YOU SIT AT HOME AND WHEN YOU WALK ON THE ROAD, WHEN YOU LIE DOWN AND WHEN YOU GET UP.

13. Summarize what parents are to say to their son when he asks, 'What is the meaning of the laws the Lord our God has commanded you?' GOD SAVED US FROM EGYPT AND GAVE US THESE COMMANDS SO WE MIGHT FEAR THE LORD AND PROSPER. ANSWERS MAY VARY.

DEUTERONOMY AND THE TEN COMMANDMENTS 2

Deuteronomy means: 'the second law giving'

1. God was going to drive out strong nations to give the land to the Israelites because ☐ the Israelites were so righteous. ■ the other nations were so wicked.

2. How did the Israelites first receive the Ten Commandments? Review Ex 20 ☐ On stone tablets. ■ Directly from the mouth of God. ☐ From Moses who heard them from God.

3. What did the Israelites do during the short time (40 days) that Moses was on Mt. Sinai? MADE AND WORSHIPPED AN IDOL

4. Do you think you would have listened and obeyed if you had heard the voice of God speaking to you? Explain. ANSWERS WILL VARY

5. What do we learn about human nature from the actions of the Israelites? ANSWERS WILL VARY: FORGETFULNESS, IMPATIENCE, UNFAITHFULNESS, ETC.

6. What did the Lord want to do to the Israelites? DESTROY THEM

7. How long without food or water did Moses pray begging God not to destroy the people? 40 DAYS AND NIGHTS Did God listen to him? YES

8. In Exodus 32, did Aaron take part in making the golden calf? YES

9. Did Aaron admit to his part in making the idol? NO How did he say it was made? HE THREW GOLD EARRINGS IN THE FIRE AND OUT CAME THE CALF!

10. Was God angry with Aaron? YES How angry was God? ENOUGH TO KILL HIM. Why did God not do it? BECAUSE MOSES PRAYED FOR HIM.

11. Moses mentions other times the Israelites made God angry. Moses describes them as ☐ uninformed ■ not trusting God ☐ weak ■ disobedient ■ rebellious ☐ poor

12. Who chiseled out the second set of stone tablets? MOSES Who wrote the Ten Commandments on the tablets? THE LORD

13. From Dt 10:12-13 write what God asks of us. TO FEAR THE LORD, TO WALK IN ALL HIS WAYS, TO LOVE HIM, TO SERVE HIM WITH ALL YOUR HEART AND SOUL, AND TO OBSERVE THE LORD'S COMMANDS AND DECREES FOR OUR OWN GOOD.

14. Dt 10:17-19 is gives two reasons for kindness to foreigners: 1. *God's attitude* - God LOVES the alien, giving him FOOD and CLOTHES. 2. *Man's experience* - The Israelites know what it is like because they WERE aliens in EGYPT.

15. Does God listen to the prayers of righteous people when they pray for God to show mercy to the wicked? YES Are there people in your life or country that you want God to show mercy to? ____ Who are they? Why do they need God's mercy?

ANSWERS MAY VARY

A SIGN ON YOUR HAND AND FOREHEAD 1

Answer sheet

This observance will be for you like a sign on your hand and a reminder on your forehead that the law of the Lord is to be on your lips. For the Lord brought you out of Egypt with a mighty hand. Exodus 13: 9 NIV

In days to come, when your son asks you, 'What does this mean?' say to him, 'With a mighty hand the Lord brought us out of Egypt, out of the land of slavery. When Pharaoh stubbornly refused to let us go, the Lord killed every firstborn in Egypt, both man and animal. This is why I sacrifice to the Lord the first male offspring of every womb and redeem each of my firstborn sons.' And it will be like a sign on your hand and a symbol on your forehead that the Lord brought us out of Egypt with His mighty hand. Exodus 13:14-16 NIV

Be careful, or you will be enticed to turn away and worship other gods and bow down to them. Then the Lord's anger will burn against you, and He will shut the heavens so that it will not rain and the ground will yield no produce, and you will soon perish from the good land the Lord is giving you. Fix these words of Mine in your hearts and minds; tie them as symbols on your hands and bind them on your foreheads. Deut. 11:16-18 NIV

Then the Lord said to Moses, "Speak to the Israelites and say to them: 'Throughout the generations to come you are to make tassels on the corners of your garments, with a blue cord on each tassel. You will have the tassels to look at and so you will remember all the commands of the Lord... Numbers 15:37-39 NIV

BIBLICAL WOMEN'S NAMES

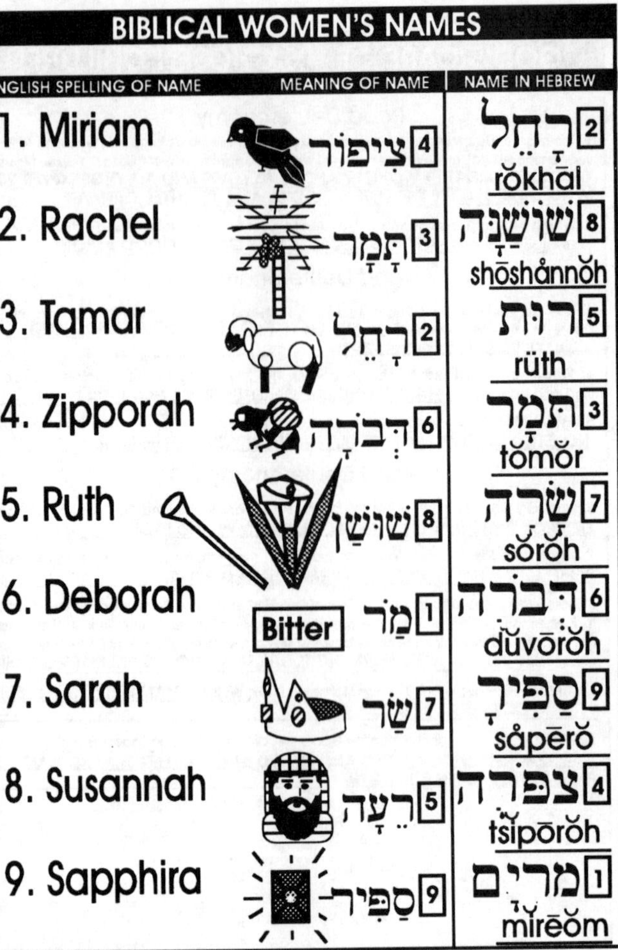

LOVING THE LORD

Read Deuteronomy 11. Fill in the blanks.

LOVE the Lord your God and KEEP His requirements, His decrees, His laws and His commands always. Dt 11: 1

Jesus said: (John 14:15) *"If you LOVE Me, you will DO what I command."*
(John 14:24) *"He who does not LOVE Me will not OBEY My teaching."*
(John 14:31) *"I LOVE the Father and ... I DO exactly what My Father has commanded Me."*

1. Tell about a relationship of yours in which love was the motivation for obedience. ANSWERS WILL VARY
2. Moses keeps telling the Israelites that it was not their CHILDREN but their OWN EYES that saw all the powerful things God had done.
3. What kind of land was God giving to them? (Verses 9-11) A LAND FLOWING WITH MILK AND HONEY
4. List as many things as you can from this chapter that God promised to do if the people were faithful to Him. ANSWERS WILL VARY BUT COULD INCLUDE: STRENGTH TO TAKE OVER THE LAND, LONG LIFE, FERTILE LAND, PLENTY OF RAIN, GOOD HARVESTS AND GRASS FOR CATTLE, SATISFACTION, VICTORY OVER LARGER NATIONS, HUGE TERRITORY, THE RESPECT OF OTHER NATIONS.
5. Fill in the blanks:
   Dt 11:8: OBSERVE *therefore all the* COMMANDS *I am giving you today.*
   Dt 11:13: *So if you* FAITHFULLY OBEY *the* COMMANDS *I am giving you...*
   Dt 11:16: BE CAREFUL, *or you will be enticed to turn...*
   Dt 11:22: *If you* CAREFULLY OBSERVE *all these* COMMANDS *I am giving you...*
   Dt 11:32: BE SURE *that you* OBEY *all the* DECREES *and* LAWS *I am setting before you today.*
6. Why does Moses emphasize this topic? ANSWERS MAY VARY
7. What can you and your family do to remind yourselves to follow the Lord? ANSWERS MAY VARY

Read chapters 12-13. Check all the correct answers.

8. God would choose a place in the land to put His Name. There they were to bring ■ burnt offerings ■ sacrifices ■ tithes ■ special gifts ■ things vowed ■ freewill offerings ■ firstborn of herds & flocks
9. In God's chosen place they were to ☐ mourn and fast ■ rejoice ■ eat and enjoy some of the offerings ■ share with the Levites
10. They were to worship ☐ as the local nations did ■ only as the Lord commanded ☐ as they pleased ☐ sacrificing animals in every town ■ presenting offerings only in the place God chose
11. They were to eat meat ☐ only at festivals ☐ only in the place God chose ■ only if drained of blood ■ any time ■ anywhere ■ as much as they wanted
12. Which of the following were the Israelites to listen to if the message was, 'Let us follow other gods'? ☐ A prophet ☐ One who foretells by dreams ☐ One doing miraculous signs (to prove his spiritual authority) ☐ Your brother ☐ Your son ☐ Your daughter ☐ Your wife ☐ Your closest friend ☐ A whole town ■ No one

Read chapter 14. Fill in the blanks. Check all the correct answers.

Dt 14:1-2 *You are the* CHILDREN *of the Lord your God. You are a* PEOPLE HOLY *to the Lord. The Lord has chosen you to be His* TREASURED POSSESSION.

13. You should eat ☐ anything you like ■ no detestable thing ■ any clean creature ☐ animals found dead
14. One tenth of all that your fields produce each year you should ☐ sell ☐ save for hard times ■ set aside ■ eat in the presence of the Lord ■ share with the Levites ☐ give to the king ☐ offer as a burnt offering
15. Every third year the tithe is to be ■ stored in towns ☐ sold to highest bidder ☐ burnt on a altar ■ given away
16. God said He would bless all their work if they give the third-year tithe to ☐ the king ■ the Levites ■ orphans ■ widows ■ aliens ☐ oppressors ☐ the important people ☐ the powerful people ☐ the rich

THE LAW OF JUSTICE AND MERCY 1

He has showed you, O man, what is good. And what does the Lord require of you? To act justly and to love mercy and to walk humbly with your God. Micah 6:8

Read Deuteronomy 15-19. On the lines write the reference for each topic. You may use a single verse or group of verses. Then decide if the law fulfills one of the three requirements of the Lord and write a letter in the box: J= JUSTICE, M= MERCY, W= WALKING with your God, and O=OTHER (any not filling the three requirements.)
NOTE: Answers may vary. Be ready to give a reason for your choice.

15:1-6 [M] Cancel debts every 7 years.
15:7-11 [M] Lend freely to the poor.
15:12-18 [M] Free slaves/servants every 7 years.
16:18-20 [J] Judges should not accept bribes.
17:2-5 [J] Thoroughly investigate and prove wrongdoing before punishing.
17:6-7 [J] There must be more than one witness.

17:8-13 [J] Contempt of court (of a judge or a priest) is forbidden.
Tell how this law is related to the incident in Acts 23:1-5. PAUL CALLS ANANIAS A WHITEWASHED WALL, BUT WHEN HE FINDS IT IS THE HIGH PRIEST, HE APOLOGIZES.

17:14-15 [O] No foreigner may be king of Israel.
17:18-20 [W] The king must make a copy of the Law for himself and read it daily.
17:20 [M] The king must not consider himself better than the rest of the people.

18:1-8 [M] The Israelites are to give to the Levites so that they may minister.
Tell how Nehemiah dealt with this law in Nehemiah 13:10-13. WHEN THE PORTIONS WERE NOT GIVEN TO THE LEVITES & SINGERS, THEY HAD TO DO WORK IN THEIR FIELDS. NEHEMIAH MADE JUDAH BRING THEIR TITHES SO THE LEVITES AND SINGERS COULD GET BACK TO MINISTRY.

18:9-13 [W] Divination, witchcraft, and consulting the dead are detestable.
How did King Saul respond to this law in 1 Samuel 28:4-10? WHEN SAUL COULD GET NO ANSWER FROM GOD, HE WENT TO A MEDIUM EVEN THOUGH HE KNEW IT WAS AGAINST GOD'S LAW.
How did King Josiah respond in 2 Kings 23:24-25? JOSIAH GOT RID OF ALL THE MEDIUMS AND SPRITISTS AND TURNED TO GOD AND THE LAW OF MOSES WITH HIS WHOLE HEART.

18:14-22 [W] A prophet of God will be recognized when his prophecies come true.
Explain the basis for Micaiah's parting remarks in 2 Chronicles 18:11-16 & 27. IF THE KING RETURNED SAFELY, THEN MICAIAH'S PROPHECY WAS NOT TRUE, AND HE WOULD NOT BE A TRUE PROPHET OF GOD.

19:1-14 [M] Cities of refuge are to protect those who accidentally kill someone.
19:15-21 [J] If one accuses another maliciously and falsely, give him the punishment he sought for the other.

THE LAW OF JUSTICE AND MERCY 2

20:1-4 [W] Trust in God; do not fear when facing an enemy stronger than you.
Read 2 Chr 14:9-12 and tell how King Asa responded to this instruction. ASA TURNED TO GOD FOR HELP AND GOD HELPED HIM CRUSH HIS ENEMIES.

20:5-9 [M] Men who are engaged are excused from military service.
20:10-15 [M] Offer peace first when you march against a city.
20:16-18 [O] Annihilate everything in the cities of your inheritance.
20:19-20 [M] Don't destroy fruit trees when you lay seige to a city.
21:1-9 [J] Innocent blood must be atoned for even if the murderer is unknown.
21:10-14 [M] You may marry a captive woman, and you must treat her well.
21:15-17 [J] You must not change the rules of inheritance for a favorite son.
21:18-21 [J] A stubborn, rebellious son must be killed.

21:23 [O] Anyone hung on a tree is under God's curse.
Relate this curse to the crucifixion of Jesus. See Gal 3:13-14 JESUS REDEEMED US FROM THE CURSE BY BECOMING A CURSE FOR US AND BRINGING US BLESSING.

22:28-29 [M] A man who rapes a girl who is not engaged must give money to the girl's father, marry the girl, and never divorce her.
Read Le 18:11 and 2 Sa 13:1-22. List the laws that Amnon broke. AMNON RAPED A GIRL, HAD SEXUAL RELATIONS WITH THE DAUGHTER OF HIS FATHER (HIS HALF-SISTER), DID NOT GIVE THE FATHER MONEY, AND DID NOT MARRY THE GIRL.
What did Tamar mean by what she said in verse 16? SHE WANTED AMNON TO MARRY HER AS THE LAW SAID, BUT HE WOULD NOT.

23:12-14 [O] Dig a hole to bury your excrement; keep the camp clean.
23:15 [M] Do not return a run-away slave to his master.

23:25 [M] You may pick a neighbor's grain with your hands (to snack on), but do not use a sickle (and carry grain away).
In Matthew 12:1-2, the Pharisees do not accuse the disciples of theft. Why? IT WAS LEGAL TO PICK GRAIN WITH YOUR HANDS AND EAT IT.

What is the accusation? BREAKING THE SABBATH. Review the Sabbath pages and explain why. IT WAS AGAINST ONE OF THEIR LAWS ABOUT NOT REAPING ON THE SABBATH.

HISTORY OF NAMES 1

Laws prohibited Jews from using non-Jewish names in Prussia, Bohemia, and Tsarist Russia. Then when the Nazi Party took over Germany, a decree in 1938 said Jews must name their children from a list of 276 names. This would let everyone know from just the name that the child was Jewish. In case there was any doubt, every boy had to use the middle name 'Israel', and every girl's middle name had to be 'Sarah'.

From the list, 185 were boys' names, and 91 names were for girls. Among the names that could be used were names that were humiliating, ludicrous, or disgraceful. Figure out why parents would not want to use these names from the list.

(1 Kings 16:30) AHAB	God of Assyria, who deported the Israelites.
(Esther 1:1) AHASUERUS or XERXES	Evil king of Israel.
(Genesis 25:24-2) ESAU	Evil queen of Judah (daughter of Ahab).
(2 Kings 16:10) ASSUR	Leader of a rebellion against Moses.
(Numbers 16) KORAH	Nephew of Abraham who had children with his daughters.
(Genesis 29:15-30) LABAN	The father-in-law of Jacob who cheated him many times.
(Genesis 19:30-38) LOT	Evil queen of Israel.
(Psalms 83:5-8) MOAB	Twin brother of Jacob whose descendants were at odds with the Israelites.
(2 Kings 11:1-4) ATHALIAH	Lot's descendants sided with Assyria against Israel.
(1 Kings 18:19) JEZEBEL	Persian king how ruled over Israel.

Cut out CAN YOU FIND THE FIFTH PIG? On History of Names 2.

1. Fold on the lines so the lines '1' and '2' touch the middle over the center line marked '1 2.'

CAN YOU FIND THE FIFTH PIG?
Glue only center square here. Make sure it can be opened and closed.

2. Fold in the other direction so that the lines 'a' and 'b' touch on the center line marked 'a b.'

3. It will make a face. Who is it?

THE LAW OF JUSTICE AND MERCY 3

24:5 [M] A recently married man is exempt from military service for a year.

24:14-15 [M] Pay a poor, hired man every day or he may cry out to God and you will be guilty of sin.
What does this law show about God's heart? GOD CARES ABOUT THE POOR AND HUNGRY.
James wrote to some Christians thousands of years later. In fact it was after Jesus died and rose from the dead. Was this law still important then? (See James 5:1-6) YES

24:19-22 [M] When you harvest, leave some produce for the alien, the fatherless, and the widow. Remember that you were slaves in Egypt.
What does this law show about God's heart? GOD CARES ABOUT FOREIGNERS, WIDOWS AND ORPHANS. WWW
Describe Boaz' actions in Ruth 2 compared with the law above. HE DID MORE THAN THE LAW SAID BY PROTECTING RUTH, LEAVING EXTRA GRAIN, AND FEEDING HER.

25:1-3 [M] Do not degrade a guilty man by flogging him with more than 40 lashes.
How careful were the Jews to obey this command even centuries later in the time of the Apostle Paul? (See 2 Corinthians 11:24) THEY WERE SO CAREFUL THAT THEY DID NOT GIVE A MAN 40 LASHES, BUT ONLY 39.

25:5-10 [M] If a man dies without an heir, his brother should marry the widow; their first son will carry the dead brother's name. Have a 'Sandal Ceremony' for the man who won't do his duty to his brother.
This law will help you understand the story of Ruth. How had the 'Sandal Ceremony' changed over the years? (Ruth 4:1-10) FROM BEING A 'SHAME ON YOU' SIGN TO A SIGN OF AN AGREEMENT THAT ONE MAN WAS TAKING ON THE DUTIES OF ANOTHER
Read Matthew 22:23-30. Why would one woman marry seven brothers, one after the other? IN ORDER TO HAVE AN HEIR IN THE NAME OF HER FIRST HUSBAND, AS PROVIDED FOR IN THE LAW.

25:13-16 [J] Have accurate, honest measurements; God detests the dishonest.
26:1-11 [W] Remember God's awesome acts when you offer your firstfruits.
26:16-19 [W] Obey the Lord with all your heart and soul, and walk in His ways.

27:1-7 [W] When you cross the Jordan, set up large stones; write the Law on them.
Check Joshua 8:30-35 to see when this was done. SOON AFTER CROSSING THE JORDAN
Who participated? JOSHUA AND ALL THE PEOPLE OF ISRAEL, ALIENS, CITIZENS, ELDERS, OFFICIALS, JUDGES, PRIESTS, MEN, WOMEN, AND CHILDREN.

THE LAW OF JUSTICE AND MERCY 4

27:9-26 [O] The people must recite the curses for disobeying the Law.
28:1-14 [M] God promised blessing upon blessing for careful obedience.

28:15-68 [M] God warned of many dreadful curses on the people for disobedience.
Why did Josiah tear his robes when he read the long-lost Book of the Law? 2 Kings 22:11-13 HE WAS VERY UPSET BECAUSE HE LEARNED OF ALL THE CURSES THAT WOULD COME ON THEM BECAUSE THE PEOPLE HAD FORSAKEN THE LORD'S WAYS.

29:1-29 [J] Abandoning the Lord will bring disaster on the land.
30:1-10 [M] If people return to the Lord, He will have compassion and bless them.

30:11-14 [O] The word is not difficult or far away but in your mouth and heart.
What 'word' was Moses talking about? THE LAW OF THE LORD
In Romans 10:6-9, what 'word' is Paul talking about? THE GOOD NEWS OF SALVATION IN JESUS

31:6 [M] Do not be afraid of your enemies; the Lord will never leave you.
Hebrews 13:5-6 states this promise with just a slight variation. What is the difference? GOD WILL TAKE CARE OF US FINANCIALLY AND WE ARE NOT TO BE AFRAID OF WHAT LIFE BRINGS. CONTRASTING POWER OF GOD WITH WEAKNESS OF MAN

31:9-13 [W] Moses told the priests to assemble the people every 7 years and to read the whole Law to them.
What happened when the people listened to the reading of the law? Nehemiah 9:3 THEY SPENT A LOT OF TIME CONFESSING THEIR SINS AND WORSHIPING GOD.

...I have set before you LIFE *and* DEATH*,*
BLESSINGS *and* CURSES*.*
Now choose LIFE*,*
so that you and your CHILDREN *may live*
and that you may LOVE *the Lord your God,*
LISTEN *to his voice, and* HOLD *fast to him.*
For the Lord is your LIFE*...*

Dt 30:19-20

BROUGHT TO YOU BY THE NUMBER FORTY

Ge 7:17 For **40** days the FLOOD kept coming on the earth; the ARK was lifted above the earth.

Ge 25:20 And ISAAC was **40** years old when he married REBEKAH.

Ge 50:2-3 It took **40** days to embalm JACOB.

Ex 16:35 The Israelites ate MANNA **40** years, until they came to the land of Canaan.

Ex 34:27, 28 And MOSES was on Mount Sinai with the Lord **40** days and **40** nights; he neither ATE bread, nor DRANK water. And he wrote on the tablets the 10 Commandments.

Dt 29:5 God led the Israelites **40** years through the DESERT; their CLOTHES and their SANDALS did not wear out.

Jos 4:13 About **40** thousand soldiers crossed the Jordan to the plains of JERICHO for WAR.

Jdg 3:11 And the land had PEACE **40** years while OTHNIEL was judge.

Jdg 5:1, 31 DEBORAH and Barak sang: "May all Your ENEMIES perish, O Lord: but may they who love You be like the sun." And the land had PEACE **40** years.

Jdg 8:28 During GIDEON'S lifetime, the land enjoyed PEACE **40** years.

Jdg 13:1 The ISRAELITES did evil in the eyes of the Lord, and He delivered them over to the PHILISTINES for **40** years.

1 Sa 4:17, 18 When the messenger told the fate of the ARK of God, ELI fell backward off the seat. He BROKE his neck, and died; for he was an old man, and heavy. He had led Israel **40** years.

2 Sa 5:4 DAVID was thirty years old when he became king, and he REIGNED **40** years.

1 Ki 6:14, 17 Solomon built the TEMPLE, and the main hall was **40** cubits long.

1 Ki 11:42 SOLOMON reigned in Jerusalem over all Israel **40** years.

1 Ki 19:2, 7, 8 JEZEBEL sent a message to ELIJAH that she was going to kill him. An angel fed him; and strengthened by the food, he TRAVELED **40** days and **40** nights to HOREB, the mount of God.

2 Chr 24:1 JOSIAH was seven when he became king, and he REIGNED **40** years in Jerusalem.

Jn 3:4 JONAH entered the city and proclaimed, "40 days and NINEVEH will be destroyed."

Mt 4:2 After FASTING **40** days and **40** nights, Jesus was hungry.

Mk 1:13 Jesus was in the DESERT **40** days, tempted by SATAN.

Jn 2:20 The Jews said, "It took **40** and six years to build this TEMPLE and You will raise it in 3 days?"

Ac 23:21 Paul was a prisoner, and more than **40** men were waiting in AMBUSH to kill him.

2 Col 11:24 Paul said he had FIVE times received from the Jews **40** LASHES minus one.

MOSES' LAST DAYS

Deuteronomy 31 Moses says 'Goodbye'

Read and fill in the blanks.

1. How old was Moses as he spoke to the Israelites for the last time? 120
2. Two reasons Moses gave for handing over leadership were: "I am no longer able to LEAD you," and "The Lord told me, 'You shall not CROSS the JORDAN.'"
3. Who would go with them? Dt 31:3 The LORD your GOD HIMSELF will cross over ahead of you.
4. In the presence of all ISRAEL Moses told Joshua that he was the one who must lead them.
5. He also gave the written LAW to the PRIESTS and entrusted them with the job of teaching it to the people and to future generations.
6. God told Moses that soon after his death, the people would begin worshiping the foreign GODS of the land and break the COVENANT He had made with them. God gave Moses a SONG to write down and teach the people for a WITNESS for God against the Israelites.

Deuteronomy 32 'The Song of Moses'

Each paragraph of the song is summarized in a sentence in the following exercise, but the lines are out of order. Read each paragraph and write its reference in the blank next to the summary.

7-9 Remember what God has done.
3-4 The Lord is great!
39-42 There is no god but the Lord.
13-14 God gave food and drink to Israel.
43 God will make atonement for His people.
15-18 The people made God jealous with idols.
36-38 God will judge them and have compassion, too.
19-22 God rejected them and will make them envious.
23-27 God will send famine, plague, beasts, and war against them.
28-33 Israel is foolish and doesn't realize that they can't succeed without God.

34-35 God must repay them.
1-2 Listen to my teaching.
10-13 God led Israel and cared for him.
5-6 His people have done great wrong.

Deuteronomy 33 'The Blessings of Moses'

Each paragraph of Dt 33 is summarized by one line in the following exercise, but the lines are out of order. Read the paragraphs and fill in the blanks. Remember that the tribe of Joseph includes Manasseh and Ephraim.

The LORD appeared at Sinai. He loves the PEOPLE.
ZEBULUN and ISSACHAR will be made rich by the sea.
GAD gets a lion's share. He carried out the Lord's will.
May REUBEN live and not die.
DAN is like a lion's cub from Bashan.
ASHER is most blessed with favor, wealth, and strength.
May God bless LEVI'S skills. He valued God's word over his own kin.
May JOSEPH'S land be blessed. He will conquer nations.
May God help JUDAH against his foes.
NAPHTALI will be full of God's blessing.
May BENJAMIN rest securely.
ISRAEL is blessed to have such a great God, their shield, helper and sword.
The tribe of SIMEON is not mentioned at all. (Check tribes on "Organization of the Camp.")

Deuteronomy 34 The Death of Moses

After instructing and encouraging the people, Moses climbed Mount Nebo. Tell of Moses' last day.

ANSWERS MAY VARY

Why did the Israelites begin to listen to Joshua? HE WAS FILLED WITH THE SPIRIT OF WISDOM BECAUSE MOSES HAD LAID HIS HANDS ON HIM.

Moses was unique. *Since then, no* PROPHET *has risen in Israel like* MOSES *whom the Lord knew* FACE *to* FACE, *who did all those* MIRACULOUS *signs and* WONDERS. Dt 34:10-11 NIV

BLESSINGS OF JACOB AND MOSES

ANSWERS MAY VARY DEPENDING ON WHAT SIMILARITIES A PERSON SEES OR INFERS.

BIRTH ORDER, NAMES, *meanings*	JACOB'S BLESSINGS FROM GENESIS 48:15-49:28
SONS OF LEAH	
1. Reuben *See, a son*	☐ You defiled my bed and will no longer excel. MAY REUBEN LIVE AND NOT DIE.
2. Simeon *One who hears*	☐ For your violence you will be scattered in Israel. NOT MENTIONED
3. Levi *Attached*	☐ For your violence you will be scattered in Israel. GOD BLESS LEVI'S SKILLS; VALUED GOD'S WORD OVER KIN.
4. Judah *Praise*	☐ Your brothers will praise you, and you will rule. MAY GOD HELP JUDAH AGAINST HIS FOES.
SONS OF BILHAH (RACHEL'S MAID)	
5. Dan *Vindicated*	■ You will provide justice, yet be like a viper. DAN IS LIKE A LION'S CUB FROM BASHAN.
6. Naphtali *My struggle*	☐ You will be like a doe set free. NAPHTALI WILL BE FULL OF GOD'S BLESSING.
SONS OF ZILPAH (LEAH'S MAID)	
7. Gad *Good fortune (or a troop)*	☐ You will be attacked, but will attack back. GAD GETS A LION'S SHARE. HE DID THE LORD'S WILL.
8. Asher *Happy*	■ You will have rich food and supply kings. MOST BLESSED WITH FAVOR, WEALTH & STRENGTH.
SONS OF LEAH	
9. Issachar *Reward*	☐ You will have pleasant land, but do forced labor. YOU WILL BE MADE RICH BY THE SEA.
10. Zebulun *Honor*	■ You will live by the sea and have harbors. YOU WILL BE MADE RICH BY THE SEA.
SONS OF RACHEL	
11. Joseph *May he add*	■ God will bless you with all kinds of blessings. LAND BE BLESSED, CONQUER NATIONS
11 a. Manasseh *Forget (trouble)*	■ God will bless you and make you great. Dt 33:17 Manasseh would number in the THOUSANDS
11 b. Ephraim *Twice fruitful*	■ God will bless you and make you greater. Dt 33:17 Ephraim would number in the TENS OF THOUSANDS
12. Benjamin (Ben-Oni) *Son of my right hand (Son of my trouble)*	☐ You are like a ravenous wolf. MAY BENJAMIN REST SECURELY

NUMBERS-TALLY IT UP

The book of Numbers is named after the fact that during it the Israelites were numbered or counted. NOTE: Only the men were counted, so the Israelites were many times larger then the numbers show.

NOTE: NAMES ARE NOT IN ORDER FOUND IN THE BIBLE.	ENTERING EGYPT GENESIS 46 8-26 THESE ARE THE NUMBER OF ISRAELITE MEN WHEN THEY WENT INTO EGYPT. (COUNT ALL OF JACOB'S LIVING SONS, GRANDSONS & GREAT-GRANDSONS.)	450 YEARS LATER NUMBERS 1:17-47 THESE ARE THE NUMBER OF THE FIRST CENSUS IN THE 2ND YEAR AFTER LEAVING EGYPT.	ENTERING CANAAN NUMBERS 26:1-51,62 THESE ARE THE NUMBER OF THE 2ND CENSUS AFTER A PLAGUE KILLED 24,000.	FIGURE OUT THE GAIN OR LOSS OF PEOPLE BY SUBTRACTING THE COUNT IN NUMBERS 1 FROM THE COUNT IN NUMBERS 26.
REUBEN	5	46,500	43,730	-2,770
SIMEON	7	59,300	22,200	-37,100
LEVI	4	NOT COUNTED	NOT COUNTED	NOT COUNTED
GAD	8	45,650	40,500	-5,150
JUDAH	6 NOTE: 2 DIED BUT TWO OF PEREZ SONS COUNT AS HIS.	74,600	76,500	+1,900
ISSACHAR	5	54,400	64,300	+9,900
ZEBULUN	4	57,000	60,500	+3,500
JOSEPH – MANASSEH	3 DO NOT INCLUDE THESE 3, THEY WERE ALREADY IN EGYPT.	32,200	52,700	+20,500
JOSEPH – EPHRAIM		40,500	32,500	-8,000
BENJAMIN	11	35,400	45,400	+10,200
DAN	2	62,700	64,400	+1,700
ASHER	8	41,500	53,400	+11,900
NAPHTALI	5	53,400	45,600	-8,000
GRAND TOTAL	ADD IN JACOB, HE ALSO WENT OT EGYPT. 66	603,550	601,730	-21,820

Read Exodus 30:11-16 and write how a census was taken.

1. What was the way the Lord told Moses to take a census? EACH ONE 20 YRS OR OLDER MUST GIVE 1/2 SHEKEL, A RANSOM (OR ATONEMENT) FOR HIS LIFE AS HE IS COUNTED.
2. Why do you think that the offering was to be exactly a half shekel for each man regardless of wealth? ALL ARE OF EQUAL VALUE TO THE LORD.
3. What was the money to be used for? THE SERVICE OF THE TENT OF MEETING, MEMORIAL, ATONEMENT

Use the chart above to answer the following questions.

4. Which tribes decreased in numbers during their time in the desert? REUBEN, SIMEON, GAD, EPHRAIM, NAPHTALI
5. Which tribe lost the largest number of men? SIMEON
6. Which tribes increased in numbers during their time in the desert? JUDAH, ISSACHAR, ZEBULUN, MANASSEH, BENJAMIN, DAN, ASHER
7. Did more people come out of slavery than went into Canaan? YES

IT WOULD HAVE BEEN

It Would Have Been Enough
Song of Grateful Israelites

1. Had He brought us out of Egypt but not executed his judgment upon their gods, it would have been enough.
2. Had He executed His judgment upon their gods but not slain their first born, it would have been enough.
3. Had He slain their first born but not given us their treasures, it would have been enough.
4. Had He given us their treasures but not led us through the desert, it would have been enough.
5. Had He led us through the desert but not divided the sea, it would have been enough.
6. Had He divided the sea but not led us through on dry ground, it would have been enough.
7. Had He led through on dry ground, but not drowned our enemies, it would have been enough.
8. Had He drowned our enemies but not supplied our needs in the desert for 40 years, it would have been enough.
9. Had He supplied our needs in the wilderness but not fed us manna, it would have been enough.
10. Had He fed us manna but not brought us to Mount Sinai, it would have been enough.
11. Had He brought us to Mount Sinai but not given us His Law, it would have been enough.
12. Had He given us His Law but not brought us to the Promised Land, it would have been enough.
13. Had He brought us to the Promised Land and not built the Temple for us, it would have been enough.

It Would Have Been More Than We Deserved
Song of Grateful Christian

[5] Had He guided us through the dry desert of our lives but not provided a path through the raging waters that overwhelm the strong, it would have been more than we deserved.

[1] Had He brought us out of our bondage to sin but had not promised to execute his judgment on the gods of this world and their followers, it would have been more than we deserved.

[3] Had He promised to slay the wicked on our behalf but not given us heavenly treasures that do not decay or rust, it would have been more than we deserved.

[4] Had He given us heavenly treasures that do not decay or rust but not guided us through the hard dry desert of our lives, it would have been more than we deserved.

[2] Had He promised to execute His judgment on the on the gods of this world and their followers, but not promised to slay the wicked on our behalf, it would have been more than we deserved.

[11] Had He brought us to mountain top where we fellowship in His presence, but not fulfilled the Law and made a New Covenant, it would have been more than we deserved.

[8] Had He wash away the strongholds of our past but not supplied our daily needs through the long desert years, it would have been more than we deserved.

[9] Had He supplied our daily needs through the long desert years but not fed us living Manna, so our souls no longer hunger, it would have been more than we deserved.

[12] Had He fulfilled the Law and made a New Covenant but is not preparing a home for us in our 'Promised Land' of Heaven, it would have been more than we deserved.

[10] Had He fed us living Manna, so our souls no longer hunger but not brought us to mountain top where we fellowship in His presence, it would have been more than we deserved.

[13] If He is not preparing a home for us in our 'Promised Land' of Heaven but did not made us His Living Temple, it would have been more than we deserved.

[6] Had He provided a path through the raging waters that overwhelm the strong but not led us step-by-step through on solid ground, it would have been more than we deserved.

[7] Had He led step-by-step through on solid ground but not wash away the strongholds of our past, it would have been more than we deserved.

FROM JOSHUA THROUGH SOLOMON

Complete these exercises to get a general feel for the people and events you will encounter in Israel's history from the time Joshua led them into Canaan through the end of Solomon's reign. Circle the correct choices in each selection.

THE TIME OF JOSHUA. Read Joshua 1:4; 24:8-13. Your land will reach from the desert to (Lebanon, the Dead Sea) and from the (Euphrates, Jordan) to the Great Sea. When you crossed the (Red Sea, Jordan), many tribes fought against you, but I gave them into your hands. I sent the (storm, hornet) ahead of you which (drove them out, demolished their homes). You (did, did not) do it with your own (sword and bow, horses and chariots). I gave you a land on which you did not (step, toil) and (caves, cities) which you did not (want, build), and now you (mope, live) in them and (eat, scrounge) from vineyards and (orange, olive) groves that you did not (plant, desire).

THE TIMES OF THE JUDGES. Read Judges 2:7-23. Israel (served, rejected) the Lord throughout the lifetimes of Joshua and the (children, elders) who outlived him. Another (leader, generation) grew up who knew neither (the Lord, Joshua) nor what he had done for Israel. They (pleased, angered) the Lord by (worshiping, forsaking) Him and (destroying, serving) Baal and the Ashtoreths. In (carelessness, anger) God handed them over to raiders. They (were, were not) in great distress. Then God provided (kings, judges, soldiers) to save them from the raiders. They (would not, would) listen to the (kings, judges, soldiers), but quickly turned to other (leaders, gods). They (were not, were) like the people of Joshua's time who obeyed the Lord... They refused to give up their (evil, righteous) practices and (obedient, stubborn) ways. In (anger, delight, carelessness) God decided to leave some of the (nations, rocks and thorns) in the land. This was to (encourage, test) Israel, to see if they would (learn to farm, keep the Lord's ways).

In those days Israel had no KING*; everyone did as he* SAW FIT. Judges 21:25

Things went from bad to worse until Israel did the horrible things recorded at the end of the book of Judges. Then God made Samuel to be a judge and prophet in Israel and to begin a better era.

DEMANDING A KING. Read 1 Sam 12:8-15. The Lord sent (kings, judges) and delivered you from your enemies, but when you saw that the (king, judge) of the Ammonites was threatening you, you said, "No, we want a king!" even though (I, the Lord) was your king. Here is your king! If you and your king obey (me, the Lord), good! If not, God will be against (me, you).

THE UNITED KINGDOM.

1. King Saul 1 Sam 15:17-19, 26	2. King David 2 Sam 7:8-16	3. King Solomon 1 Kings 4:29-34; 10:23-29; 11:1-13
You were once (great, small) in your own eyes; yet God made you king over (all, some) of Israel. You have (obeyed, rejected) the word of the Lord, and the Lord has (established, rejected) you as king.	I took you from the (palace, pasture) and made you ruler over my people. I have been (with, against) you wherever you have gone, and I have (helped, cut off) all your enemies. Now I will make your name (great, a curse). I (will, will not) give Israel a home. Wicked people (will, will not) oppress them anymore. I will give you (rest, no rest) from all your enemies. Your house and your kingdom will (die out, endure forever) before Me, and your throne (will, will not) be established forever.	God made Solomon wiser than any other man. He spoke 3,000 (languages, proverbs) and made 1005 (songs, temples). He (dissected, described) plant life, animals, birds, reptiles and fish. Kings all over the world sent men to (argue with, listen to) him. He was (richer, crueler) than all the other kings. He had 1,400 (captured kings, chariots) and 12,000 (slaves, horses). He also married many (godly, foreign) wives who turned his heart (after, away from) other gods. God was (angry, pleased) with him and said He would take the (enemies, kingdom) from him. For David's sake, He would do it (immediately, later).
Saul reigned for many years after this and relentlessly hunted David who was anointed to be the next king. God withdrew from Saul and he died in battle.	David was a man after God's own heart. God enabled him to defeat the neighboring tribes who had oppressed the Israelites for hundreds of years. He wrote many of the Psalms. His descendants formed a dynasty that lasted until Judah was finally exiled to Babylon. Jesus, the eternal king would be of David's royal line.	

SIMPLE HEBREW SENTENCES 1

Read each word. Draw a line to its pronunciation and then from the pronunciation to its meaning.

He remembered	zŏkhŏr	נָתַן
He saw	nŏthăn	שָׁפַט
He heard	mŏlăk	שָׁמַע
He judged	shŏfăt	רָאָה
He ruled	rŏ'ŏh	מָלַךְ
He gave	shŏmă'	זָכַר

Written under each word and then write the number of each Hebrew sentence in the box in front of the English sentence translation.

[3] A brother heard. — 1. בֵּן זָכַר (zŏkhăr běn)

[5] A judge judged. — 2. אָב נָתַן (nŏthăn ŏv)

[6] A friend saw. — 3. אָח שָׁמַע (shŏmă' ŏkh)

[1] A son remembered. — 4. מֶלֶךְ מָלַךְ (mŏlăk mělěk)

[4] A king ruled. — 5. דָּן שָׁפַט (shŏfăt doň)

[5] A father gave. — 6. רֵעָה רָאָה (rŏ'ŏh ră'ŏh)

Write each sentence in Hebrew.

A king saw. מֶלֶךְ רָאָה

A friend heard. רֵעָה שָׁמַע

A son ruled. בֵּן מָלַךְ

A brother judged. אָח שָׁפַט

A judge remembered. דָּן זָכַר

JOSHUA'S HEART

1. Ex 17:9 The first time we meet Joshua, what is he doing? HEADING UP ISRAEL'S ARMY TO FIGHT THE AMALEKITES.
2. Ex 24:13 Where was Joshua when Moses went up Mt Sinai? HE WENT WITH HIM AS HIS AIDE.
3. Ex 32:15-17 Why did Joshua not stop the people from worshipping the golden calf? HE DIDN'T KNOW IT WAS HAPPENING. HE WAS ON THE MOUNTAIN WITH MOSES.
4. Ex 33:11 Where was Joshua when Moses went into the Tent of Meetings? IN OR NEAR THE TENT.
   What did Joshua do when Moses left the Tent of Meetings? STAYED THERE.
5. Nu 14:5-10 Who were the two men who spied out the promised land and gave a good report? JOSHUA AND CALEB
   Why did Joshua tell the people not to be afraid? THE PROTECTION OF THE CANAANITES IS GONE, BUT THE LORD IS WITH US.
6. Nu 32:11-12 Who would be spared death in the wilderness? JOSHUA AND CALEB
   Why? BECAUSE THEY HAD FOLLOWED THE LORD WHOLEHEARTEDLY.
7. De 1:38 What did the Lord instruct Moses to do? ENCOURAGE JOSHUA TO LEAD THE PEOPLE TO INHERIT THE LAND.
8. De 31:7-8 What were Moses' words of encouragement? BE STRONG AND COURAGEOUS. THE LORD GOES BEFORE YOU AND WILL NOT FORSAKE YOU.
9. De 34:9 What was Joshua's character? HE WAS FILLED WITH THE SPIRIT OF WISDOM
10. Jos 1:1,5 After Moses died what did the Lord say to Joshua? NO ONE WILL BE ABLE TO STAND UP TO YOU. AS I WAS WITH MOSES, I WILL BE WITH YOU AND NEVER FORSAKE YOU
11. Jos 2:1 Did Joshua show wisdom in sending only 2 spies to Jericho? YES Why? ANSWERS WILL VARY.
12. Jos 3:14-17 What does this story remind you of? CROSSING THE RED SEA
    Had any of these people been there at the crossing of the Red Sea? YES Who were they? THE CHILDREN UNDER 20 YRS OLD AT THE TIME & THOSE BORN LATER.
13. Jos 4:20-24 What was set up? A PILE OF STONES Why? TO TELL FUTURE GENERATIONS ABOUT GOD'S POWER SO THEY WOULD ALWAYS FEAR HIM.
14. Genesis 17:10-14 What was the purpose of circumcision? A SIGN OF THE COVENANT BETWEEN GOD AND ABRAHAM AND HIS DESCENDANTS.
15. Jos 5:3-8 Why did Joshua have to circumcise the men? THE PEOPLE BORN IN THE DESERT IN THE LAST 40 YEARS HAD NOT BEEN CIRCUMCISED.
16. Summarize Joshua's heart and character. ANSWERS WILL VARY.

COMMANDED TO KILL?!

God's command to destroy all the inhabitants of the Promised Land seems harsh and unfair. How could a God of love order the Israelites to kill everyone, including women and children? We are not sure of all the reasons for the harshness, but we get a hint in Genesis 15:13-16.

Then the LORD said to him (Abraham), "Know for certain that your **DESCENDANTS** *will be* **STRANGERS** *in a country not their own, and they will be* **ENSLAVED** *and mistreated four* **HUNDRED** *years. But I will punish the nation they serve as* **SLAVES** *, and afterward they will come out with great* **POSSESSIONS** *. You, however, will go to your fathers in peace and be buried at a good old age. In the fourth generation your* **DESCENDANTS** *will come back* **HERE** *, for the* **SIN** *of the Amorites has* **NOT YET** *reached its* **FULL** *measure."*

God was giving the inhabitants of Canaan over 400 years to change their ways, but they only became more cruel and depraved.

Their gods had no moral standards, so the people could do whatever they wanted. Their gods controlled fertility, the weather, love, war and chaos and could be affected by magical rites. For example, by having sex, the priests and priestesses could cause the gods to make the land fertile and produce good crops.

The people also committed all kinds of sexual sins; in fact, sexual sin was a big part of worship in their religions. Nearly every man visited the male and female temple prostitutes. Parents made their children become prostitutes at the temples.

They also offered human sacrifices, the most horrible of which is referred to in the Bible as "causing their children to pass through the fire." Latin and Greek writers say that the god Molech had a human figure with the head of a bull. His idol was of metal with outstretched arms. It was heated red-hot by a fire inside it, and then children were placed on its arms as gifts to this god, and flutes and drums were played to drown out their screams as they burned to death.

Deut. 12:31 *You must not worship the LORD your God in their way, because in worshiping their gods, they do all kinds of detestable things the LORD hates. They even burn their sons and daughters in the fire as sacrifices to their gods.*

Molech comes from מֶלֶךְ which is *melek* and means "king." He was the pagan god of the Ammonites and other people of the area. The people who worshiped this god were calling him "king," but the Israelites refused to call this evil god a name of respect or honor. Since the name is written without vowels, they substituted the vowels from the Hebrew word *bosheh* which means "shame" or "abhorrence." Thus they showed contempt for this horrid god by calling him *Molech* instead of *Melek*.

As in any abuse situation, the victims cry out to God for justice (whether they know Him or not). God does hear their cries. The cries from within a nation bring about destruction and war.

Read Lev. 18:3, 24, 28 to learn how much these cruel and depraved practices displeased the Lord.

"You must not do as they do in **EGYPT** *, where you used to live, and you must not do as they do in the land of* **CANAAN** *, where I am bringing you. Do not follow their* **PRACTICES** *. Do not* **DEFILE** *yourselves in any of these* **WAYS** *, because this is how the* **NATIONS** *that I am going to drive out before you became* **DEFILED** *. And if you* **DEFILE** *the land, it will* **VOMIT** *you out as it* **VOMITED** *out the* **NATIONS** *that were before you."*

Deut. 18:9-13 *When you enter the land the LORD your God is giving you, do not learn to imitate the detestable ways of the nations there. Let no one be found among you who sacrifices his son or daughter in the fire, who practices* **DIVINATION** *or* **SORCERY** *, interprets* **OMENS** *, engages in* **WITCHCRAFT** *, or casts* **SPELLS** *, or who is a* **MEDIUM** *or* **SPIRITIST** *or who consults the* **DEAD** *. Anyone who does these things is detestable to the LORD, and because of these detestable practices the LORD your God will drive out those nations before you. You must be* **BLAMELESS** *before the LORD your God.*

Ex. 23:33 *Do not let them* **LIVE** *in your land, or they will cause you to* **SIN** *against Me, because the* **WORSHIP** *of their* **GODS** *will certainly be a* **SNARE** *to you."*

ARMOR OF GOD 1

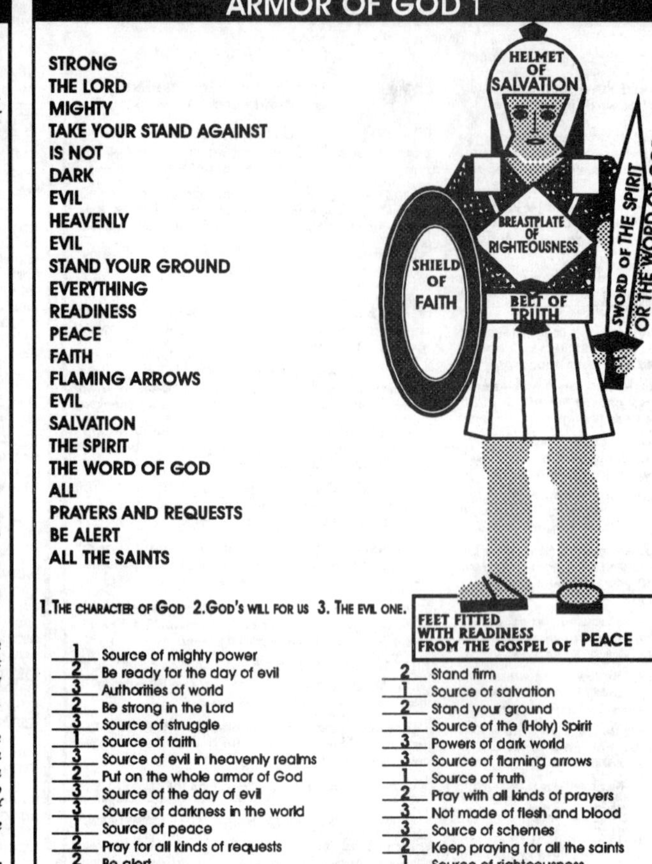

STRONG
THE LORD
MIGHTY
TAKE YOUR STAND AGAINST
IS NOT
DARK
EVIL
HEAVENLY
EVIL
STAND YOUR GROUND
EVERYTHING
READINESS
PEACE
FAITH
FLAMING ARROWS
EVIL
SALVATION
THE SPIRIT
THE WORD OF GOD
ALL
PRAYERS AND REQUESTS
BE ALERT
ALL THE SAINTS

FEET FITTED WITH READINESS FROM THE GOSPEL OF PEACE

1. THE CHARACTER OF GOD 2. GOD'S WILL FOR US 3. THE EVIL ONE.

1 Source of mighty power
2 Be ready for the day of evil
3 Authorities of world
2 Be strong in the Lord
3 Source of struggle
1 Source of faith
3 Source of evil in heavenly realms
2 Put on the whole armor of God
3 Source of the day of evil
3 Source of darkness in the world
1 Source of peace
2 Pray for all kinds of requests
2 Be alert
3 Spiritual forces of evil

2 Stand firm
1 Source of salvation
2 Stand your ground
1 Source of the (Holy) Spirit
3 Powers of dark world
3 Source of flaming arrows
1 Source of truth
2 Pray with all kinds of prayers
3 Not made of flesh and blood
3 Source of schemes
2 Keep praying for all the saints
1 Source of righteousness
3 Rulers of this world

ADDING 'THE' IN HEBREW 1

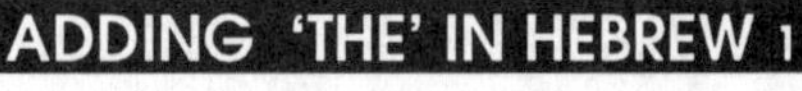

'dagesh' → doubles consonant sound
?הַ hå = 'the'
First letter of the word

START

הַמֶּלֶךְ = מֶלֶךְ + ?הַ ⇐
the king (hămmĕlĕk) = king (mĕlĕk) + the (hå)

הַבֵּן = בֵּן + ?הַ ⇐
the son (hăbbān) = son (bān) + the (hå)

דֶּלֶת הַדֶּלֶת håddŏlŏth the door	גָּמָל הַגָּמָל håggŏmŏl the camel	בַּיִת הַבַּיִת håbbayith the house
שַׂר הַשַּׂר håssår the prince	תָּמָר הַתָּמָר håttŏmŏr the palm tree	שֵׁן הַשֵּׁן håssān the tooth
דָּן הַדָּן håddŏn the judge	בַּת הַבַּת håbbåth the daughter	פֶּה הַפֶּה håppĕh the mouth
מַיִם הַמַּיִם håmmåyim the water	לֶחֶם הַלֶּחֶם hållĕkhĕm the bread	כַּף הַכַּף håkkåf the palm of hand

THE TALE TOLD BY A TELL 1

A 'tell' is a mound of dirt, sand, and rubble over an abandoned city. Over the years, fires, floods, earthquakes, and wars swept over the cities destroying the mud-bricks walls and buildings. Other times buildings were knocked down and flattened so that new, large structures could be built on top of the old. Each time, the city was rebuilt on top of the remains of the older structures. Finally the city was abandoned and the rain, wind, and searing sun slowly eroded it, creating an artificial hill known as a 'tell.' Archeologists can dig down through the layers of the 'tell' and discover the history of the city. In the Middle East there are numerous tells. Iraq alone has over 6,000 tells.

Cut Tell page 2 on the dotted lines. Glue into a book on the bottom of this page. Make up a history for the 'tell' and write it on the lines provided. Draw the different stages on each page, with A showing the oldest scene and F the current scene. In the grey area of the mound, draw the ruins of the previous stage. Some parts have been done for you.

A. Thousands of years ago, a small village began around a spring feed well. Their homes were small dome like structures. Their pottery was large and thick. Little is known about why these people left.

B. These houses were flat and square.

C.

ANSWERS MAY VARY

D.

E. The city was at its height around the time of Christ. It was a walled city with many houses. At that time the Romans attacked and burnt city and killed most of the people.

F. The bodies of the dead were not buried and the city was never rebuilt. Now-a-days the hot winds blow over the 'tell' as shepherd graze their flocks on what at one time was a great city.

GLUE B HERE

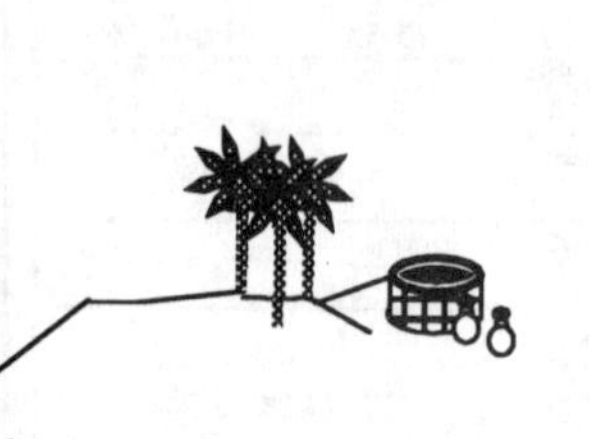

A

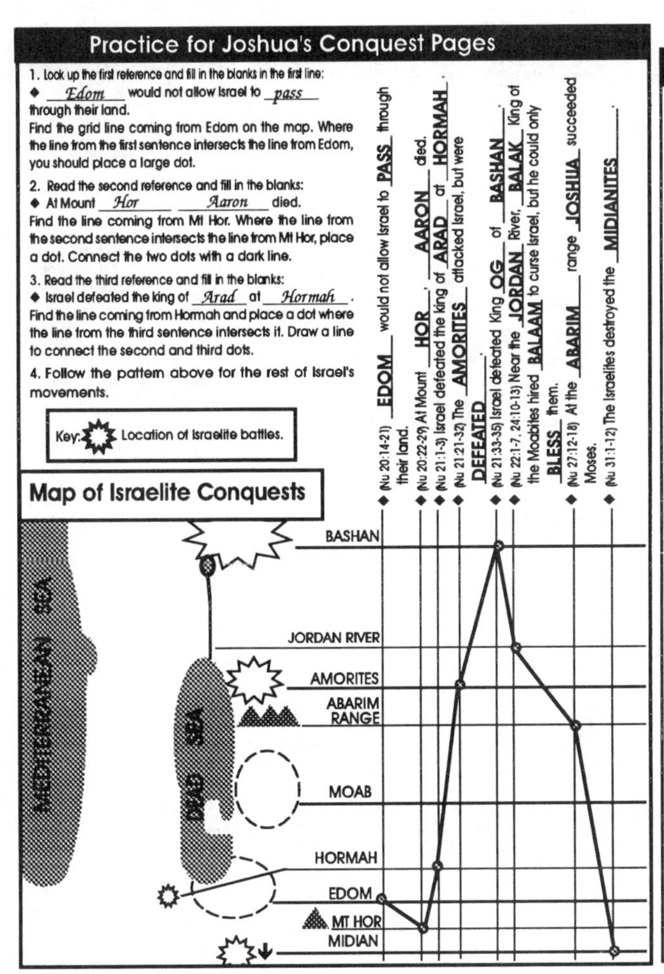

Practice for Joshua's Conquest Pages
1. Look up the first reference and fill in the blanks in the first line:
◆ Edom would not allow Israel to pass through their land.
Find the grid line coming from Edom on the map. Where the line from the first sentence intersects the line from Edom, you should place a large dot.
2. Read the second reference and fill in the blanks:
◆ At Mount Hor Aaron died.
Find the line coming from Mt Hor. Where the line from the second sentence intersects the line from Mt Hor, place a dot. Connect the two dots with a dark line.
3. Read the third reference and fill in the blanks:
◆ Israel defeated the king of Arad at Hormah.
Find the line coming from Hormah and place a dot where the line from the third sentence intersects it. Draw a line to connect the second and third dots.
4. Follow the pattern above for the rest of Israel's movements.
Key: Location of Israelite battles.
Map of Israelite Conquests
◆ (Nu 20:14-21) EDOM would not allow Israel to PASS through their land.
◆ (Nu 20:22-29) At Mount HOR AARON died.
◆ (Nu 21:1-3) Israel defeated the king of ARAD at HORMAH
◆ (Nu 21:21-32) The AMORITES attacked Israel, but were DEFEATED.
◆ (Nu 21:33-35) Israel defeated King OG of BASHAN
◆ (Nu 22:1-7, 24:10-13) Near the JORDAN River, BALAK King of the Moabites hired BALAAM to curse Israel, but he could only BLESS them.
◆ (Nu 27:12-18) At the ABARIM range JOSHUA succeeded Moses.
◆ (Nu 31:1-12) The Israelites destroyed the MIDIANITES.
BASHAN
JORDAN RIVER
AMORITES
ABARIM RANGE
MOAB
HORMAH
EDOM
MT HOR
MIDIAN
MEDITERRANEAN SEA
DEAD SEA

THE CITY OF JERICHO

When doing excavation it is often hard to know for sure which ancient settlement you are digging up. The ancient world did not have extensive use of written names on cities or streets. So deciding what you have uncovered is often guesswork. A tell named es-Sultan has been identified as Jericho.

This site was first excavated in 1907. There is disagreement among archeologists as to where the walls fell or even if the city had many people in the time of Joshua.

Dr. Garstang, who excavated the ruins from 1926-36, states that he believes the walls did fall flat. He said that the outer wall fell outward and pulled the inner wall with it. He also said there was evidence that the city was burned with vast quantities of food in storage left undisturbed. There are still various other tells in the area that have not been explored.

City of Jericho with double walls and plastered slope.

The wall surrounding the city was made of two walls built 15 feet apart. The outer wall was 6 feet thick; the inner wall, 12. Both were 30 feet high, built of bricks that were 4 inches thick and 1 to 2 feet long. The slope of the hill between the two walls was covered with plaster, making it slippery and difficult for attackers to climb. Often houses were built across the two walls linking them together. Rahab's house would have been one built on the walls.

ITEMS FOUND AT JERICHO

There are numerous finds from this site. Some human skulls were found where the features of the person were made in clay. They were painted flesh-color and had shells for eyes.

A vast grave site was found with baskets and wooden furniture in remarkably well-preserved condition. Scientists suggest that gases seeped into the tomb and killed all the bacteria. This was suggested to have been because of earthquake activity at the time the city fell.

Jericho is considered the oldest continually lived-in city on earth. The first city was a small city with round mud brick houses surrounded by a stone wall. Jericho's greatest period was during the Bronze Age (1850-1550 BC).

Clay molded over skull

Ivory combs

Pottery vase from Jericho

Joshua 6:26 After Jericho was destroyed. What did Joshua say about Jericho? GOD WOULD CURSE ANYONE WHO TRIED TO REBUILD JERICHO. THE FOUNDATION WOULD COST HIM HIS FIRSTBORN SON, AND THE GATES WOULD COST HIM HIS YOUNGEST SON.

1 Kings 16:34 Did the curse happen? Explain. YES. DURING THE REIGN OF AHAB, AHIEL OF BETHEL REBUILT JERICHO. THE FOUNDATION COST HIM HIS FIRSTBORN SON ABIRAM, AND THE GATES COST HIM HIS YOUGEST SON SEGUB.

JOSHUA'S CONQUESTS 1

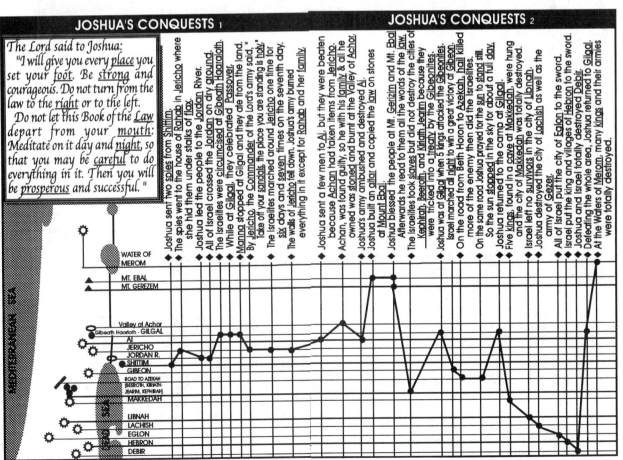

The Lord said to Joshua:
"I will give you every place you set your foot. Be strong and courageous. Do not turn from the law to the right or to the left.
Do not let this Book of the Law depart from your mouth: Meditate on it day and night, so that you may be careful to do everything in it. Then you will be prosperous and successful."

- ◆ Joshua sent two spies from Shittim.
- ◆ The spies went to the house of Rahab in Jericho where she hid them under stalks of flax.
- ◆ Joshua led the people to the Jordan River.
- ◆ All of Israel crossed the Jordan on dry ground.
- ◆ The Israelites were circumcised at Gibeath Haaraloth.
- ◆ While at Gilgal, they celebrated Passover.
- ◆ Manna stopped at Gilgal and they ate from the land.
- ◆ By Jericho, the Commander of the Lord's army said, "Take off your sandals, the place you are standing is holy."
- ◆ The Israelites marched around Jericho one time for six days and seven times on the seventh day.
- ◆ The walls of Jericho fell down. Joshua's army burned everything in it except for Rahab and her family.

WATER OF MEROM
MT. EBAL
MT. GEREZEM
Valley of Achor
Gibeath Haarloth - GILGAL
AI
JERICHO
JORDAN R.
SHITTIM
GIBEON
ROAD TO AZEKAH (BEEROTH, KIRIATH-JEARIM, KEPHIRAH)
MAKKEDAH
LIBNAH
LACHISH
EGLON
HEBRON
DEBIR
MEDITERRANEAN SEA
DEAD SEA

JOSHUA'S CONQUESTS 2

- ◆ Joshua sent a few men to Ai, but they were beaten because Achan had taken items from Jericho.
- ◆ Achan, was found guilty, so he with his family & all he owned was stoned and burnt at the Valley of Achor.
- ◆ Joshua's army ambushed and destroyed Ai.
- ◆ Joshua built an altar and copied the law on stones at Mount Ebal.
- ◆ Joshua blessed the people at Mt. Gerizim and Mt. Ebal. Afterwards he read to them all the words of the law.
- ◆ The Israelites took slaves but did not destroy the cities of Kephirah, Beeroth, and Kiriath Jearim because they were tricked into a treaty by the Gibeonites.
- ◆ Joshua was at Gilgal when 5 kings attacked the Gibeonites.
- ◆ Israel marched all night to win a great victory at Gibeon.
- ◆ On the road from Beth Horon to Azekah, hail killed more of the enemy than did the Israelites.
- ◆ On the same road Joshua prayed for the sun to stand still.
- ◆ So the sun stopped in the sky for about a full day.
- ◆ Joshua returned to the camp at Gilgal.
- ◆ Five kings, found in a cave at Makkedah, were hung and the city of Makkedah was totally destroyed.
- ◆ Israel left no survivors in the city of Libnah.
- ◆ Joshua destroyed the city of Lachish as well as the army of Gezer.
- ◆ All of Israel put the city of Eglon to the sword.
- ◆ Israel put the king and villages of Hebron to the sword.
- ◆ Joshua and Israel totally destroyed Debir.
- ◆ Defeating the whole area, Joshua returned to Gilgal.
- ◆ At the Waters of Merom, many kings and their armies were totally destroyed.

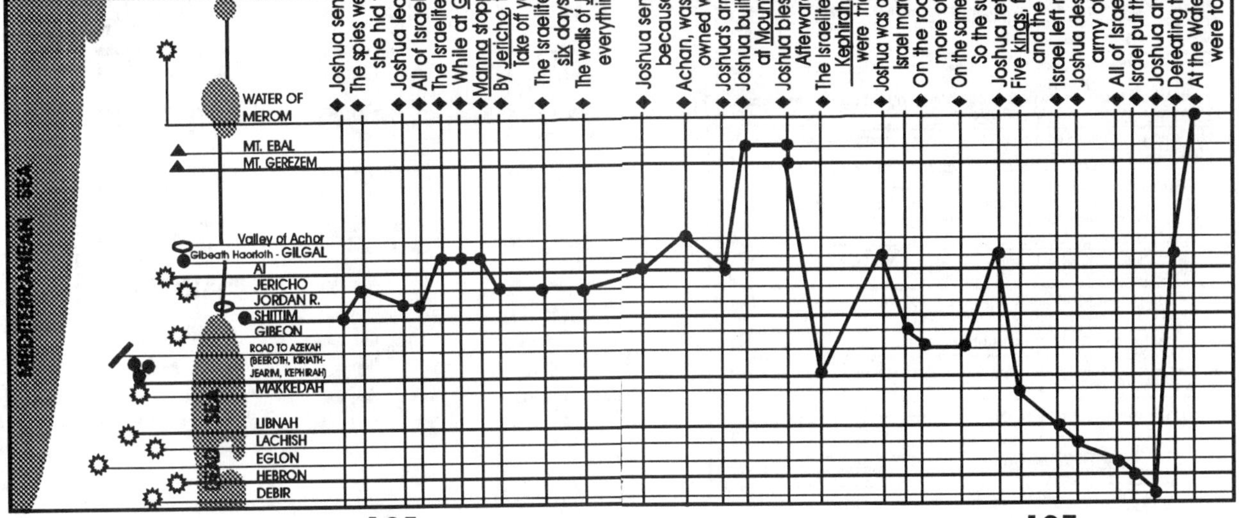

HE SAID, SHE SAID

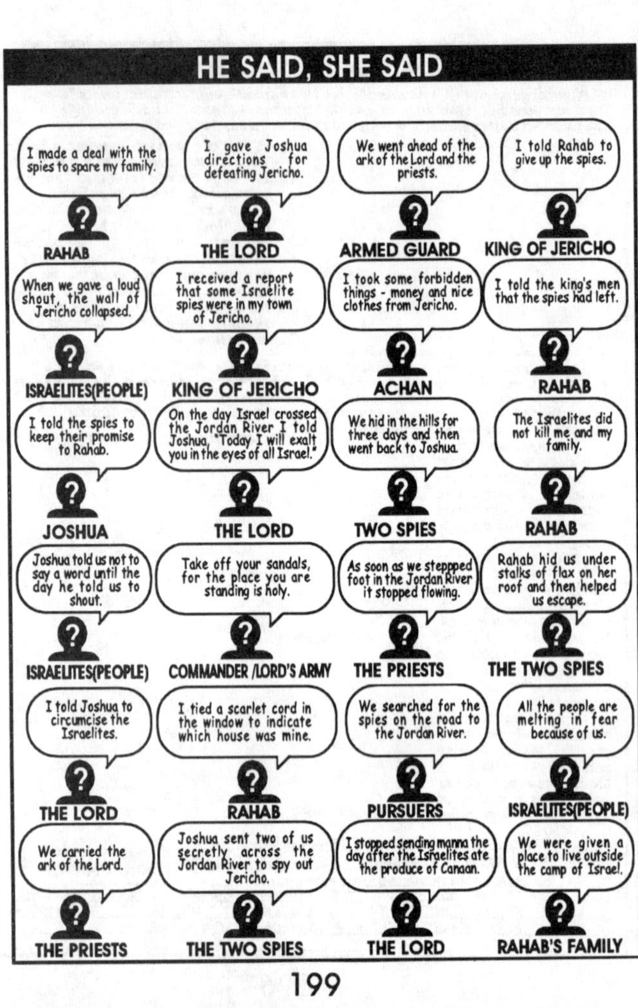

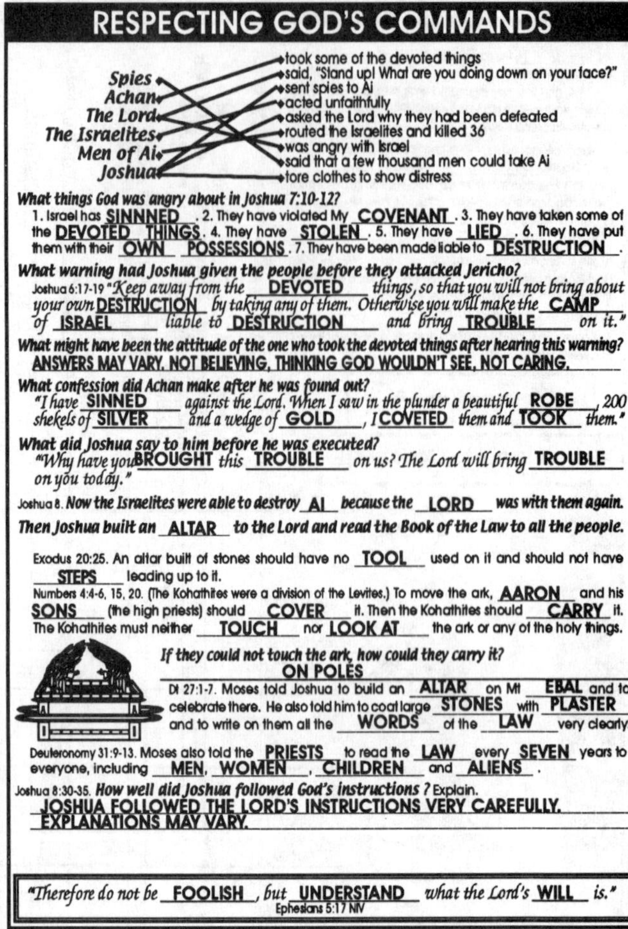

RESPECTING GOD'S COMMANDS

Spies
Achan
The Lord
The Israelites
Men of Ai
Joshua

- took some of the devoted things
- said, "Stand up! What are you doing down on your face?"
- sent spies to Ai
- acted unfaithfully
- asked the Lord why they had been defeated
- routed the Israelites and killed 36
- was angry with Israel
- said that a few thousand men could take Ai
- tore clothes to show distress

What things God was angry about in Joshua 7:10-12?
1. Israel has SINNNED. 2. They have violated My COVENANT. 3. They have taken some of the DEVOTED THINGS. 4. They have STOLEN. 5. They have LIED. 6. They have put them with their OWN POSSESSIONS. 7. They have been made liable to DESTRUCTION.

What warning had Joshua given the people before they attacked Jericho?
Joshua 6:17-19 "Keep away from the DEVOTED things, so that you will not bring about your own DESTRUCTION by taking any of them. Otherwise you will make the CAMP of ISRAEL liable to DESTRUCTION and bring TROUBLE on it."

What might have been the attitude of the one who took the devoted things after hearing this warning?
ANSWERS MAY VARY. NOT BELIEVING, THINKING GOD WOULDN'T SEE, NOT CARING.

What confession did Achan make after he was found out?
"I have SINNED against the Lord. When I saw in the plunder a beautiful ROBE, 200 shekels of SILVER and a wedge of GOLD, I COVETED them and TOOK them."

What did Joshua say to him before he was executed?
"Why have you BROUGHT this TROUBLE on us? The Lord will bring TROUBLE on you today."

Joshua 8. Now the Israelites were able to destroy AI because the LORD was with them again.
Then Joshua built an ALTAR to the Lord and read the Book of the Law to all the people.

Exodus 20:25. An altar built of stones should have no TOOL used on it and should not have STEPS leading up to it.
Numbers 4:4-6, 15, 20. (The Kohathites were a division of the Levites.) To move the ark, AARON and his SONS (the high priests) should COVER it. Then the Kohathites should CARRY it. The Kohathites must neither TOUCH nor LOOK AT the ark or any of the holy things.
If they could not touch the ark, how could they carry it?
ON POLES
Dt 27:1-7. Moses told Joshua to build an ALTAR on Mt EBAL and to celebrate there. He also told him to coat large STONES with PLASTER and to write on them all the WORDS of the LAW very clearly.
Deuteronomy 31:9-13. Moses also told the PRIESTS to read the LAW every SEVEN years to everyone, including MEN, WOMEN, CHILDREN and ALIENS.
Joshua 8:30-35. How well did Joshua followed God's instructions? Explain.
JOSHUA FOLLOWED THE LORD'S INSTRUCTIONS VERY CAREFULLY. EXPLANATIONS MAY VARY.

"Therefore do not be FOOLISH, but UNDERSTAND what the Lord's WILL is."
Ephesians 5:17 NIV

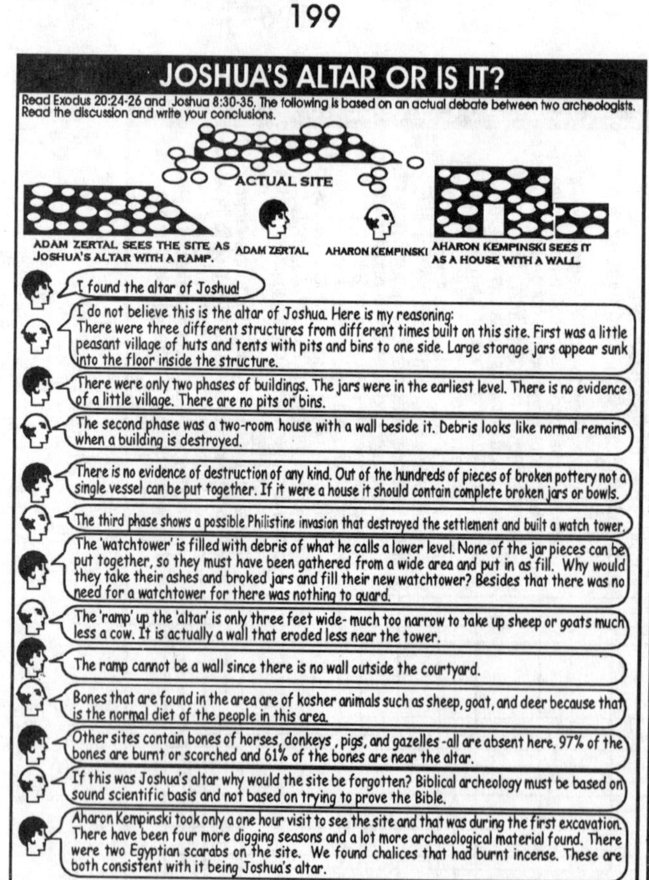

JOSHUA'S ALTAR OR IS IT?

Read Exodus 20:24-26 and Joshua 8:30-35. The following is based on an actual debate between two archeologists. Read the discussion and write your conclusions.

ACTUAL SITE

ADAM ZERTAL SEES THE SITE AS JOSHUA'S ALTAR WITH A RAMP. ADAM ZERTAL AHARON KEMPINSKI AHARON KEMPINSKI SEES IT AS A HOUSE WITH A WALL.

- I found the altar of Joshua!
- I do not believe this is the altar of Joshua. Here is my reasoning: There were three different structures from different times built on this site. First was a little peasant village of huts and tents with pits and bins to one side. Large storage jars appear sunk into the floor inside the structure.
- There were only two phases of buildings. The jars were in the earliest level. There is no evidence of a little village. There are no pits or bins.
- The second phase was a two-room house with a wall beside it. Debris looks like normal remains when a building is destroyed.
- There is no evidence of destruction of any kind. Out of the hundreds of pieces of broken pottery not a single vessel can be put together. If it were a house it should contain complete broken jars or bowls.
- The third phase shows a possible Philistine invasion that destroyed the settlement and built a watch tower.
- The 'watchtower' is filled with debris of what he calls a lower level. None of the jar pieces can be put together, so they must have been gathered from a wide area and put in as fill. Why would they take their ashes and broked jars and fill their new watchtower? Besides that there was no need for a watchtower for there was nothing to guard.
- The 'ramp' up the 'altar' is only three feet wide- much too narrow to take up sheep or goats much less a cow. It is actually a wall that eroded less near the tower.
- The ramp cannot be a wall since there is no wall outside the courtyard.
- Bones that are found in the area are of kosher animals such as sheep, goat, and deer because that is the normal diet of the people in this area.
- Other sites contain bones of horses, donkeys, pigs, and gazelles -all are absent here. 97% of the bones are burnt or scorched and 61% of the bones are near the altar.
- If this was Joshua's altar why would the site be forgotten? Biblical archeology must be based on sound scientific basis and not based on trying to prove the Bible.
- Aharon Kempinski took only a one hour visit to see the site and that was during the first excavation. There have been four more digging seasons and a lot more archaeological material found. There were two Egyptian scarabs on the site. We found chalices that had burnt incense. These are both consistent with it being Joshua's altar.

Almost every site excavated has a lot of controversy. After reading the debate, tell if you feel this site could be Joshua's altar. Explain.

ANSWERS MAY VARY

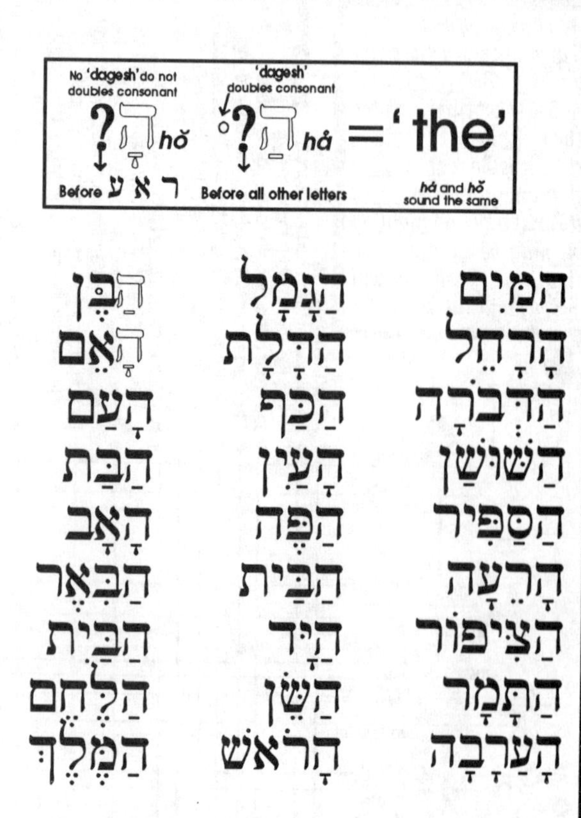

ADDING 'THE' IN HEBREW 2

No 'dagesh' do not doubles consonant [hŏ] 'dagesh' doubles consonant [hă] = 'the'
Before ... Before all other letters hă and hŏ sound the same

הַמַּיִם הַגָּמָל הַבֵּן
הָרָחֵל הַדֶּלֶת הָאֵם
הַדְּבֹרָה הַכַּף הָעָם
הַשּׁוּשָׁן הָעַיִן הַבַּת
הַסַּפִּיר הַפֶּה הָאָב
הָרָעָה הַבַּיִת הַבְּאֵר
הַצִּפּוֹר הַיָּד הַבַּיִת
הַתָּמָר הַשֵּׁן הַלֶּחֶם
הָעֲרָבָה הָרֹאשׁ הַמֶּלֶךְ

KEEPING PROMISES

THE SET-UP:

Why did the kings west of the Jordan plan an attack on the Israelites? THEY HEARD WHAT ISRAEL HAD DONE TO JERICHO AND AI, AND WANTED TO STOP THEM.

Which one group did not join to attack the Israelites? THE GIBEONITES.

How did they trick Joshua? THEY TOOK OLD CLOTHES AND FOOD TO PRETEND THEY WERE FROM FAR AWAY.

Why did they trick Joshua? THEY HEARD THAT ISRAEL WAS TO DESTROY EVERYONE IN THE LAND.

What mistake did the men of Israel make in 9:14? THEY DID NOT INQUIRE OF THE LORD.

THE TREATY:

What did Joshua promise in the initial treaty? TO LET THEM LIVE.

Who ratified the treaty? THE LEADERS OF ISRAEL.

What would happen to God's Name if the Israelites attacked the Gibeonites after taking the oath? IT WOULD BE SHOWN TO MEAN NOTHING TO THE ISRAELITES.

What does this have to do with Exodus 20:7? USING GOD'S NAME AND MEANING NOTHING BY IT, SHOWING DISRESPECT FOR IT. ANSWERS MAY VARY.

Why were the leaders afraid to break their promise? WRATH WOULD FALL ON ISRAEL.

What did Joshua add to the treaty when he found out where the Gibeonites lived? THEY WOULD BE WATER CARRIERS AND WOODCUTTERS FOR ISRAEL, FOR THE HOUSE OF GOD.

How might this be a blessing for the Gibeonites? THEY WOULD BE NEAR THE TABERNACLE AND LEARN OF GOD'S WAYS.

Josh. 18:1 and 1Sam. 1:24 show that the Tabernacle was in Shiloh during the times of Joshua and the judges.

What was in Gibeon in the time of David? 1 Chronicles 16:39-40 TABERNACLE & ALTAR OF BURNT OFFERINGS.

In the time of Solomon? 2 Chronicles 1:3-5 TABERNACLE AND BRONZE ALTAR.

KEEPING THE PROMISE:

Why was the king of Jerusalem alarmed? BECAUSE THE ISRAELITES HAD DESTROYED JERICHO AND AI; AND GIBEON, A POWERFUL CITY, WAS ALLIED WITH ISRAEL.

How many kings with their armies attacked Gibeon? FIVE.

How did Joshua respond to Gibeon's cry for help? HE IMMEDIATELY WENT TO HELP THEM.

HELPED BY GOD:

What did the Lord tell Joshua? DO NOT BE AFRAID. I HAVE GIVEN THEM INTO YOUR HANDS. NONE WILL BE ABLE TO WITHSTAND YOU.

What did the Lord do for Joshua in verse 10? THREW ENEMIES INTO CONFUSION.

In verse 11? HURLED LARGE HAILSTONES ON THE ENEMIES.

In verses 12-14? MADE THE SUN STAND STILL. GAVE THE AMORITES OVER TO ISRAEL.

> *"Do not be* AFRAID *; do not be* DISCOURAGED.
> *Be* STRONG *and* COURAGEOUS.*"* Joshua 10:25 NIV

The reason they were so successful was that THE LORD WAS WITH THEM AND HELPED THEM.

From what you learned from Achan, why was the Lord on Israel's side in this campaign? THEY WERE OBEYING THE LORD, DOING THINGS THE WAY HE TOLD THEM.

Check all that are true:

WE SHOULD MAKE PROMISES ☒ after careful thought ☒ after seeking God's guidance ☐ whenever asked to.

WE SHOULD KEEP OUR PROMISES ☐ if we were not tricked ☐ if it is easy ☒ to the best of our ability.

AS CHRISTIANS, IF WE BREAK A PROMISE, ☒ we dishonor the Lord ☐ it's ok because we are only human.

MALE AND FEMALE WORDS IN HEBREW

MALE NOUNS No ending	Meaning Draw a line to the Hebrew word.	FEMALE NOUNS Add ָה?
גָּמָל	queen	שׁוֹשַׁנָּה
צִיפּוֹר	king	שָׂרָה
שַׂר	prince	גְּמַלָּה
אֵל	princess	מַלְכָּה
מֶלֶךְ	god	צִיפֹּרָה
שׁוּשַׁן	goddess	אֵלָה
	lily (male)	
	lily (female)	
	camel (male and female)	
	little bird (male)	
	little bird (female)	

MALE VERBS Add ???	Meaning Draw a line to the Hebrew word.	FEMALE VERBS Add ָה???
נָתַן	(he) gave	נָתְנָה
שָׁפַט	(she) gave	שָׁפְטָה
שָׁמַע	(he) ruled	שָׁמְעָה
יָשַׁע	(she) ruled	יָשְׁעָה
מָלַךְ	(he) heard	מָלְכָה
זָכַר	(she) heard	זָכְרָה
רָאָה	(he) remembered	רָאֲהָה
	(she) remembered	
	(he) saw	
	(she) saw	
	(he) saved	
	(she) saved	
	(he) judged	
	(she) judged	

SIMPLE HEBREW SENTENCES 2

Write the pronunciation under each word and then write the number of each Hebrew sentence in the box in front of the English sentence translation.

[8] A queen heard. — 1. הַמַּלְכָּה רָאֲהָה (rō'ŭhŏh hȧmmŏlŭkŏh)

[4] The goddess judged. — 2. צִיפֹּרָה שָׁמְעָה (shŏmŭ'ŏh tsĕfŏrŏh)

[1] The queen saw. — 3. הַמֶּלֶךְ נָתַן (nŏthȧn hȧmmĕlĕk)

[7] The son remembered. — 4. הָאֵלָה שָׁפְטָה (shŏfŭtŏh hŏ'ālŏh)

[3] The king gave. — 5. צִיפּוֹר שָׁמַע (shŏmȧ' tsĕfŏr)

[2] A sparrow (female) heard. — 6. מֶלֶךְ נָתַן (nŏthȧn mĕlĕk)

[6] A king gave. — 7. הַבֵּן זָכַר (zŏkhȧr hȧbbĕn)

[5] A sparrow (male) heard. — 8. מַלְכָּה שָׁמְעָה (shŏmŭ'ŏh mŏlŭkŏh)

Write each sentence in Hebrew.

The prince saw. הַשַּׂר רָאָה

A princess saved. שָׂרָה יָשְׁעָה

The son heard. הַבֵּן שָׁמַע

A son judged. בֵּן שָׁפַע

A camel (male) remembered. גָּמָל זָכַר

The sparrow (female) saw. הַצִּיפֹּרָה רָאֲהָה

EMBLEMS OF THE TRIBES OF ISRAEL

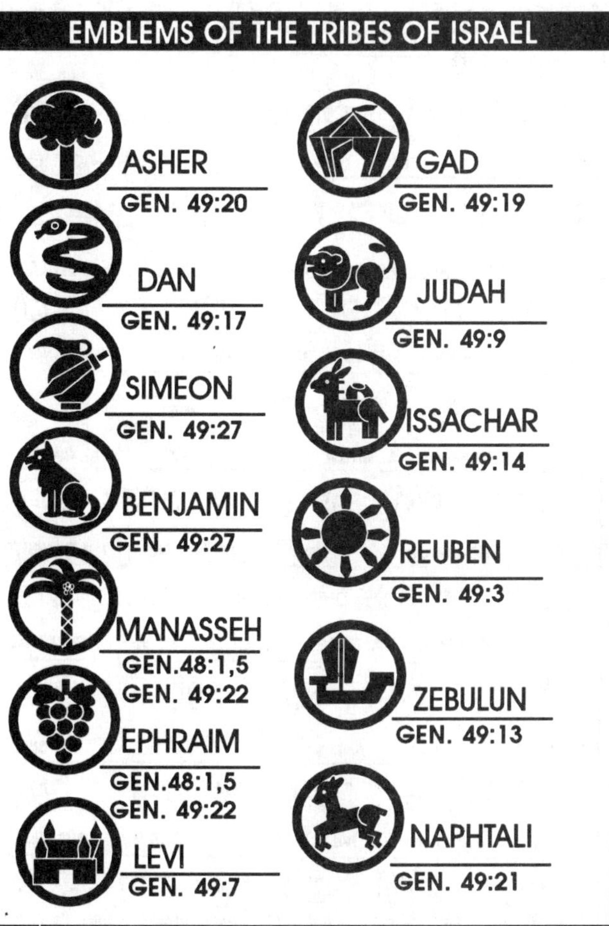

DIVISION OF THE PROMISED LAND

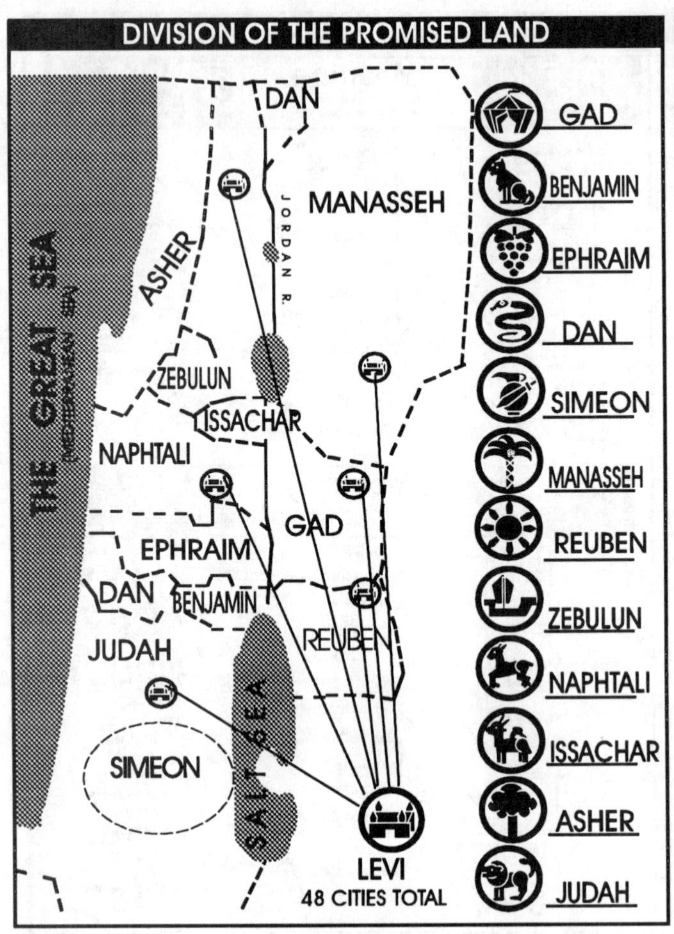

THE GREAT SEA (MEDITERRANEAN)

DAN
MANASSEH
JORDAN R.
ASHER
ZEBULUN
ISSACHAR
NAPHTALI
EPHRAIM
GAD
DAN
BENJAMIN
JUDAH
REUBEN
SALT SEA
SIMEON

- GAD
- BENJAMIN
- EPHRAIM
- DAN
- SIMEON
- MANASSEH
- REUBEN
- ZEBULUN
- NAPHTALI
- ISSACHAR
- ASHER
- JUDAH

LEVI
48 CITIES TOTAL

208

MORE HEBREW

If there is a 'dagesh' it is taken out.   If there is a 'dagesh' it is taken out.

וְ ŭ or וּ ŭ = 'and'

Before בּ, מ, פּ.   Before most consonants.

START
וְ × = ŭ   and
גָּמָל = a camel gŏmŏl
וּגָמָל and a camel ŭgŏmŏl

START
וּ × = ŭ   and
בֵּן = a son bān
וּבֵן and a son ŭvān

אֵת = Answers: What? Whom? Direct object marker

מֶלֶךְ רָאָה אֶת גָּמָל
A king saw a camel (what?)

1. אָח רָאָה אֶת רָחֵל (וְאֶת) עַם
PEOPLE. AND (WHAT?)   A SHEEP (WHAT?)   SAW   A BROTHER

2. הַמֶּלֶךְ שָׁמַע (וְרָאָה) אֶת רֵעָה
A FRIEND (WHAT?)   AND SAW   HEARD   THE KING

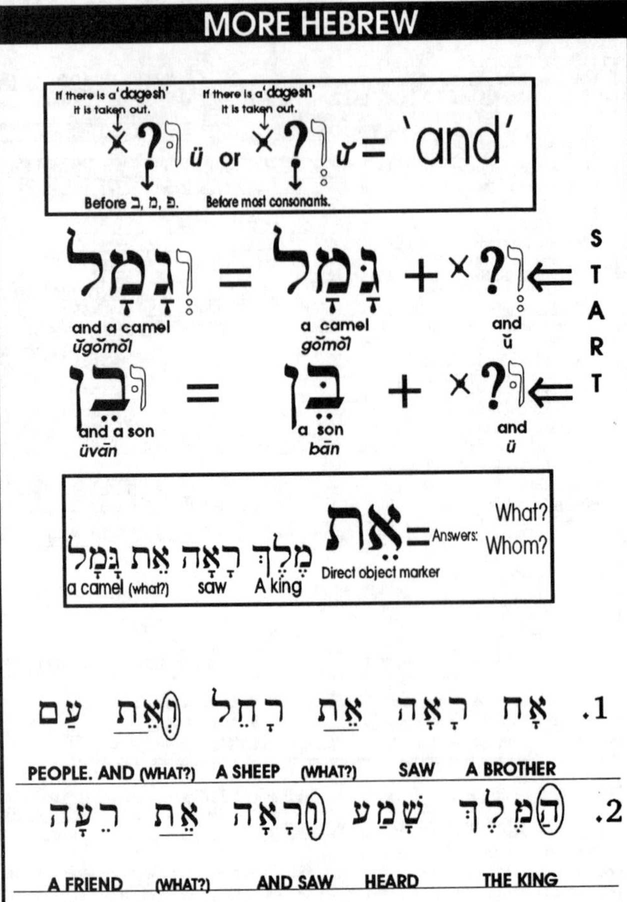

209

SIMPLE SENTENCES 3

1. הַדָּן שָׁפַט אֶת מֶלֶךְ (וְאֶת) מַלְכָּה
a queen. (what?) and   a king (what?)   judged   The judge

2. הָאֵם נָתְנָה אֶת לֶחֶם (וְאֶת) מַיִם
WATER. AND (WHAT?)   BREAD   (WHAT?)   GAVE   THE MOTHER

3. הַמֶּלֶךְ שָׁמַע (וְשָׁפַט) אֶת שַׂר
A PRINCE. (WHAT?)   AND JUDGED   HEARD   THE KING

7. הַגָּמָל יָשַׁע אֶת אָב (וְאֶת) בֵּן
A SON. AND (WHAT?)   A FATHER (WHAT?)   SAVED   THE CAMEL

4. הַבַּת רָאֲתָה אֶת צִיפּוֹר (וְאֶת) דְּבוֹרָה
A BEE. AND (WHAT?)   A BIRD (WHAT?)   SAW   THE DAUGHTER

5. בַּת נָתְנָה אֶת סַפִּיר (וְאֶת) שׁוּשַׁנָּה
A LILY. AND (WHAT?)   A SAPPHIRE (WHAT?)   GAVE   A DAUGHTER

6. הַצִּיפּוֹר שָׁמַע (וְרָאָה) אֶת הָרָחֵל
THE SHEEP. (WHAT?)   AND SAW   HEARD   THE BIRD

8. גָּמָל רָאָה אֶת תָּמָר (וְאֶת) בְּאֵר
A WELL. AND (WHAT?)   A PALM TREE (WHAT?)   SAW   A CAMEL

9. אָב זָכַר אֶת בַּיִת (וְאֶת) דֶּלֶת
A DOOR AND (WHAT?)   A HOUSE (WHAT?)   REMEMBERED   A FATHER

210

INTERACTING WITH PERSECUTION

Review the pages about the persecution of the Jews over the centuries. First put in order the following nations and groups by writing them in order from 1 to 8. See the example.

1 ASSYRIA
2 BABYLON
3 PERSIA
4 GREECE
5 ROME
6 SYRIA
7 THE MUSLIMS
8 EUROPE

Now show which era each of the following facts belongs to by writing the era's number (from your work above) by each fact. The first one is done for you.

- 8   The Holocaust took the lives of six million Jews.
- 6   Pompey conquered Jerusalem, killing 12,000 Jews.
- 8   The Jews were forced to be baptized.
- 6   Hadrian banned the Jews from Jerusalem.
- 1   In 722 BC, Sennacherib attacked Jerusalem.
- 4   Hellenism caused much conflict among the Jews.
- 3   Haman plotted to kill all the Jews in the empire.
- 1   Several kings including Ahab were able to push this nation back.
- 2   Nebuchadnezzar took captives including Daniel and Ezekiel.
- 3   Cyrus allowed the Jews to return to their land.
- 8   Plagues and epidemics of "possession" were blamed on the Jews.
- 6   When Titus besieged Jerusalem, one million Jews were killed.
- 7   They put a building on the Temple Mount where the Temple belongs.
- 4   Alexander wanted all his subjects to adopt the Greek language and culture.
- 5   Antiochus V Epiphanes sacrificed a pig on the altar in Jerusalem.
- 7   This religious group made people chose their way or the sword.
- 3   Queen Esther risked her life to save her people.
- 4   The whole empire learned a common language. This later enabled the gospel to spread quickly.
- 5   Mattathias and his 5 sons led a revolt and recaptured Jerusalem.
- 8   The Jews were exiled from country after country.
- 2   The Jews were not treated poorly, but they mourned for their land.
- 1   In 732 BC, Tiglath-Pileser III defeated the northern kingdom of Israel and took the people captive.
- 8   The ghetto was first created.
- 5   This country dominated Israel from 204-165 BC.
- 1   These ferocious warriors were cruel to all they conquered.
- 6   Soldiers destroyed the Temple as Jesus had predicted.

221

PERSECUTION CROSSWORD

Across: 2 PENNILESS · 4 RHINE · 7 HOLOCAUST · 8 JEROME · 9 POSSESSION · 12 NAZI · 14 CRUSADE · 15 PLAGUE · 16 KRISTALLNACHT · 17 RABBI · 18 POGROM · 19 MARTINLUTHER

Down: 1 ORIGEN · 3 SYNAGOGUE · 5 GHETTO · 6 SLAVERY · 10 STAUGUSTINE · 11 INQUISITION · 12 NICEA · 13 EASTER

223

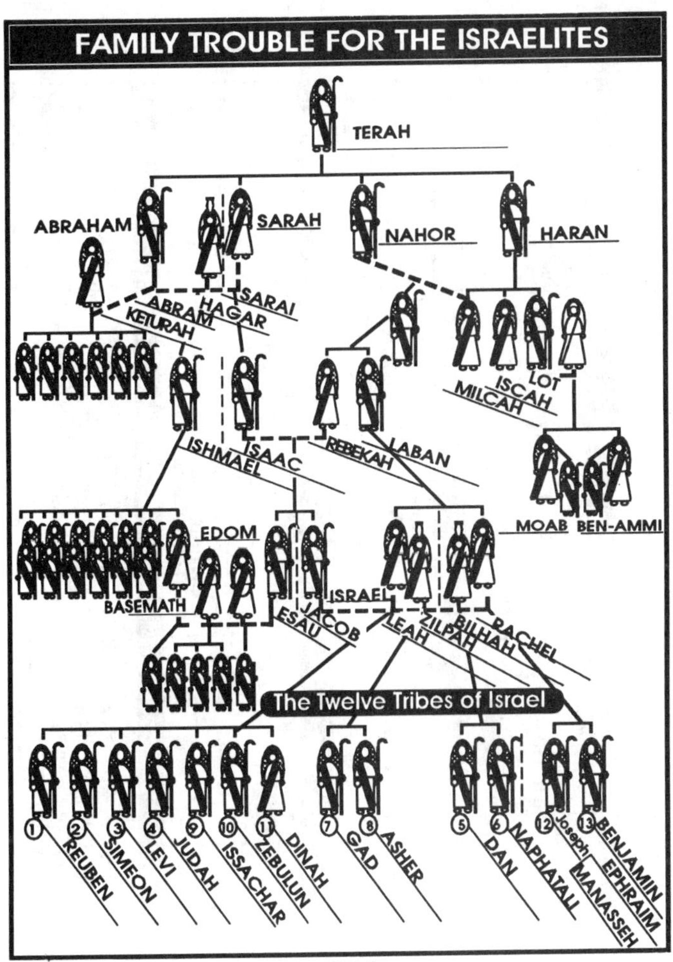

224

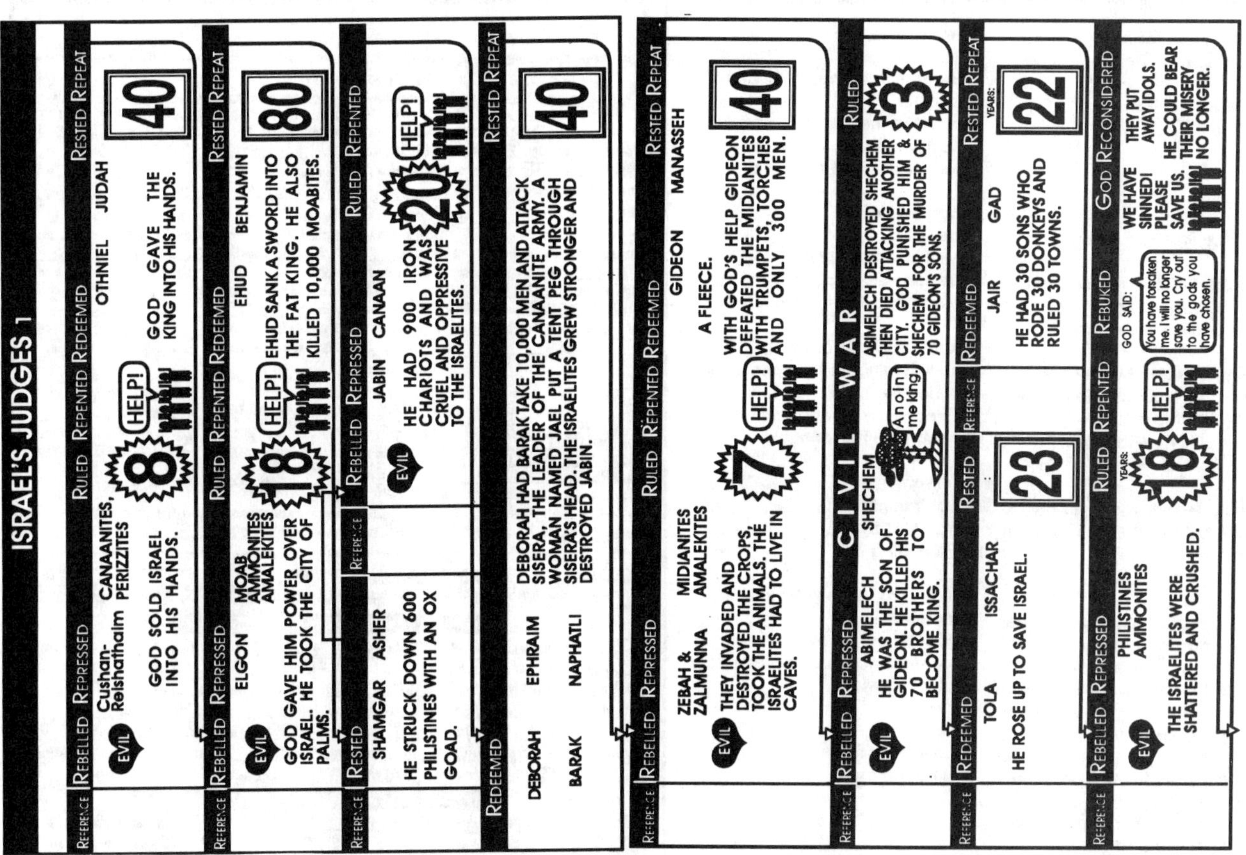

ISRAEL'S JUDGES 1
REBELLED REPRESSED RULED REPENTED REDEEMED RESTED REPEAT
EVIL
Cushan-Reishathaim CANAANITES PERIZZITES
GOD SOLD ISRAEL INTO HIS HANDS.
8
HELP!
OTHNIEL JUDAH
GOD GAVE THE KING INTO HIS HANDS.
40
ELGON MOAB AMMONITES AMALEKITES
GOD GAVE HIM POWER OVER ISRAEL. HE TOOK THE CITY OF PALMS.
18
EHUD BENJAMIN
EHUD SANK A SWORD INTO THE FAT KING. HE ALSO KILLED 10,000 MOABITES.
80
SHAMGAR ASHER
HE STRUCK DOWN 600 PHILISTINES WITH AN OX GOAD.
JABIN CANAAN
HE HAD 900 IRON CHARIOTS AND WAS CRUEL AND OPPRESSIVE TO THE ISRAELITES.
20
DEBORAH EPHRAIM
BARAK NAPHATLI
DEBORAH HAD BARAK TAKE 10,000 MEN AND ATTACK SISERA, THE LEADER OF THE CANAANITE ARMY. A WOMAN NAMED JAEL PUT A TENT PEG THROUGH SISERA'S HEAD. THE ISRAELITES GREW STRONGER AND DESTROYED JABIN.
40
ZEBAH & ZALMUNNA MIDIANITES AMALEKITES
THEY INVADED AND DESTROYED THE CROPS, TOOK THE ANIMALS. THE ISRAELITES HAD TO LIVE IN CAVES.
7
GIDEON MANASSEH
A FLEECE.
WITH GOD'S HELP GIDEON DEFEATED THE MIDIANITES WITH TRUMPETS, TORCHES AND ONLY 300 MEN.
40
CIVIL WAR
ABIMELECH SHECHEM
HE WAS THE SON OF GIDEON. HE KILLED HIS 70 BROTHERS TO BECOME KING.
Anoint me king.
ABIMELECH DESTROYED SHECHEM THEN DIED ATTACKING ANOTHER CITY. GOD PUNISHED HIM & SHECHEM FOR THE MURDER OF 70 GIDEON'S SONS.
3
TOLA ISSACHAR
HE ROSE UP TO SAVE ISRAEL.
23
JAIR GAD
HE HAD 30 SONS WHO RODE 30 DONKEYS AND RULED 30 TOWNS.
22
REBELLED REPRESSED RULED REPENTED REBUKED GOD RECONSIDERED
PHILISTINES AMMONITES
THE ISRAELITES WERE SHATTERED AND CRUSHED.
18
GOD SAID: You have forsaken me. I will no longer save you. Cry out to the gods you have chosen.
WE HAVE SINNED! PLEASE SAVE US.
THEY PUT AWAY IDOLS. HE COULD BEAR THEIR MISERY NO LONGER.

225

227

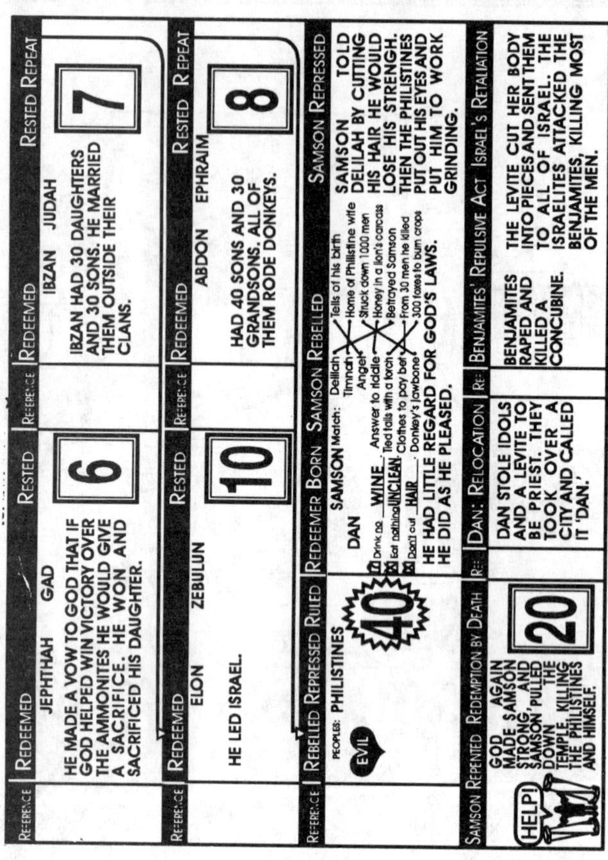

Reference | Redeemed | Rested | Reference | Redeemed | Rested Repeat
JEPHTHAH GAD
HE MADE A VOW TO GOD THAT IF GOD HELPED WIN VICTORY OVER THE AMMONITES HE WOULD GIVE A SACRIFICE. HE WON AND SACRIFICED HIS DAUGHTER.
6
IBZAN JUDAH
IBZAN HAD 30 DAUGHTERS AND 30 SONS. HE MARRIED THEM OUTSIDE THEIR CLANS.
7
ELON ZEBULUN
HE LED ISRAEL.
10
ABDON EPHRAIM
HAD 40 SONS AND 30 GRANDSONS. ALL OF THEM RODE DONKEYS.
8
Reference | Rebelled | Repressed | Ruled | Redeemer Born | Samson Rebelled | Samson Repressed
PEOPLES: PHILISTINES
EVIL
40
SAMSON Match:
DAN
Drink no WINE
Eat nothing UNCLEAN
Don't cut HAIR
Delilah / Timnah / Angel / Answer to riddle / Tied tails with a torch / Clothes to pay bet / Donkey's jawbone
Tells of his birth / Home of Philistine wife / Struck down 1000 men / Honey in a lion's carcass / Betrayed Samson / From 30 men he killed / 300 foxes to burn crops
HE HAD LITTLE REGARD FOR GOD'S LAWS. HE DID AS HE PLEASED.
SAMSON TOLD DELILAH BY CUTTING HIS HAIR HE WOULD LOSE HIS STRENGH. THEN THE PHILISTINES PUT OUT HIS EYES AND PUT HIM TO WORK GRINDING.
Samson Repented | Redemption by Death | Dan: Relocation | Benjamites' Repulsive Act | Israel's Retaliation
HELP!
GOD AGAIN MADE SAMSON STRONG, AND SAMSON PULLED DOWN THE TEMPLE, KILLING THE PHILISTINES AND HIMSELF.
20
DAN STOLE IDOLS AND A LEVITE TO BE PRIEST. THEY TOOK OVER A CITY AND CALLED IT 'DAN.'
BENJAMITES RAPED AND KILLED A CONCUBINE.
THE LEVITE CUT HER BODY INTO PIECES AND SENT THEM TO ALL OF ISRAEL. THE ISRAELITES ATTACKED THE BENJAMITES, KILLING MOST OF THE MEN.

229

226

SAMSON'S HEART

- an angel of the Lord
- No razor may be used on his head
- set apart to God
- begin
- blessed

- Philistine
- get
- Get the Philistine for me

- the Spirit of the Lord came upon him in power and
- scooped it out and ate it

- complained to him that he hated her because he refused to tell her the answer
- cried until he finally told her
- told

- struck down thirty men and gave their clothes to the wedding guests
- Burning with anger.

- had thought Samson hated her and had given her to his friend.
- he had the right to get even
- He tied torches to three hundred foxes and set them loose in the Philistine fields

- "I merely did to them what they did to me"
- The Spirit of the Lord came on him in power and

- twenty years

- He went in to spend the night with her
- he lifted the city gate and its posts on his shoulders and carried them to the top of a hill.

- named Delilah
- decided
- I will become weak
- Delilah said, "You made a fool of me and lied to me."

- Again Delilah complained that he was lying and making a fool of her.
- "Weave my seven braids into the fabric of the loom."

- Delilah
- won't confide in
- was tired to death
- everything

- sent word to the Philistines
- the Lord
- gouged out his eyes, put him in bronze shackles and made him grind in prison

- Dagon
- remember me
- just once more
- die with

ANSWERS WILL VARY

231

PRIEST FOR HIRE

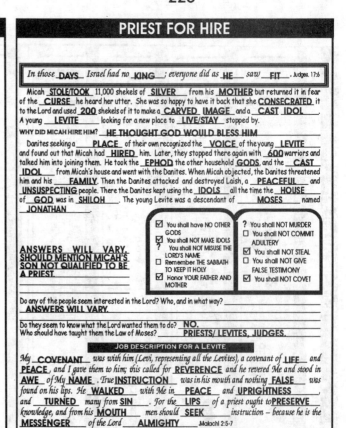

In those DAYS *Israel had no* KING *; everyone did as* HE *saw* FIT . Judges 17:6

Micah STOLE/TOOK 11,000 shekels of SILVER from his MOTHER but returned it in fear of the CURSE he heard her utter. She was so happy to have it back that she CONSECRATED it to the Lord and used 200 shekels of it to make a CARVED IMAGE and a CAST IDOL . A young LEVITE looking for a new place to LIVE/STAY stopped by.

WHY DID MICAH HIRE HIM? HE THOUGHT GOD WOULD BLESS HIM

Danites seeking a PLACE of their own recognized the VOICE of the young LEVITE and found out that Micah had HIRED him. Later, they stopped there again with 600 warriors and talked him into joining them. He took the EPHOD the other household GODS, and the CAST IDOL from Micah's house and went with the Danites. When Micah objected, the Danites threatened him and his FAMILY. Then the Danites attacked and destroyed Laish, a PEACEFUL and UNSUSPECTING people. There the Danites kept using the IDOLS all the time the HOUSE of GOD was in SHILOH . The young Levite was a descendant of MOSES named JONATHAN .

ANSWERS WILL VARY. SHOULD MENTION MICAH'S SON NOT QUALIFIED TO BE A PRIEST.

- ☑ You shall have NO OTHER GODS
- ☑ You shall NOT MAKE IDOLS
- ? You shall NOT MISUSE THE LORD'S NAME
- ☐ Remember THE SABBATH TO KEEP IT HOLY
- ☑ Honor YOUR FATHER AND MOTHER
- ? You shall NOT MURDER
- ☐ You shall NOT COMMIT ADULTERY
- ☑ You shall NOT STEAL
- ☐ You shall NOT GIVE FALSE TESTIMONY
- ☑ You shall NOT COVET

Do any of the people seem interested in the Lord? Who, and in what way? ANSWERS WILL VARY.

Do they seem to know what the Lord wanted them to do? NO.
Who should have taught them the Law of Moses? PRIESTS/ LEVITES, JUDGES.

JOB DESCRIPTION FOR A LEVITE

My COVENANT *was with him (Levi, representing all the Levites), a covenant of* LIFE *and* PEACE, *and I gave them to him; this called for* REVERENCE *and he revered Me and stood in* AWE *of My* NAME. *True* INSTRUCTION *was in his mouth and nothing* FALSE *was found on his lips. He* WALKED *with Me in* PEACE *and* UPRIGHTNESS, *and* TURNED *many from* SIN . *For the* LIPS *of a priest ought to* PRESERVE *knowledge, and from his* MOUTH *men should* SEEK *instruction – because he is the* MESSENGER *of the Lord* ALMIGHTY Malachi 2:5-7

JOB DESCRIPTION FOR A JUDGE

(Moses said)...the people come to me to SEEK *God's* WILL . *Whenever they have a* DISPUTE , *it is brought to me, and I* DECIDE *between the parties and* INFORM *them of God's* DECREES *and* LAWS . Exodus 18:15-16

232

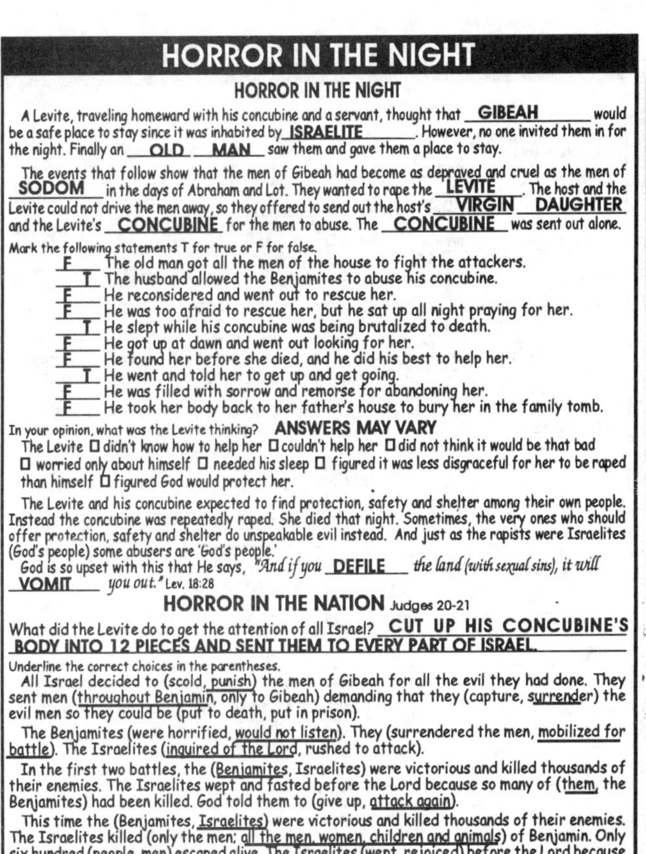

HORROR IN THE NIGHT

HORROR IN THE NIGHT

A Levite, traveling homeward with his concubine and a servant, thought that **GIBEAH** would be a safe place to stay since it was inhabited by **ISRAELITE**. However, no one invited them in for the night. Finally an **OLD MAN** saw them and gave them a place to stay.

The events that follow show that the men of Gibeah had become as depraved and cruel as the men of **SODOM** in the days of Abraham and Lot. They wanted to rape the **LEVITE**. The host and the Levite could not drive the men away, so they offered to send out the host's **VIRGIN DAUGHTER** and the Levite's **CONCUBINE** for the men to abuse. The **CONCUBINE** was sent out alone.

Mark the following statements T for true or F for false.

- F The old man got all the men of the house to fight the attackers.
- T The husband allowed the Benjamites to abuse his concubine.
- F He reconsidered and went out to rescue her.
- F He was too afraid to rescue her, but he sat up all night praying for her.
- T He slept while his concubine was being brutalized to death.
- F He got up at dawn and went out looking for her.
- F He found her before she died, and he did his best to help her.
- T He went and told her to get up and get going.
- F He was filled with sorrow and remorse for abandoning her.
- F He took her body back to her father's house to bury her in the family tomb.

In your opinion, what was the Levite thinking? **ANSWERS MAY VARY**
The Levite ☐ didn't know how to help her ☐ couldn't help her ☐ did not think it would be that bad ☐ worried only about himself ☐ needed his sleep ☐ figured it was less disgraceful for her to be raped than himself ☐ figured God would protect her.

The Levite and his concubine expected to find protection, safety and shelter among their own people. Instead the concubine was repeatedly raped. She died that night. Sometimes, the very ones who should offer protection, safety and shelter do unspeakable evil instead. And just as the rapists were Israelites (God's people) some abusers are 'God's people.'

God is so upset with this that He says, *"And if you* **DEFILE** *the land (with sexual sins), it will* **VOMIT** *you out."* Lev. 18:28

HORROR IN THE NATION Judges 20-21

What did the Levite do to get the attention of all Israel? **CUT UP HIS CONCUBINE'S BODY INTO 12 PIECES AND SENT THEM TO EVERY PART OF ISRAEL.**

Underline the correct choices in the parentheses.

All Israel decided to (scold, punish) the men of Gibeah for all the evil they had done. They sent men (throughout Benjamin, only to Gibeah) demanding that they (capture, surrender) the evil men so they could be (put to death, put in prison).

The Benjamites (were horrified, would not listen). They (surrendered the men, mobilized for battle). The Israelites (inquired of the Lord, rushed to attack).

In the first two battles, the (Benjamites, Israelites) were victorious and killed thousands of their enemies. The Israelites wept and fasted before the Lord because so many of (them, the Benjamites) had been killed. God told them to (give up, attack again).

This time the (Benjamites, Israelites) were victorious and killed thousands of their enemies. The Israelites killed (only the men; all the men, women, children and animals) of Benjamin. Only six hundred (people, men) escaped alive. The Israelites (wept, rejoiced) before the Lord because so many of (them, the Benjamites) had been killed. They were afraid that the tribe of Benjamin would (become strong again, die out).

The Israelites had taken an oath not to give their daughters to the Benjamites for wives. So they did the best they knew how. This involved the (massacre of, treaty with) Jabesh Gilead, and the (wooing, kidnapping) of virgins there and at Shiloh.

What a lot of suffering occured for the evil acts of a few!

233

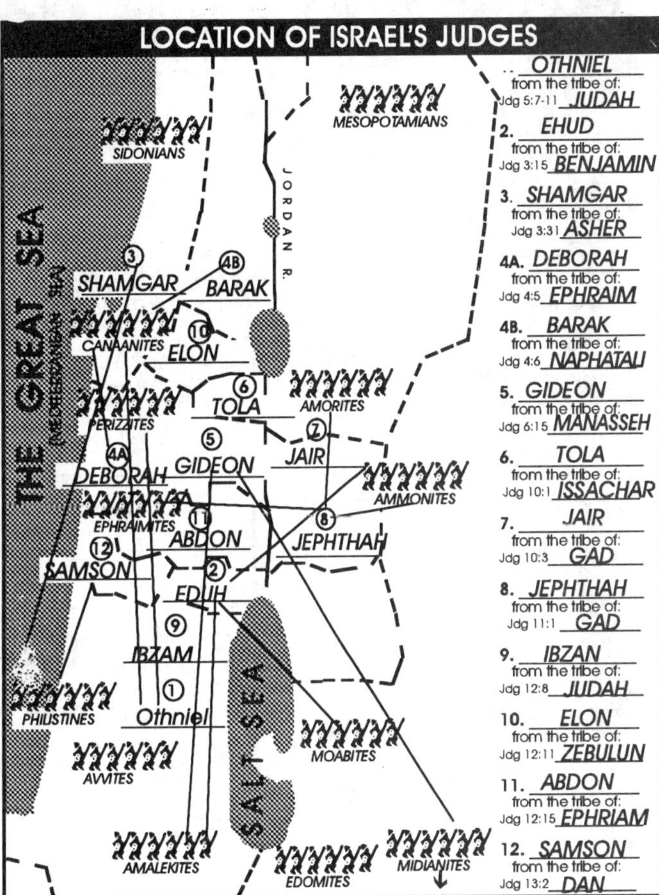

234

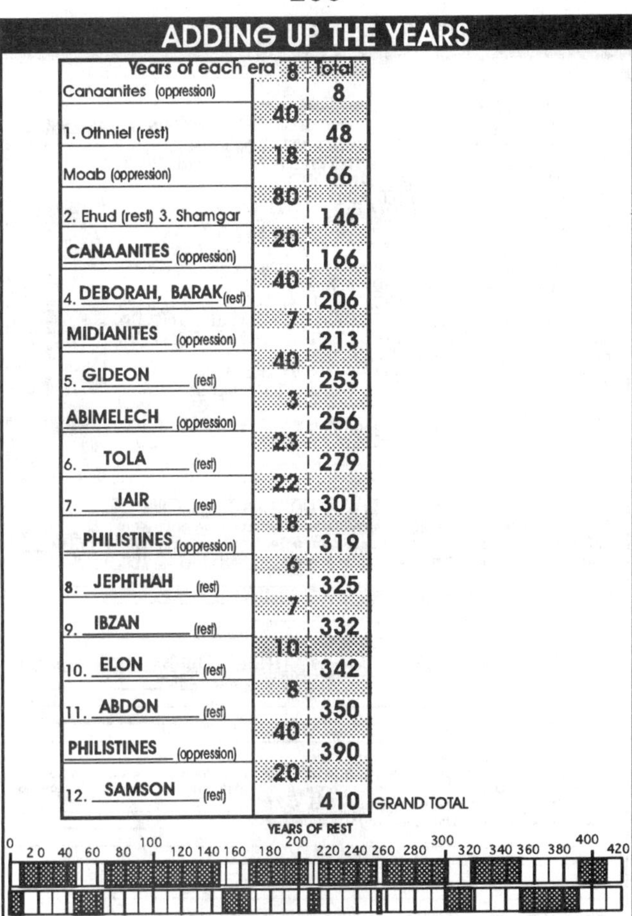

ADDING UP THE YEARS

Years of each era		Total
Canaanites (oppression)	8	8
1. Othniel (rest)	40	48
Moab (oppression)	18	66
2. Ehud (rest) 3. Shamgar	80	146
CANAANITES (oppression)	20	166
4. DEBORAH, BARAK (rest)	40	206
MIDIANITES (oppression)	7	213
5. GIDEON (rest)	40	253
ABIMELECH (oppression)	3	256
6. TOLA (rest)	23	279
7. JAIR (rest)	22	301
PHILISTINES (oppression)	18	319
8. JEPHTHAH (rest)	6	325
9. IBZAN (rest)	7	332
10. ELON (rest)	10	342
11. ABDON (rest)	8	350
PHILISTINES (oppression)	40	390
12. SAMSON (rest)	20	410 GRAND TOTAL

235

NAME THAT JUDGE

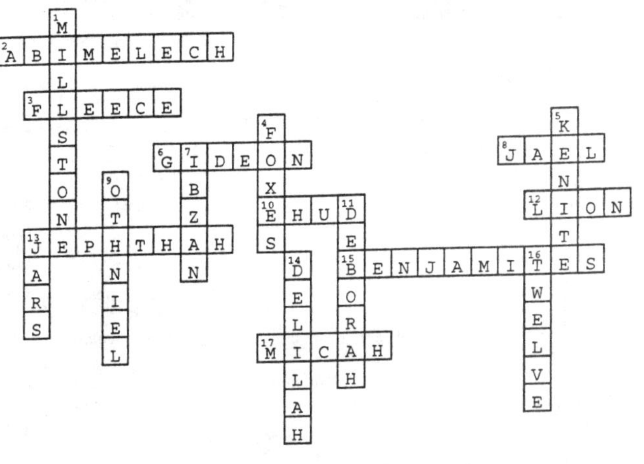

236

OVERVIEW OF RUTH

Read the book of Ruth in one sitting. How long did it take? **ANSWERS WILL VARY**

What kind of literature is it? ☐ Poetry ■ Narrative (story) ☐ History (of nations, kings, wars) ☐ Letter ■ Genealogy (family tree) ☐ Persuasive (logical argument) ☐ Instruction ☐ Fable ☐ Parable ☐ Proverb

Briefly describe the main characters. **ANSWERS WILL VARY. SOME POSSIBILITIES:**

Naomi **SAD, WIDOWED, BEREAVED OF SONS, BLAMES GOD, LOVES AND GUIDES RUTH IN THE ISRAELITE CULTURE.**

Ruth **DEVOTED DAUGHTER-IN-LAW, WIDOW, CHILDLESS, HARD-WORKING, VERY GOOD, HUMBLE, LISTENED TO ADVICE.**

Boaz **RICH, GOD-LOVING, GENEROUS, KIND, OBSERVANT, QUICK TO ACT ON PLANS.**

Describe the following places, including the main events that occurred at each.

Israel before the family left **FAMINE, JUDGES RULING**

Moab during the family's stay there **THREE MEN DIED LEAVING THE THREE WIDOWS**

Israel after ten years **GOD CAME TO THEIR AID, PROVIDING FOOD**

The town of Bethlehem **HAD FIELDS OF GRAIN. NEWS SPREAD QUICKLY. PEOPLE KNEW EVERYONE. MUCH EXCITEMENT OVER RETURN AND MARRIAGE.**

Boaz' fields **QUITE LARGE & PRODUCTIVE. HE EMPLOYED MEN & WOMEN. RUTH GLEANED THERE, PROTECTED BY BOAZ. RUTH PROPOSED THERE.**

The town gate **BOAZ FOUND THE NEARER KINSMAN AND OFFERED NAOMI'S FIELD FOR SALE, BUT MAN GAVE UP RIGHT. BOAZ MARRIED RUTH.**

Trace the route the family might have taken to Moab. Estimate the distance they traveled. **45 MILES**

At 15 miles a day (with all their possessions) how many days might the journey have taken? **3 DAYS**

How was Moab related to Israel? (See "Family Trouble for the Israelites.") **DESCENDANTS OF LOT**

Note any interesting observations you made. Example: Naomi urged Ruth to follow Orpah and return to their own gods.

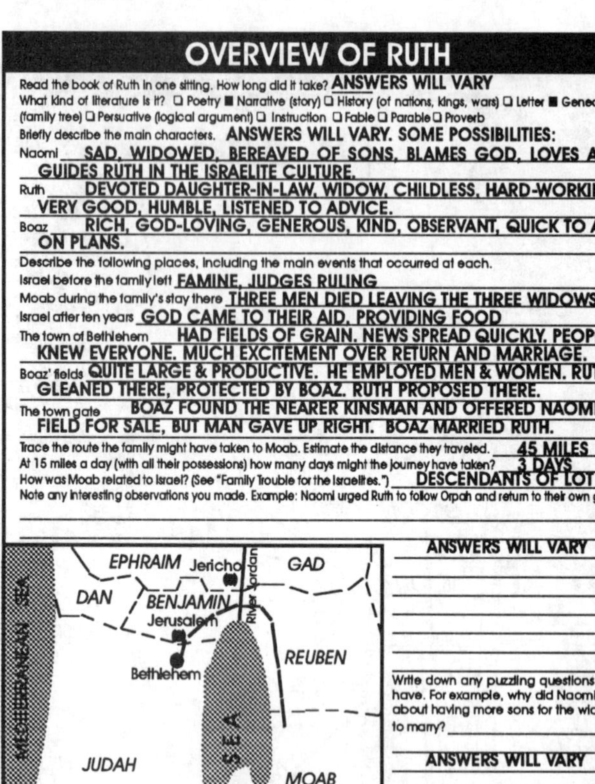

ANSWERS WILL VARY

Write down any puzzling questions you have. For example, why did Naomi talk about having more sons for the widows to marry?

ANSWERS WILL VARY

GLEANINGS FROM RUTH 1

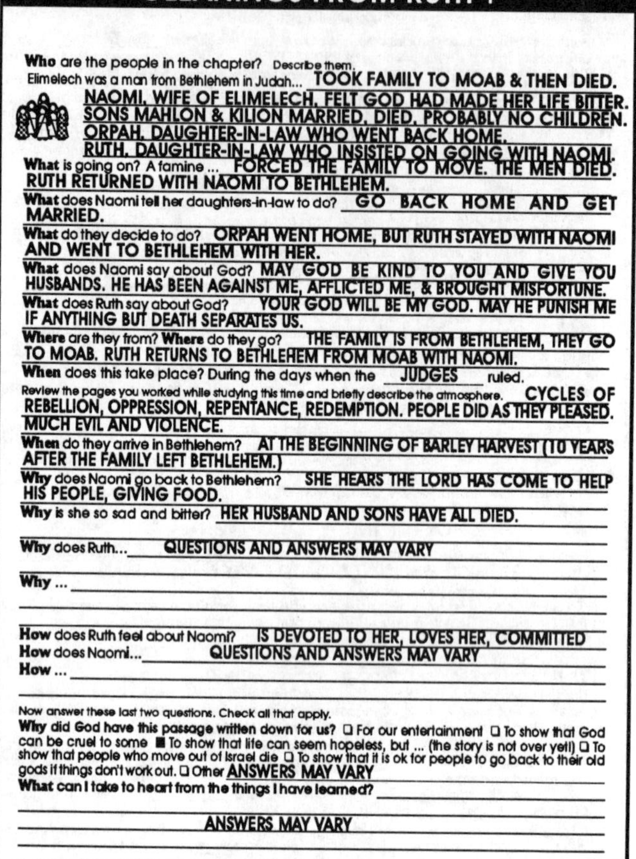

Who are the people in the chapter? Describe them.

Elimelech was a man from Bethlehem in Judah... **TOOK FAMILY TO MOAB & THEN DIED.**

NAOMI, WIFE OF ELIMELECH, FELT GOD HAD MADE HER LIFE BITTER.

SONS MAHLON & KILION MARRIED, DIED, PROBABLY NO CHILDREN.

ORPAH, DAUGHTER-IN-LAW WHO WENT BACK HOME.

RUTH, DAUGHTER-IN-LAW WHO INSISTED ON GOING WITH NAOMI.

What is going on? A famine ... **FORCED THE FAMILY TO MOVE. THE MEN DIED. RUTH RETURNED WITH NAOMI TO BETHLEHEM.**

What does Naomi tell her daughters-in-law to do? **GO BACK HOME AND GET MARRIED.**

What do they decide to do? **ORPAH WENT HOME, BUT RUTH STAYED WITH NAOMI AND WENT TO BETHLEHEM WITH HER.**

What does Naomi say about God? **MAY GOD BE KIND TO YOU AND GIVE YOU HUSBANDS. HE HAS BEEN AGAINST ME, AFFLICTED ME, & BROUGHT MISFORTUNE.**

What does Ruth say about God? **YOUR GOD WILL BE MY GOD. MAY HE PUNISH ME IF ANYTHING BUT DEATH SEPARATES US.**

Where are they from? **Where** do they go? **THE FAMILY IS FROM BETHLEHEM, THEY GO TO MOAB. RUTH RETURNS TO BETHLEHEM FROM MOAB WITH NAOMI.**

When does this take place? During the days when the **JUDGES** ruled.

Review the pages you worked while studying this time and briefly describe the atmosphere. **CYCLES OF REBELLION, OPPRESSION, REPENTANCE, REDEMPTION. PEOPLE DID AS THEY PLEASED. MUCH EVIL AND VIOLENCE.**

When do they arrive in Bethlehem? **AT THE BEGINNING OF BARLEY HARVEST (10 YEARS AFTER THE FAMILY LEFT BETHLEHEM.)**

Why does Naomi go back to Bethlehem? **SHE HEARS THE LORD HAS COME TO HELP HIS PEOPLE, GIVING FOOD.**

Why is she so sad and bitter? **HER HUSBAND AND SONS HAVE ALL DIED.**

Why does Ruth... **QUESTIONS AND ANSWERS MAY VARY**

Why ...

How does Ruth feel about Naomi? **IS DEVOTED TO HER, LOVES HER, COMMITTED**

How does Naomi... **QUESTIONS AND ANSWERS MAY VARY**

How ...

Now answer these last two questions. Check all that apply.

Why did God have this passage written down for us? ☐ For our entertainment ☐ To show that God can be cruel to some ■ To show that life can seem hopeless, but ... (the story is not over yet!) ☐ To show that people who move out of Israel die ☐ To show that it is ok for people to go back to their old gods if things don't work out. ☐ Other **ANSWERS MAY VARY**

What can I take to heart from the things I have learned?

ANSWERS MAY VARY

RUTH

ר.ע.ה. 'associate'

The root רָעָה meant to tend, to pasture, or to rule over the flock. The words that have come from this root include shepherd, pasture, graze, but also a whole array of words that contain the meaning 'associate.'

Hebrew word	Definition	Relates to root meaning 'associate'
1. רָעָה	**6** ru'Uth means 'additional wife'	**10** Ruth, a permanent *associate* of Naomi
2. רְעוּאֵל	**1** ro'oh means 'pastor'	**1** The leader who closely *associates* with church members
3. רֵיעַ	**7** rO'E means 'shepherd'	**6** An additional female *associated*
4. רֵעַ	**4** rA' means 'a thought'	**9** A close female who is *associated* with love
5. רֵעֶה	**5** rA'oh means 'friend' (male)	**4** An *association* of ideas
6. רְעוּת	**3** rAyÖ' means 'brother,' 'boyfriend,' husband,'	**2** Reuel, the father-in-law of Moses who gave good advice because of his *assocation* with God.
7. רֹעִי	**2** ru'UAl a boy's name that means 'friend of God'	**8** Where sheep graze together in close *association*
8. רְעִי	**8** ru'E means 'pasture'	
9. רַעְיָה	**10** rUth a girl's name that means 'friend' **5**	**3** A close male *associate*
10. רוּת	**9** rä'uyoh means 'girlfriend'	**7** The leader who closely *associates* with a flock

Ruth's vow: / **Ruth chose to permanently associate with Naomi:**

1. *"Don't urge me to leave you* — **8** *by planning to be buried with her.*
2. *or to turn back from you.* — **2** *by having no plans to go back even if times were tough.*
3. *Where you go I will go,* — **5** *by leaving her own people.*
4. *and where you stay I will stay.* — **3** *by saying she would go wherever Naomi lead.*
5. *Your people will be my people* — **6** *by rejecting the gods of her people for the one true God.*
6. *and your God my God.* — **7** *by making a lifetime vow. 'Til' death do us part.'*
7. *Where you die I will die,* — **1** *by committing herself to Naomi regardless of Naomi's urgings.*
8. *and there I will be buried...."* — **4** *by staying with her regardless of an uncertain future.*

How did Ruth's choice to permanently *associate* with Naomi work out? **SHE MARRIED A GOOD AND WEALTHY MAN AND BECAME THE GREAT-GRANDMOTHER OF KING DAVID.**

GLEANINGS FROM RUTH 2

Who are the people in the chapter? Describe them.

Boaz... **WAS A MAN OF STANDING** and was related to Naomi ... **ON HUSBAND'S SIDE**

Naomi who **SAW THINGS WERE GOING WELL FOR RUTH**

Ruth who **IS DEVOTED, HARDWORKING, HUMBLE, GRATEFUL**

The foreman who seems **HONEST AND KIND**

The men harvesting **OBEYED BOAZ**

The servant girls **RUTH KEPT CLOSE TO THEM IN THE FIELDS**

What is going on? Review Leviticus 19:9-10. Ruth is **GLEANING AS A POOR, WIDOWED FOREIGNER, TO GET FOOD FOR HERSELF AND NAOMI.**

What is Boaz doing at a time when "everyone did as he saw fit?" **OBEYING THE LAW ABOUT GLEANING, AND MORE -- BEING KIND.**

What does Boaz do for Ruth? **INVITES HER TO GLEAN IN HIS FIELDS THE WHOLE SEASON, TELLS THE MEN TO LEAVE HER ALONE, GIVES ACCESS TO WATER, GIVES LUNCH, TELLS MEN TO DROP STALKS OF GRAIN FOR HER, NOT TO EMBARRASS OR REBUKE HER.**

What do we find out about the character of Boaz? **KIND, GENEROUS, RESPECTFUL, OBSERVANT, HAS THE OBEDIENCE OF HIS EMPLOYEES.**

What does Naomi say about Ruth's first day of work? **GOD BLESS THE MAN WHO NOTICED YOU! HE IS OUR RELATIVE. IT WILL BE GOOD FOR YOU.**

What ... **QUESTIONS AND ANSWERS WILL VARY.**

What ...

Where does all this take place? **IN BOAZ' FIELDS AND IN BETHLEHEM**

When does this take place? **BARLEY HARVEST** How many days are covered in verses 1-22? **ONE**

How long does Ruth continue to glean? (See Seasons and Feasts calendar) **ALMOST 4 MONTHS**

Why is Naomi surprised when Ruth returns from work? **SHE HAS SO MUCH FOOD**

Why ... **QUESTIONS AND ANSWERS WILL VARY.**

Why ...

How much does Ruth bring home that first day? **AN EPHAH - 22 LITERS - ALMOST 6 GALLONS**

How ... **QUESTIONS AND ANSWERS WILL VARY.**

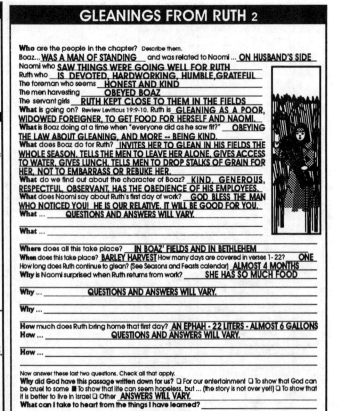

How ...

Now answer these last two questions. Check all that apply.

Why did God have this passage written down for us? ☐ For our entertainment ☐ To show that God can be cruel to some ■ To show that life can seem hopeless, but ... (the story is not over yet!) ☐ To show that it is better to live in Israel ☐ Other **ANSWERS WILL VARY.**

What can I take to heart from the things I have learned?

ANSWERS WILL VARY.

GLEANINGS FROM RUTH 3

Who are the people in the chapter? NAOMI, BOAZ, RUTH

What new qualities of each do we discover? NAOMI SEEKS RUTH'S SECURITY, GIVES ADVICE TO RUTH; RUTH FOLLOWS NAOMI'S ADVICE. NOBLE CHARACTER IS RECOGNIZED ALL OVER TOWN. BOAZ TAKES PART IN THE WORK, UNDERSTANDS RUTH'S MESSAGE, QUICK TO TAKE ACTION, VERY PLEASED WITH RUTH'S PROPOSAL, DISCREET.

What do the townsmen think of Ruth? NOBLE CHARACTER

What is going on? Naomi is trying to find a HUSBAND AND HOME FOR RUTH

Read Leviticus 25:25 and Deuteronomy 25:5-10

What should a near relative redeem? LAND THAT A POOR RELATIVE HAS TO SELL

What should a man do for his brother who dies childless? MARRY HIS WIDOW. HER FIRST SON WILL CARRY ON THE DEAD MAN'S NAME.

What does Naomi instruct Ruth to do? GO TO THE THRESHING FLOOR. WHEN BOAZ LIES DOWN, UNCOVER HIS FEET AND LIE DOWN. HE'LL TELL YOU WHAT TO DO.

What did Ruth mean when she asked Boaz to spread the corner of his garment over her? SHE WAS ASKING HIM TO MARRY HER.

Where ...

Where ...

When ...

When ...

Why does Boaz want to keep the nighttime meeting a secret? ANSWERS WILL VARY. PERHAPS SO PEOPLE WOULD NOT THINK EVIL OF THEM.

Why ... QUESTIONS AND ANSWERS WILL VARY.

Why ...

How does Boaz feel about Ruth's proposal? DELIGHTED. BLESSES HER FOR NOT RUNNING AFTER YOUNGER MEN. WANTS TO MARRY HER.

How can you know that Ruth's actions were not indecent? NAOMI ADVISED HER TO DO THIS. SHE WAS TO GET INSTRUCTIONS FROM BOAZ. BOAZ TOLD HER HIS PLAN.

How ... QUESTIONS AND ANSWERS WILL VARY.

How ...

Now answer these last two questions. Check all that apply.

Why did God have this passage written down for us? ☐ For our entertainment ■ To show the value of a noble reputation ☐ To show that people must slyly work out their own problems ☐ Other ANSWERS WILL VARY.

What difference would it make if I took to heart the things I have learned?

ANSWERS WILL VARY.

GLEANINGS FROM RUTH 4

Who is involved in the redemption transaction, and how?

Boaz OFFERING LAND TO NEXT OF KIN, THEN REDEEMING IT AND RUTH

The unnamed kinsman-redeemer GIVES UP RIGHT OF REDEMPTION

The elders WITNESSES TO TRANSACTION

The people WITNESSES TO TRANSACTION

What do the people say about the proposed marriage? WE ARE WITNESSES. MAY GOD GIVE RUTH MANY CHILDREN. MAY BOAZ BE FAMOUS.

Who ... QUESTIONS AND ANSWERS WILL VARY.

Who ...

What is going on? Boaz is redeeming RUTH & FAMILY LAND

Read Deuteronomy 25:5-10 again.

What is the purpose of marrying a brother's widow? TO PRODUCE A SON TO CARRY ON THE DEAD MAN'S NAME

What should happen to a man who refuses to do this? WIDOW PULLS HIS SANDAL OFF, SPITS IN HIS FACE. "THIS IS WHAT IS DONE TO THE MAN WHO WILL NOT TO BUILD UP HIS BROTHER'S FAMILY LINE."

How is the ceremony in Ruth different? NO SPITTING. THE MAN REMOVED HIS OWN SANDAL AND GAVE IT TO BOAZ. NO SHAME INVOLVED.

What ...

Where ... QUESTIONS AND ANSWERS WILL VARY.

Where ...

When ...

When ...

Why does Boaz offer the land to the other man? THE OTHER MAN IS MORE CLOSELY RELATED TO NAOMI AND HAS FIRST RIGHTS.

Why ... QUESTIONS AND ANSWERS WILL VARY.

Why ...

How can this passage help explain genealogies in which the names don't seem to match? Hint: Name four people who were called Obed's parents. PERSON MAY BE CALLED THE CHILD OF SOMEONE OTHER THAN BIRTH PARENTS. RUTH & BOAZ, LEGALLY MAHLON, ALSO NAOMI.

How ...

Now answer these last two questions. Check all that apply.

Why did God have this passage written down for us? ☐ For our entertainment ■ To show the wisdom of the Law ■ To show how a believing Moabite became the great-grandmother of King David ☐ Other ANSWERS MAY VARY

What difference would it make if I took to heart the things I have learned?

ANSWERS MAY VARY

REDEEMING RUTH

1. Boaz fulfilled the law and became the kinsman-redeemer when a close relative refused to.
2. Ruth went on and on to Naomi about one blessing after another that she had received from Boaz. Boaz had given her food, water, safety, companions, extra provisions, and even a place to sit down and rest.
3. Boaz was honored to bring Ruth into his household even though a lesser man would have looked down on her for being a foreigner, an alien, a widow, childless, and poor.
4. Boaz spread the corner or wings of his garment over Ruth, as a sign of his willingness to care for her.
5. Naomi's life was empty of hope until Boaz redeemedit by marrying Ruth.
6. Boaz took Ruth as his bride.
7. Boaz gave Ruth a home.

__4__ (Jesus said,) "O Jerusalem, Jerusalem, you who kill the prophets and stone those sent to you, how often I have longed to gather your children together, as a hen gathers her chicks under her wings, but you were not willing!" Luke 13:34

__7__ (Jesus said,) "Do not let your hearts be troubled. Trust in God; trust also in Me. In My Father's house are many rooms; if it were not so, I would have told you. I am going there to prepare a place for you. And if I go and prepare a place for you, I will come back and take you to be with Me that you also may be where I am." John 14:1-3

__6__ I saw the Holy City, the new Jerusalem, coming down out of heaven from God, prepared as a bride beautifully dressed for her husband. And I heard a loud voice from the throne saying, "Now the dwelling of God is with men, and He will live with them. They will be His people, and God Himself will be with them and be their God. Revelation 21:2-3

__1__ (Jesus said,) "Do not think that I have come to abolish the Law or the Prophets; I have not come to abolish them but to fulfill them." Matthew 5:17

__2__ From the fullness of His grace we have all received one blessing after another. John 1:16

__5__ For you know that it was not with perishable things such as silver or gold that you were redeemed from the empty way of life handed down to you from your forefathers, but with the precious blood of Christ, a lamb without blemish or defect. 1 Peter 1:18

__3__ Now in Christ Jesus you who once were far away have been brought near through the blood of Christ ... Consequently you are no longer foreigners and aliens, but fellow citizens with God's people and members of God's household... Ephesians 2:12-13, 19

Write an entry in Ruth's journal for the day Boaz redeemed her. She should write about the past hardships, her wonderful kinsman-redeemer, and her hope for the future.

ANSWERS WILL VARY

RUTH

EXAMPLE ONLY. ANSWERS MAY VARY.

Where you GO I will GO, and where you STAY I will STAY. Your people will be MY people and your GOD my GOD.

May the Lord REPAY you for what you have DONE. May you be richly REWARDED by the Lord, the God of Israel, under whose wings you have COME to take REFUGE.

RUTH GIVES LOVE AND COMMITMENT

Chapter 1 — RUTH HELPS NAOMI — RUTH CHOOSES GOD & NAOMI

- NAOMI & FAMILY LEAVE BETHLEHEM FOR MOAB
- NAOMI'S HUSBAND DIES
- NAOMI'S SONS MARRY MOABITE WOMEN
- NAOMI'S SONS DIE
- NAOMI PREPARES TO RETURN HOME
- ONE DAUGHTER-IN-LAW STAYS; ONE GOES
- NAOMI AND RUTH RETURN TO BETHLEHEM

Chapter 2 — BOAZ HELPS RUTH — RUTH IS HARD-WORKING & HUMBLE

- RUTH GOES TO THE BARLEY FIELDS
- RUTH ENDS UP IN THE FIELDS OF BOAZ
- BOAZ TELLS HER TO STAY IN HIS FIELDS
- RUTH IS SURPRISED AT HIS KINDNESS
- BOAZ IS IMPRESSED WITH HER DEDICATION
- BOAZ FEEDS HER AND GIVES EXTRA GRAIN
- RUTH HAS MUCH TO GIVE NAOMI
- RUTH IS PROTECTED BY BOAZ' ORDER
- RUTH STAYS IN BOAZ' FIELDS FOR THE WHEAT HARVEST

RUTH RECEIVES LOVE AND COMMITMENT

Chapter 3 — RUTH SEEKS OUT BOAZ — RUTH'S CHARACTER ATTRACTS BOAZ

- NAOMI TELLS RUTH TO TRY TO MARRY BOAZ
- RUTH LIES AT BOAZ' FEET ON THE THRESHING FLOOR
- BOAZ DISCOVERS RUTH
- RUTH ASKS BOAZ TO REDEEM HER
- BOAZ IS SURPRISED AT HER KINDNESS
- BOAZ SENDS RUTH BACK WITH BARLEY

Chapter 4 — BOAZ MARRIES RUTH — RUTH JOINS THE ROYAL LINE

- BOAZ GOES AND FINDS THE KINSMAN-REDEEMER
- BOAZ TELLS HIM OF THE SALE OF NAOMI'S FIELDS
- THE KINSMAN SAYS HE WANTS THEM
- BOAZ SAYS THAT RUTH IS PART OF THE DEAL
- THE KINSMAN BACKS OUT
- BOAZ BUYS THE LAND AND ACQUIRES RUTH
- THE ELDERS GIVE A BLESSING TO RUTH
- BOAZ MARRIES RUTH
- RUTH GIVES BIRTH TO A SON
- WOMEN PRAISE GOD FOR RUTH
- THE SON IS NAMED OBED
- OBED IS THE FATHER OF JESSE
- JESSE IS THE FATHER OF KING DAVID

BIRTH OF SAMUEL

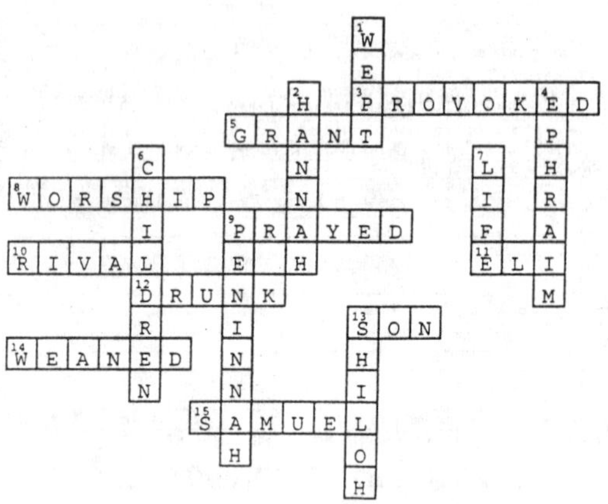

RATS! FOILED AGAIN!

The Israelites went to (make peace, **fight**) the Philistines. The (**Philistines**, Israelites) killed 4,000 on the battlefield. The people sent for (more soldiers, **the ark of the Lord**). Eli's sons were with the ark.

When the ark of the Lord came into camp, (**all Israel**, the Philistines) raised such a great shout that the ground shook. The Philistines were (**afraid**, excited). They knew that the God of Israel struck the Egyptians with all kinds of (blessings, **plagues**). So they decided (to leave while they had a chance, **fight so they would not be slaves of the Hebrews**).

In the battle the (Israelites, **Philistines**) defeated the (**Israelites**, Philistines). They killed (**30,000**, 25) Israelites. They captured the ark and (captured, **killed**) Hophni and Phinehas. When Eli, who was (40, **98**) years old, heard what happened he fell backwards and broke his neck. He had led Israel (**40**, 98) years.

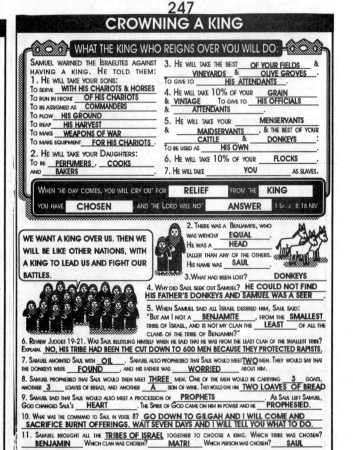

9. THE ISRAELITES ASSEMBLED AT MIZPAH FOR PRAYER, AND THE PHILISTINES ATTACKED. BUT GOD THUNDERED SO LOUDLY THAT THE PHILISTINES WERE FRIGHTENED AND RAN.

1. THE PHILISTINES' CAMP. THEY BEAT THE ISRAELITES, KILLING 4,000. THEN THEY KILLED 30,000 AND TOOK THE ARK.

2. ISRAEL'S CAMP.

3. PEOPLE TOOK THE ARK FROM SHILOH INTO BATTLE. ELI DIED HERE WHEN HE HEARD THE ARK WAS CAPTURED.

1. Aphek
2. Ebenezer
3. Shiloh
4. Ashdod
5. Gath
6. Ekron
7. Beth-Shemesh
8. Kiriath Jearim
9. Mizpah

6. THEY SENT THE ARK TO EKRON NEXT WHICH FRIGHTENED THE RESIDENTS. THEY PUT IT IN A CART DRAWN BY 2 COWS & LET THE COWS GO FREE.

4. THE PHILISTINES TOOK THE ARK TO ASHDOD, INTO DAGON'S TEMPLE. DAGON KEPT FALLING DOWN IN FRONT OF THE ARK, AND THE PEOPLE GOT TUMORS.

5. THEY TOOK THE ARK TO GATH NEXT. GOD THREW THE CITY INTO A PANIC AND GAVE EVERYONE TUMORS.

7. THE COWS BROUGHT THE ARK TO BETH-SHEMESH. THE ISRAELITES RECEIVED IT WITH JOY, BUT GOD KILLED 70 MEN FOR LOOKING INSIDE IT.

8. THE MEN OF KIRIATH JEARIM TOOK THE ARK TO ABINADAB'S HOUSE AND CONSECRATED HIS SON, ELEAZAR TO GUARD IT.

THE HEARTS OF FATHERS AND SONS

Birth and Dedication of Samuel

Samuel's father was **ELKANAH**. He had two wives, **PENINAH** who had sons and daughters, and **HANNAH** who was **BARREN**.

The wife with children provoked the other wife until she **WEPT** and would not **EAT**. In bitterness of **SOUL** Hannah **WEPT** much and **PRAYED** to the Lord.

What happened next? **ELI THOUGHT SHE WAS DRUNK BUT HEARD HER STORY AND SAID, "THE LORD GRANT YOUR WISH." SHE WENT HOME AND LATER HAD A SON.**

Hannah said, "I have **PRAYED** for this **CHILD**, and the Lord has granted me what I asked of Him. So now I **GIVE** him to the Lord. For his **WHOLE LIFE** he will be given over to the Lord." Hannah had **3** more sons and **2** daughters.

❤Contrast the Hearts of Fathers and Sons❤

1. Eli
2. Hophni
3. Abijah
4. Samuel
5. Phinehas
6. Joel

1	Recognized the Lord was speaking and told Samuel what to say.
2, 5	Had no regard for the Lord.
4	Anointed kings.
2, 5	Took raw meat and fat as it was being offered as a sacrifice.
1	Told the boy to tell him everything the Lord had said and not to hold back.
4	Never cheated or oppressed the people.
2, 5	Threatened to take what they wanted by force.
1	Rebuked his sons when he heard of their wicked ways.
3, 6	Got dishonest gain, accepted bribes, and perverted justice.
4	Grew in stature and in favor with the Lord and with men.
2, 5	Slept with women at the entrance to the Tent of Meetings.
4	The Lord was with him and did not let any of his words fall to the ground.
4	A faithful priest who will do according to what was in the Lord's heart.
1	Said, "If a man sins against the Lord, who will intercede for him?"
3, 6	Because of their unfaithfulness to the Lord, the people demanded a king.
2, 5, 1	All died in one day.
2, 5	Took the ark of God into battle.
1, 2, 5	Because of their sins, the family line would have to beg for bread.
4	The people recognized he was a prophet of the Lord.
5	Had a son after he died whose name meant 'Israel's glory has departed.'
1	Fell over backwards and broke his neck and died.
1	The Lord asked why he honored his sons more than Him.
2, 5	Were killed and the ark was captured by the Philistines.
4	Said, "Speak, for your servant is listening."
1	His sin was that he did not restrain his sons.
3, 6	They did not walk in the ways of Samuel.
1	Humbly said, "He is the Lord; let Him do what is good in His eyes."

Speak, for your servant is listening.

I will raise up for myself a **FAITHFUL** *priest, who will do according to what is in my* **heart** *and mind.* 1 Samuel 2:35A NIV

CROWNING A KING

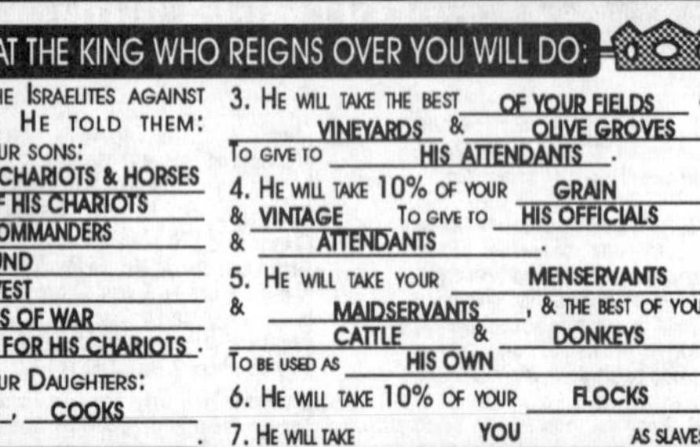

WHAT THE KING WHO REIGNS OVER YOU WILL DO:

SAMUEL WARNED THE ISRAELITES AGAINST HAVING A KING. HE TOLD THEM:

1. HE WILL TAKE YOUR SONS:
   - TO SERVE **WITH HIS CHARIOTS & HORSES**
   - TO RUN IN FRONT **OF HIS CHARIOTS**
   - TO BE ASSIGNED AS **COMMANDERS**
   - TO PLOW **HIS GROUND**
   - TO REAP **HIS HARVEST**
   - TO MAKE **WEAPONS OF WAR**
   - TO MAKE EQUIPMENT **FOR HIS CHARIOTS**.
2. HE WILL TAKE YOUR DAUGHTERS: TO BE **PERFUMERS**, **COOKS** AND **BAKERS**.
3. HE WILL TAKE THE BEST **OF YOUR FIELDS** & **VINEYARDS** & **OLIVE GROVES**. TO GIVE TO **HIS ATTENDANTS**.
4. HE WILL TAKE 10% OF YOUR **GRAIN** & **VINTAGE** TO GIVE TO **HIS OFFICIALS** & **ATTENDANTS**.
5. HE WILL TAKE YOUR **MENSERVANTS** & **MAIDSERVANTS**, & THE BEST OF YOUR **CATTLE** & **DONKEYS**: TO BE USED AS **HIS OWN**.
6. HE WILL TAKE 10% OF YOUR **FLOCKS**.
7. HE WILL TAKE **YOU** AS SLAVES.

WHEN THE DAY COMES, YOU WILL CRY OUT FOR **RELIEF** FROM THE **KING** YOU HAVE **CHOSEN**, AND THE LORD WILL NOT **ANSWER** 1 SAM 8:18 NIV

WE WANT A KING OVER US. THEN WE WILL BE LIKE OTHER NATIONS, WITH A KING TO LEAD US AND FIGHT OUR BATTLES.

2. THERE WAS A BENJAMITE, WHO WAS WITHOUT **EQUAL**. HE WAS A **HEAD** TALLER THAN ANY OF THE OTHERS. HIS NAME WAS **SAUL**.
3. WHAT HAD BEEN LOST? **DONKEYS**
4. WHY DID SAUL SEEK OUT SAMUEL? **HE COULD NOT FIND HIS FATHER'S DONKEYS AND SAMUEL WAS A SEER**.
5. WHEN SAMUEL SAID ALL ISRAEL DESIRED HIM, SAUL SAID: "BUT AM I NOT A **BENJAMITE**, FROM THE **SMALLEST** TRIBE OF ISRAEL, AND IS NOT MY CLAN THE **LEAST** OF ALL THE CLANS OF THE TRIBE OF BENJAMIN?"
6. REVIEW JUDGES 19-21. WAS SAUL BELITTLING HIMSELF WHEN HE SAID THAT HE WAS FROM THE LEAST CLAN OF THE SMALLEST TRIBE? EXPLAIN. **NO, HIS TRIBE HAD BEEN THE CUT DOWN TO 600 MEN BECAUSE THEY PROTECTED RAPISTS.**
7. SAMUEL ANOINTED SAUL WITH **OIL**. SAMUEL ALSO PROPHESIED THAT SAUL WOULD MEET **TWO** MEN. THEY WOULD SAY THAT THE DONKEYS WERE **FOUND**, AND HIS FATHER WAS **WORRIED** ABOUT HIM.
8. SAMUEL PROPHESIED THAT SAUL WOULD THEN MEET **THREE** MEN. ONE OF THE MEN WOULD BE CARRYING **3** GOATS, ANOTHER **3** LOAVES OF BREAD, AND ANOTHER **A** SKIN OF WINE. THEY WOULD GIVE HIM **TWO LOAVES OF BREAD**
9. SAMUEL SAID THAT SAUL WOULD ALSO MEET A PROCESSION OF **PROPHETS**. AS SAUL LEFT SAMUEL, GOD CHANGED SAUL'S **HEART**. THE SPIRIT OF GOD CAME ON HIM IN POWER AND HE **PROPHESIED.**
10. WHAT WAS THE COMMAND TO SAUL IN VERSE 8? **GO DOWN TO GILGAH AND I WILL COME AND SACRIFICE BURNT OFFERINGS. WAIT SEVEN DAYS AND I WILL TELL YOU WHAT TO DO.**
11. SAMUEL BROUGHT ALL THE **TRIBES OF ISRAEL** TOGETHER TO CHOOSE A KING. WHICH TRIBE WAS CHOSEN? **BENJAMIN** WHICH CLAN WAS CHOSEN? **MATRI** WHICH PERSON WAS CHOSEN? **SAUL**
12. WHERE WAS SAUL? **HIDING IN THE BAGGAGE** WHAT DID THE PEOPLE SHOUT? **'LONG LIVE THE KING!'**
13. WHO WENT HOME WITH SAUL? **VALIANT** MEN WHOSE **HEARTS** GOD HAD **TOUCHED**.
14. WHAT DID THE TROUBLEMAKERS SAY? **'HOW CAN THIS FELLOW SAVE US?'** HOW DID SAUL'S RESPOND? **HE WAS SILENT**

SAUL'S FAMILY TREE

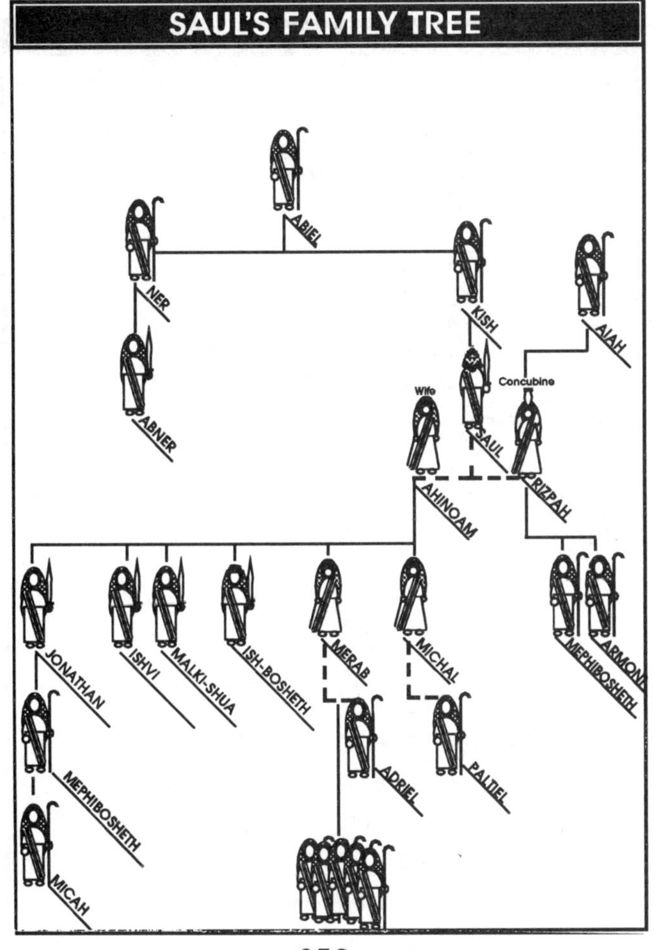

SAUL'S FAMILY TREE CROSSWORD

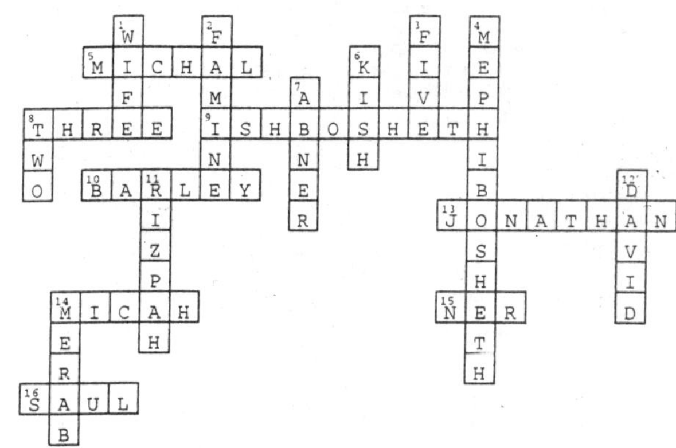

FIRST KING OF ISRAEL

KING SAUL

BIBLE REFERENCES: 1 Samuel 11, 13, 14, 31
Age when became King: 30
Length of reign: 40
Wife's name: AHINOAM
Children's names: Boys: JONATHAN ISHVI (ABINADAB) MALKI-SHUA
Girls: MERAB, MICHAL
Saul's cousin & army commander: ABNER
How did Saul die? HE WAS WOUNDED IN BATTLE AND KILLED HIMSELF BY FALLING ON HIS SWORD.
Buried: BURNED AND BURIED AT JABESH UNDER A TAMARISK TREE.

BEGAN REIGN: ☐ RIGHTEOUS ■ EVIL
ENDED REIGN: ☐ RIGHTEOUS ■ EVIL

Check the boxes that reveal Saul's heart.

"You have done all this **EVIL** *; yet do* **NOT** *turn away from the Lord, but* **SERVE** *the Lord with all your* (heart). *Do not turn away after* **USELESS** *idols... For the sake of His* **GREAT** *name the Lord will* **NOT** *reject His people, because the Lord was* **PLEASED** *to make you His* **OWN** *...But be sure to* **FEAR** *the Lord and* **SERVE** *Him* **FAITHFULLY** *with all your* (heart) *;...Yet if you persist in doing* **EVIL** *, both you and your* **KING** *will be* **SWEPT** *away."* 1 Samuel 12:20-24

SAUL'S BATTLES: EXPLAIN THEM:

1st BATTLE Chapter 11

Jabesh Gilead: ISRAELITE TOWN ATTACKED BY AMMON.
Ammonites: THE PEOPLE ATTACKING THE TOWN. THEY AGREED TO A PEACE TREATY ON ONE CONDITION.
: ALL IN JABESH GILEAD WOULD HAVE TO HAVE THEIR RIGHT EYES GOUGED OUT.
: SAUL CUT UP OXEN AND SENT PIECES TO GET ISRAEL TO FIGHT.
Three divisions: SAUL DIVIDED HIS ARMY INTO THREE DIVISIONS.
Last watch of night: ATTACKED AMMONITES
No two together: AMMONITES WERE BEATEN.
"No one shall be put to death." SAUL DID NOT PUNISH THOSE WHO HAD OPPOSED HIM.
Gilgal: WHERE THE PEOPLE CONFIRMED SAUL AS KING.

2nd BATTLE Chapter 13

Soldiers: 2,000 with SAUL 1,000 with JONATHAN
Outpost at Geba: JONATHAN ATTACKED
: 3,000 PHILISTINE CHARIOTS
Seashore sand: NUMBER OF PHILISTINE SOLDIERS
Hid: ISRAEL HID IN CAVES, THICKETS, ROCKS, PITS & CISTERNS
Quaking with fear: ISRAELITE SOLDIERS.
7 day wait: SAUL WAITED FOR SAMUEL TO COME TO MAKE THE BURNT SACRIFICES.
: SAUL MADE THE SACRIFICES HIMSELF.
Samuel: CAME AND SAID, "YOU DISOBEYED GOD."
600: NUMBER OF SOLDIERS LEFT TO FIGHT.
2 swords & 2 spears: JONATHAN AND SAUL WERE THE ONLY ONES IN ALL ISRAEL THAT HAD WEAPONS.

3rd BATTLE Chapter 14

Micmash (1 Samuel 13:16): PHILISTINES CAMPED HERE
Philistines: A DETACHMENT WENT TO THE PASS.
Ahijah: PRIEST
Jonathan & armor-bearer WENT TO THE PHILISTINE OUTPOST TO SEE WHAT GOD WOULD DO.
The sign: IF THE PHILISTINES SAID, "COME UP HERE," THAT WOULD BE THE SIGN GOD WOULD GIVE THEM INTO THEIR HANDS.
20: JONATHAN & HIS ARMOR BEAR KILLED 20 PHILISTINES.
Curse: SAUL SAID ANYONE WHO ATE BEFORE THE BATTLE WAS OVER WOULD DIE.
: JONATHAN ATE SOME HONEY BECAUSE HE HAD NOT HEARD THE CURSE.
Ate blood: THE ISRAELITES WERE SO HUNGRY THEY ATE MEAT WITH ITS BLOOD.
Jonathan's life: THE PEOPLE DID NOT LET SAUL KILL HIM. HE HAD WON THE VICTORY.

WARS & CONFLICTS

MEDITERRANEAN SEA · ISRAEL · PHILISTIA
☐ SYRIA
☒ AMMON
☒ MOAB
☒ EDOM
☒ AMALEK
☒ ZOBAH?
☒ (PHILISTIA)

Put an X in the boxes of the people who had strife with Saul.

SAUL'S HEART

What God Said: (The Lord said...) *"Go attack the Amalekites and* **TOTALLY** *destroy* **EVERYTHING** *that belongs to them. Do* **NOT** *spare them; Put to* **DEATH** *men and women, children and infants,* **CATTLE** *and* **SHEEP** *, camels and donkeys"* 1 Samuel 15:3

Saul's Actions:

Obeyed	Disobeyed	
■	☐	Saul summoned an army of 210,000 soldiers.
■	☐	Saul set ambush to the city of Amalek.
■	☐	Saul attacked from Havilah to Shur to east of Egypt.
■	☐	Saul started to destroy the Amalekites.
☐	■	Saul took Agag the king of the Amalekites alive.
☐	■	Saul and the armies spared the best of the sheep and cattle.
☐	■	Saul kept the fat calves and lambs.
☐	■	Everything that was good was spared.
■	☐	They destroyed what was despised and weak.

Saul's Character:

1. Saul immediately built a monument (in God's honor, in his own honor).
2. Saul told Samuel, "I have carried out (the Lord's instructions, part of the Lord's instruction)."
3. When Samuel said that he heard the bleating of sheep and the lowing of cattle, Saul (admitted that he had spared them, blamed the soldiers for sparing them).
4. Saul (admitted to taking the plunder, said the sheep and cattle were for a sacrifice to Lord).
5. Saul implied (that he should have obeyed God and what he had done was wrong, that he had a better idea than God so what he did was a good thing).
6. Saul, when talking to Samuel, referred to God, as (the Lord my God, the Lord your God).
7. When Samuel repeated what God had instructed, Saul (broke down in sorrow and repentance, insisted that he had obeyed the Lord).
8. Saul argued he had obeyed the Lord by completely destroying the Amalekites (including the king, except for the king).
9. Saul (repeated that it was the soldiers who kept the plunder, said he as king was responsible for making the soldiers obey God).
10. After Samuel said that God had rejected Saul as king, Saul said, " (I have sinned by violating the Lord's command, I obeyed God's instructions)."
11. Saul said, " I am (responsible as King to lead my people, afraid of the people so I gave in to them)."
12. Because of his heart attitude, the Lord (tore the kingdom from Saul, gave more land to Saul).
13. When Saul admitted his sin, he wanted to worship with Samuel (to look good in the people's eyes, to seek forgiveness from the Lord his God).
14. All the rest of Samuel's life, he (mourned, rejoiced) for Saul.
15. The Lord was (grieved, delighted) that He had made Saul king over Israel.

Saul's (heart): BLUE

■ Rash ■ Arrogant ☐ Honest ■ Proud ☐ Humble ■ Compromising
☐ Obedient ■ Greedy ■ Arguing ■ Deceitful ■ Blaming ☐ Grateful

The Lord's (heart):

"Does the Lord delight in burnt **OFFERINGS** *and* **SACRIFICE** *as much as in* **OBEYING** *the voice of the* **LORD** *? To* **OBEY** *is better than* **SACRIFICE** *... For* **REBELLION** *is like the sin of* **DIVINATION** *and* **ARROGANCE** *like the evil of* **IDOLATRY** *."*

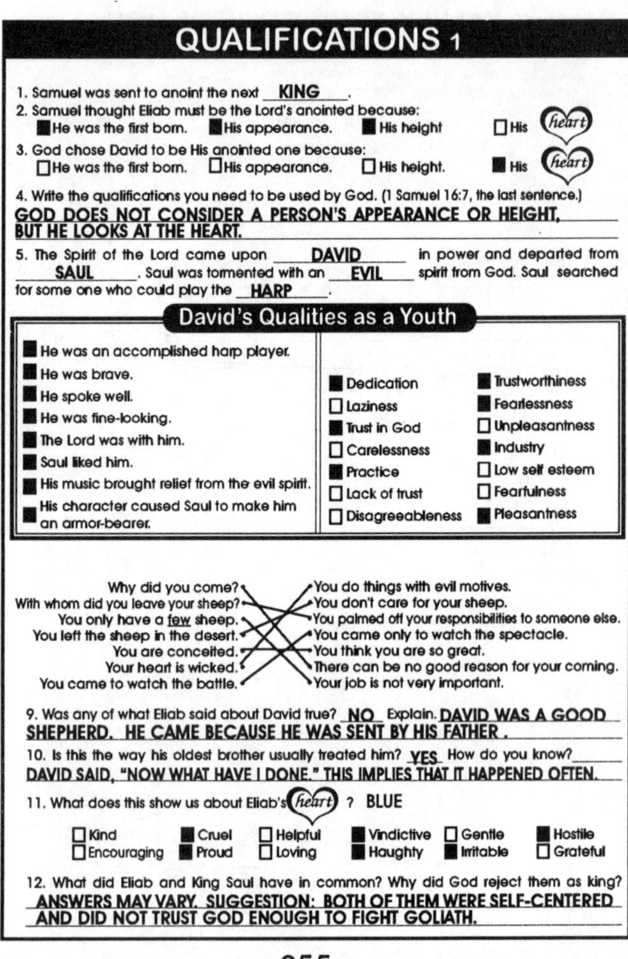

QUALIFICATIONS 1

1. Samuel was sent to anoint the next KING.
2. Samuel thought Eliab must be the Lord's anointed because:
   ■ He was the first born. ■ His appearance. ■ His height ☐ His heart
3. God chose David to be His anointed one because:
   ☐ He was the first born. ☐ His appearance. ☐ His height. ■ His heart
4. Write the qualifications you need to be used by God. (1 Samuel 16:7, the last sentence.)
   GOD DOES NOT CONSIDER A PERSON'S APPEARANCE OR HEIGHT, BUT HE LOOKS AT THE HEART.
5. The Spirit of the Lord came upon DAVID in power and departed from SAUL. Saul was tormented with an EVIL spirit from God. Saul searched for some one who could play the HARP.

David's Qualities as a Youth

- ■ He was an accomplished harp player.
- ■ He was brave.
- ■ He spoke well.
- ■ He was fine-looking.
- ■ The Lord was with him.
- ■ Saul liked him.
- ■ His music brought relief from the evil spirit.
- ■ His character caused Saul to make him an armor-bearer.

■ Dedication	■ Trustworthiness
☐ Laziness	■ Fearlessness
■ Trust in God	☐ Unpleasantness
☐ Carelessness	■ Industry
■ Practice	☐ Low self esteem
☐ Lack of trust	☐ Fearfulness
☐ Disagreeableness	■ Pleasantness

Why did you come? / With whom did you leave your sheep? / You only have a few sheep. / You left the sheep in the desert. / You are conceited. / Your heart is wicked. / You came to watch the battle.

You do things with evil motives. / You don't care for your sheep. / You palmed off your responsibilities to someone else. / You came only to watch the spectacle. / You think you are so great. / There can be no good reason for your coming. / Your job is not very important.

9. Was any of what Eliab said about David true? NO Explain. DAVID WAS A GOOD SHEPHERD. HE CAME BECAUSE HE WAS SENT BY HIS FATHER.
10. Is this the way his oldest brother usually treated him? YES How do you know? DAVID SAID, "NOW WHAT HAVE I DONE." THIS IMPLIES THAT IT HAPPENED OFTEN.
11. What does this show us about Eliab's heart? BLUE
   ☐ Kind ■ Cruel ☐ Helpful ■ Vindictive ☐ Gentle ■ Hostile
   ☐ Encouraging ■ Proud ☐ Loving ■ Haughty ■ Irritable ☐ Grateful
12. What did Eliab and King Saul have in common? Why did God reject them as king?
   ANSWERS MAY VARY. SUGGESTION: BOTH OF THEM WERE SELF-CENTERED AND DID NOT TRUST GOD ENOUGH TO FIGHT GOLIATH.

255

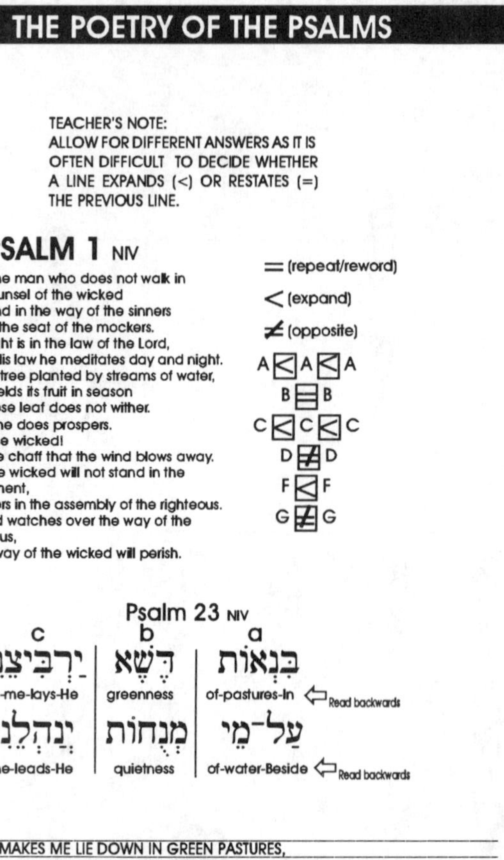

THE POETRY OF THE PSALMS

TEACHER'S NOTE:
ALLOW FOR DIFFERENT ANSWERS AS IT IS OFTEN DIFFICULT TO DECIDE WHETHER A LINE EXPANDS (<) OR RESTATES (=) THE PREVIOUS LINE.

PSALM 1 NIV

A. Blessed is the man who does not walk in the counsel of the wicked
A who stand in the way of the sinners
A or sits in the seat of the mockers.
B. But his delight is in the law of the Lord,
B and on His law he meditates day and night.
C. He is like a tree planted by streams of water,
C which yields its fruit in season
C and whose leaf does not wither.
D. What ever he does prospers.
D Not so the wicked!
E. They are like chaff that the wind blows away.
F. Therefore the wicked will not stand in the judgement,
F nor sinners in the assembly of the righteous.
G. For the Lord watches over the way of the righteous,
G but the way of the wicked will perish.

= (repeat/reword)
< (expand)
≠ (opposite)

A < A < A
B = B
C < C < C
D ≠ D
F < F
G ≠ G

Psalm 23 NIV

c	b	a	
יַרְבִּיצֵנִי	דֶּשֶׁא	בִּנְאוֹת	
.down-me-lays-He	greenness	of-pastures-In	⇦ Read backwards
יְנַהֲלֵנִי	מְנֻחוֹת	עַל־מֵי	
.me-leads-He	quietness	of-water-Beside	⇦ Read backwards

HE MAKES ME LIE DOWN IN GREEN PASTURES,
HE LEADS ME BESIDE QUIET WATERS.

ANSWERS WILL VARY

256

THE GOOD SHEPHERD

Good Shepherd/God/Jesus/Just leaders	Hired Hand/Bad Shepherd/Stranger/Thief
•He calls the sheep by NAME. •He is the gate. Who ever enters by him will be SAVED. •He comes that the sheep may have LIFE and have it to the full. •He lays down his LIFE for the sheep. •He has other sheep and they shall be one FLOCK with one SHEPHERD. •His sheep LISTEN to his voice; and FOLLOW him. •He will give them ETERNAL life, and no one can SNATCH them out of his hand.	•He does not ENTER the sheep pen by the GATE. •He CLIMBS in some other way. •The sheep WILL NEVER follow him. •The sheep run AWAY because they do not RECOGNIZE his voice. •He comes only to STEAL, KILL and DESTROY. •He does not OWN the sheep. •When he sees a wolf coming, he ABANDONS the sheep and runs AWAY. •He cares NOTHING for the sheep.
Jeremiah 23:1-4	
•He will GATHER a remnant of his flocks out of all the COUNTRIES. •He will BRING them back to their pastures where they will be FRUITFUL and INCREASE IN NUMBERS. •He will place shepherds over them so they will no longer be AFRAID or TERRIFIED, and NONE will be missing.	•They DESTROY and SCATTER the sheep. •They have DRIVEN them away, and not CARED for them. •God will PUNISH them for the EVIL they have done.
Ezekiel 34:1-16	
•He will RESCUE them from all the places they were LOST. •He will BRING them into their own land. •He will PASTURE them on the mountains. •He himself will TEND his sheep and have them LIE down. •He will SEARCH for the LOST and bring BACK the strays. •He will bind up the INJURED and STRENGTHEN the weak.	•They EAT the curds, clothe themselves with WOOL, and SLAUGHTER the choice animals. •They haven't STRENGTHENED the weak or HEALED the sick or BOUND up the injured. •They ruled them HARSHLY and BRUTALLY. •They SCATTERED the sheep so they became FOOD for the wild animals. •They have not SEARCHED for the lost sheep.
Isaiah 40:11	
•He TENDS his flocks. •He GATHERS the lambs in his arms. •He CARRIES them close to his heart. •He gently LEADS those with young.	

257

QUALIFICATIONS 2

Man's Qualifications for the Battle

1. What qualifications did Goliath have to challenge Israel?	2. What were Saul's qualifications to possibly accept Goliath's challenge?	3. What were David's qualifications to possibly accept Goliath's challenge?
■ He was tall.	■ He was tall.	☐ He was tall.
■ He had a bronze helmet.	■ He had a bronze helmet.	☐ He had a bronze helmet.
■ He had a coat of armor.	■ He had a coat of armor.	☐ He had a coat of armor.
■ He had large weapons.	■ He had large weapons.	☐ He had large weapons.
■ He had a shield/armor bearer.	■ He had a shield/armor bearer.	☐ He had a shield/armor bearer.
■ He was an experienced fighting man	■ He was an experienced fighting man.	☐ He was an experienced fighting man.
☐ None of the above.	☐ None of the above.	■ None of the above.

God's Qualifications for the Battle

4. Saul's reasons for why David did not qualify to fight Goliath:	5. David's reasons why he did qualify to fight Goliath:
■ He was a boy.	☐ He was a boy.
☐ He had fought and killed bears.	■ He had fought and killed bears.
■ Goliath was a warrior from his youth.	☐ Goliath was a warrior from his youth.
☐ David had fought and killed lions.	■ David had fought and killed lions.
☐ The Lord would deliver him.	■ The Lord would deliver him.

Armor for Battle

6. Write a 'G' by whatever Goliath used in battle. Write a 'D' by whatever David used in battle.

G A bronze helmet
G A coat of armor
D A shepherd's bag
G A bronze javelin
D A staff
D Five smooth stone
G A large spear
G A shield bearer
G Bronze greaves
D A slingshot
G A sword
D The living God

AM I A DOG, THAT YOU COME TO ME TO ME WITH STICKS? 1 SAMUEL 17:43
COME HERE, AND I WILL GIVE YOUR FLESH TO THE BIRDS OF THE AIR AND THE BEASTS OF THE FIELDS. 1 SAMUEL 17:44
YOU COME WITH SWORD, SPEAR AND JAVELIN, BUT I COME IN THE NAME OF THE GOD YOU DEFIED. 1 SAMUEL 17:45
THE LORD WILL GIVE YOU TO ME. I'LL CUT OFF YOUR HEAD AND FEED THE PHILISTINE ARMY TO THE BIRDS AND BEASTS. THE WHOLE WORLD WILL KNOW THERE IS A GOD. 1 SAMUEL 17:46

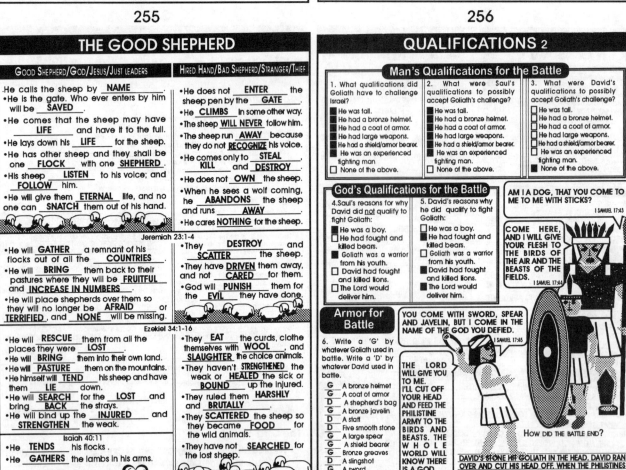

How did the battle end?
DAVID'S STONE HIT GOLIATH IN THE HEAD. DAVID RAN OVER AND CUT HIS HEAD OFF. WHEN THE PHILISTINES SAW HE WAS DEAD THEY FLED. THE ISRAELITES CHASED THEM AND PLUNDERED THEIR CAMP.

260

PSALM OF PRAISE

PRAISE - The praise of God

1. **Praise:** Praising God.
   (Example: I will sing a new song to the Lord. Praise the Lord all you people.)
2. **Praiseworthiness:** Telling why God is worthy of praise.
   (Example: For the Lord is great. Worthy is the Lord who made heaven and earth.)

PSALM 103 NIV

1 [A. Praise the Lord, O my soul;
__A__ all my inmost being, praise His holy name.
__A__ Praise the Lord, O my soul,]

2 [B. and forget not all His benefits-
__B__ who forgives all your sins
__B__ and heals all your diseases,
__B__ who redeems your life from the pit
__B__ & crowns you with love & compassion,
__B__ who satisfies your desires with good things so that your youth is renewed like the eagle's.
C. The Lord is compassionate and gracious,
__C__ slow to anger, abounding in love.
D. He will not always accuse,
__D__ nor will He harbor His anger forever;
E. He does not treat us as our sins deserve
__E__ or repay us according to our iniquities.
F. For as high as the heavens are above the earth,
G. so great is His love for those who fear Him;
__F__ as far as the east is from the west,
__G__ so far has He removed our transgressions from us.
H. As a father has compassion on his children,
__H__ so the Lord has compassion on those who fear Him;
I. for He knows how we are formed,
__I__ He remembers that we are dust.
J. But from everlasting to everlasting
K. the Lord's love is with those who fear Him,
__K__ and His righteousness with their children's children--
__K__ with those who keep His covenant
__K__ and remember to obey His precepts.]

1 [L. Praise the Lord, all His heavenly hosts,
__L__ You His servants who do His will.
__L__ Praise the Lord, all His works everywhere in His dominion.
__L__ Praise the Lord, O my soul.]

PSALM 19:1, 7-11,14 NIV

1 [A. The heavens declare the glory of God;
__A__ the skies proclaim the work of His hands.]

2 [B. The Law of the Lord is perfect,
C. reviving the soul.
__B__ The statutes of the Lord are trustworthy,
__C__ making wise the simple.
__B__ The precepts of the Lord are right,
__C__ giving joy to the heart.
__B__ The commands of the Lord are radiant,
__C__ giving light to the eyes.
__B__ The fear of the Lord is pure,
__C__ enduring forever.
__B__ the ordinances of the Lord are sure
__C__ and altogether righteous.
D. They are more precious than gold,
__D__ than much fine gold;
E. they are sweeter than honey from the comb.
F. By them is your servant warned;
__F__ in keeping them there is great reward.]

1 [G. May the words of my mouth
__G__ and the meditations of my heart be pleasing in Your sight,
H. O Lord, my Rock
____ and my Redeemer.]

PSALM 100 NIV

1 [A. Shout for joy to the Lord, all the earth.
__A__ Serve the Lord with gladness;
__A__ come before Him with joyful songs.]

2 [B. Know that the Lord is God.
__B__ It is He who has made us,
__B__ and we are His,
__B__ we are His people,
__B__ the sheep of His pastures.]

1 [C. Enter His gates with thanksgiving
__C__ and His courts with praise;
D. give thanks to Him
__D__ and praise His name.]

2 [E. For the Lord is good
__E__ and His love endures forever;
__E__ His faithfulness continues though all generations.]

262

SAUL'S JEALOUSY 1

Read 1 Samuel 11-19. Write the number of each of Saul's words and covenants in front of the sentences that go with it in the second and third columns. Quotes are from the NIV. They have been shortened to fit the space.

Saul's Words & Covenants:	Saul's ❤ in the matter:	The end results:
1. "This is what will be done to the oxen of anyone who does not follow."	__6__ Jealous because the women's song praised David over him, Saul bribed him to fight the Philistines, hoping David would die in battle.	__7__ David brought back 200 foreskins, and Saul was forced to gave him Michal in marriage.
2. "I felt compelled to offer the burnt offering."	__5__ Saul was dismayed and terrified by Goliath, so he proposed a huge gift to motivate someone to fight him.	__1__ The people came in terror as one man.
3. "Cursed be any man who eats food before I avenge myself on my enemies!"	__4__ Saul's rash curse put him in the position of having to kill his own son or lose face.	__2__ His foolish actions cost his descendants the kingship.
4. "May God deal with me, be it ever so severely, if you do not die, Jonathan."	__3__ Saul tried to motivate his soldiers to fight harder by making them go hungry.	__6__ David did fight the Philistines and won because the Lord was with him, but Merab was given in marriage to Adriel instead of to David.
5. "The king will give great wealth to the man that kills (Goliath). He will also give him his daughter in marriage. His father's family will be exempt from paying taxes.	__2__ Saul saw the men leaving and was anxious, so he took matters into his own hands and disobeyed God.	__3__ The soldiers were faint with hunger, and Jonathan had a taste of honey.
6. "Here is my oldest daughter Merab. I will give her to you in marriage; only serve me bravely and fight the battles of the Lord."	__7__ Saul wanted David to die, and he did not care how David's death would impact his daughter Michal.	__4__ The Israelites had to oppose their king in order to save Jonathan's life.
7. "Look, the king is pleased with you, now become his son-in-law. The king wants no other price for the bride than a hundred Philistine foreskins."	__1__ From the city that cut the dead concubine into pieces, Saul threatened Israel so that they would fear him more than the enemy.	__5__ David did not get the king's daughter in marriage. The Bible does not say whether Saul kept the other promises.

Saul thought he had to do these things to be successful as a king and to maintain control. It seemed necessary and right to him. Find out what God says about such thinking.

There is a __WAY__ *that seems* __RIGHT__ *to a man, but in the* __END__ *it leads to* __DEATH__. *Proverbs 14:12*

Give a present-day example of the truth of this verse. __ANSWERS MAY VARY__

264

DAVID ON THE RUN 1 / DAVID ON THE RUN 2

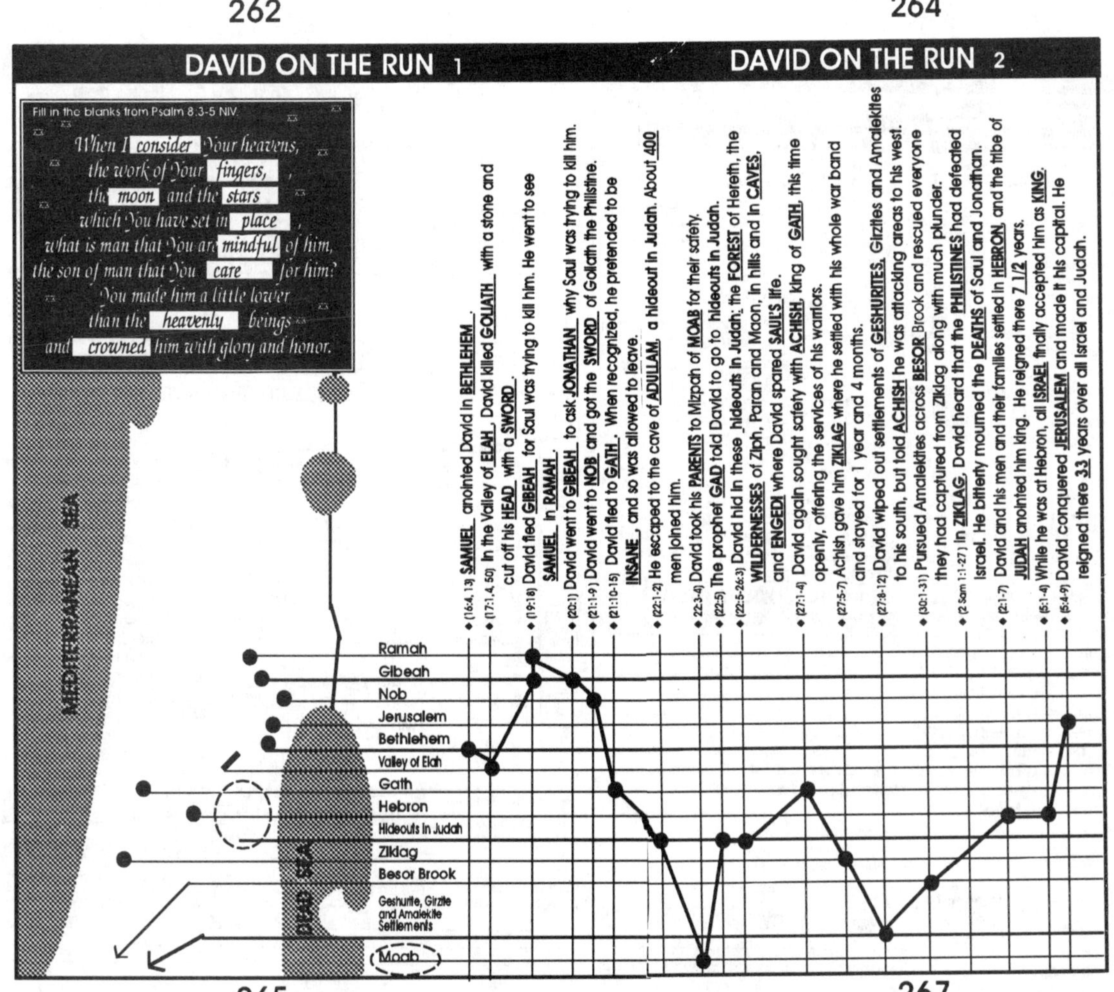

Fill in the blanks from Psalm 8:3-5 NIV.
When I consider Your heavens,
the work of Your fingers,
the moon and the stars
which You have set in place,
what is man that You are mindful of him,
the son of man that You care for him?
You made him a little lower
than the heavenly beings
and crowned him with glory and honor.
MEDITERRANEAN SEA
DEAD SEA
Ramah
Gibeah
Nob
Jerusalem
Bethlehem
Valley of Elah
Gath
Hebron
Hideouts in Judah
Ziklag
Besor Brook
Geshurite, Girzite and Amalekite Settlements
Moab
(16:4, 13) SAMUEL anointed David in BETHLEHEM.
(17:1, 4, 50) In the Valley of ELAH, David killed GOLIATH with a stone and cut off his HEAD with a SWORD.
(19:18) David fled GIBEAH for Saul was trying to kill him. He went to see SAMUEL in RAMAH.
(20:1) David went to GIBEAH to ask JONATHAN why Saul was trying to kill him.
(21:1-9) David went to NOB and got the SWORD of Goliath the Philistine.
(21:10-15) David fled to GATH. When recognized, he pretended to be INSANE, and so was allowed to leave.
(22:1-2) He escaped to the cave of ADULLAM, a hideout in Judah. About 400 men joined him.
(22:3-4) David took his PARENTS to Mizpah of MOAB for their safety.
(22:5) The prophet GAD told David to go to hideouts in Judah.
(22:5-26:3) David hid in these hideouts in Judah; the FOREST of Hereth, the WILDERNESSES of Ziph, Paran and Maon, in hills and in CAVES, and ENGEDI where David spared SAUL'S life.
(27:1-4) David again sought safety with ACHISH, king of GATH, this time openly, offering the services of his warriors.
(27:5-7) Achish gave him ZIKLAG where he settled with his whole war band and stayed for 1 year and 4 months.
(27:8-12) David wiped out settlements of GESHURITES, Girzites and Amalekites to his south, but told ACHISH he was attacking areas to his west.
(30:1-31) Pursued Amalekites across BESOR Brook and rescued everyone they had captured from Ziklag along with much plunder.
(2 Sam 1:1-27) In ZIKLAG, David heard that the PHILISTINES had defeated Israel. He bitterly mourned the DEATHS of Saul and Jonathan.
(2:1-7) David and his men and their families settled in HEBRON, and the tribe of JUDAH anointed him king. He reigned there 7 1/2 years.
(5:1-4) While he was at Hebron, all ISRAEL finally accepted him as KING.
(5:4-9) David conquered JERUSALEM and made it his capital. He reigned there 33 years over all Israel and Judah.

265 267

PSALM TO TEACH WISDOM 1

WISDOM - Instruction on how to be wise and avoid evil.

1. **Wisdom of the author:** The speaker's wisdom and why he desires to teach it. (Example: I will instruct you and teach you in the way you should go.)
2. **What to do:** Instruction on what it takes to be wise and righteous. (Example: He whose walk is blameless. He delights in the Law of the Lord.)
3. **What NOT to do:** Instruction on what to avoid or NOT to do to be wise and righteous. (Example: He who does not accept a bribe. In his spirit is no deceit.)
4. **What the righteous will receive:** Instruction on what God will do for the wise. (Example: The Lord's unfailing love surrounds the man who trusts in Him.)
5. **What the wicked will receive:** Instruction on what God will do to the wicked. (Example: Many are the woes of the wicked.)

PSALM 32:8-11 NIV

Written by DAVID.

1 A. I will instruct you and teach you in the way you should go;
A I will counsel you and watch over you.
3 B. Do not be like the horse or the mule, which have no understanding
B but must be controlled by bit and bridle or they will not come to you.
5 C. Many are the woes of the wicked,
4 C but the Lord's unfailing love surrounds the man who trusts in Him.
4 D. Rejoice in the Lord and be glad, you righteous;
D sing, all you who are upright in heart!

PSALM 15 NIV

4 A. Lord, who may dwell in Your sanctuary?
A Who may live on Your holy hill?
2 B. He whose walk is blameless
B and who does what is righteous,
C. who speaks the truth from his heart
C and who has no slander on his tongue,
3 D. who does his neighbor no wrong
D and casts no slur on his fellowman,
E. who despises a vile man
E but honors those who fear the Lord.
2 F. who keeps his oath even when it hurts,
3 F who lends his money without usury
F and does not accept a bribe against the innocent.
4 G. He who does these things will never be shaken.

PSALM 34:3-16 NIV

Written by DAVID When? WHEN HE PRETENDED TO BE CRAZY & WAS SENT AWAY BY ABIMELECH.

2 A. Glorify the Lord with me;
A let us exalt His name together;
4 B. I sought the Lord and He answered me;
B He delivered me from all my fears.
C. Those who look to Him are radiant;
C their faces are never covered with shame.
D. This poor man called, the Lord heard him;
D and saved him out of his troubles.
E. The angel of the Lord encamps around those who fear Him;
E and delivers them.
2 F. Taste and see that the Lord is good;
4 F blessed is the man who takes refuge in Him.
2 G. Fear the Lord, you His saints,
4 G for those who fear Him lack nothing.
4 H. The lion grows weak and hungry,
H but those who seek the Lord lack no good thing.
1 I. Come, my children, listen to me;
I I will teach you the fear of the Lord.
4 J. Whoever of you loves life and
J desires to see many good days,
3 K. keep your tongue from evil
K and your lips from speaking lies.
2,3 L. Turn from evil and do good;
2 L seek peace and pursue it.
4 M. The eyes of the Lord are on the righteous
M and His ears are attentive to their cry;
5 N. The face of the Lord is against those who do evil,
N to cut off the memory of them from the earth.

PSALM TO TEACH WISDOM 2

WISDOM - Instruction on how to be wise and avoid evil.

1. **Wisdom of the author:** The speaker's wisdom and why he desires to teach it. (Example: I will instruct you and teach you in the way you should go.)
2. **What to do:** Instruction on what it takes to be wise and righteous. (Example: He whose walk is blameless. He delights in the Law of the Lord.)
3. **What NOT to do:** Instruction on what to avoid or NOT to do to be wise and righteous. (Example: He who does not accept a bribe. In his spirit is no deceit.)
4. **What the righteous will receive:** Instruction on what God will do for the wise. (Example: The Lord's unfailing love surrounds the man who trusts in Him.)
5. **What the wicked will receive:** Instruction on what God will do to the wicked. (Example: Many are the woes of the wicked.)

Written by DAVID

PSALM 37:1-9,25,38,39 NIV

3 A. Do not fret because of evil men
A or be envious of those who do wrong;
5 B. for like the grass they will soon wither,
B like green plants they will soon die away.
2 C. Trust in the Lord and do good;
4 C dwell in the land and enjoy safe pastures.
2 D. Delight yourself in the Lord
4 E. and He will give you the desires of your heart.
2 D Commit your way to the Lord;
E trust in Him and He will do this:
4 F. He will make your righteousness shine like the dawn,
F the justice of your cause like the noonday sun.
2 G. Be still before the Lord
G and wait patiently for Him;
H. do not fret when men succeed in their ways,
H when they carry out their wicked schemes.
3 I. Refrain from anger and turn from wrath;
I do not fret--it leads only to evil.
5 J. For evil men will be cut off,
4 J but those who hope in the Lord will inherit the land.
K. I was young and now I am old,
1 L. yet I have never seen the righteous forsaken
L or their children begging bread.
5 M. But all sinners will be destroyed;
M the future of the wicked will be cut off.
4 N. The salvation of the righteous comes from the Lord;
N He is their stronghold in time of trouble.

Written by DAVID
When? WHEN DOEG KILLED THE PRIESTS

PSALM 52 NIV

A. Why do you boast of evil,
B. you mighty man?
A Why do you boast all day long,
B You who are a disgrace in the eyes of God?
C. Your tongue plots destruction;
3 C it is like a sharpened razor,
B you who practice deceit.
E. you love evil rather than good,
E falsehood rather than speaking the truth.
F. You love every harmful word,
F O you deceitful tongue!
5 G. Surely God will bring you down to everlasting ruin;
G He will snatch you up and tear you from your tent;
G He will uproot you from the land of the living.
4 H. The righteous will see and fear;
H they will laugh at him, saying,
5 I. "Here now is the man who did not make God his stronghold
I but trusted in his great wealth and grew strong by destroying others!"
2 J. But I am like an olive tree flourishing in the house of God;
J I trust in God's unfailing love for ever and ever.
4 K. I will praise You forever for what You have done;
K in Your name I will hope, for Your name is good.
K I will praise You in the presence of Your saints.

Read 1 Samuel 21, 22. What had Doeg done? TOLD SAUL THAT AHIMELECH HAD HELPED DAVID, AND THEN AT SAUL'S COMMAND KILLED 85 PRIESTS AND EVERYONE IN HIS TOWN.

JONATHAN'S HEART

Read 1 Samuel 14-23. Write the number of each of Jonathan's words and covenants in front of the sentences that go with it in the second and third columns. Quotes are from the NIV. They have been shortened to fit the space.

Jonathan's Words & Covenants:	Jonathan's ♥ in the matter:	The end results:
1. "Come, let's go over to fight. Nothing can hinder the Lord from saving, whether by many or a few."	4 Jonathan shared his heart with his father telling him how wrong he was to try to kill David.	3 David hid while Jonathan reasoned with his father.
2. Upon their first encounter, Jonathan made a covenant with David.	3 Jonathan had a two-fold plan to help the two he loves -- to save David, and to stand up to his father to reason with him.	6 In spite of Jonathan's friendship, David was now on the run and would be for many years.
3. "My father Saul is looking for a chance to kill you. Go into hiding and stay there. I will stand with my father in the field where you are and speak to him about you."	7 Jonathan went out into the desert to encourage David and help him find strength in God, so David would be able to endure Saul's relentless pursuit.	7 David did become king, but Jonathan was killed in battle.
4. "Let not the king do wrong to his servant David; he has not harmed you, and what he has done has benefited you greatly."	5 Jonathan's character was such that his father Saul always confided in him. It shocked him to think his father would plan something without his knowledge.	4 Jonathan had his father vow not to kill David.
5. "Never! You are not going to die! Look, my father doesn't do anything, great or small, without confiding in me. Why would he hide this from me?"	6 Jonathan sent David away with his peace and friendship. He had no jealousy, fear or anger towards David.	1 Some twenty Philistines fell before Jonathan and his armor-bearer. The Philistine army went into a panic, and the Israelites won the battle.
6. "Go in peace, for we have sworn friendship with each other in the name of the Lord, between you and me, and between your descendants and my descendants forever."	1 Jonathan's bravery and complete trust in the Lord made him fearless in battle	5 Saul was still trying to kill David but did not tell Jonathan since it would have upset him.
7. "Don't be afraid. My father Saul will not lay a hand on you. You will be king over Israel, and I will be second to you. Even my father Saul knows this."	2 Jonathan saw in David the same valor and devotion to God as he had, and loved David as himself.	2 Jonathan gave David his robe, tunic, sword, bow and belt.

David's Lament for Saul and Jonathan

When Saul and Jonathan died, David wrote a lament for them. Write out 2 Samuel 1:23, 25-27.

Saul and Jonathan --
in life they were loved and gracious,
and in death they were not parted.
They were swifter than eagles,
they were stronger than lions.
How the mighty have fallen in battle!
Jonathan lies slain on our heights.
I grieve for you, Jonathan my brother; you were very dear to me.
Your love for me was wonderful, more wonderful than that of women.
How the mighty have fallen!
The weapons of war have perished!

How did David feel toward Saul even though Saul had many times tried to kill him? ANSWERS MAY VARY

How did David feel towards Jonathan? ANSWERS MAY VARY

Have you ever had a good friend who moved away or died? ____ How did you feel? ANSWERS MAY VARY

PSALM OF THANKSGIVING

THANKSGIVING - Thanking God for His help

1. **Thanksgiving:** Praising God for who He is. (Example: Shout to the Lord! Praise the Lord.)
2. **Trial Past:** A past illness, disaster, war, danger, sin. (Example: I was in the snare of death. My enemies were camped all around me.)
3. **Trust:** Tell how trust had been placed in God's hands. (Example: In the Lord I placed my trust.)
4. **Testimony:** A statement of what He has done. (Example: The Lord saved me from my enemies. He lifted me up.)
5. **Thankfulness in the Future:** Future thanks and praise to God. (Example: I will praise your name. I will tell others of Your greatness.)

PSALM 18:1-6,16-19,46-50 NIV

Written by DAVID. When? WHEN GOD SAVED HIM FROM SAUL.

1 A. I love you, O Lord, my strength.
B. The Lord is my rock, my fortress and my deliverer;
3 B my God is my rock, in whom I take refuge.
B He is my shield and the horn of my salvation, my stronghold.
C. I call to the Lord, who is worthy of praise,
C and I am saved from my enemies.
D. The cords of death entangled me;
D the torrents of destruction overwhelmed me.
2 D The cords of the grave coiled around me;
D the snares of death confronted me.
E. In my distress I called to the Lord;
E I cried to my God for help.
F. From His Temple He heard my voice;
4 F my cry came to Him, into His ears.
H. He reached down from on high
H and took hold of me;
H He drew me out of deep waters.
I. He rescued me from my powerful enemy,
4 I from my foes, who were too strong for me.
I They confronted me in the day of my disaster,
J. but the Lord was my support.
J He brought me out into a spacious place;
J He rescued me because He delighted in me.
1 K. The Lord lives! Praise be to my Rock!
K Exalted be God my Savior!
L. He is the God who avenges me,
L Who subdues nations under me,
4 L Who saved me from my enemies.
L You exalted me above my foes;
L from violent men you rescued me.
5 M. Therefore I will praise you among the nations, O Lord;
M I will sing praises to your name.
3 N. He gives His king great victories;
O He shows unfailing kindness to His anointed,
O to David and his descendants forever.

Read 1 Samuel 24. How many men did Saul have with him to catch David? 3,000 How close did David get to Saul? CLOSES ENOUGH TO CUT A PIECE OFF HIS ROBE.

What do you think David's men thought David would do? KILL SAUL.

What did David do? HE SHOWED SAUL THE PIECE. Why? TO PROVE HE MEANT HIM NO HARM.

What was Saul's reaction? SAUL WEPT AND BLESSED DAVID AND HIS FAMILY.

Whom did David put his trust in? THE LORD. What does Psalm 18 tell us about David's trust and love for the Lord? ANSWERS MAY VARY.

AHEAD OF THE GAME

רֹאשׁ =HEAD, FIRST IN TIME, PLACE, OR RANK. CHIEF, EXCELLENT, FIRST, FOREFRONT, HIGHEST.

רוֹשׁ .1	2 rîshōh- A BEGINNING
רֵאשָׁה .2	4 rāshēn bikūrāy- FIRST OF FIRSTFRUITS
רֵאשֹׁת .3	9 rōsh pinnōh- CORNERSTONE
רֵאשִׁית בִּכּוּרֵי .4	10 Rōsh HăShōnōh- NEW YEAR
רִאשׁוֹן .5	11 rōshōn- A TADPOLE (Looks like a swimming head.)
רֹאשׁ .6	15 rōsh simūkhōh- HIGHEST JOY
כֹּהֵן הָרֹאשׁ .7	13 mārōsh- FROM THE BEGINING
רֹאשׁ חֹדֶשׁ .8	14 rōsh vŭsōmĕm- MOST PRECIOUS SPICES
רֹאשׁ פִּנָּה .9	12 rōshēm- SOURCE OF A STREAM
רֹאשׁ הַשָּׁנָה .10	7 lhān hrōsh- HIGH PRIEST
רֹאשָׁן .11	3 răshōth- PILLOW
רָאשִׁים .12	6 rōsh- CHIEF
מֵרֹאשׁ .13	1 rōsh- VENOM, OPIUM (poison from the head of the poppy)
רֹאשׁ בְּשָׂמִים .14	5 rîshōn- ANCESTORS
רֹאשׁ שִׂמְחָה .15	8 rōsh khōdāsh- NEW MOON

11, 3, 1 having to do with the HEAD
2, 4, 10, 13, 12, 8, 5 having to do with FIRST IN TIME, A BEGINNING
15, 14, having to do with being the MOST EXCELLENT or HIGHEST
7, 9 having to do with being the MOST IMPORTANT
7, 6 having to do with being the LEADER

As you come to Him (Jesus), the LIVING STONE - REJECTED *by men but* CHOSEN *by God and* PRECIOUS *to Him-you also, like living* STONES, *are being built into a* SPIRITUAL *house... For in Scripture it says: "See, I lay a* STONE *in Zion, a* CHOSEN *and precious* CORNERSTONE, *and the one who* TRUSTS *in him will* NEVER *be put to* SHAME*."*

Now to you who BELIEVE, *this stone is* PRECIOUS. *But to those who do* NOT *believe, "The stone the* BUILDERS *rejected has become the* CORNERSTONE.*" and "A* STONE *that causes* MEN *to* STUMBLE *and a* ROCK *that makes them* FALL.*"* 1 Peter 2:4-8a NIV

274

SAUL'S JEALOUSY 2

Saul's Words & Covenants:	Saul's ❤ in the matter:	The end results:
1 "As surely as the Lord lives, David will not be put to death."	7 Saul admitted his folly and blessed David; but David knew better than to trust him.	2 Michal helped David escape out a window and put an idol in bed to make it appear that David was sick.
2 "Now bring (David) to me in his bed so that I can kill him."	1 Jealous of David's victory, Saul broke his vow to Jonathan.	7 After Saul's "repentance," David continued to hide from him. Saul only stopped hunting for him when he went to Gath.
3 "You son of a perverse and rebellious woman! Don't I know you have sided with the son of Jesse? As long as he lives you and your kingdom will not be established."	9 Saul feared the Philistines would abuse and kill him.	5 Just as he was closing in on David, a Philistine attack caused Saul to return home. Later he renewed his search.
4 "You shall surely die, Ahimelech, you and your father's whole family."	4 Paranoid, Saul believed the priest had conspired against him and helped David.	8 Samuel's spirit said that Saul and his three sons would die in the battle.
5 "Find out all the hidden places he uses. I will track him down."	5 Saul hunted David in the Desert of Maon. He was determined to kill him.	3 Saul threw his spear at Jonathan to kill him.
6 "Is that your voice, David my son? You are more righteous than I. You did not kill me. I know you will surely be king. Swear you will not cut off my descendants."	6 Saul finally acknowledged that God has chosen David and not him. He worried about his descendants.	1 As David played his harp, Saul tried to kill him.
7 "I have sinned. Come back, David my son. You considered my life precious today. I will not try to harm you again."	8 Terror filled his heart, and God would not advise, so he turned to a medium.	9 His armor-bearer would not kill him, so Saul fell on his own sword and died.
8 "Consult a spirit for me and bring up the one I name."	2 Saul was so blinded by fear that he made Michal choose between her father and her husband.	4 None of the king's officials would strike the priests, so Doeg the Edomite killed 85 men and all that lived in Nod.
9 "Draw your sword and run me through."	3 It was God who tore the kingdom from him, but Saul thought he could change that by killing David. He was furious that Jonathan sided with David.	6 Saul went home with David's oath to spare his family but later returned with 3000 men to hunt him down.

Write a paragraph describing one aspect of Saul's heart and how it affected his behavior.

ANSWERS MAY VARY

275

HEAR AND OBEY 1

שָׁמַע =hear, listen, pay attention, grant request, and obey. שְׁמוּאֵל =heard of God

שְׁמוּאֵל
1:20 Hannah bore a son and called his name *Samuel*, saying, "Because I have asked him of Jehovah."

שֹׁמֵעַ
2:22 Eli was very old, and *had heard* all that his sons did.

שֹׁמֵעַ שֹׁמֵעַ
2:23 Eli said to his sons, "For I *am hearing* of your evil deeds. My sons, the report I am *hearing* is not good."

יִשְׁמְעוּ
2:25 But not *did they listen* to the voice of their father.

שְׁמוּאֵל שֹׁמֵעַ
3:10 And *Samuel* said, "Speak for your servant *hears* you."

כָּל־שֹׁמְעוֹ
3:11 And Jehovah said, "I am doing a thing in Israel at which the ears of *everyone hearing* it shall tingle."

וַיִּשְׁמַע
4:14 *And heard* Eli the noise of the cry, and said, "What is the noise of this tumult?"

8:8, 9 "What they have done to Me since I brought them out of Egypt, even to this day, so they

שְׁמַע
are also doing to you. Now *listen* to their voice."

לִשְׁמֹעַ שְׁמוּאֵל
8:19 And the people *refused to listen* to the voice of *Samuel*, and said, "No, but a king shall be over us."

וַיִּשְׁמַע שְׁמוּאֵל
8:21 *And heard Samuel* all the words of the people, and spoke them in the ears of Jehovah.

שְׁמוּאֵל שְׁמַע
8:22 And Jehovah said to *Samuel*, "*Listen to* their voice and you shall cause a king to reign over them."

שְׁמוּאֵל שָׁמַעְתִּי
12:1 And *Samuel* said to all Israel, "Behold, *I have heard* your voice, and I made a king to reign over you."

וּשְׁמַעְתֶּם
12:14 " If you fear Jehovah and serve Him, *and listen* to His voice, and do not rebel... then you and also the king who reigns over you shall follow Jehovah your God."

שְׁמוּאֵל לֹא־שָׁמַעְתָּ
28:16-19 And *Samuel* said, "Because *you did not listen* to the voice of Jehovah,... Jehovah is giving Israel into the hands of the Philistines, along with you."

276

FAMILY TREE OF DAVID

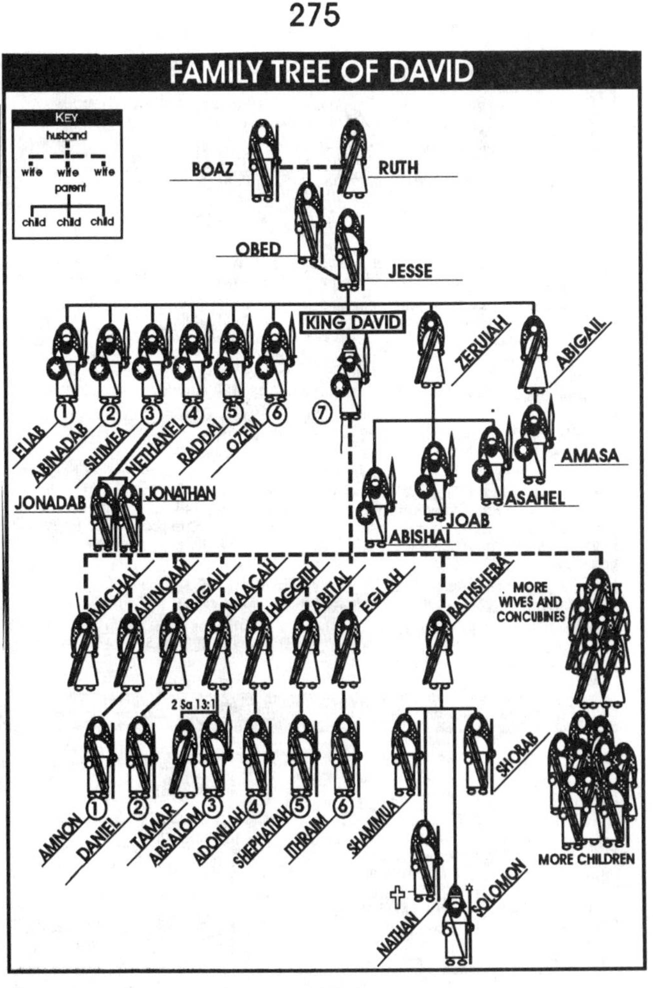

278

DAVID'S FAMILY TREE CROSSWORD

Across: 5 GOLIATH · 7 EVIL · 8 KILLED · 9 SONS · 10 OLD · 11 RUTH · 14 ASAHEL · 16 MOTHER · 17 SAUL · 18 BROTHER

Down: 1 WIFE · 2 FATHER · 3 FIRST · 4 WISDOM · 6 MICHAL · 9 SISTER · 12 NATHAN · 13 JESSE · 15 NABAL

GOD GIVES DAVID THE KINGDOM 1

2 Sa 1:1-16 The Amalekite tells David that he had caused Saul's death. Why does he claim to have killed Saul? ☐ out of revenge ☐ in self-defense ☐ reluctantly ☐ while at war with him ■ Saul was in pain ■ to gain favor from David

David is not glad that Saul is dead even though Saul hunted him for years. Instead his is shocked and angry that the Amalekite has killed the **LORD'S ANOINTED**. David executes the man.

After **INQUIRING** of the Lord, David settles with his two **WIVES** and all his **MEN** and their **FAMILIES** in **HEBRON** and the surrounding towns. David is anointed king by the men of **JUDAH**. He sends a blessing to those who buried **SAUL**.

What had Saul done for the people of Jabesh-Gilead? **SAVED THEM FROM THE AMMONITES WHO WANTED THE MEN TO PUT THEIR RIGHT EYES OUT.**

2 Sa 2:8-32 Abner leads the army of Israel in support of Saul's son, Ish-Bosheth, and fights Joab and David's men. Who usually inherits the throne when a king dies? **THE OLDEST SON** Study Saul's Family Tree and tell why Abner supports Ish-Bosheth. **ISH-BOSHETH IS NEXT IN LINE FOR THE THRONE. THE 3 OLDER SONS ARE DEAD.**

Beside the pool of Gibeon, the troops meet. The commanders have twelve men from each side fight hand to hand. The result is **ALL 24 KILL EACH OTHER. NOBODY WINS.**

The two armies start fighting again, and **COUSINS** and the men of **ISRAEL** are defeated by **DAVID'S** men. Look at David's Family Tree. How are Joab, Abishai and Asahel related to David? **DAVID'S COUSINS**

Abner kills Asahel ☐ out of revenge ■ reluctantly ☐ with deceit or secrecy ■ in self-defense ■ after warning him away ☐ in peacetime ■ while at war with him

2 Sa 3:1-21 Verse 6 may give a clue to a second reason for Abner's support of Ish-Bosheth. Look at Saul's Family Tree. Tell how Abner is related to Saul, and what he might be working towards in 3:6. **SAUL'S COUSIN. MAY BE TRYING TO BECOME KING.**

Abner gets angry with Ish-Bosheth and decides to help David become king of all Israel. Why is Abner angry? **ISH-BOSHETH ACCUSED HIM OF SLEEPING WITH SAUL'S CONCUBINE. (A WAY OF CLAIMING THE THRONE.)**

Abner knows that **GOD** has promised to transfer the kingdom from the **HOUSE** (dynasty) of Saul to **DAVID** and to establish his **THRONE** over Israel and **JUDAH** from **DAN** to **BEERSHEBA** Abner also knows that for some time, the **ELDERS** of **ISRAEL** have wanted to make **DAVID** their king. He reports to David all the people want to do, he gets permission to assemble everyone to make a **COMPACT** with David. David sends him on his mission in **PEACE**.

2 Sa 3:22-25 Joab distrusts Abner. He says to David, "You know **ABNER** son of Ner; he came to **DECEIVE** you and observe your **MOVEMENTS** and find out **EVERYTHING** you are doing." In your opinion, was Joab right about Abner? Explain your answer **ANSWERS WILL VARY**

GOD GIVES DAVID THE KINGDOM 2

Joab kills Abner ■ out of revenge ■ with deceit or secrecy ☐ in self-defense ☐ reluctantly ☐ after trying to warn him away ☐ while at war with him ■ in peace-time

Name five or more ways David shows his grief over Abner's death. **1. DECLARES HIS INNOCENCE. 2.CURSES JOAB AND HIS HOUSE, 3. TELLS ALL TO MOURN, 4. WALKS BEHIND THE BIER, WEEPS ALOUD, 5. GIVES ABNER AN HONORABLE BURIAL, 6. SINGS A LAMENT, 7. FASTS THE REST OF THE DAY, 8. ASKS THAT GOD PUNISH THE EVILDOERS.**

The people are convinced that David had **NO PART** in the **MURDER** of Abner.

Recab and Baanah kill Ish-Bosheth ☐ out of revenge ■ with deceit or secrecy ☐ in self-defense ☐ reluctantly ☐ while at war with him ■ in peace-time ■ to gain favor from David

Learning nothing from the experience of the Amalekite, they take Ish-Bosheth's **HEAD** to **DAVID**. What do they think David's reaction will be? **GLAD, GRATEFUL**

Even though Ish-Bosheth has been fighting David for the kingdom, David counts him as an **INNOCENT** man. David executes the wicked men, hangs their **BODIES** by the pool in **HEBRON**, and **BURIES** Ish-Bosheth's **HEAD** in **ABNER'S** tomb. When the people hear what David did to Ish-Bosheth's murderers and what he did with his remains, they will be convinced that David ■ had not taken part in Ish-Bosheth's murder.

All the tribes of **ISRAEL** accept **DAVID** as king. They know the **LORD** had said David would **SHEPHERD** His people **ISRAEL**. The king makes a **COMPACT** with them, and they **ANOINT** him king over **ISRAEL**.

The Jebusites are confident of their fortress. "You will not get in here; even the blind and the lame can ward you off." They had good reason to brag. Read Judges 1:21. The **BENJAMITES** had tried and failed to drive them out hundreds of years earlier, and no one else had ever succeeded. However, David conquers Jerusalem and moves in. It is at this time that Joab officially earns his position of **COMMANDER - IN - CHIEF**. David builds up the **CITY** around the **FORTRESS**, and Joab restores the **REST** of the **CITY**.

David builds a **PALACE** with the help of King **HIRAM** of **TYRE**. David takes more **WIVES** and **CONCUBINES**, and has more sons and **DAUGHTERS**.

2 Sa 5:17-25 (1 Ch 14:8-17) When the **PHILISTINES** hear that David has been **ANOINTED** king, they go to **SEARCH** for him. First he escapes to the **STRONGHOLD**. When he **INQUIRES** of the Lord, he receives guidance and success.

MURDER VICTIM & HIS RELATIONSHIP TO DAVID	MURDERER(S) & RELATIONSHIP TO DAVID	DAVID'S FEELINGS	DAVID'S ACTIONS	DAVID'S STATEMENTS ABOUT THE VICTIM
SAUL ■ ENEMY ☐ FRIEND ■ KING ☐ COMMANDER ■ FOUGHT AGAINST DAVID	THE AMALEKITE, OR SO HE SAID. ■ NONE ☐ COUSINS ☐ ENEMY TURNCOATS ☐ IN DAVID'S ARMY	GREAT SORROW, ANGER	HAD HIM EXECUTED MOURNED	HE WAS THE LORD'S ANOINTED
ABNER ☐ ENEMY ☐ FRIEND ☐ KING ■ COMMANDER ■ FOUGHT AGAINST DAVID	JOAB & ABISHAI ☐ NONE ■ COUSINS ☐ ENEMY TURNCOATS ■ IN DAVID'S ARMY	ANGER, SORROW, FRUSTRATION	CURSED JOAB AND HIS HOUSE, MOURNED	A PRINCE & A GREAT MAN
ISH-BOSHETH ■ ENEMY ☐ FRIEND ■ KING ☐ COMMANDER ■ FOUGHT AGAINST DAVID	RECAB & BAANAH ☐ NONE ☐ COUSINS ■ ENEMY TURNCOATS ☐ IN DAVID'S ARMY	ANGER	HAD THEM EXECUTED	AN INNOCENT MAN

PSALM 119 - AN ACROSTIC

PUT PSALM 119 WORDS IN ALPHABETIC ORDER:		ENGLISH DEFINITIONS:	
חֶלְקִי	8	10	your hands
טוֹב	9	14	a lamp to my feet
גְּמֹל	3	15	halfhearted, double-minded
בַּמֶּה	2	16	I have done
עָשִׂיתִי	16	6	let come near
קְרָאתִי	19	19	I cry, call
רִיבָה	20	1	blessed
שָׂרִים	21	9	good
תִּקְרַב	22	4	clings, latd low
פְּלָאוֹת	17	21	princes, rulers
צַדִּיק	18	3	grant,do good
יָדֶיךָ	10	8	my portion
כָּלְתָה	11	5	teach me
סֵעֲפִים	15	2	by what, how
מָה־אָהַבְתִּי	13	22	let come near
דָּבְקָה	4	7	remember your word
לְעֹלָם	12	12	Forever, eternal
הוֹרֵנִי	5	13	O how I love
אַשְׁרֵי	1	17	wonderful
נֵר־לְרַגְלִי	14	18	righteous
וִיבֹאֻנִי	6	20	contend, look upon
זְכָר־דָּבָר	7	11	being consumed, faints

DAVID GETS THE ARK

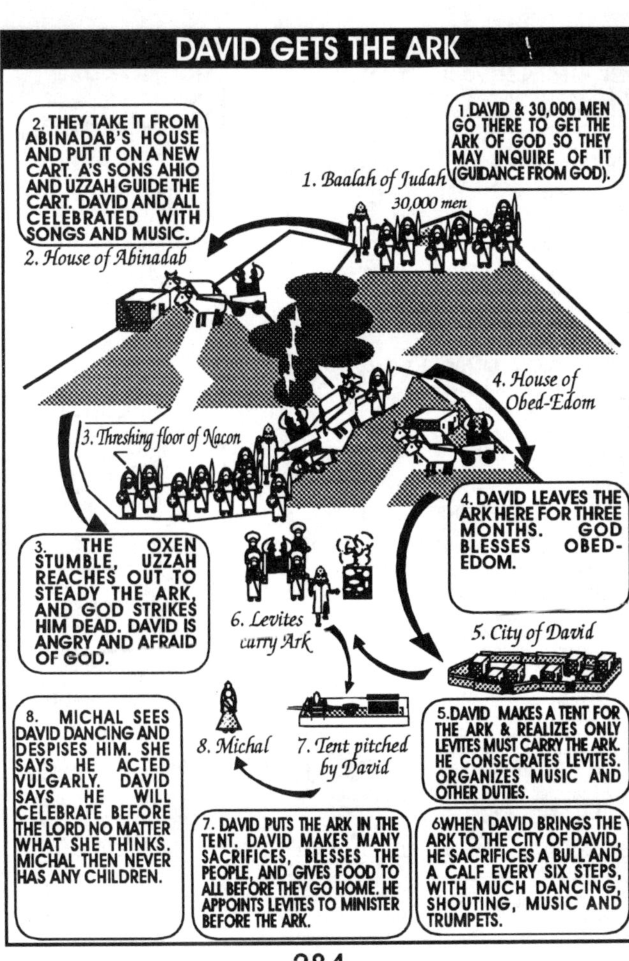

1.DAVID & 30,000 MEN GO THERE TO GET THE ARK OF GOD SO THEY MAY INQUIRE OF IT (GUIDANCE FROM GOD).
2. THEY TAKE IT FROM ABINADAB'S HOUSE AND PUT IT ON A NEW CART. A'S SONS AHIO AND UZZAH GUIDE THE CART. DAVID AND ALL CELEBRATED WITH SONGS AND MUSIC.
1. Baalah of Judah
30,000 men
2. House of Abinadab
3. Threshing floor of Nacon
4. House of Obed-Edom
3. THE OXEN STUMBLE, UZZAH REACHES OUT TO STEADY THE ARK, AND GOD STRIKES HIM DEAD. DAVID IS ANGRY AND AFRAID OF GOD.
4. DAVID LEAVES THE ARK HERE FOR THREE MONTHS. GOD BLESSES OBED-EDOM.
6. Levites carry Ark
5. City of David
8. MICHAL SEES DAVID DANCING AND DESPISES HIM. SHE SAYS HE ACTED VULGARLY. DAVID SAYS HE WILL CELEBRATE BEFORE THE LORD NO MATTER WHAT SHE THINKS. MICHAL THEN NEVER HAS ANY CHILDREN.
8. Michal
7. Tent pitched by David
5.DAVID MAKES A TENT FOR THE ARK & REALIZES ONLY LEVITES MUST CARRY THE ARK. HE CONSECRATES LEVITES. ORGANIZES MUSIC AND OTHER DUTIES.
7. DAVID PUTS THE ARK IN THE TENT. DAVID MAKES MANY SACRIFICES, BLESSES THE PEOPLE, AND GIVES FOOD TO ALL BEFORE THEY GO HOME. HE APPOINTS LEVITES TO MINISTER BEFORE THE ARK.
6WHEN DAVID BRINGS THE ARK TO THE CITY OF DAVID, HE SACRIFICES A BULL AND A CALF EVERY SIX STEPS, WITH MUCH DANCING, SHOUTING, MUSIC AND TRUMPETS.

GOD BUILDS DAVID'S HOUSE

David desires to build a HOUSE for the ARK of God. NATHAN thinks that is a great idea, but God speaks to Nathan in the night: "Tell David that I will build a house for him!"

GOD'S PROMISES TO DAVID

1. I will make your name GREAT.
2. I will provide a PLACE for Israel so that they can have a HOME of their own and no longer be DISTURBED . WICKED men will not OPPRESS them anymore. I will give you REST from all your ENEMIES .
3. I will establish the KINGDOM of your offspring. He will build a HOUSE for My NAME . I will establish his THRONE forever. When he does WRONG , I will PUNISH him, but My LOVE will never be TAKEN away from him. Your HOUSE and your KINGDOM will endure FOREVER before Me; your THRONE will be established FOREVER .

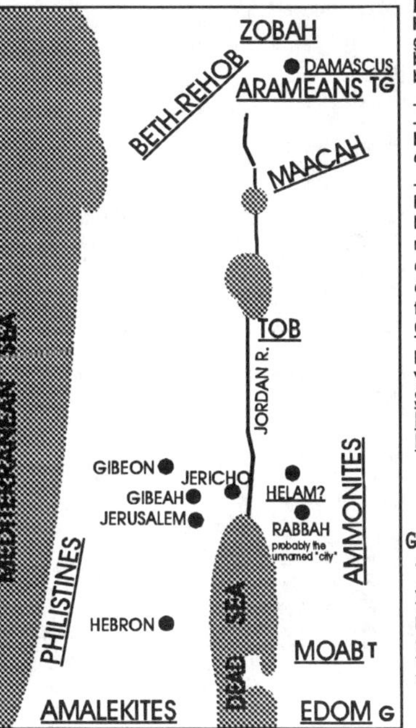

DAVID'S RESPONSE TO GOD

He is stunned and awed by God's generosity. Who am I, that You have brought me so far? How far had God brought him ?
FROM SHEPHERD
TO KING OF ISRAEL

He praises God for His greatness. What does David repeatedly call God?
O SOVEREIGN LORD

He is amazed by the wonderful things God has done in the past for Israel. He has redeemed them from EGYPT to be a people for HIMSELF, and has driven out NATIONS and their GODS from before them. He has become their GOD .

He accepts God's promise with gratitude. You, O SOVEREIGN Lord, have SPOKEN, and with Your blessing the HOUSE of Your servant will be BLESSED forever.

GOD IS STILL FULFILLING PROMISES

"Your throne will be established forever." Jesus fulfills this. When the angel told Mary that she would bear Jesus, he said, "The Lord God will give him the THRONE of his father David, and He will reign over the house of Jacob forever; his kingdom will never END ." Luke 1:32-33

HOUSE OF DAVID

This is a picture of a broken tablet, written in 900 BC and found in the Tell of Dan.

1. Use your Hebrew Alphabet Chart to rewrite the fifth line in modern Hebrew.
2. Some people do not accept the Bible as a historical document. The only proof of a person's existence that they will accept is to find references to him in several places other than the Bible. Write 'house (of) David' (byt dvd) in modern Hebrew. (Write from right to left.) בית דוד
3. Find the line on the tablet that reads 'house (of) David.' Line 9
4. What does the mention of the 'house of David' on this tablet imply? THAT DAVID WAS A REAL KING, NOT MADE UP.
5. The 'house of David' and other expressions about King David are used in the Bible. Read the verses and write the missing words in the blanks. In each box write the letter of the meaning of the completed phrase. You may use more than one letter.

Meanings: A. Bethlehem B. Descendant C. Jesus D. Royalty

B	Luke 1:27	DESCENDANT	of David	
D	Luke 1:32	THRONE	of David	
B	Luke 1:69	HOUSE	of David	
A	Luke 2:4a	TOWN	of David	
BCD	Luke 18:38	SON	of David	
BD	Luke 2:4b	HOUSE	and LINE	of David
B	Revelation 22:16	ROOT	and OFFSPRING	of David

1.
2.
3.
4.
5.
6.
7.
8.
9.
10.
11.
12.
13.

The words that come from ד.ו.ד. carry the meaning of 'love' or 'beloved.' Write the number from each Hebrew word by its English translation and again by its meaning.

		Translation		Meaning
1. דּוֹד	5	dūdōēm - mandrake plant	1	Your father's or mother's brother whom you love.
2. דָּוִד	4	dōdēm - caress	3	Anyone with whom you have a close, loving relationship.
3. יְדִיד	2	dōvīd - David	4	A loving hug.
4. דּוֹדִים	3	yūdēd - friend	2	A name meaning 'beloved.'
5. דּוּדָאִים	1	dōd - uncle	5	A plant believed to help in conceiving a child

GOD'S KINDNESS

David reigned over all Israel,
doing what was just and right for all his people
2 Samuel 8:15

Name David's officials. Check the boxes in front of the ones who continued to serve into the reign of Solomon. (See 1 Kings 4:1-6)

- ❑ Commander of the army: JOAB son of ZERUIAH.
  How was he related to David? COUSIN
- ■ Recorder: JEHOSHAPHAT son of AHILUD.
- ■ Priest: ZADOK son of Ahitub
- ❑ Priest: AHIMELECH son of Abiathar
- ❑ Secretary: SERAIAH, also called SHAVSHA.
- ■ Commander of the Kerethites and Pelethites: BENAIAH son of JEHOIADA
- ❑ Royal advisers: David's SONS

Read 2 Sa 9. As a grandson of King Saul, Mephibosheth could have been a political enemy. For whose sake does David seek him out? JONATHAN'S What promise had he made? (See 1 Sa 20:12-15) TO SHOW UNFAILING KINDNESS LIKE THAT OF THE LORD TO JONATHAN & HIS FAMILY, NEVER TO KILL HIM

Who's kindness does he want to show? GOD'S . What is Ziba's position? SERVANT of Saul's HOUSEHOLD . As such he is the manager of Saul's property and workers, much as Joseph was in Potiphar's house. Ziba has 15 sons and 20 servants. He is not a poor man. David has the right to seize all King Saul's property and his servants and kill any heirs. In your opinion, how must Mephibosheth feel as he is summoned to appear before the king?
ANSWERS MAY VARY

David restores Saul's property to MEPHIBOSHETH and authorizes ZIBA to continue working the land to provide for Mephibosheth's needs. He invites Mephibosheth to eat with him at his TABLE like one of his own SONS. Mephibosheth moves to JERUSALEM with his young son, MICAH.

For you did not RECEIVE *a spirit*
that makes you a SLAVE *again to* FEAR ,
but you RECEIVED *the Spirit of* SONSHIP .
Romans 8:15

In your opinion, how might Ziba feel? ❑ Relieved to have a job. ❑ Relieved to be alive. ❑ Angry that he didn't get to use Saul's fields for himself. ❑ Disgusted with having a cripple for a master.
Contrast God's kind of love with the way people normally act.
ANSWERS WILL VARY

DAVID'S DOWNFALL

DAVID'S ACTIONS

7 David pulls Bathsheba's husband, Uriah, from the war. He plies him with food and presents to entice him to go home to sleep with his wife.

4 Although David finds out she is a married woman, he still sends for her.

1 King David is at the palace.

2 David gets out of his bed and walks around the roof.

8 David gets Uriah drunk to destroy his resolve to do what is right.

5 Bathsheba comes to David and he sleeps with her.

9 David boldly sends Uriah back to the battle carrying his own death warrant.

10 When David hears that several good men were killed needlessly, he is only relieved that Uriah died too.

11 David marries Bathsheba after her time of mourning over the death of her husband has past.

3 David sees a beautiful woman bathing, and asks about her.

6 When David finds out that Bathsheba is pregnant, he is upset and decides to cover it up.

FATAL STEPS TO DESTRUCTION

1. IN THE WRONG PLACE
2. ALONE AND RESTLESS
3. LINGERS WITH TEMPTATION
4. LUST OVERRIDES CONSCIENCE
5. SINS IN SECRET
6. DISTRAUGHT WITH NATURAL CONSEQUENCE
7. FAKES FRIENDSHIP TO COVER UP SIN
8. USES ALCOHOL TO LOWER RESOLVE
9. BETRAYS AN INDIVIDUAL OF VALOR
10. CAUSES THE DEMISE OF INNOCENT BYSTANDERS
11. CARRIES OUT PLANS SO LIFE WILL APPEAR NORMAL

A WAY OF ESCAPE

5 When Bathsheba comes to David, he reconsiders and sends her home.

2 David goes to the roof and kneels in prayer for the men on the battle field.

10 When David hears that several good men were killed, he is in great sorrow over their needless deaths.

1 King David goes to the battle front with the Ark of the Covenant and all the men of Israel.

8 After David gets Uriah drunk, he is ashamed of himself and has Uriah sleep it off in the palace.

9 Upon seeing that his two attempts to get Uriah to compromise have failed, David is convicted and resolves to be honest.

11 After marrying Bathsheba, David is horrified at how low he has sunk and seeks God's direction.

7 David gets godly counsel and pulls Bathsheba's husband, Uriah, from the war to confess and make amends.

4 When David finds out she is a married woman, he goes into the palace to be with one of his own wives.

6 When David finds out that Bathsheba is pregnant, he falls down in repentance to God.

3 David turns away as soon as he sees a woman bathing.

And God is FAITHFUL; *he will not let you be* TEMPTED *beyond what you can* BEAR. *But when you are* TEMPTED *He will also* PROVIDE *a way out so that you can* STAND *up under it.*

288

DRUGS AND THE BODY 2

BRAIN/NERVOUS SYSTEM

□■■ Sense of well-being, joy, relief, euphoria, relaxed, giddiness
□□□ Enhanced mental & physical capacity
■□■ Permanent damage
■□□ Unconscious/coma
□□□ Crazy/schizophrenia
■□□ Mood change
□□□ 'Hear' voices
■□■ Hallucinations
■□□ Impaired judgment
□□□ Thought disturbance
■□□ Loss of memory
□□□ Drowsiness/sleepiness
■□□ Dizziness/poor coordination
□□■ Confusion/ sensory distortion
■□□ Trembling
□□□ Sleeplessness
□□□ Personality problems
■□□ Slow reaction/reflexes
□□■ Altered sense of time
□□□ Nervousness/anxiety
□□□ Speed up mentally
■□□ Slurred speech
□□□ Fear/paranoia
□□□ Violent/angry
□□□ Depression
■■■ Addictive
□□□ Suicidal
■■■ Death
□□■ High

BODY/SKIN/MUSCLES

□□□ Temporary gain in strength
□□□ Skin "crawling" (like bugs)
□□□ Severe acne
□□□ Weight loss
□□□ Weight gain
□□□ Tumors
□□□ Balding

STOMACH/INTESTINES

□□□ No appetite
□□□ Vomiting/nausea
□□□ Inflammation/swelling
□□□ Cramps
□□□ Ulcers
□□□ Diarrhea

REPRODUCTIVE ORGANS

□□□ Harmful to unborn babies
□□□ Impairs development
□□□ Lowers sperm count
□□□ Loss of fertility
□□□ Impotence

MOUTH/NOSE

□□□ Cancer
□■□ Bad breath
□□■ Nose bleeds
□□□ Loose teeth
□□□ Runny nose
□□■ Sneezing
□□□ Chronic cough

EYES

□□□ Bloodshot/ red
□□□ Yellow
□□□ Dilated pupils
□□□ Double vision
□□□ Severely swollen eyes

HEART/BLOOD VESSELS

□□□ Rapid heart beat
□□□ Irregular beat
□■□ Heart attack
□□□ Stroke
■■□ High blood pressure
□□□ Builds up cholesterol

LUNGS

□□■ Death by suffocation
□□□ Respiration slowed
■□□ Inflammation/swelling
□■□ Chronic bronchitis
□■□ Emphysema
□■□ Pneumonia
□■□ Wheezing
□■□ Shortness of breath
□■□ Permanent damage
□■□ Cancer
□■□ Asthma

KIDNEY/LIVER

□□■ Kidney damage
■□■ Liver damage
■□□ Cirrhosis of the liver
■□□ Inflammation/swelling

ALCOHOL
IN THE US, SOMEONE IS KILLED IN AN ALCOHOL-RELATED ACCIDENT EVERY 22 MINUTES; CAUSES TROUBLE CONTROLLING EMOTIONS

TOBACCO
CAN CAUSE A SPONTANEOUS ABORTION; PERSON MAY GO BACK TO A PREVIOUS SMOKING LEVEL AFTER QUITTING FOR YEARS

INHALANTS
CAN KILL WITH ONE USE; MANY ARE HOUSEHOLD ITEMS

293

DRUGS AND THE BODY 4

BRAIN/NERVOUS SYSTEM

■□■ Sense of well-being, joy, relief, euphoria, relaxed, giddiness
■□□ Enhanced mental & physical capacity
■□□ Permanent damage
□□□ Unconscious/coma
□□■ Crazy/schizophrenia
■□■ Mood change
■□□ 'Hear' voices
□□■ Hallucinations
□□□ Impaired judgment
□□□ Thought disturbance
□□□ Loss of memory
■□□ Drowsiness/sleepiness
□□□ Dizziness/poor coordination
□□□ Confusion/ sensory distortion
□□□ Trembling
■□■ Sleeplessness
□□□ Personality problems
□□□ Slow reaction/reflexes
□□□ Altered sense of time
□□□ Nervousness/anxiety
□□■ Speed up mentally
□□□ Slurred speech
□□□ Fear/paranoia
□□□ Violent/angry
□□□ Depression
■□■ Addictive
■□□ Suicidal
□□■ Death
□□□ High

BODY/SKIN/MUSCLES

□■□ Temporary gain in strength
□□■ Skin "crawling" (like bugs)
□■□ Severe acne
■□■ Weight loss
□■□ Weight gain
□■□ Tumors
□■□ Balding

STOMACH/INTESTINES

■□□ No appetite
■□□ Vomiting/nausea
□□□ Inflammation/swelling
□□□ Cramps
□□□ Ulcers
□□■ Diarrhea

REPRODUCTIVE ORGANS

■□□ Harmful to unborn babies
□□□ Impairs development
□■□ Lowers sperm count
□□□ Loss of fertility
□□□ Impotence

MOUTH/NOSE

□□□ Cancer
□□□ Bad breath
■□□ Nose bleeds
□□□ Loose teeth
■□□ Runny nose
□□□ Sneezing
■□□ Chronic cough

EYES

□□□ Bloodshot/ red
□■□ Yellow
□□■ Dilated pupils
□□□ Double vision
□□□ Severely swollen eyes

HEART/BLOOD VESSELS

■□■ Rapid heart beat
■□□ Irregular beat
■□□ Heart attack
■□□ Stroke
□■■ High blood pressure
□■□ Builds up cholesterol

LUNGS

□□□ Death by suffocation
□□□ Respiration slowed
□□□ Inflammation/swelling
□□□ Chronic bronchitis
□□□ Emphysema
□□□ Pneumonia
□□□ Wheezing
□□□ Shortness of breath
□□□ Permanent damage
□□□ Cancer
□□□ Asthma

KIDNEY/LIVER

□■□ Kidney damage
□■□ Liver damage
□□□ Cirrhosis of the liver
□□□ Inflammation/swelling

COCAINE
FEVER CONVULSIONS USE OF NEEDLES MAY GET AIDS

STEROIDS
ATHLETES USE THEM ALTHOUGH THEY ARE BANNED; WE USED TO HELP CONCENTRATION CAMPS VICTIMS BUILD UP THEIR STARVED BODIES

AMPHETAMINES
ANXIETY CAN SMOKE, SWALLOW OR INJECT

297

DRUGS AND THE BODY 6

BRAIN/NERVOUS SYSTEM

■■■ Sense of well-being, joy, relief, euphoria, relaxed, giddiness
□□□ Enhanced mental & physical capacity
□□□ Permanent damage
■□□ Unconscious/coma
□□□ Crazy/schizophrenia
■□□ Mood change
□□□ 'Hear' voices
□■□ Hallucinations
■□□ Impaired judgment
□■□ Thought disturbance
■■□ Loss of memory
■■■ Drowsiness/sleepiness
■■□ Dizziness/poor coordination
□■□ Confusion/ sensory distortion
□□□ Trembling
□□□ Sleeplessness
□□■ Personality problems
■□□ Slow reaction/reflexes
□■□ Altered sense of time
□■□ Nervousness/anxiety
□□□ Speed up mentally
■□□ Slurred speech
□■□ Fear/paranoia
□□□ Violent/angry
□□□ Depression
■■■ Addictive
□□□ Suicidal
■□□ Death
□□□ High

BODY/SKIN/MUSCLES

□□□ Temporary gain in strength
□□□ Skin "crawling" (like bugs)
□□□ Severe acne
□□□ Weight loss
□□□ Weight gain
□□□ Tumors
□□□ Balding

STOMACH/INTESTINES

□□□ No appetite
■□□ Vomiting/nausea
□□□ Inflammation/swelling
□□□ Cramps
□□□ Ulcers
□□□ Diarrhea

REPRODUCTIVE ORGANS

□■■ Harmful to unborn babies
□■□ Impairs development
□□□ Lowers sperm count
□■□ Loss of fertility
□□□ Impotence

MOUTH/NOSE

□□□ Cancer
□□□ Bad breath
□□□ Nose bleeds
□□□ Loose teeth
□□□ Runny nose
□□□ Sneezing
□□□ Chronic cough

EYES

□■□ Bloodshot/ red
□□□ Yellow
□□□ Dilated pupils
■□□ Double vision
□□□ Severely swollen eyes

HEART/BLOOD VESSELS

□■□ Rapid heart beat
□□□ Irregular beat
□□□ Heart attack
□□□ Stroke
□□□ High blood pressure
□□□ Builds up cholesterol

LUNGS

□□□ Death by suffocation
■□□ Respiration slowed
□□□ Inflammation/swelling
□□□ Chronic bronchitis
□□□ Emphysema
□□□ Pneumonia
□□□ Wheezing
□□□ Shortness of breath
□■□ Permanent damage
□□□ Cancer
□□□ Asthma

KIDNEY/LIVER

□□□ Kidney damage
□□□ Liver damage
□□□ Cirrhosis of the liver
□□□ Inflammation/swelling

BARBITUATES
MOST ABUSED, ONE THIRD OF ALL DRUG RELATED DEATHS, LACK MOTIVATION, IMPAIRED MOTOR CONTROL, HORRIBLE WITHDRAWAL SYMPTOMS

MARIJUANA
"GATEWAY" DRUG- LEADS TO HEROIN, COCAINE AND ALCOHOL, REDUCES CONCENTRATION, LACK OF MOTIVATION, HARMS LUNGS, PANIC

HEROIN
LAZINESS, POOR DIET, POOR HYGIENE, DANGER OF AIDS AND HEPATITIS

299

THE HIGH PRICE OF DRUGS AND ALCOHOL

These are some of the costs of using drugs and alcohol. There are many more, but these are just to get the ideas flowing and a discussion going. Some of these costs apply to all the substances, and some to only one or two. Some substances are far more damaging than others. Underline those that have affected someone you know.

1. Deny and hide problems.
2. Need for secrecy.
3. Leads to hard drugs.
4. Taken advantage of while drunk or high.
5. Inhibitions weaken.
6. Do things while drunk or high that you would never do sober.
7. Can't remember what happened.
8. May harm someone else while drunk or high.
9. May wreck car, injure or kill friends while drunk or high.
10. Loss of self-esteem.
11. Loss of self-control.
12. Do not learn to take responsibility for self.
13. Have sex when you otherwise would not.
14. May get raped or may rape someone.
15. May get into unnecessary fights.
16. Constant fear of getting caught.
17. Paranoid.
18. Addiction.
19. Difficulty in stopping habit.
20. Lifelong struggle with addiction.
21. May lose friends.
22. May lose boyfriend or girlfriend.
23. Dulling of conscience.
24. Cannot admit to the problem.
25. Cause others to follow example.
26. Affects relationship with God.
27. Cause those who know you as a Christian to mock your God.
28. Doubt God's willingness to forgive you.
29. Doubt God's ability to change you.
30. Doubt God's existence.
31. Loss of ministry.
32. Others discuss you.
34. Guilt.
35. Shame.
36. Loneliness.
37. Hopelessness.
38. Poverty.
39. Destroyed marriage.
40. Ruined lives of children.
41. Poor performance at school.
42. Disrespectful and angry.
43. Failing grades.
44. Loss of privileges.
45. Get kicked off team or out of club.
46. Loss of scholarship.
47. Lateness at school or work.
48. Lack of concentration.
49. Loss of motivation.
50. May drop out of school or college.
51. Poor performance at work.
52. Distrusted by employer.
53. Loss of job.
54. May do illegal things to get illegal drugs.
55. Fines.
56. Jail-time.
57. May steal from friends or family to support addition.
58. Turn to robbery or other crimes to get money.
59. Breaking and entering to support habit.
60. Breaking the law.
61. Police records.
62. Time in prison.
63. The habit is very expensive.
64. Stained fingers and teeth.
65. Bloodshot eyes.
66. Odor.
67. Vomiting, unconsciousness.
68. Scars.
69. Painful hangovers.
70. Bad trip.
71. Overdose.
72. HIV-AIDS and hepatitis from sharing needles.
73. Liver disease.
74. Seizures
75. Brain damage.
76. Death
77. Damage to your reproductive system.
78. Damage to your future children.

VOCABULARY OF PSALM 51

bloodguilt	wipe out.
blot out	crushed by sorrow or grief.
broken heart	throw aside, reject, discard.
cast	make by giving a new character.
compassion	responsible for murder.
contrite	take great pleasure in.
create	help, sympathy, pity.
declare	a broken spirit because of guilt.
delight	announce publicly, proclaim.
desire	something given as an act of worship & devotion.
despise	wickedness or sin.
gladness	look down on with contempt.
hide	wish for strongly.
hyssop	happiness, joy.
iniquity	keep away, put out of sight.
inmost	a plant used to sprinkle water in Jewish ceremonies.
justifiy	clear of any blame or guilt.
offerings	deepest, most intimate.
pleasure	perfectly clean, spotless.
presence	be glad, full of joy.
pure	a saving from destruction or ruin.
rejoice	make spiritually new, a new beginning.
renew	bring back to former condition.
restore	upright conduct, moral rightness.
righteousness	in the place where someone is.
salvation	a feeling of being pleased, enjoyment, delight.
spirit	breaking a law or command.
steadfast	knowledge, good judgement, wise conduct.
sustain	loyal, unwavering, firmly fixed, immoveable.
tongue	to keep up, keep going.
transgression	ready, cheerful, consenting.
truth	power of speech.
willing	man's moral, religious or emotional nature.
wisdom	what is true, real or actual.

Read what is written just under the title of Psalm 51. Who wrote Psalm 51? **DAVID** What had happened?
THE PROPHET NATHAN CONFRONTED HIM ABOUT ADULTERY WITH BATHSHEBA.
How did God use David's past as a shepherd to have David condemn himself?
HE USED A STORY ABOUT A RICH MAN STEALING A BELOVED SHEEP FROM A POOR MAN.
Was David forgiven? **YES** What did God's enemies show towards Him? **CONTEMPT.**
Were there any consequences for what David did? **YES** What were they? (2 Samuel 12:10,11,14)
DAVID'S BABY WOULD DIE. CALAMITY WILL COME FROM HIS OWN FAMILY.
THE SWORD WOULD NOT DEPART FROM HIS FAMILY.
How did David's response differ from Saul's after each was confronted about sinning? (1 Sam 15)
SAUL ARGUED AND BLAMED OTHERS. DAVID ASKED FORGIVENESS.
What consequence of sin did Saul experience that David wanted to avoid? (Ps 51:11)
HE DID NOT WANT THE HOLY SPIRIT TO LEAVE HIM NOR FOR GOD TO REJECT HIM.

300

PSALM OF PETITION 1

PETITION - Asking for God's help

1. **Plea:** Calling out for God to listen. (Example: Hear my prayer, O God. Have mercy on me, O Lord.)
2. **Problem:** An illness, a disaster, war, danger, sin. (Example: My enemies are camped around me. Ruthless men seek my life.)
3. **Prayer Request:** Tell God what is needed of Him. (Example: Save me. Forgive me. Protect me.)
4. **Profession:** A statement of trust and faith in Who God is and what He has done and will do. (Example: Surely God is my help. The Lord is the One who sustains me.)
5. **Promise:** Promise to thank God in the future for His answer to the prayer. (Example: I will praise your name. I will declare Your works.)

PSALM 51 NIV

Written by **DAVID**. When? **WHEN NATHAN CONFRONTED HIM ABOUT ADULTERY AND MURDER.**

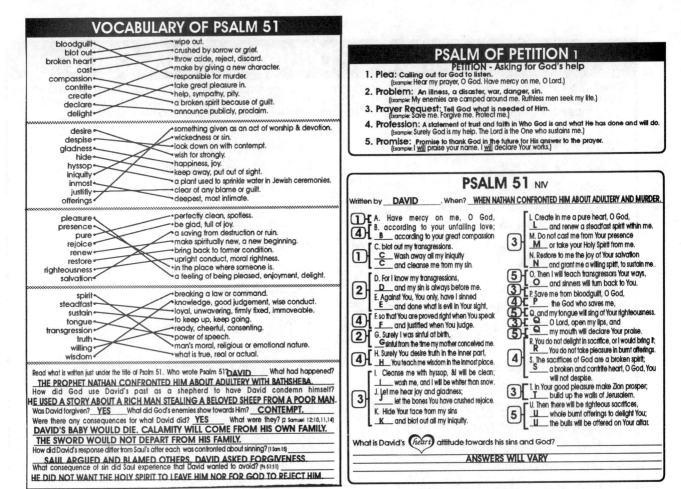

[1] A. Have mercy on me, O God,
[4] B. according to your unfailing love; **B** according to your great compassion
[1] C. blot out my transgressions. **C** Wash away all my iniquity **C** and cleanse me from my sin.
[2] D. For I know my transgressions, **D** and my sin is always before me. E. Against You, You only, have I sinned **E** and done what is evil in Your sight,
[4] F. so that You are proved right when You speak **F** and justified when You judge.
[2] G. Surely I was sinful at birth, **G** sinful from the time my mother conceived me.
[4] H. Surely You desire truth in the inner part, **H** You teach me wisdom in the inmost place.
[3] I. Cleanse me with hyssop, & I will be clean; **I** wash me, and I will be whiter than snow. J. Let me hear joy and gladness; **J** let the bones You have crushed rejoice. K. Hide Your face from my sins **K** and blot out all my iniquity.
[3] L. Create in me a pure heart, O God, **L** and renew a steadfast spirit within me. M. Do not cast me from Your presence **M** or take your Holy Spirit from me. N. Restore to me the joy of Your salvation **N** and grant me a willing spirit, to sustain me..
[5] O. Then I will teach transgressors Your ways, **O** and sinners will turn back to You.
[3] P. Save me from bloodguilt, O God,
[4] **P** the God who saves me,
[5] Q. and my tongue will sing of Your righteousness.
[3] **Q** O Lord, open my lips, and
[5] **Q** my mouth will declare Your praise.
[4] R. You do not delight in sacrifice, or I would bring it; **R** You do not take pleasure in burnt offerings. S. The sacrifices of God are a broken spirit; **S** a broken and contrite heart, O God, You will not despise.
[3] T. In Your good pleasure make Zion prosper; **T** build up the walls of Jerusalem.
[5] U. Then there will be righteous sacrifices, **U** whole burnt offerings to delight You; **U** the bulls will be offered on Your altar.

What is David's (heart) attitude towards his sins and God?
ANSWERS WILL VARY

301

TROUBLE IN DAVID'S FAMILY 1

Read 2 Samuel 12:26-31 and chapter 13. Write in the name of the speakers on the line below the statements.

I named my daughter after my poor, desolate sister.
__ABSALOM__

I was grateful that the king had granted my request to bring Absalom back.
__JOAB__

I felt sorry for the widow and promised to issue an order protecting her son, the murderer.
__DAVID__

I forced my half-sister to have sex with me. I hated her afterwards.
__AMNON__

I fled to my mother's hometown and stayed there three years.
__ABSALOM__

I sent for my son, but I did not talk with him about the tragic events that led to his banishment. I just kissed him.
__DAVID__

I invited the king and all my brothers to my sheep-shearing feast, but I had revenge on my mind.
__ABSALOM__

I told a wise woman from Tekoa to pretend she was in mourning and to speak to the king.
__JOAB__

I told a story of a hunted murderer.
__TEKOA WOMAN__

After I mourned for my dead son for a long time, I longed to see Absalom again, but I did nothing about it.
__DAVID__

I tore my ornamented robe in grief and despair, for I was no longer a virgin.
__TAMAR__

I knew what was going on and reassured the king that only one son was killed at the feast.
__JONADAB__

I guessed correctly who had invented the story the woman told.
__DAVID__

It had been five years since I had seen my father, yet our reunion was not much to talk about.
__ABSALOM__

I ignored the king's son until he set my fields on fire.
__JOAB__

I was furious when I heard the news of my daughter's rape, but did nothing.
__DAVID__

I was extremely handsome and had great hair.
__ABSALOM__

I went to live with my brother. He has said nothing to my half-brother although he is furious and hates him.
__TAMAR__

I did not allow Absalom to see me even after he had been gone three years.
__DAVID__

I went to Geshur to bring Absalom back to Jerusalem.
__JOAB__

I summoned Joab thinking he could get me in to see my father.
__ABSALOM__

I fought the city of Rabbah, and told David if he did not come I would take the city and name it after myself.
__JOAB__

I applied my story to Absalom's plight.
__TEKOA WOMAN__

I told Amnon to pretend to be sick in order to have his sister come to him.
__JONADAB__

303

TROUBLE IN DAVID'S FAMILY 2

Read 2 Samuel 15-17. Draw a line from the person or persons to what they did.

🙿 ABSALOM'S CONSPIRACY ◌ CHAPTER 15

Hushai the Arkite
Absalom
Ittai the Gittite
Kerethites & Pelethites
Ahithophel
Zadok and Abiathar
A messenger
David

He sends secret messengers throughout Israel to proclaim himself king.
David sends him back to frustrate Ahithophel's counsel.
He goes to take over Jerusalem after David leaves.
David takes his family and these groups of people.
David encourages him to go back, but he and his people stay with David.
David prays, "O Lord, turn his counsel into foolishness."
He gets permission from the king to "fulfill a vow" in Hebron.
David tells them to go back to Jerusalem to send messages by their sons.
He stole the hearts of the men of Israel.
He leaves behind 10 concubines.
He was to give messages to David by the sons of Zadok and Abiathar.
These priests carry the ark of God and offer sacrifices while David flees.
David's wisest counselor joins Absalom.
He tells David, "The hearts of the men of Israel are with Absalom."
David tells them to take the ark back into the city.
He said, "If I find favor in the Lord's eyes, he will bring me back.."
He realizes how dangerous Absalom is and announces they must all flee.

🙿 FRIEND OR FOE? ◌ CHAPTER 16

Ziba
Abishai
Hushai
Absalom
Shimei
Ahithophel
David

He offers to kill Shimei, but David says, "Maybe God told him to curse me."
He meets David with donkeys and provisions.
He takes Ahithophel's advice.
David gives him all Mephibosheth's property, and he accepts.
He explains to Absalom that he came to serve the one "chosen by the Lord."
He says, "My own son is trying to kill me. Let the Benjamite curse!"
He tells David that Mephibosheth stayed back hoping to become king.
He and his group continue toward Bahurim.
Absalom asks him for his advice.
He says, "Maybe God will see my distress and give me a blessing instead."
He tells Absalom to sleep with his father's concubines.
He is from Saul's clan, and pelts David's group with stones and curses.

🙿 HUSHAI SAVES THE DAY ◌ CHAPTER 17

Absalom
Hushai
Ahithophel
Amasa
Shobi, Makir & Barzillai
David
Jonathan & Ahimaaz

He crosses the Jordan and camps in Gilead.
He sends a warning to David to cross the Jordan that very night.
He hangs himself.
He advises Absalom to muster every man in Israel.
He and the men of Israel like Hushai's advice better than that of Ahithophel.
He advises an overwhelming attack and to kill everyone.
He tells Absalom to take 12,000 men and kill David that very night.
He advises to kill David but spare everyone else.
He asks Hushai for his advice.
Absalom appoints him over the army.
They go secretly to deliver the message to David, but are spotted.
They hide in a well until the searchers leave, then are able to reach David.
He and his followers flee to Mahanaim.
They took bedding, bowls, and food to David and his people.
Absalom and the elders like his advice best.

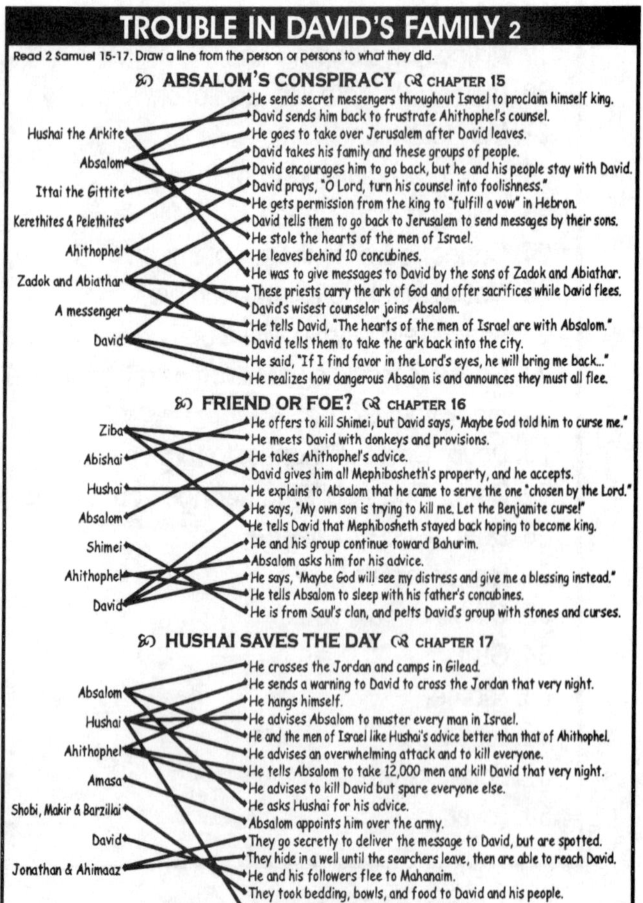

306

PRICE OF SEX OUTSIDE OF MARRIAGE

Below are some of the costs of sex outside marriage. Circle the numbers of the costs that you realize have already affected friends or family. Use as a jumping off point for a discussion.

1. Loss of self esteem.
2. Attachment without commitment.
3. Fear kills ability to enjoy the sex.
4. One person more attached than other.
5. Causes far more inner turmoil than a nonsexual relationship does.
6. Cheapens sex and marriage.
7. Judgment clouded -- many rash decisions.
8. Constant fear of abandonment.
9. Partner casually moves on.
10. Loss of ability to bond with another.
11. Heart and soul ripped apart when it ends.
12. Feeling used.
13. Gift of yourself may be broken or destroyed.
14. Breaking up becomes very painful.
15. Makes other relationships easier to break up.
16. Sneak around for quick interludes.
17. Not able to discuss relationship with others.
18. Fear of getting caught.
19. Disappoint parents.
20. Loss of trust.
21. May need to tell lies upon lies to cover up.
22. May not learn how to work through problems.
23. Communication stops.
24. Not the real world -- a fantasy that falls apart.
25. Hard or impossible to change the relationship to a healthy one.
26. Lack of trust.
27. Feel trapped.
28. Must hold back part of self.
29. May loathe self and partner.
30. May not know how to end the relationship.
31. Guilt.
32. Must live a lie.
33. Betrayal of family and friends.
34. Being gossiped about.
35. Others belittle you.
36. Many disdain you, call you names.
37. Burden of sin breaks you.
38. Affects relationship with God.
39. Loss of ministry.
40. Public humiliation for whole family or church.
41. Cause others to follow your example.
42. Cause those who trusted you to question God.
43. Breaks up the family.
44. Divorce.
45. Destroys children's lives.
46. Affects your future children.

DISEASE

1. Constant fear of disease or pregnancy.
2. Chance of getting AIDS, herpes or 65 other sexually transmitted diseases.
3. Some diseases are incurable; you may carry it the rest of your life.
4. Pass disease on to others.
5. Death from disease or from complications of an abortion.
6. Diseases cause damage that prevent having children in the future.

PREGNANCY

1. Abortion, with all its danger, guilt, depression.
2. Quick marriage.
3. May have to give up baby for adoption.
4. Affects the rest of your life.
5. May lose independence.
6. May feel obligated to get married.
7. Causes you to stay with wrong person.
8. Feel forced to marry.
9. Don't get to know the other person well.
10. May not be able to raise your own child.
11. Must put off education, college or career.
12. May never graduate from high school or college.
13. Being a child raising a child.
14. Loss of your childhood -- have to grow up fast.
15. May have to live at poverty level.
16. May have to raise child by yourself.
17. May have to pay child support.
18. May have to live with in-laws.
19. Must rely on parents for survival & for help with baby.
20. Must rely on government help to raise the baby.
21. No time for yourself.
22. Your body is forever changed by the pregnancy.
23. May have little say in the raising the child.
24. May not be able to protect the child from bad or harmful situations.
25. Think baby will give unconditional love, and are not prepared for the constant demands.
26. Having a child lessens chances of marriage.

PSALM OF PETITION 2

PETITION - Asking for God's help

1. **Plea:** Calling out for God to listen. (Example: Hear my prayer, O God. Have mercy on me, O Lord.)
2. **Problem:** An illness, a disaster, war, danger, sin. (Example: My enemies are camped around me. Ruthless men seek my life.)
3. **Prayer Request:** Tell God what is needed of Him. (Example: Save me. Forgive me. Protect me.)
4. **Profession:** A statement of trust and faith in Who God is and what He has done and will do. (Example: Surely God is my help. The Lord is the One who sustains me.)
5. **Promise:** Promise to thank God in the future for His answer to the prayer. (Example: I will praise your name. I will declare Your works.)

PSALM 3 NIV

Written by **DAVID**
When? **WHEN HE FLED FROM ABSALOM**

[1] A. O Lord,
[2] how many are my foes!
A How many rise up against me!
A Many are saying, "God will not deliver him."
[4] B. But You are a shield around me, O Lord;
B My Glorious One, Who lifts up my head.
C. To the Lord I cry aloud,
C and He answers me from His holy hill.
D. I lie down and sleep;
D I wake again, because the Lord sustains me.
E. I will not fear the tens of thousands
E drawn up against on every side.
[3] F. Arise, O Lord!
F Deliver me, O my God!
G. Strike all my enemies on the jaw;
G Break the teeth of the wicked.
[4] **G** From the Lord comes deliverance.

PSALM 40:5,11-14,16-17 NIV

[4] A. Many, O Lord my God are the wonders You have done.
A The things you planned for us no one can recount to You;
A were I to speak and tell of them, they would be too many to declare.
[3] B. Do not withhold your mercy from me, O Lord;
B may Your love and Your truth always protect me.
[2] C. For troubles without number surround me;
C my sins have overtaken me, and I cannot see.
C They are more than the hairs of my head,
C and my heart fails within me.
[3] D. Be pleased, O Lord, to save me;
D O Lord, come quickly to help me.
E. May all who seek to take my life be put to shame and confusion;
E may all who desire my ruin be turned back in disgrace.
[5] F. But may all those who seek You rejoice and be glad in You;
F may those who love Your salvation always say, 'The Lord be exalted!"
[2] G. Yet I am poor and needy;
[3] **G** may the Lord think of me.
[4] H. You are my help and my deliverer;
[3] **H** O my God, do not delay.

Read 2 Samuel chapters 14-18

How did Absalom win the people's favor? **BY ACTING AS IF HE CARED ABOUT THEIR PROBLEMS.**
What did David and his family have to do? **FLEE FOR THEIR LIVES.** Which adviser was most trusted by both David and Absalom? **AHITHOPHEL** What advice did he give in 17:1-4? **ATTACK NOW AND KILL ONLY DAVID.**
What did he do when Absalom didn't follow it? **HE HUNG HIMSELF.**
Whom did David send to give Absalom bad advice? **HUSHAI** What was the bad advice? **GATHER ALL ISRAEL TO HUNT DAVID AND HIS MEN DOWN AND DESTROY THEM ALL**
How was Absalom caught? **HIS HEAD GOT CAUGHT IN AN OAK TREE.**
Did Joab obey David's orders not to harm him? **NO** Why do you think he disobeyed? **ANSWERS MAY VARY**
What did David say when he heard of Absalom's death? **"OH ABSALOM! IF ONLY I HAD DIED INSTEAD OF YOU"!**

307

THE CONSPIRACY FAILS

JOAB KILLS ABSALOM

David organizes his men under three commanders: **JOAB, ABISHAI, ITTAI THE GITTITE**
Knowing Ahithophel's advice to Absalom, the men do not let **DAVID** go with them. David warns them in the presence of all to be gentle with **ABSALOM**. The **ISRAELITE** army is defeated by **DAVID'S** army. Absalom gets caught in a **TREE** by his **HEAD**. A messenger reports the situation to Joab. Joab asks him why he didn't **KILL** Absalom. The reply is: **DAVID SAID NOT TO KILL HIM. I WOULD BE EXECUTED.** Joab goes and kills Absalom.

Joab kills Absalom ■ contrary to David's will ☐ with deceit or secrecy ☐ in self-defense ☐ in peace-time ■ while Absalom is helpless ☐ to gain favor from David ■ while at war with him ☐ reluctantly

What happened to the last few men who brought David news of the death of his enemies? **EXECUTED**
In your opinion, why does Ahimaaz want to be the messenger? **ANSWERS MAY VARY**

JOAB ADVISES DAVID TO ENCOURAGE HIS MEN

David is so devastated by the death of his son, that he thinks of nothing else. Joab goes to him and warns him of disaster. In your own words, explain the problem and Joab's solution. **ANSWERS MAY VARY BUT SHOULD INCLUDE HOW DAVID'S BEHAVIOR AFFECTS HIS LOYAL WARRIORS**

FRIENDS AND FOES WELCOME DAVID BACK AS KING

As you read through 2 Samuel 19:8b-43, list what each of the following did to welcome David back to Jerusalem.

The men of Israel **ARGUED WITH EACH OTHER ABOUT WHAT TO DO. HALF THE TROOPS TOOK HIM OVER THE JORDAN. ARGUED WITH JUDAH.**
The men of Judah **SENT INVITATION. WENT TO MEET HIM. ALL THE TROOPS TOOK HIM OVER THE JORDAN. ARGUED WITH ISRAEL.**
Shimei **HURRIED WITH 1000 MEN TO HELP. CONFESSED SIN. BEGGED FORGIVENESS. CLAIMED TO BE THE FIRST OF HOUSE OF JOSEPH TO WELCOME HIM BACK.**
Mephibosheth **WENT TO MEET HIM. HADN'T GROOMED SINCE DAVID LEFT. EXPLAINED WHY HE HADN'T GONE WITH DAVID. RELIEVED TO SEE HIM ALIVE. DIDN'T WANT LAND.**
Barzillai **WENT TO CROSS THE JORDAN AND SEE DAVID OFF IN SPITE OF BEING 80 YRS OLD. SENT KIMKAM WITH DAVID TO REPRESENT HIM.**

JOAB KILLS AMASA AND TAKES COMMAND OF THE ARMY

When Israel and Judah argue, **SHEBA** of the tribe of Benjamin sounds a **TRUMPET** and shouts "We have no share in David!" All the men of **ISRAEL** desert David and follow him. All the men of **JUDAH** stay with David and bring him to Jerusalem. David bypasses Joab and puts **AMASA** in charge of summoning an army, but he takes too long. Then David sends **ABISHAI** after Sheba to prevent a rebellion worse than Absalom's. Joab goes, too. They meet Amasa in **GIBEON**.

Joab kills Amasa ■ contrary to David's will ■ with deceit or secrecy ☐ in self-defense ☐ reluctantly ☐ to stop a rebellion ☐ while at war with him ■ while in the same army with him

In your opinion why does Joab kill his cousin? ☐ He thinks Amasa is actually working for Sheba as he did for Absalom ☐ He thinks he deserves to die for fighting against David ☐ Joab doesn't want to be replaced as commander of the army. ☐ Other **ANSWERS MAY VARY**

JOAB KILLS SHEBA AND ENDS THE REBELLION

Joab and **ABISHAI** continue after Sheba, who has a large following and has gone into the city of **ABEL BETH MAACAH**. The men of Judah besiege the city. A wise woman of that city talks with Joab and stops the attack by getting the people of the city to **KILL** Sheba and throw his **HEAD** over to Joab. Joab sounds the **TRUMPET** and sends the army home.

Joab has Sheba killed ☐ contrary to David's will ☐ with deceit or secrecy ☐ while in the same army with him ☐ in self-defense ☐ reluctantly ■ to stop a rebellion ■ while at war with him

Compare 20:23-26 with 8:15-18. List any new officials and their jobs.
ADONIRAM - FORCED LABOR, SHEVA - SECRETARY, IRA - DAVID'S PRIEST

309

NATHAN

You did it in **SECRET**, but I will do this thing in broad **DAYLIGHT**. 2 Sa 12:12

REFERENCE:	SPEAKER: SPOKEN TO:	WHAT WAS SAID	WHAT HAPPENED:
1 Chr 17:1	King David to Nathan	"Here I am, living in a **PALACE** of **CEDAR**, while the **ARK** of the Lord is under a **TENT**."	Nathan said to go ahead and do what he had in mind, for the Lord was with him.
1 Chr 17:3-4	GOD TO NATHAN	"Go tell my servant **DAVID**, 'This is what the Lord says: You are **NOT** the one to build me a **HOUSE** to dwell in."	1 Chr 22 **DAVID PREPARED THE MATERIALS BUT GAVE THE JOB OF BUILDING TO SOLOMON**
1 Chr 17:7-8	GOD TO DAVID	"I took you from the **PASTURE** and from following the **FLOCK**, to be **RULER** over my **PEOPLE** Israel. Now I will make your name like the names of the **GREATEST** men of the earth."	2 Sa 22:38-51, 1 Chr 29:26-30 **DAVID LIVED LONG, HAD WEALTH, HONOR AND VICTORIES OVER HIS ENEMIES, RULED MANY GROUPS.**
1 Chr 17:11-12	GOD TO DAVID	"I will raise up your **OFFSPRING** and I will establish his **KINGDOM**. He is the one who will build a **HOUSE** for me."	1 Ki 5, 6 **SOLOMON BUILT A GRAND TEMPLE FOR THE LORD.**
1 Chr 17:14	GOD TO DAVID	"I will **SET** him over my **HOUSE** and my **KINGDOM** forever; his **THRONE** will be established **FOREVER**."	1 Ki 2:12 **GOD ESTABLISHED SOLOMON'S KINGDOM**
2 Sa 12:1-4	NATHAN TO DAVID	"A **RICH** man had a large number of **SHEEP** and cattle, but the **POOR** man had nothing but **ONE** ewe lamb he had bought. It grew up with his **CHILDREN** It shared his **FOOD**, drank from his cup and **SLEPT** in his arms."	**DAVID WAS VERY UPSET THAT ANYONE COULD DO SUCH A THING.**
2 Sa 12:5-6	DAVID TO NATHAN	"As surely as the **LORD** lives, the man who did this deserves to **DIE**! He must **PAY** for that lamb **FOUR** times over, because he did such a thing and had no **PITY**."	**DAVID WAS THE ONE WHO HAD 'STOLEN THE LAMB' BY TAKING BATHSHEBA, SO HE WAS THE ONE WHO DESERVED TO DIE.**
2 Sa 12: 10-12	GOD TO DAVID	"Now the **SWORD** will never depart from your **FAMILY**. Out of your household I am going to bring **CALAMITY** upon you. I will take your **WIVES** and give them to one who is **CLOSE** to you. You did it in **SECRET** but I will do this thing in broad daylight,"	2 Sa 13-16 **ABSALOM KILLED AMNON AND LATER ATTACKED DAVID. HE SLEPT WITH HIS FATHER'S CONCUBINES IN BROAD DAYLIGHT.**
2 Sa 12:13-14	NATHAN TO DAVID	"The Lord has taken away your **SIN**. You are not going to **DIE**. But because by doing this you have made **ENEMIES** of the Lord show utter **CONTEMPT**, the son born to you will **DIE**."	**DAVID'S SON DIED AT AGE SEVEN DAYS.**
1 Ki 1:11	NATHAN TO BATHSHEBA	"Have you not heard **ADONIJAH** has become **KING** without the lord David's knowing it? Say to King David,' Did you not swear to me ,"Surely **SOLOMON** will be king after me"?	**BATHSHEBA WENT TO DAVID ABOUT IT, AND NATHAN BACKED HER UP.**
1 Ki 1:32-34	DAVID TO BATHSHEBA	"Have Zadok, the priest and **NATHAN** the prophet anoint **SOLOMON** king over Israel."	**THEY ANOINTED SOLOMON KING OF ISRAEL**

311

DAVID'S PART IN BUILDING THE TEMPLE

DAVID GIVES OF HIS PLUNDER

What did David do with all the plunder from the nations he conquered? **HE DEDICATED IT TO THE LORD.**
What kinds of metals did he take? **GOLD, BRONZE, SILVER**

DAVID SETS LOCATION

WHAT did Satan incite David to do? **TO TAKE A CENSUS OF ISRAEL.**
HOW did Joab feel about it? **HE WAS REPULSED.**
WHAT did David say after he had taken the census? **DAVID TOLD GOD THAT HE HAD SINNED.**
WHAT punishment did Israel get? **THREE DAYS OF PLAGUES.**
HOW many men died? **70,000 MEN DIED.**
HOW did that affect the census? **THE CENSUS IS NO LONGER ACCURATE.**
WHAT did David see at the threshing floor of Araunah? **THE ANGEL OF THE LORD.**
WHAT did David buy? **THE THRESHING FLOOR OF ARAUNAH.**
WHY did he not want to get it for nothing? **HE DID NOT GIVE GOD SOMETHING THAT COST HIM NOTHING.**
WHAT was the cost? **600 SHEKELS OF GOLD.**
WHAT did David do at that spot? **DAVID BUILT AN ALTAR AND GAVE AN OFFERING.**
HOW did the Lord answer him? **THE LORD ANSWERED WITH FIRE THAT BURNT UP THE OFFERING.**
WHAT did the angel do? **THE ANGEL PUT HIS SWORD AWAY.**
WHERE was the Tabernacle at this time? **THE TABERNACLE WAS AT GIBEON.**
WHERE would the Temple of Solomon be built? 2 Ch 3:1 **ON THE THRESHING FLOOR OF ARAUNAH.**

DAVID MAKES ARRANGEMENTS

- **F** David could do nothing to help get ready for the building of the Temple.
- **F** Stonecutters were taken from the Israelites.
- **F** There were no such things as nails in those times.
- **T** David made extensive preparations for the Temple before his death.
- **F** David could not build the House for the Lord because he was too old.
- **F** David provided gold, silver, bronze, and steel.
- **T** David had the workmen beyond number ready to work.
- **T** David told Solomon to devote his heart and soul to seeking the Lord his God.
- **F** The ark of the covenant would stay in the Tabernacle.
- **T** David had the Levites supervise the work of the Temple.
- **T** 4,000 Levites were to praise the Lord with music.
- **F** Their musical instruments were cymbals, lyres, organs, and harps.
- **F** There would be six Levites a day guarding the east, north, and south gates.
- **T** There were 12 army commanders that were on duty each for one month.
- **F** Each army division had 27,000 men.
- **F** David counted the twenty year old men because the Lord had promised to make Israel as numerous as the stars.
- **F** Wrath came upon the Israelites for the numbering after the number was entered into the annals of King David.

DAVID TURNS PLANS OVER TO SOLOMON

What does David tell Solomon in 1 Ch 28:9-10? **DAVID TOLD SOLOMON TO ACKNOWLEDGE & SERVE GOD WITH WHOLEHEARTED DEVOTION. HE WAS TO BE STRONG AND BUILD THE TEMPLE.**

COMPARING THE TEMPLE AND THE TABERNACLE

	TEMPLE	TABERNACLE
To whom did God give the plans?	DAVID	MOSES
What was put into the Holy of Holies?	ARK AND 2 CHERUBIM	ARK
What was in the Ark of the Covenant?	2 STONE TABLETS	MANNA, AARON'S ROD, STONE TABLETS
The attitude of those who gave was:	FREELY & WHOLEHEARTEDLY	THEIR HEARTS WERE MOVED
What did God do at its dedication?	GLORY & CLOUD OF THE LORD	GLORY & CLOUD OF THE LORD
Who worked on the construction?	24,000 LEVITES, 153,600 ALIENS	EVERY SKILLED PERSON
What were the dimensions of the structure? 1 Kings 6:2	length: 60 cubits width: 20 cubits height: 30 cubits	length: 30 cubits width: 10 cubits height: 10 cubits

312

SWORD WILL NEVER DEPART

"You struck down Uriah with the sword of the Ammonites. Now, therefore, the sword will never depart from your house..."
"This is what the Lord says; 'Out of your own household I am going to bring calamity upon you. Before your very eyes I will take your wives and give them to one who is close to you, and he will lie with your wives in broad daylight. You did it in secret, but I will do this thing in broad daylight before all Israel.'"

DAVID'S ACTIONS	THE SWORD WILL NEVER DEPART YOUR HOUSE
David (■ sends for □ sends) Bathsheba to come to him.	David (□ sends for ■ sends) Tamar to go to her brother Amnon.
David sleeps with a forbidden woman, Bathsheba who is (■ a married woman □ a virgin half-sister).	Amnon sleeps with a forbidden woman, Tamar who is (□ a married woman ■ a virgin half-sister).
Bathsheba (■ is □ is not) married, comforted, and given children.	Tamar (□ is ■ is not) married, comforted, and given children.
Joab kills Uriah, (■ an innocent □ a guilty) man (■ at □ against) the orders of David.	Joab kills Absalom, (□ an innocent ■ a guilty) man (□ at ■ against) the orders of David.
Nathan (□ does not ■ does) confront David and David (■ repents □ does not repent).	David (■ does not □ does) confront Amnon and Amnon (□ repents ■ does not repent).
David (■ puts to death □ allows to live) (■ an innocent □ a guilty) Uriah.	David (□ puts to death ■ allows to live) (□ an innocent ■ a guilty) Amnon.
David's innocent new-born son dies at the hand of (■ God □ Absalom).	David's guilty-first born son, Amnon, dies at the hand of (□ God ■ Absalom).
David's relationship with God (■ is □ is not) restored.	David's relationship with Absalom (□ is ■ is not) restored.
David sleeps with another man's wife (□ in broad day light ■ at night). He does it (■ in secret □ in the sight of all Israel).	Absalom sleeps with David's concubines (■ in broad day light □ at night). He does it (□ in secret ■ in the sight of all Israel).
David is punished by the death of (■ his baby son □ himself).	Amnon is punished by the death of (□ his baby son ■ himself).
David's concubines who were raped by Absalom (□ were restored and comforted ■ lived the rest of their lives as desolate women).	David's daughter Tamar, who was raped by Amnon (□ was restored and comforted ■ lived the rest of her life as a desolate woman).
David (■ was □ was not) given (■ Saul's wives □ David's wife, Abishag) as a sign he was king.	Adonijah (□ was ■ was not) given (□ Saul's wives ■ David's wife, Abishag) as a sign he was king. Instead Solomon killed him.

CONSEQUENCES OF SIN

What was the sin?	Why did God take it so seriously?	Whom did it affect, and how?
Numbers 14 *The people were afraid and refused to enter* CAANAN/THE PROMISED LAND (Grumble)	Nu 14:11 CONTEMPT/REFUSE TO BELIEVE 14:22, 23 DISOBEYED, TESTED ME 14:27, 29 WICKED COMMUNITY, GRUMBLE, COMPLAIN 14:33 UNFAITHFULNESS 14:35 BANDED TOGETHER AGAINST THE LORD	Nu 14:29 ALL AGE 20 AND UP WOULD DIE IN THE DESERT 14:33 YOUR CHILDREN WILL SUFFER IN DESERT *Other* ANSWERS MAY VARY. E.G. JOSHUA, CALEB, MOSES, AND AARON HAD TO SUFFER AND WAIT40 YEARS.
Joshua 6, 7 *Achan took things that were* DEVOTED *to God.*	Jos 7:1 UNFAITHFUL 7:11 SINNED, VIOLATED MY COVENANT, TOOK DEVOTED THINGS, STOLE, LIED	Jos 7:4, 5 36 WARRIORS DIED, ISRAEL - DEFEATED 7:24-26 ACHAN & FAMILY KILLED *Other* ANSWERS MAY VARY
2 Samuel 11, 12 *David committed* ADULTERY *with Bathsheba and then ordered that her husband be* KILLED	2 Sa 12:8 LACK OF GRATITUDE? 12:9 DESPISED THE WORD OF THE LORD 12:10 DESPISED ME 12:14 MADE ENEMIES OF THE LORD SHOW CONTEMPT	2 Sa 12:10 DESCENDANTS WOULD SUFFER "THE SWORD" 12:11 WIVES/CONCUBINES WOULD BE RAPED 12:14 SON WOULD DIE *Other* ANSWERS MAY VARY
Joshua 9:15-21; 2 Sa 21:1-14 *The Israelites took an* OATH *by the* LORD *that they would let the Gibeonites* LIVE *but some 400 years later Saul tried to* ANNIHILATE *them.*	2 Sa 21:1 SAUL AND HIS BLOODSTAINED HOUSE PUT GIBEONITES TO DEATH *How did the Gibeonites describe the sin?* DESTROYED US, PLOTTED AGAINST US, DECIMATED US SO WE HAVE NO PLACE IN ISRAEL	21:1 FAMINE ON ISRAEL 3 YEARS - HUNGER 21:6 7 OF SAUL'S DESCENDANTS KILLED *Other* ANSWERS MAY VARY, E.G. SORROW/MADNESS? OF RIZPAH, SORROW OF OTHER FAMILY MEMBERS.

SAUL	ISRAELITES	ACHAN	DAVID
God told us to wipe out all the inhabitants of the land. Besides Joshua was a fool to make a treaty with these liars.	There are giants and fortified cities in the lands! There is no way we can beat them! It is suicide to try!	Why should something this beautiful be burned? I want it - and look at this! I could be rich. I'll hide it; no one will ever know.	I am king. I can take what I want...Oops! I don't want to be found out. I'll cover it up.

DAVID'S LIFE

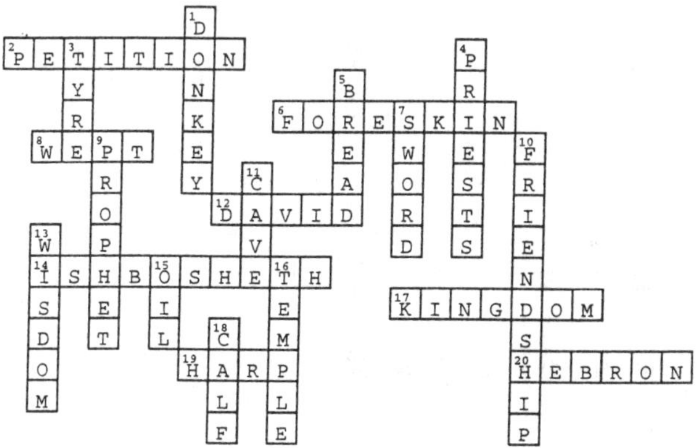

MEMORABLE SONGS

Read 2 Samuel 21:15-22. These victories give a background to David's song of victory in chapter 22 (also Psalm 18.) It may have been a favorite which David sang every time the Lord helped him. David's life was often in danger from enemies. What kind of "battles" keep coming up in your life? Write a song or prayer to use every time the Lord gives you victory. Include three elements: God's character and power as in 2 Sa 22:2-16; how your heart is toward the Lord as in 2 Sa 22:21-30; and your rescue by God as in 2 Sa 22:17-20, 31-51.

♫ SONG OF VICTORY ♫

ANSWERS WILL VARY

AN IMPORTANT MESSAGE FROM GOD

Read 2 Sa 23:1-7. What is it that the Rock of Israel said to David?

"When one RULES *over men in* RIGHTEOUSNESS
... he is like the brightness after RAIN *that brings the* GRASS *from the earth."*

A famous person about to speak often gets a very long, glowing introduction. How many lines does David use to introduce this statement from God? 9 What is something important that you have learned from God? Introduce your statement with powerful phrases that tell how you know it is true and how important it is. Work on other paper and write your final draft here.

ANSWERS WILL VARY

RIGHT WITH GOD

At the end of his life, after so many family problems, David is able to say that his house is right with God. What do you see as the main difference between David and Saul? They both sinned. Why did God reject Saul but establish David's house? ANSWERS WILL VARY BUT SHOULD INCLUDE MENTION THAT DAVID REPENTED, HAD A HEART TOWARD GOD, WHEREAS SAUL DID NEITHER.

THE PRICE OF LYING

Lying is costly. There are emotional, spiritual, financial, physical, and social costs. Underline those that make lying too expensive for you.

1. Loss of self-esteem.
2. Constant fear of getting caught.
3. Must keep inventing more lies to cover up previous lies.
4. Loss of intimacy with friends and family for fear they will discover the truth.
5. Must conceal activities.
6. Disappoint parents.
7. Loss of parents' trust.
8. Loss of friends' trust.
9. View others with suspicion.
10. Difficult to change habit of lying.
11. Begin to believe own lies.
12. Cannot distinguish between lies and the truth.
13. Loss of ministry.
14. Coming clean will be painful.
15. Loss of friends.
16. Loss of boyfriend or girlfriend.
17. May feel trapped in web of lies.
18. Dulling of conscience.
19. Loss of self-respect.
20. Feel like you are living a lie and others truly don't know you.
21. No one believes you even when you tell the truth.
22. The dishonesty of lying leads to other wrong choices like cheating and stealing.
23. Cannot be completely honest with anyone for fear of revealing a lie.
24. Cause others to follow example.
25. Loss of ability to bond with others.
26. Affects relationship with God.
27. Others discuss you.
28. Do not learn to face reality.
29. Do not learn to work through difficult issues.
30. Do not learn to take responsibility for your own actions.
31. Punishment is worse than if you came clean up front.
32. It is harder to tell the truth as time goes on.
33. When caught in a lie, everything about you is called into question.
34. Distrust by employer.
35. Loss of job.
36. Cause those who know you as a Christian to mock your God.
37. May doubt God's willingness to forgive you.
38. May doubt God's ability to change you.
39. May doubt God's existence.
40. Feel dirty, unclean, sad or lonely.

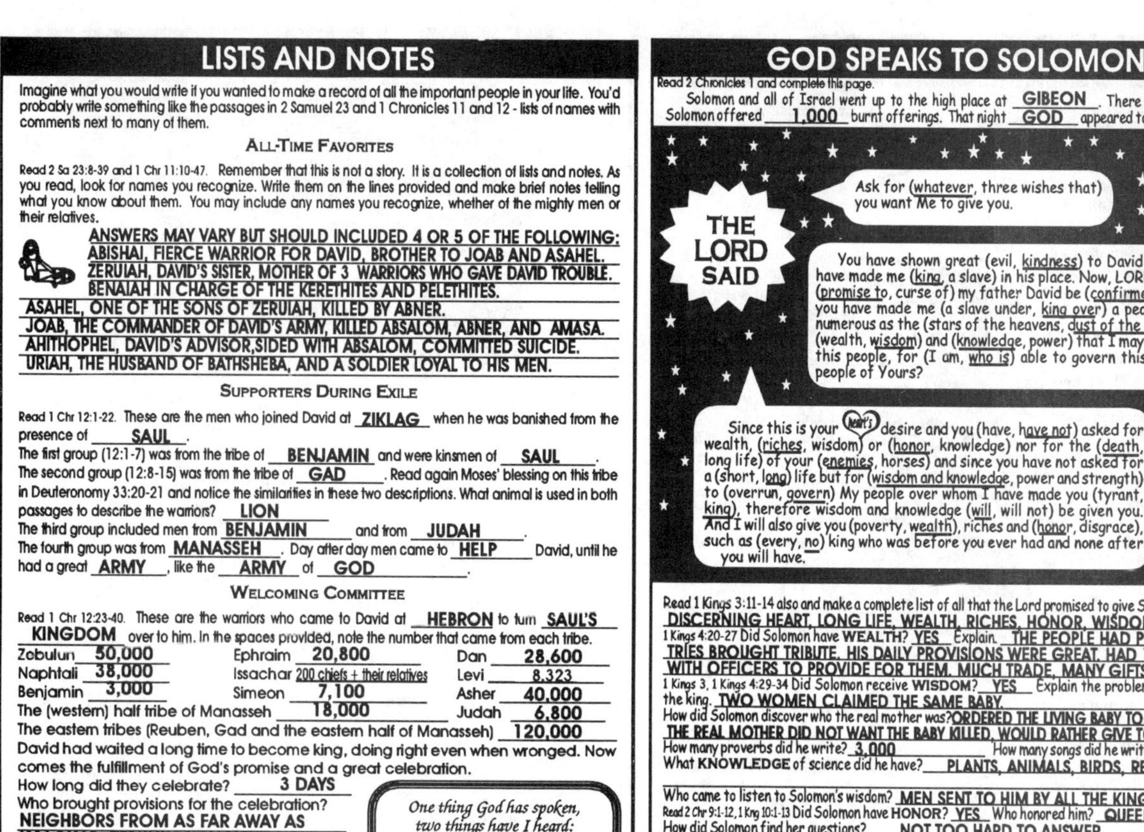

LISTS AND NOTES

Imagine what you would write if you wanted to make a record of all the important people in your life. You'd probably write something like the passages in 2 Samuel 23 and 1 Chronicles 11 and 12 - lists of names with comments next to many of them.

All-Time Favorites

Read 2 Sa 23:8-39 and 1 Chr 11:10-47. Remember that this is not a story. It is a collection of lists and notes. As you read, look for names you recognize. Write them on the lines provided and make brief notes telling what you know about them. You may include any names you recognize, whether of the mighty men or their relatives.

ANSWERS MAY VARY BUT SHOULD INCLUDED 4 OR 5 OF THE FOLLOWING:
ABISHAI, FIERCE WARRIOR FOR DAVID, BROTHER TO JOAB AND ASAHEL.
ZERUIAH, DAVID'S SISTER, MOTHER OF 3 WARRIORS WHO GAVE DAVID TROUBLE.
BENAIAH IN CHARGE OF THE KERETHITES AND PELETHITES.
ASAHEL, ONE OF THE SONS OF ZERUIAH, KILLED BY ABNER.
JOAB, THE COMMANDER OF DAVID'S ARMY, KILLED ABSALOM, ABNER, AND AMASA.
AHITHOPHEL, DAVID'S ADVISOR,SIDED WITH ABSALOM, COMMITTED SUICIDE.
URIAH, THE HUSBAND OF BATHSHEBA, AND A SOLDIER LOYAL TO HIS MEN.

Supporters During Exile

Read 1 Chr 12:1-22. These are the men who joined David at ZIKLAG when he was banished from the presence of SAUL.
The first group (12:1-7) was from the tribe of BENJAMIN and were kinsmen of SAUL.
The second group (12:8-15) was from the tribe of GAD. Read again Moses' blessing on this tribe in Deuteronomy 33:20-21 and notice the similarities in these two descriptions. What animal is used in both passages to describe the warriors? LION
The third group included men from BENJAMIN and from JUDAH.
The fourth group was from MANASSEH. Day after day men came to HELP David, until he had a great ARMY, like the ARMY of GOD.

Welcoming Committee

Read 1 Chr 12:23-40. These are the warriors who came to David at HEBRON to turn SAUL'S KINGDOM over to him. In the spaces provided, note the number that came from each tribe.

Zebulun	50,000	Ephraim	20,800	Dan	28,600
Naphtali	38,000	Issachar	200 chiefs + their relatives	Levi	8,323
Benjamin	3,000	Simeon	7,100	Asher	40,000

The (western) half tribe of Manasseh 18,000 Judah 6,800
The eastern tribes (Reuben, Gad and the eastern half of Manasseh) 120,000

David had waited a long time to become king, doing right even when wronged. Now comes the fulfillment of God's promise and a great celebration.
How long did they celebrate? 3 DAYS
Who brought provisions for the celebration? NEIGHBORS FROM AS FAR AWAY AS ISSACHAR, ZEBULUN & NAPHTALI
What foods did they bring? FLOUR, FIGS, RAISINS, WINE, OIL, CATTLE AND SHEEP

One thing God has spoken, two things have I heard: that You, O God, are strong, and that You, O Lord, are loving. Surely You will reward each person according to what he has done. Psalm 62:11-12 NIV

318

GOD SPEAKS TO SOLOMON 1

Read 2 Chronicles 1 and complete this page.
Solomon and all of Israel went up to the high place at GIBEON. There on the bronze altar Solomon offered 1,000 burnt offerings. That night GOD appeared to SOLOMON.

THE LORD SAID

Ask for (whatever, three wishes that) you want Me to give you.

You have shown great (evil, kindness) to David my father and have made me (king, a slave) in his place. Now, LORD God, let Your (promise to, curse of) my father David be (confirmed, broken), for you have made me (a slave under, king over) a people who are as numerous as the (stars of the heavens, dust of the earth). Give me (wealth, wisdom) and (knowledge, power) that I may (scourge, lead) this people, for (I am, who is) able to govern this (great, sorry) people of Yours?

Since this is your heart's desire and you (have, have not) asked for wealth, (riches, wisdom) or (honor, knowledge) nor for the (death, long life) of your (enemies, horses) and since you have not asked for a (short, long) life but for (wisdom and knowledge, power and strength) to (overrun, govern) My people over whom I have made you (tyrant, king), therefore wisdom and knowledge (will, will not) be given you. And I will also give you (poverty, wealth), riches and (honor, disgrace), such as (every, no) king who was before you ever had and none after you will have.

SOLOMON

Read 1 Kings 3:11-14 also and make a complete list of all that the Lord promised to give Solomon. A WISE & DISCERNING HEART, LONG LIFE, WEALTH, RICHES, HONOR, WISDOM, KNOWLEDGE
1 Kings 4:20-27 Did Solomon have WEALTH? YES Explain. THE PEOPLE HAD PLENTY. COUNTRIES BROUGHT TRIBUTE. HIS DAILY PROVISIONS WERE GREAT. HAD 12,000 HORSES WITH OFFICERS TO PROVIDE FOR THEM. MUCH TRADE. MANY GIFTS FROM VISITORS.
1 Kings 3, 1 Kings 4:29-34 Did Solomon receive WISDOM? YES Explain the problem which came before the king. TWO WOMEN CLAIMED THE SAME BABY.
How did Solomon discover who the real mother was? ORDERED THE LIVING BABY TO BE DIVIDED, BUT THE REAL MOTHER DID NOT WANT THE BABY KILLED, WOULD RATHER GIVE TO OTHER WOMAN
How many proverbs did he write? 3,000 How many songs did he write? 1005
What KNOWLEDGE of science did he have? PLANTS, ANIMALS, BIRDS, REPTILES, FISH
Who came to listen to Solomon's wisdom? MEN SENT TO HIM BY ALL THE KINGS OF THE WORLD
Read 2 Chr 9:1-12, 1 Kng 10:1-13 Did Solomon have HONOR? YES Who honored him? QUEEN OF SHEBA
How did Solomon find her questions? NOT TOO HARD TO ANSWER
What was her response? OVERWHELMED. PRAISE HIM AND PRAISED THE LORD.
What did she give Solomon? 120 TALENTS OF GOLD, MUCH SPICE AND PRECIOUS STONES
What did Solomon give her in return? WHATEVER SHE WANTED, MORE THAN SHE GAVE HIM.
2 Chronicles 9:29-31 Did Solomon have a LONG LIFE? YES How long did he rule? 40 YEARS

319

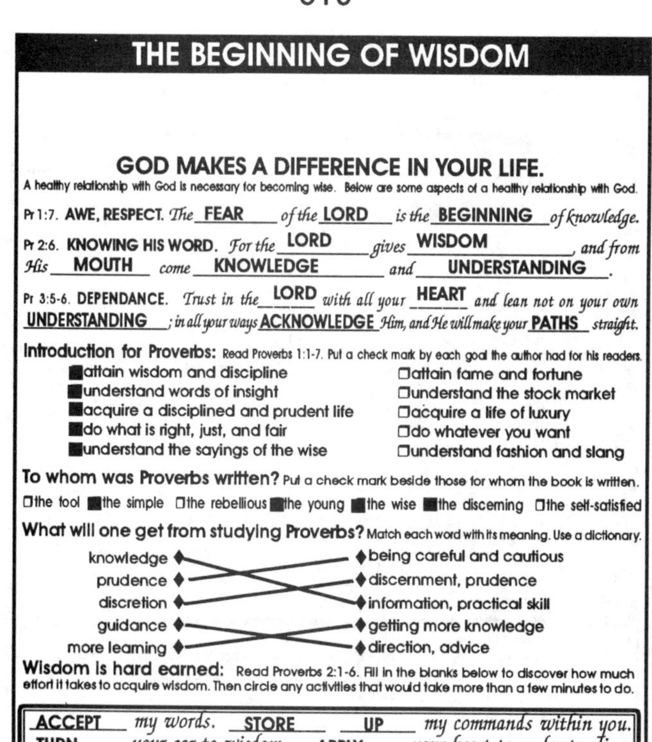

THE BEGINNING OF WISDOM

GOD MAKES A DIFFERENCE IN YOUR LIFE.

A healthy relationship with God is necessary for becoming wise. Below are some aspects of a healthy relationship with God.

Pr 1:7. AWE, RESPECT. *The* FEAR *of the* LORD *is the* BEGINNING *of knowledge.*

Pr 2:6. KNOWING HIS WORD. *For the* LORD *gives* WISDOM, *and from His* MOUTH *come* KNOWLEDGE *and* UNDERSTANDING.

Pr 3:5-6. DEPENDANCE. *Trust in the* LORD *with all your* HEART *and lean not on your own* UNDERSTANDING*; in all your ways* ACKNOWLEDGE *Him, and He will make your* PATHS *straight.*

Introduction for Proverbs: Read Proverbs 1:1-7. Put a check mark by each goal the author had for his readers.

- [x] attain wisdom and discipline
- [x] understand words of insight
- [x] acquire a disciplined and prudent life
- [x] do what is right, just, and fair
- [x] understand the sayings of the wise
- [ ] attain fame and fortune
- [ ] understand the stock market
- [ ] acquire a life of luxury
- [ ] do whatever you want
- [ ] understand fashion and slang

To whom was Proverbs written? Put a check mark beside those for whom the book is written.
[ ] the fool [x] the simple [ ] the rebellious [x] the young [x] the wise [x] the discerning [ ] the self-satisfied

What will one get from studying Proverbs? Match each word with its meaning. Use a dictionary.

- knowledge — information, practical skill
- prudence — being careful and cautious
- discretion — discernment, prudence
- guidance — direction, advice
- more learning — getting more knowledge

Wisdom is hard earned: Read Proverbs 2:1-6. Fill in the blanks below to discover how much effort it takes to acquire wisdom. Then circle any activities that would take more than a few minutes to do.

ACCEPT *my words.* STORE UP *my commands within you.* TURN *your ear to wisdom.* APPLY *your heart to understanding.* CALL OUT *for insight.* CRY ALOUD *for understanding.* LOOK FOR *it as for silver.* SEARCH FOR *it as for hidden treasure.* From Pr 2:1-6

Hard work: Something worth this much effort must be wonderful. Have you ever worked this hard for anything? Describe what you wanted and how hard you worked.
ANSWERS WILL VARY

320

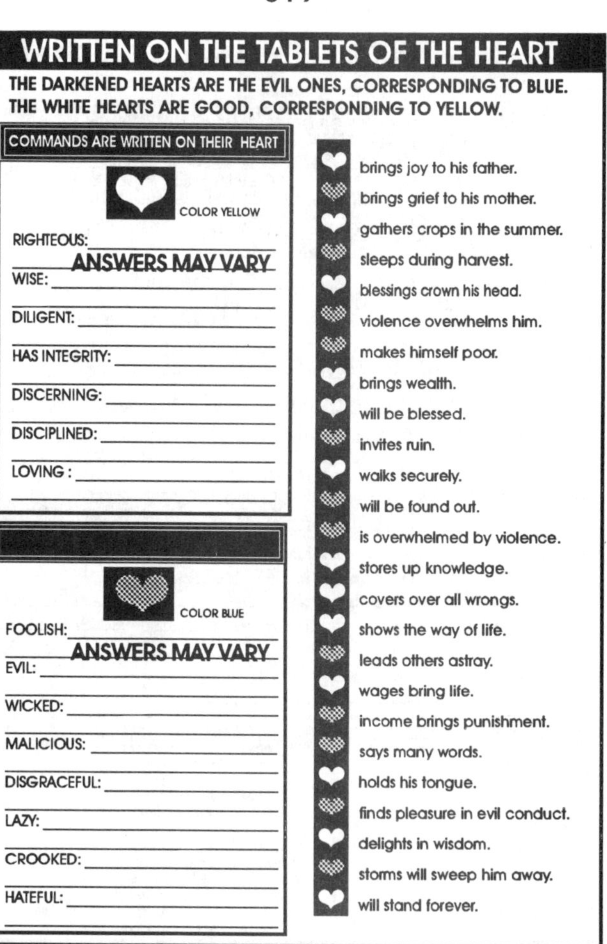

WRITTEN ON THE TABLETS OF THE HEART

THE DARKENED HEARTS ARE THE EVIL ONES, CORRESPONDING TO BLUE.
THE WHITE HEARTS ARE GOOD, CORRESPONDING TO YELLOW.

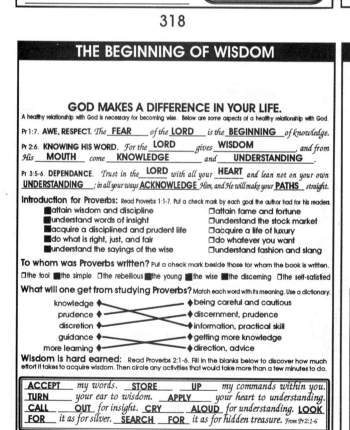

COMMANDS ARE WRITTEN ON THEIR HEART

COLOR YELLOW

RIGHTEOUS:
ANSWERS MAY VARY
WISE:
DILIGENT:
HAS INTEGRITY:
DISCERNING:
DISCIPLINED:
LOVING :

COLOR BLUE

FOOLISH:
ANSWERS MAY VARY
EVIL:
WICKED:
MALICIOUS:
DISGRACEFUL:
LAZY:
CROOKED:
HATEFUL:

brings joy to his father.
brings grief to his mother.
gathers crops in the summer.
sleeps during harvest.
blessings crown his head.
violence overwhelms him.
makes himself poor.
brings wealth.
will be blessed.
invites ruin.
walks securely.
will be found out.
is overwhelmed by violence.
stores up knowledge.
covers over all wrongs.
shows the way of life.
leads others astray.
wages bring life.
income brings punishment.
says many words.
holds his tongue.
finds pleasure in evil conduct.
delights in wisdom.
storms will sweep him away.
will stand forever.

325

A VIRTUOUS WOMAN

Read Proverbs 31:10-31. Then reread it line by line as you draw a line connecting the start of each verse to the ending.

A wife of noble character	eager hands.
She is worth	good, not harm, all her days.
Her husband has	who can find?
She brings him	full confidence in her.
She selects	far more than rubies.
She works with	wool and flax.
She is like	while it is still dark.
She gets up	for her servant girls.
She provides	a field and buys it.
and portions	the merchant ships.
She considers	food for her family.
Out of her earnings	plants a vineyard.
She sets about her work	vigorously.
Her arms are	does not go out at night.
She sees that her trading	strong for her tasks.
Her lamp	is profitable.
In her hand she holds	the spindle with her fingers.
She grasps	the distaff.
She opens her arms	to the needy.
She extends her hand	no fear for her household.
When it snows she has	to the poor.
All of them are clothed	with strength and dignity.
She makes	in scarlet.
She is clothed	coverings for her bed.
She can laugh at	the affairs of her household.
She speaks	the bread of idleness.
She watches over	the days to come.
She does not eat	arise and call her blessed.
Her children	with wisdom.
Her husband	praises her.
Many women do	surpass them all.
But you	fears the Lord is to be praised.
Charm is	bring her praise in the city.
Beauty is	deceptive.
A women who	noble things.
Let her works	fleeting.

Using a dictionary or thesaurus, describe the virtuous woman. ANSWERS MAY VARY

327

SOLOMON'S TEMPLE

THE TEMPLE was **60** cubits long, **20** cubits wide and **20** cubits high. 1 Ki 6:29 On the walls were carved **CHERUBIM**, **PALM** **TREES**, and open **FLOWERS**.
THE MAIN HALL was paneled in **PINE** and covered with **GOLD**.
THE MOST HOLY PLACE was overlaid with **600** talents of fine **GOLD**. (23 tons of gold.) The nails used were of **GOLD**. The upper parts were overlaid with **GOLD**. In the Most Holy Place was a **PAIR** of sculptured **CHERUBIM** that were overlaid with **GOLD**. The total wingspan was **20** cubits.
THE CURTAIN was made of **BLUE**, **PURPLE**, and **CRIMSON** yarn and fine **LINEN**. It had **CHERUBIM** worked into it.
THE FRONT OF THE TEMPLE had two **PILLARS**, One was named **JAKIN** (*He establishes*) and the other **BOAZ** (*In Him is strength*).
THE ALTAR was made of **BRONZE**. It was **20** cubits long, **20** cubits wide and **10** cubits high.
THE SEA was of **CAST** metal, it was **CIRCULAR** in shape. It stood on **12** bulls, **3** facing each direction. It held **3,000** baths (17,5000 gallons).
There were **10** **BASINS** for washing. There were **10** gold **LAMPSTANDS** placed in the Temple. There were **10** **TABLES** placed in the Temple. He also made 100 **GOLD** sprinkling **BOWLS**.
THE FURNISHINGS FOR GOD'S TEMPLE were: The **GOLDEN** altar; tables for the **BREAD** of the **PRESENCE**; the **LAMPSTANDS** of pure **GOLD** to burn in front of the **INNER** sanctuary; And these other things of gold **FLORAL WORK, LAMPS, TONGS, WICK TRIMMERS, SPRINKLING BOWLS, DISHES, CENSERS, DOORS**
1 Ki 6:5-7 Against the main hall and inner sanctuary was a **STRUCTURE** around the **BUILDING**.
DURING THE BUILDING OF THE TEMPLE, there was no sound of **HAMMER**, **CHISEL** or any other iron **TOOL** at the Temple site. 1 Ki 7:51 When the Temple were done, the things **DAVID** had dedicated were placed in the **TREASURIES**.

329

SOLOMON DEDICATES THE TEMPLE

WHEN did the Israelites come together to dedicate the Temple? **ISRAEL CAME TOGETHER TO THE KING AT THE TIME OF THE FESTIVAL IN THE SEVENTH MONTH.**
WHO carried all the sacred furnishings and the Ark? **THE PRIESTS, WHO WERE LEVITES CARRIED THEM UP.**
HOW many sheep and cattle were sacrificed? **SO MANY SHEEP AND CATTLE THAT THEY COULD NOT BE RECORDED OR COUNTED.**
WHAT room was the the new home of the Ark of the Covenant? **THE INNER SANCTUARYOF THE TEMPLE, THE MOST HOLY PLACE.**
WHAT was over the Ark? **THE WINGS OF THE CHERUBIM.**
WHAT was in the Ark? **THERE WAS NOTHING IN THE ARK EXCEPT THE TWO TABLETS THAT MOSES HAD PLACED IN IT.**
WHAT instruments were played? **CYMBALS, HARPS AND LYRES. TRUMPETS.**
WHAT did the Lord do? **THE TEMPLE OF THE LORD WAS FILLED WITH A CLOUD, FOR THE GLORY OF THE LORD FILLED THE TEMPLE OF GOD.**
WHAT couldn't the priests do and why? **PRIESTS COULD NOT PERFORM THEIR SERVICE BECAUSE OF THE CLOUD.**

2 CHR. 6:18 *"But will God really dwell on earth with men? The heavens, even the highest heavens, cannot contain you. How much less this temple I have built!"*

SOLOMON PRAYS THAT WHEN THIS HAPPENS:	IF THE PEOPLE DO THIS: WRITE IN LETTERS FROM THE FIRST BOX BELOW.	THEN LORD, PLEASE DO THIS: WRITE IN NUMBERS FROM THE SECOND BOX BELOW
When a man wrongs his neighbor,	A	8, 3, 1, 10
When Israel is defeated by an enemy because of sin,	B OR G, J, D, I, F	8, 5, 4
When the heavens are shut up because of sin,	D, F, B	8, 5, 9, 2
When whatever disaster or disease may come,	C, D, H, F	8, 5, 11
When a foreigner prays toward this temple,	D, F	8, 7
When Your people go to war against their enemies,	D, F	8, 6
When they are captured by enemies because of sin,	K, E, C, G, F, D	8, 6, 5

IF THE PEOPLE DO THIS:	THEN LORD, PLEASE DO THIS:
A. if he takes an oath,	1. then Lord, repay the guilty.
B. if they turn from sin,	2. then Lord, send rain on the land.
C. if they plead,	3. then Lord, judge between them.
D. if they pray,	4. then Lord, bring them back to the land.
E. if they repent,	5. then Lord, forgive the sin.
F. if they turn towards the Temple,	6. then Lord, uphold their cause.
G. if they turn back to You,	7. then Lord, do whatever he asks of You.
H. if they spread out their hands,	8. then Lord, hear from heaven.
I. if they make supplication,	9. then Lord, teach them the right way.
J. if they confess Your Name,	10. then Lord, declare the innocent not guilty.
K. if they change their hearts,	11. then Lord, deal according to all he does.

330

GOD SPEAKS TO SOLOMON 2

Read 2 Chronicles 7 and complete this page.
When Solomon had **FINISHED** the Temple of the **LORD** and the royal **PALACE** and had succeeded in carrying out all he had in mind to do in the **TEMPLE** of the LORD and in his own **PALACE**, the LORD **APPEARED** to Solomon at **NIGHT**.

THE LORD SAID

I have heard your (complaints, prayer) and have (chosen, rejected) this place for Myself as a Temple for (prostitution, sacrifices). When I (open, shut up) the heavens so that there is no rain, or command locusts to (depart, devour) the land or send a (plague, revival) among My people, *IF My* **PEOPLE**, *who are called by* **MY** *Name, will* **HUMBLE** *themselves and* **PRAY** *and* **SEEK** *My* **FACE** *and* **TURN** *from their* **WICKED** *ways, then will I* **HEAR** *from* **HEAVEN** *and will* **FORGIVE** *their* **SIN** *and will* **HEAL** *their land.*
Now My eyes will be (closed, open) and My ears (attentive, inattentive) to the prayers offered in this place. I have (chosen, rejected) and (consecrated, scorned) this Temple so that My Name may be there (forever, for now). My (eyes, ears) and My (heart) will always be there.

As for you, if you **WALK** before me as David your father did, and do **ALL** I command, and **OBSERVE** My decrees and **LAWS**, I will **ESTABLISH** your royal throne, as I **COVENANTED** with David your father when I said, "You shall **NEVER** fail to have a **MAN** to **RULE** over Israel."
But if you **TURN** away and **FORSAKE** the decrees and **COMMANDS** I have given you and go off to **SERVE** other **GODS** and **WORSHIP** them, then I will **UPROOT** Israel from My land, which I have given them, and will **REJECT** this temple I have consecrated for My **NAME**. I will make it a **BYWORD** and an object of **RIDICULE** among **ALL** peoples. And though this **TEMPLE** is now so **IMPOSING**, all who **PASS** by will be appalled and say, "**WHY** has the LORD done such a thing to this **LAND** and to this **TEMPLE**?" People will answer, "Because they have **FORSAKEN** the LORD, the **GOD** of their fathers, who brought them out of **EGYPT**, and have **EMBRACED** other gods, worshipping and **SERVING** them – that is why He brought **ALL** this **DISASTER** on them."

SOLOMON

Read 1 Kings 11:1-13 and fill in the blanks.
King Solomon, however, loved many **FOREIGN** women besides Pharaoh's **DAUGHTER** - M **MOABITES**, A **AMMONITES**, E **EDOMITES**, S **SIDONIANS** and H **HITTITES**.
They were from **NATIONS** about which the Lord had told the Israelites, *"You must not* **INTERMARRY** *with them, because they will surely* **TURN** *your (heart) after their* **GODS**."
Nevertheless, Solomon held fast to them in **LOVE**. As Solomon grew old, his **WIVES** turned his (heart) after other **GODS** and his (heart) was not fully **DEVOTED** to the Lord.
The Lord said to him, *"Since this is your* **ATTITUDE** *... I will most certainly tear the* **KINGDOM** *away from you... For the sake of* **DAVID** *I will not do it during* **YOUR** *lifetime. I will tear it out of the hand of your* **SON**, *but I will give him one* **TRIBE** *for the sake of* **DAVID** *My servant and for the sake of* **JERUSALEM**, *which I have chosen."*
In spite of all God had done for Solomon, he did not please God in his old age. What was his downfall, and how did it come about? **HE TURNED AWAY FROM GOD AFTER MANY OTHER GODS. THIS WAS BECAUSE HE LOVED HIS MANY FOREIGN (HEATHEN) WIVES AND WORSHIPED THEIR GODS RATHER THAN BEING FAITHFUL TO THE LORD.**

331

SONG OF SONGS 1

The Hebrew title is Solomon's Song of Songs, which means "the best of songs by (or for or about) Solomon." There are many unanswered questions about the Song of Songs, including: Who wrote it? When was it written? What kind of literature is it? And what does it mean?

Many believe that the Song of Songs was written by or for Solomon to be sung at a wedding. Some see the book as a drama with two main characters, the bride and groom, namely the Shulammite and Solomon. Others feel that there are three main characters, Solomon, the Shulammite girl, and her beloved shepherd. Some think the book is a series of songs for a week-long wedding celebration.

People have interpreted it as an **ALLEGORY** of **GOD'S LOVE FOR ISRAEL**, and **CHRIST'S LOVE FOR THE CHURCH.** We may see similarities between romantic love and God's love, for He is the Lover of our Soul. He longs for us to have a passionate, unwavering love for Him.

The Song of Songs is also a celebration of human love between a man and a woman. It reminds us of what is written in Genesis 1:31a: "God saw all that He had made, and it was very good." Having this book included in Scripture keeps us from two extremes: **ASCETICISM** which teaches that **PLEASURE IS EVIL**; and **LUST** which **USES PEOPLE AND THINGS SELFISHLY**. Sex in marriage is a special and wonderful gift from God.

People outline the book in different ways, and none of them are totally satisfactory. Below are two examples:

OUTLINE ONE
SOLOMON AND HIS BRIDE

1. Solomon and his Bride Fall in Love
2. The Bride Responds to Solomon
3. The First Dream: A NightSearch
4. Solomon's Procession
5. Solomon's Song to his Bride
6. Solomon's Second Song

OUTLINE TWO
A SHEPHERD AND HIS BRIDE

1. The Girl Shuns Solomon for Shepherd
2. The Shepherd Visits the Girl
3. The First Dream: A NightSearch
4. Solomon's Procession
5. Shepherd's Song to his True Love
6. Shepherd Urges Girl Away from Solomon

Solomon Marries Girl

Shepherd Marries Girl

7. The Wedding Night
8. The 2nd Dream: Hesitatiton Brings Loss
9. The Groom Praises his Bride
10. The Bride Delights in the Groom
11. The Pledge of Love
12. Purity Keeps Love Fresh

In the Hebrew language, all the pronouns show gender and number. Because of this, the translators were able to make notes in the text showing who is speaking: the lover (the man), the beloved (the woman), or the friends who act as a chorus. By the way, the word lover means one who gives love. Recently many people have used it to mean one who gives sex, but this is not the real meaning of the word.

SOLOMON AND HIS BRIDE FALL IN LOVE OR GIRL IS LOYAL TO HER SHEPHERD

Read chapter 1:1-2:7 She meets Solomon in the palace. She seems delighted. Then she describes herself as __DARKENED__ by the sun and forced to take care of the __VINEYARDS__. Then she either describes Solomon in metaphor or she shuns him and goes in search of the shepherd. The lovers exchange compliments.

Check the boxes next to the foods that are mentioned in 2:3-7
☐ steak ■ apples ☐ chips ■ raisins ☐ steamed rice ☐ cake ■ fruit

THE BRIDE RESPONDS TO SOLOMON OR THE SHEPHERD VISITS

SPRINGTIME

Read chapter 2:8-17. Check the boxes next to the signs of spring that are mentioned.
■ singing ☐ harvest ■ rains are gone ☐ ripening fruit ■ blossoms
☐ storms ☐ heat ■ fragrance ■ cooing of doves ■ flowers
☐ plowing ■ winter is past ■ early fruit is forming ☐ rains are frequent

How does the girl describe the one she loves?
☐ fighting ☐ toiling ■ leaping ☐ plundering
■ bounding ■ gazing ■ browsing ☐ conquering
☐ like a king ☐ like a warrior ■ like a gazelle ■ like a young stag

What does the lover ask of the girl? ☐ to hunt doves ■ to see her face ■ to hear her voice
☐ to go mountain climbing ■ to catch destructive foxes ☐ to run away together

SONG OF SONGS 2

THE FIRST DREAM: A NIGHT SEARCH

Read 3:1-5. This passage seems to tell about a dream. The dream may mean that the girl is afraid of losing her true love. Where does she search? ☐ palace ☐ temple ■ city ■ streets ■ squares ☐ pastures ☐ hills

In the dream, where does she take him when she finds him?
☐ palace ☐ temple ☐ city ☐ her apartment ■ her mother's home ☐ pastures ☐ hills

SOLOMON'S PROCESSION

Read 3:6-11. Thought questions: Is this when the girl marries Solomon? Or is he trying to impress her to steal her away from her beloved shepherd? Make a list of the materials used in Solomon's carriage.
__WOOD FROM LEBANON, SILVER, GOLD, PURPLE UPHOLSTERY__

What other things made his approach impressive?
__CLOUD OF DUST (LIKE A COLUMN OF SMOKE) PERFUMES, ESCORT OF SIXTY EXPERIENCED, WELL-ARMED WARRIORS, THE CROWN ON HIS HEAD__

SOLOMON'S SONG TO HIS BRIDE OR SHEPHERD'S SONG TO HIS TRUE LOVE

Read 4:1-7 This may be what Solomon sang to his bride, or what the shepherd sang to his true love as they watched the grand approach of Solomon. It describes the physical beauty of the girl.

OUTDOORS

List the springtime, outdoorsy things the man uses to praise her.
__DOVES, GOATS, SHEEP, TWINS, POMEGRANATE, FAWNS, LILIES, DAY BREAKING, SHADOWS FLEEING, MOUNTAIN OF MYRRH, HILL OF INCENSE__

SOLOMON'S SECOND SONG OR SHEPHERD URGES GIRL AWAY FROM SOLOMON

Read 4:8-15. This song might be a second by Solomon to his new bride, or by the shepherd urging his beloved to come away from Solomon. Although this song describes the girl physically, it praises her personality as well. The garden locked up probably refers to her sexual purity. On a scale of 1 to 10, how in love with her is he? __ANSWERS WILL VARY__

The Wedding Night

Read 4:16-5:1. She invites him into the garden, and he comes. The friends celebrate. List the outdoorsy things.
__WIND, GARDEN, FRAGRANCE, FRUITS, MYRRH, SPICE__

Now list the food and drink from this passage.
__FRUITS, HONEYCOMB, HONEY, WINE, MILK__

THE SECOND DREAM: HESITATION BRINGS LOSS

Read 5:2-8 This seems to be a second dream. The girl is reluctant and too slow to open the door, and her beloved disappears. How do the watchmen treat her in this dream? __BEAT, BRUISED, TOOK CLOAK__

Does she find her beloved as she did in the first dream? __NO__ Who helps her? __DAUGHTERS OF JERUSALEM__

Read 5:9-6:3 Now it is her turn to describe him. She uses plants, animals and minerals in her praise of him. Fill in the columns below. (Include any materials that come from plants or animals under those categories.)

PLANT	ANIMAL	MINERAL
BEDS OF SPICE	RAVEN	GOLD
LILIES	DOVES	WATER
MYRRH	MILK	CHRYSOLITE
CEDARS	IVORY	SAPPHIRES
		MARBLE

When friends ask her where he has gone, she seems to remember. He has gone down to his __GARDEN__ to gather __LILIES__. In the end she is sure of this: *"I am* __MY LOVER'S__ *and my* __LOVER__ *is mine."*

YOUR EYES ARE DOVES

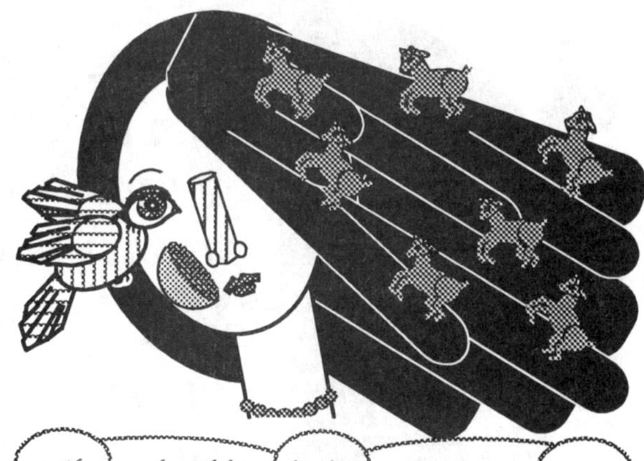

Ah, you are beautiful, my Beloved! Your eyes are doves.
Your hair is like a flock of goats streaming down the mountains.
Your lips are like a scarlet strand. Your check is like a half-pomegranate.
Your nose is a like the tower of Lebanon.

Explain what the similes and metaphors express about each of the following.

Eyes __ANSWERS MAY VARY__
Cheeks ____
Lips ____
Hair ____
Nose ____

Use similes and metaphors to describe someone's face. Then illustrate it in the space on the right.

Your eyes are __ANSWERS MAY VARY__
Your cheeks are ____
Your lips are ____
Your hair is ____
Your nose is ____

DRAWINGS MAY VARY

SONG OF SONGS 3

THE GROOM PRAISES HIS BRIDE

Read 6:4-12. Either Solomon or the shepherd describes the girl. She is as __BEAUTIFUL__ as Tirzah, as __LOVELY__ as Jerusalem, as __MAJESTIC__ as troops with __BANNERS__. He also describes her face including her __EYES__, __HAIR__, __TEETH__ and __TEMPLES.__. None of the __60__ queens, __80__ concubines, or virgins without __NUMBER__ can compare with her.

Read 6:13-7:9a. The lover is enthralled with his bride and describes her from head to toe, but doesn't want others to stare. List the descriptions under the following headings:

NATURAL WONDERS	MAN-MADE WONDERS
MOUND OF WHEAT	JEWEL, GOBLET
LILIES, TWO FAWNS	IVORY TOWER
MOUNT CARMEL, PALM	POOLS OF HESHBON
CLUSTERS OF FRUIT	TOWER OF LEBANON
CLUSTERS OF THE VINE	ROYAL TAPESTRY
APPLES, WINE?	WINE?

BRIDE DELIGHTS IN THE GROOM

Read 7:9b-8:4. The bride's response to her groom in verses 10-13 is,

"I belong to __MY LOVER__, *and his* __DESIRE__ *is for* __ME__." She invites her lover, *"Let us go to the* __COUNTRYSIDE__, *let us spend the night in the* __VILLAGES__... *There I will* __GIVE__ *you my* __LOVE__ *...At our* __DOOR__ *is every delicacy, both* __NEW__ *and* __OLD__, *that I have* __STORED__ *up for* __YOU__, *my lover."*

She wishes she could kiss him in public and no one would __DESPISE__ her.

THE PLEDGE OF LOVE

Read 8:5-7. This passage contains a well-known declaration of love. Who is the speaker? __BRIDE/GIRL__.
Fill in the blanks to complete the verses.

Place me like a __seal__ over your __heart__,
like a __seal__ on your __arm__;
for __love__ is as strong as __death__,
its __jealousy__ unyielding as the __grave__.
It __burns__ like __blazing__ fire,
like a __mighty__ flame.
Many __waters__ cannot __quench__ love;
__rivers__ cannot wash it __away__.
If one were to give __all__ the __wealth__ of his house for __love__,
it would be utterly __scorned__.

SONG OF SONGS 8:6,7 NIV

PURITY KEEPS LOVE FRESH

Read 8:8-14. **THE CONCLUSION.** In verses 8-9, the bride may be remembering how her brothers protected her purity as she was growing up. In verses 10-12 she may be saying she is not part of Solomon's vineyard (or harem).

Then her true love calls to her, and she responds,

" __COME__ *away, my lover, and be like a* __GAZELLE__
or like a young __STAG__ *on the spice-laden* __MOUNTAINS__ *."*

SOLOMON'S CHECK LIST

Check List for a King
God to Choose the King:
Appoint the king the Lord your God chooses.
Must be a Israelite, not a foreigner.
Laws for the King:
He must not acquire a great number of horses.
He must not make the people go back to Egypt.
He must not take many wives or his heart will stray.
He must not accumulate large amounts of silver & gold.
He must not consider himself better than his brothers.
He must not turn from the law to the right or to the left.
A Scroll of the Law for the King:
He must copy the scroll himself when he takes the throne.
He must read it all the days of his life.
He must learn from it to revere the Lord his God.
He must carefully follow all the words of this law.
Deuteronomy 17:15-18

What was the weight of gold that Solomon received yearly? **666 TALENTS (25 TONS)**

Solomon accumulated how many horses? **12,000** And how many chariots? **1,400**

Where did Solomon's people go to get his horses? **EGYPT, KUE AND OTHER COUNTRIES**

How many years did it take to build the Temple? **7** How many years did it take to build his palace? **13**

What was as common in Jerusalem as stones? **SILVER AND GOLD**

Describe Solomon's throne. **INLAID WITH IVORY, OVERLAID WITH GOLD, WITH 6 STEPS & A GOLD FOOTREST. 2 LIONS BESIDE THE ARMRESTS & 2 LIONS ON EACH OF THE 6 STEPS.**

How many wives and concubines did Solomon have? **700 WIVES & 300 CONCUBINES**

Where did Solomon's wives come from? **EGYPT, MOAB, AMMON, EDOM, SIDON, THE HITTITES**

What did his wives cause him to do? **TURN HIS HEART & BUILD HIGH PLACES TO OTHER GODS**

What gods did he follow? 1Ki 11:33 **ASHTORETH, CHEMOSH, MOLECH**

What does Solomon's son say about how King Solomon treated the people? 2 Chr 10:14 **MADE THEIR YOKE HEAVY AND BEAT THEM WITH WHIPS.**

How many of the instructions for a king did Solomon break? On the check list above from Deuteronomy, put an × on the ones that the Bible says he broke and a ✓ on the ones he most likely broke. The summarize you findings. **ANSWERS MAY VARY**

Ecclesiastes is thought to have been written near the end of Solomon's life. Fill in Ecclesiastes 12:13b-14.

Here is the **CONCLUSION** *of the matter:* **FEAR** *God and keep His* **COMMANDMENTS** *for this is the whole* **DUTY** *of man. For* **GOD** *will bring* **EVERY** *deed into* **JUDGMENT**, *including every* **HIDDEN** *thing, whether it is good or* **EVIL**.

What does this verse tell you about Solomon's heart towards God at the end? **ANSWERS MAY VARY**

DOUBLE TROUBLE

The Bible does not condemn *polygamy* (having more than one wife), but it does encourage *monogamy*. Review the following passages and check the boxes that were true in each family.

ABRAHAM WITH SARAH AND HAGAR. Genesis 16, 21, 25.

A general statement of what happened: **HAGAR GOT PREGNANT & DESPISED BARREN SARAH. SARAH MISTREATED HER & SENT HER AWAY. HAGAR'S CHILD TEASED SARAH'S.**

■ Mistreatment of one wife/concubine by the other. ■ Despair. ☐ Rivalry for husband's love. ■ Weeping. ■ Unequal treatment of wives. ☐ Husband loves one more than other. ☐ Competition over having children. ■ Pride of one over having children. ☐ Husband led astray by wives. ☐ Unequal treatment of children based on who their mother was. ■ Rivalry between children of different mothers. ☐ Killing or attempted killing of children from other mothers.

JACOB WITH RACHEL AND LEAH. Genesis 29, 30, 37

A general statement of what happened: **JACOB LOVED RACHEL MORE, BUT LEAH HAD MORE CHILDREN. RACHEL'S SON WAS JACOB'S FAVORITE. BROTHERS WANTED TO KILL HIM**

☐ Mistreatment of one wife/concubine by the other. ■ Despair. ■ Rivalry for husband's love. ■ Weeping. ☐ Unequal treatment of wives. ■ Husband loves one more than other. ■ Competition over having children. ☐ Pride of one over having children. ☐ Husband led astray by wives. ■ Unequal treatment of children based on who their mother was. ■ Rivalry between children of different mothers. ■ Killing or attempted killing of children from other mothers.

GIDEON (JERUB-BAAL) AND HIS CHILDREN FROM DIFFERENT MOTHERS. Judges 9

A general statement of what happened: **ABIMELECH MURDERED HIS 70 (69) HALF-BROTHERS SO HE COULD RULE.**

☐ Mistreatment of one wife/concubine by the other. ☐ Despair. ☐ Rivalry for husband's love. ☐ Weeping. ☐ Unequal treatment of wives. ☐ Husband loves one more than other. ☐ Competition over having children. ☐ Pride of one over having children. ☐ Husband led astray by wives. ☐ Unequal treatment of children based on who their mother was. ☐ Rivalry between children of different mothers. ■ Killing or attempted killing of children from other mothers.

ELKANAH WITH HANNAH AND PENINNAH. 1 Samuel 1.

A general statement of what happened: **PENINNAH TEASED BARREN HANNAH AND MADE HER LIFE MISERABLE.**

■ Mistreatment of one wife/concubine by the other. ■ Despair. ☐ Rivalry for husband's love. ■ Weeping. ■ Unequal treatment of wives. ■ Husband loves one more than other. ■ Competition over having children. ■ Pride of one over having children. ☐ Husband led astray by wives. ☐ Unequal treatment of children based on who their mother was. ☐ Rivalry between children of different mothers. ☐ Killing or attempted killing of children from other mothers.

DAVID AND HIS CHILDREN FROM DIFFERENT MOTHERS. 2 Samuel 13; 1 Kings 1-2.

A general statement of what happened: **ABSALOM KILLED AMNON FOR RAPING TAMAR. DAVID'S SON'S COMPETED FOR THE THRONE. SOLOMON KILLED RIVAL ADONIJAH.**

☐ Husband led astray by wives. ■ Unequal treatment of children based on who their mother was. ■ Rivalry between children of different mothers. ■ Killing or attempted killing of children from other mothers.

SOLOMON AND HIS MANY WIVES. 1 Kings 11.

A general statement of what happened: **SOLOMON MARRIED MANY HEATHEN WIVES AND EVENTUALLY BEGAN TO WORSHIP THEIR GODS.**

■ Husband led astray by wives. ☐ Unequal treatment of children based on who their mother was. ☐ Rivalry between children of different mothers. ☐ Killing or attempted killing of children from other mothers.

Based on your study, what problems are likely to come up in polygamous marriages? **ANSWERS MAY VARY, SHOULD INCLUDE MANY OF THE ITEMS WHOSE BOXES ARE MARKED**

UNDER THE SUN 1

Is there any meaning in life? Read Ecclesiastes 1.

Ecclesiastes is Greek for 'preacher.' Who wrote it? **A SON OF DAVID** (Probably Solomon)

What are the first words from the author? **MEANINGLESS! MEANINGLESS!**

In Solomon's search for the meaning in life, what did he decide about the following?

What does a man **GAIN** from all his labor at which he **TOILS** UNDER THE SUN?

Draw a line to connect the items below.

Everything	Never full
Generations	Never enough
Earth	South, north, round & round
Sun	Come and go
Wind	Much sorrow
Streams	Flow away and then return
Sea	Nothing new
Ears & eyes	More grief
Under the sun	Rises and sets & rises again
New	Not remembered
Men of old	Here before
Much wisdom	Remains forever
More knowledge	Utterly meaningless

Meaninglessness of Pleasure: Read Ecclesiastes 2.

Solomon decided to explore pleasure. What did he decide about the following?

Pleasure	Foolish
Laughter	Embracing folly
Wine	Meaningless

What material things did Solomon gain in his search for meaning in life? **HOUSES, VINEYARDS, GARDENS, PARKS, FRUIT TREES, RESERVOIRS, SLAVES, HERDS, FLOCKS, SILVER, GOLD, TREASURES, SINGERS, HAREMS.** He became **GREATER** by far than anyone in Jerusalem.

Fill in the blanks from Ecclesiastes 2:10-11

I **DENIED** myself **NOTHING** my eyes **DESIRED**; I **REFUSED** my heart no **PLEASURE**

Yet when I **SURVEYED** what I had **TOILED** to achieve,

everything was **MEANINGLESS**, A CHASING AFTER THE WIND; nothing was **GAINED** UNDER THE SUN

Solomon decides wisdom is better than **MADNESS** or **FOLLY**. But like the **FOOL**, the **WISE** man too must **DIE**. All the work he has done with wisdom, knowledge, skill, pain and grief, will be left to the one who **COMES** after him whether he was a **WISE** man or a **FOOL**.

Which of the following comes from the HAND OF GOD?

■ Eat & drink ■ Work satisfaction
■ Enjoyment ■ Wisdom
■ Knowledge ■ Happiness.

A TIME FOR EVERYTHING

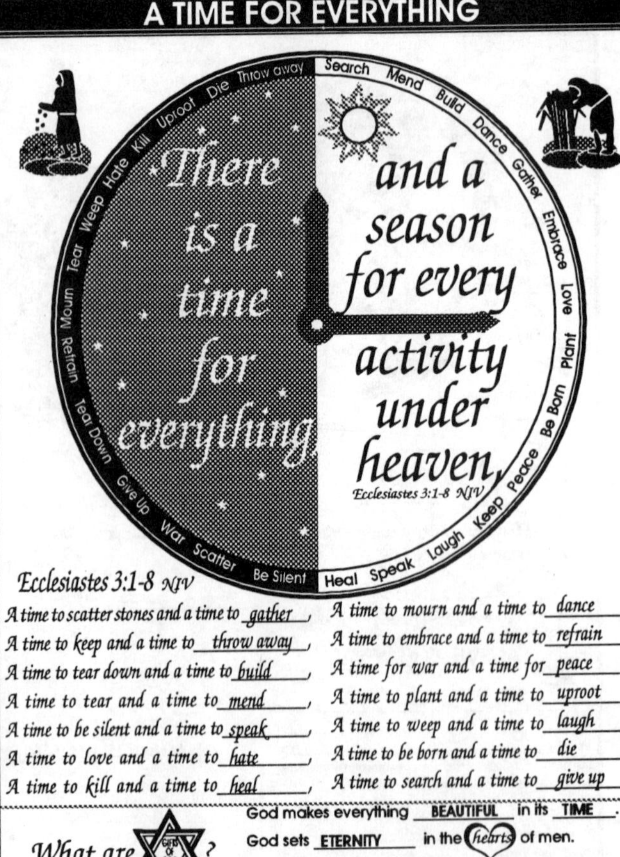

Ecclesiastes 3:1-8 NIV

A time to scatter stones and a time to gather,
A time to keep and a time to throw away,
A time to tear down and a time to build,
A time to tear and a time to mend,
A time to be silent and a time to speak,
A time to love and a time to hate,
A time to kill and a time to heal,
A time to mourn and a time to dance,
A time to embrace and a time to refrain,
A time for war and a time for peace.
A time to plant and a time to uproot,
A time to weep and a time to laugh,
A time to be born and a time to die,
A time to search and a time to give up,

What are GIFTS OF GOD?

God makes everything **BEAUTIFUL** in its **TIME**.

God sets **ETERNITY** in the hearts of men.

God gives **SATISFACTION** in ones toil.

God gives food and **DRINK**.

There is nothing better for man than to be **HAPPY** and **DO GOOD**.

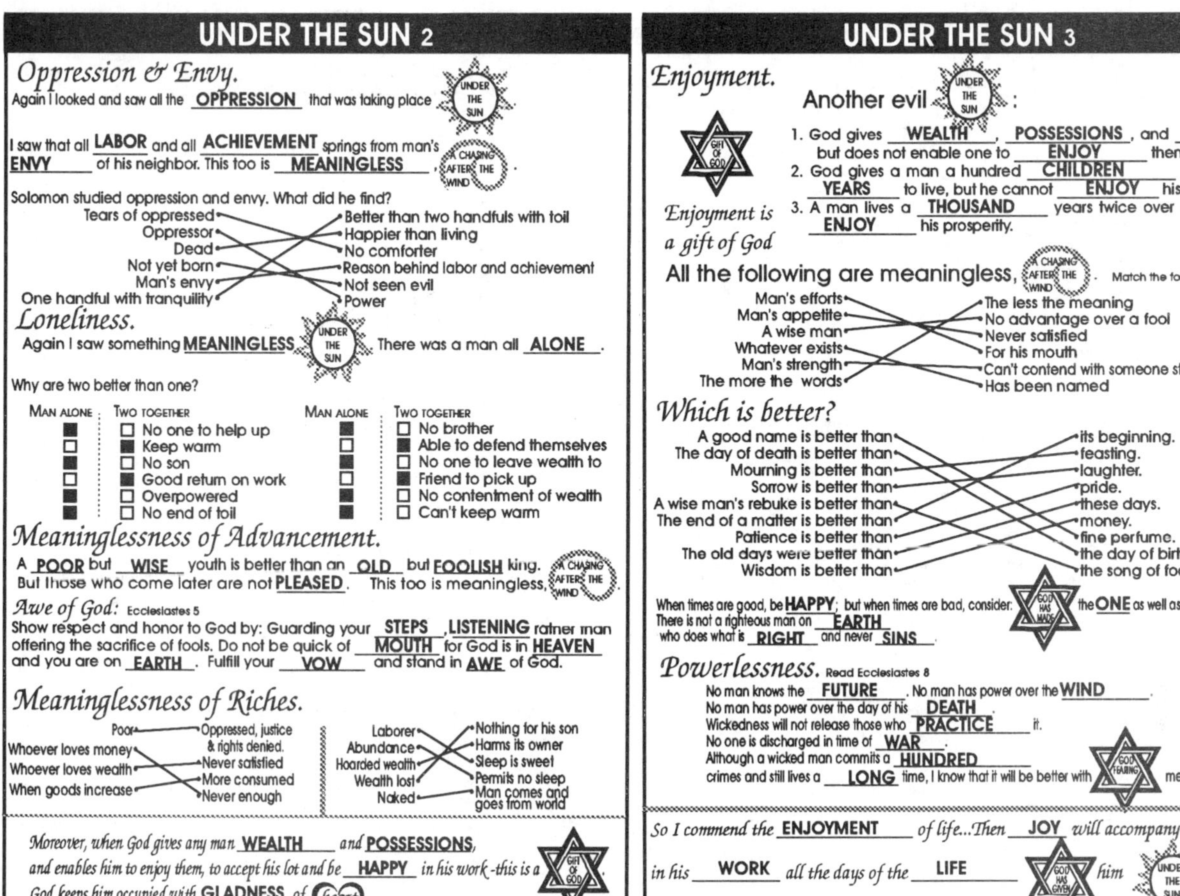

UNDER THE SUN 2

Oppression & Envy.

Again I looked and saw all the OPPRESSION that was taking place UNDER THE SUN.

I saw that all LABOR and all ACHIEVEMENT springs from man's ENVY of his neighbor. This too is MEANINGLESS, CHASING AFTER THE WIND.

Solomon studied oppression and envy. What did he find?

Tears of oppressed / Oppressor / Dead / Not yet born / Man's envy / One handful with tranquility

Better than two handfuls with toil / Happier than living / No comforter / Reason behind labor and achievement / Not seen evil / Power

Loneliness.

Again I saw something MEANINGLESS UNDER THE SUN. There was a man all ALONE.

Why are two better than one?

MAN ALONE	TWO TOGETHER	MAN ALONE	TWO TOGETHER
■	☐ No one to help up	☐	☐ No brother
☐	■ Keep warm	☐	■ Able to defend themselves
■	☐ No son	■	☐ No one to leave wealth to
☐	■ Good return on work	☐	■ Friend to pick up
■	☐ Overpowered	■	☐ No contentment of wealth
■	☐ No end of toil	☐	☐ Can't keep warm

Meaninglessness of Advancement.

A POOR but WISE youth is better than an OLD but FOOLISH king. But those who come later are not PLEASED. This too is meaningless, CHASING AFTER THE WIND.

Awe of God: Ecclesiastes 5

Show respect and honor to God by: Guarding your STEPS, LISTENING rather than offering the sacrifice of fools. Do not be quick of MOUTH for God is in HEAVEN and you are on EARTH. Fulfill your VOW and stand in AWE of God.

Meaninglessness of Riches.

Poor / Whoever loves money / Whoever loves wealth / When goods increase

Oppressed, justice & rights denied. / Never satisfied / More consumed / Never enough

Laborer / Abundance / Hoarded wealth / Wealth lost / Naked

Nothing for his son / Harms its owner / Sleep is sweet / Permits no sleep / Man comes and goes from world

Moreover, when God gives any man WEALTH *and* POSSESSIONS, *and enables him to enjoy them, to accept his lot and be* HAPPY *in his work -this is a* GIFT OF GOD. *God keeps him occupied with* GLADNESS *of* heart.

340

UNDER THE SUN 3

Enjoyment.

Another evil UNDER THE SUN:

1. God gives WEALTH, POSSESSIONS, and HONOR, but does not enable one to ENJOY them.
2. God gives a man a hundred CHILDREN and many YEARS to live, but he cannot ENJOY his prosperity.
3. A man lives a THOUSAND years twice over but fails to ENJOY his prosperity.

Enjoyment is a gift of God (GIFT OF GOD)

All the following are meaningless, CHASING AFTER THE WIND. Match the following.

Man's efforts / Man's appetite / A wise man / Whatever exists / Man's strength / The more the words

The less the meaning / No advantage over a fool / Never satisfied / For his mouth / Can't contend with someone stronger / Has been named

Which is better?

A good name is better than / The day of death is better than / Mourning is better than / Sorrow is better than / A wise man's rebuke is better than / The end of a matter is better than / Patience is better than / The old days were better than / Wisdom is better than

its beginning. / feasting. / laughter. / pride. / these days. / money. / fine perfume. / the day of birth. / the song of fools.

When times are good, be HAPPY; but when times are bad, consider: GOD HAS MADE the ONE as well as the OTHER.

There is not a righteous man on EARTH who does what is RIGHT and never SINS.

Powerlessness. Read Ecclesiastes 8

No man knows the FUTURE. No man has power over the WIND.

No man has power over the day of his DEATH.

Wickedness will not release those who PRACTICE it.

No one is discharged in time of WAR.

Although a wicked man commits a HUNDRED crimes and still lives a LONG time, I know that it will be better with GOD FEARING men.

So I commend the ENJOYMENT *of life...Then* JOY *will accompany him (a man) in his* WORK *all the days of the* LIFE GOD HAS GIVEN *him* UNDER THE SUN.

341

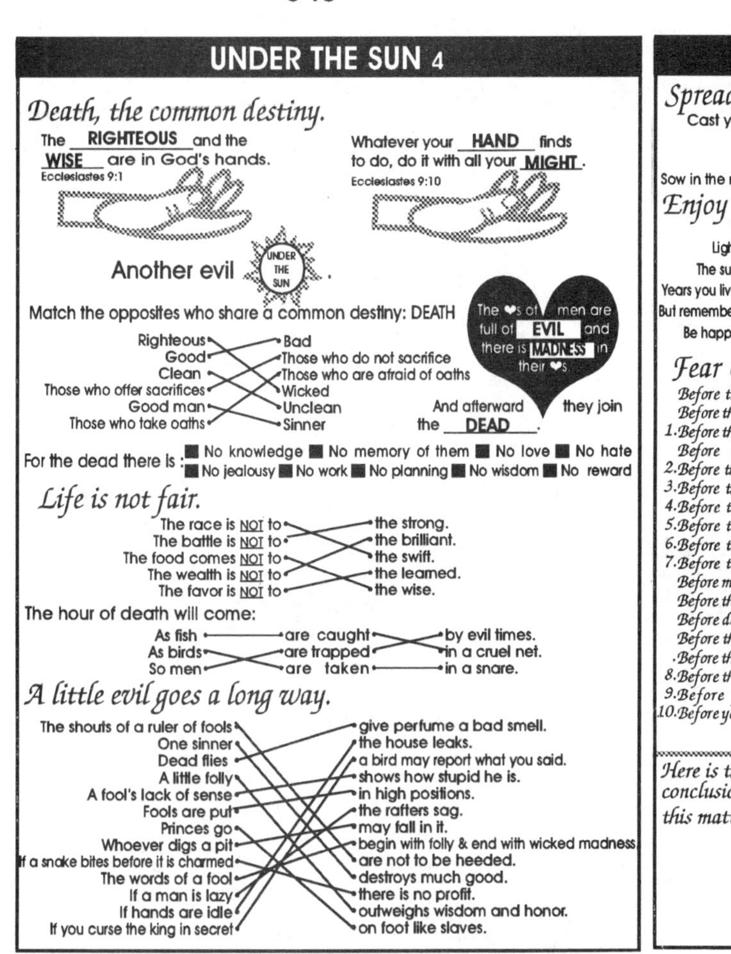

UNDER THE SUN 4

Death, the common destiny.

The RIGHTEOUS and the WISE are in God's hands. Ecclesiastes 9:1

Whatever your HAND finds to do, do it with all your MIGHT. Ecclesiastes 9:10

Another evil UNDER THE SUN.

Match the opposites who share a common destiny: DEATH

Righteous / Good / Clean / Those who offer sacrifices / Good man / Those who take oaths

Bad / Those who do not sacrifice / Those who are afraid of oaths / Wicked / Unclean / Sinner

The ♥s of men are full of EVIL and there is MADNESS in their ♥s. And afterward they join the DEAD.

For the dead there is: ■ No knowledge ■ No memory of them ■ No love ■ No hate ■ No jealousy ■ No work ■ No planning ■ No wisdom ■ No reward

Life is not fair.

The race is NOT to / The battle is NOT to / The food comes NOT to / The wealth is NOT to / The favor is NOT to

the strong. / the brilliant. / the swift. / the learned. / the wise.

The hour of death will come:

As fish / As birds / So men — are caught / are trapped / are taken — by evil times. / in a cruel net. / in a snare.

A little evil goes a long way.

The shouts of a ruler of fools / One sinner / Dead flies / A little folly / A fool's lack of sense / Fools are put / Princes go / Whoever digs a pit / If a snake bites before it is charmed / The words of a fool / If a man is lazy / If hands are idle / If you curse the king in secret

give perfume a bad smell. / the house leaks. / a bird may report what you said. / shows how stupid he is. / in high positions. / the rafters sag. / may fall in it. / begin with folly & end with wicked madness. / are not to be heeded. / destroys much good. / there is no profit. / outweighs wisdom and honor. / on foot like slaves.

342

UNDER THE SUN 5

Spread the wealth.

Cast your bread upon the water / Give portions away / If clouds are full of water / A tree falls / Sow in the morning, work in the evening

where it falls it lies. / after many days you will find it. / they pour on the earth. / you don't know which will succeed. / you don't know when disaster may come.

Enjoy your youth.

While you are young:

Light / The sun / Years you live / But remember / Be happy

the dark days will be many. / pleases the eye. / enjoy all of them. / is sweet. / while you are young.

Let your heart / Follow the ways / But know / Banish anxiety / Cast off the troubles

of your heart. / God will judge all you do. / from your heart. / of your body / give you joy in your youth.

Fear God. Remember your Creator in the days of your youth:

Before the days of TROUBLE *come.*

Before the years are without PLEASURE.

1. *Before the sun, moon & stars grow* DARK. *Before clouds* RETURN.
2. *Before the house keepers* TREMBLE.
3. *Before the strong men* STOOP.
4. *Before the grinders* CEASE.
5. *Before the* WINDOW *view dims.*
6. *Before the doors are* CLOSED.
7. *Before the songs of birds grow* FAINT. *Before men are* AFRAID *of heights & dangers.. Before the grasshopper* DRAGS *himself along. Before desire no longer* STIRS. *Before the golden bowl is* BROKEN. *Before the pitcher is* SHATTERED.
8. *Before the wheel of the well is* BROKEN.
9. *Before you* TURN *to dust.*
10. *Before your spirit* RETURNS *to God.*

1.–11. ANSWERS MAY VARY

What gives meaning to life?

Here is the conclusion of this matter: FEAR GOD *and keep His* COMMANDMENTS. *For this is the* WHOLE *duty of man. For God will bring every* DEED *into judgment, including every* HIDDEN *thing, whether it is* GOOD *or* EVIL.

343